Competition and Profitability in European Financial Services

Financial services firms play a key role in the European economy. The efficiency and profitability of these firms and the competition among them have an impact on allocation of savings, financing of investment, economic growth, the stability of the financial system and the transmission of monetary policy.

Competition and Profitability in European Financial Services is a collection of research contributions which includes evaluations of trends in the European financial services industry and examines the driving forces of efficiency, competition and profitability of financial firms and institutions in Europe. The papers have been written by leading academics and researchers in the field who specialise in strategic, systematic and policy issues related to the European financial services industry.

This edited collection will be essential reading for students and academics and will also be of interest to financial practitioners and government officials interested in acquiring a deeper understanding of this complex issue.

Morten Balling is Professor of Finance at the Aarhus School of Business, Denmark.

Frank Lierman is Chief Economist at Dexia Bank, Belgium.

Andy Mullineux is Professor of Global Finance at the University of Birmingham, United Kingdom.

Routledge International Studies in Money and Banking

Competition and Profitability in European Financial Services

Strategic, systemic and policy issues

Edited by Morten Balling,
Frank Lierman and
Andy Mullineux

Routledge
Taylor & Francis Group

LONDON AND NEW YORK

First published 2006
by Routledge
2 Park Square, Milton Park, Abingdon, Oxon OX14 4RN

Simultaneously published in the USA and Canada
by Routledge
270 Madison Ave, New York, NY 10016

Routledge is an imprint of the Taylor & Francis Group

© 2006 SUERF

Typeset in Times New Roman by
Newgen Imaging Systems (P) Ltd, Chennai, India
Printed and bound in Great Britain by
Biddles Ltd, King's Lynn

British Library Cataloguing in Publication Data
A catalogue record for this book is available
from the British Library

Library of Congress Cataloging in Publication Data
A catalog record for this book has been requested

ISBN 0–415–38494–X

Contents

Figures

Tables

Contributors

Lieven Baele is a Lecturer in the Faculty of Economics and Business Administration at Tilburg University, The Netherlands.

Morten Balling is a Professor in the Department of Accounting, Finance and Logistics at the Aarhus School of Business, Denmark, a member of the SUERF Council of Management and Chairman of the SUERF Editorial Board.

Martin T. Bohl is the Chairman of the Department of Finance and Capital Market Theory at the Europa University Viadrina in Frankfurt an der Oder, Germany.

Wim Boonstra is Chief Economist at the Rabobank Group, Amsterdam, The Netherlands, and an Observer on the SUERF Council of Management.

John P. Calverley is Chief Economist and Strategist at the American Express Bank, London, United Kingdom.

Jordi Canals is the Dean of IESE Business School and Professor of Economics and General Management in Madrid, Spain.

Santiago Carbó Valverde is the Director of the Department of Economic Theory and History, University of Granada, Spain, and Director of the Financial Analysis Department of the Fundación de las Cajas de Ahorros (FUNCAS).

Jaime Caruana has been the Governor of the Banco de España since 2000 and is also Chairman of the Basel Committee on Banking Supervision.

Josef Christl is the Executive Director of the Oesterreichische Nationalbank, having previously been Chief Economic Advisor to the Austrian Minister of Finance and Chief Economist of Creditanstalt.

Olivier De Jonghe is a Research Assistant of the Fund for Scientific Research Flanders at the University of Ghent, Belgium.

Javier Delgado, Banco de España, Madrid.

Jean Dermine is Professor of Banking and Finance at INSEAD, Fontainebleau, France.

Johannes M. Groeneveld is Senior Vice President of Corporate Strategy to the Executive Board and Deputy Chief Economist at the Rabobank Group, Amsterdam, The Netherlands.

Philipp Hartmann is Head of the Financial Research Division at the European Central Bank, Frankfurt am Main, Germany.

Olena Havrylchyk is a member of the Department of Economics at the Europa University Viadrina in Frankfurt an der Oder, Germany.

Ignacio Hernando, Banco de España, Madrid.

David B. Humphrey is Professor of Finance at the Department of Finance, Florida State University, Tallahassee, USA.

Malcolm D. Knight has been General Manager of the Bank for International Settlements since 1 April 2003. From 1999 to 2003 he was Senior Deputy Governor of the Bank of Canada.

Michael Koetter is a Postgraduate at the Utrecht School of Economics, The Netherlands.

Marko Košak is an Assistant Professor at the Faculty of Economics at the University of Ljubljana, Slovenia.

Frank Lierman is Chief Economist at Dexia Bank, Belgium, and a member of the SUERF Council of Management.

Rafael Lopez del Paso is Professor in the Department of Economic Theory and History, University of Granada, Spain.

Simone Manganelli, Financial Research Division at the European Central Bank, Frankfurt am Main, Germany.

Cyril Monnet, Financial Research Division at the European Central Bank, Frankfurt am Main, Germany.

Andy Mullineux is Professor of Global Finance at the University of Birmingham, United Kingdom.

María J. Nieto is an Advisor at the Banco de España, Madrid.

Francisco Rodríguez Fernández is the Assistant Director of the Department of Economic Theory and History, University of Granada, Spain.

Anthony M. Santomero is the President of the Federal Reserve Bank of Philadelphia. Previously he was the Richard K. Mellon Professor of Finance at the University of Pennsylvania's Wharton School.

Dirk Schiereck is Professor in the Department of Finance at the European Business School, Oestrich-Winkel, Germany.

Rudi Vander Vennet is Professor of Financial Economics at the University of Ghent, Belgium.

Peter Zajc is an Assistant Professor at the Faculty of Economics at the University of Ljubljana, Slovenia.

Acknowledgements

The editors would like to gratefully acknowledge the excellent support they have received in producing this book from the SUERF Secretariat based at the Oesterreichische Nationalbank in Vienna, particularly Michael Bailey and Beatrix Krones, and from Gabrielle Kelly, Andy Mullineux's secretary of the Department of Accounting and Finance in the Birmingham Business School at the University of Birmingham.

Abbreviations

ACH	Automated Clearing House
AIG	Accord Implementation Group
ANZ	Australia and New Zealand Banking Group Limited
ARC	Accounts Receivable Check
ATM	Automatic Teller Machine
BGC	Bankgiro Centrale
BIS	Bank for International Settlements
BR	Bank Branches
CAPM	Capital Asset Pricing Model
CARs	Cumulative Abnormal Returns
CDO	Collateralised Debt Obligation
CE	Cost Efficiency
CEE	Central and Eastern Europe
CFS	Centre for Financial Studies
C&G	Cheltenham and Gloucester
CGFS	Committee on the Global Financial System
C–I ratio	Cost–Income ratio
CPI	Consumer Price Index
CSD	Central Securities Depositories
CV	Coefficient of Variation
DEA	Data Envelopment Analysis
DFA	Distribution-Free Approach
EAD	Exposure at Default
ECB	European Central Bank
ECB-CFS	ECB-Centre for Financial Studies
ECU	European Currency Unit
EFTPOS	Electronic Funds Transfer at Point of Sale
EMU	European Monetary Union
EP	Economic Profit
EPS	Earnings Per Share
ESCB	European System of Central Banks
EUR	Euro
FA	Fixed Assets

FDH	Free Disposable Hull
FSAP	Financial Sector Assessment Programs/Financial Services Action Plan
GDP	Gross Domestic Product
GLS-RE	Generalized Least Squares Random Effects
GMM	Generalized Method of Moments
HHI	Herfindahl–Hirschman Index
HKMA	Hong Kong Market Authority
HSBC	Hong Kong and Shanghai Banking Corporation
HVB	HypoVereinsbank
ICT	Information and Communications Technology
IESE	Institute for Experimental Software Engineering
i.i.d.	Independently Identical Distribution
IMF	International Monetary Fund
ING	ING Group
INTMG	Interest Margins
IO	Industrial Organization
IOSCO	International Organization of Securities Commissions
IPO	Initial Public Offering
IRB	Internal Ratings Based
IT	Information Technology
LDC	Lesser Developed Countries
LGD	Loss Given Default
LMSPR	Loan Market Rate Spread
LTA	Loan-to-Asset Ratio
LTCM	Long Term Capital Management
LTV	Loan-to-Value Ratios
M&A	Mergers and Acquisitions
MADC	Mean Average Deviations for Country
MADI	Mean Average Deviations for Industry
MEW	Mortgage Equity Withdrawal
MTS	MTS (European Bond Market)
NEIO	New Empirical Industrial Organization
OBS	Off-Balance Sheet Activities
OC	Operating Costs
OECD	Organisation for Economic Co-operation and Development
OFHEO	Office of Federal Housing Enterprise Oversight
OLS	Ordinary Least Squares
PD	Probability of Default
PE	Price–Earnings ratio/Profit Efficiency
PIN	Personal Identification Number
P&L	Profit and Loss
POP	Per Person
PR	Panzar and Rosse Model
RAROC	Risk-Adjusted Return on Capital

ROA	Return on Assets
ROE	Return on Equity
SBC	Swiss Bank Corporation
SCP	Structure–Conduct–Performance
SD	Standard Deviation
SFA	Stochastic Frontier Analyses/Approach
SMEs	Small and Medium-Sized Enterprises
TA	Total Assets
TARGET 2	TARGET 2 system
TFA	Thick Frontier Approach
TOC	Total Operating Cost
TSB	Trustees Savings Bank
UBS	Union Bank of Switzerland
USD	US Dollars
VAT	Value Added Tax
VC	Venture Capital
WIG	Warsaw Stock Exchange Share Index

Introduction

Morten Balling

The chapters in this volume are papers that were presented at a Colloquium organized in Madrid, Spain 14–16 October 2004 by the *Societé Universitaire Européenne de Recherches Financières* (*SUERF*) in cooperation with *IESE Business School* and in association with *Banco de España*. The theme of the Colloquium was 'Competition and Profitability in European Financial Services: Strategic, Systemic and Policy Issues'. The first four chapters are keynote speeches that cover strategic and organizational issues, financial stability issues, regulatory capital requirements and macroeconomic perspectives. Chapter 5 is the 2004 Marjolin Lecture concerning patterns of payments in the United States compared with Europe.

The remaining eleven chapters are papers presented in one of the three Commissions of the Colloquium. They deal with banking efficiency, economies of scale and scope in financial institutions, privatization of banks, changing technology, pricing strategies, competition, the impact of internet banking and the connection between business cycles, asset price fluctuations, monetary policy and banking risks.

In Chapter 1, Jordi Canals, IESE Business School, looks at the strategic and organizational challenges that must be faced by banks in Europe. He considers the task of European bankers to be very demanding. The implementation of the European single market in financial services is still far from being complete. American banks are on average more efficient and profitable. Economic prospects in Europe look gloomy. Banks in Europe are in a transformation process, but the process is slow. Financial margins have been declining between 1999 and 2003. Banks are diversifying from traditional intermediation and interest-based transactions to fee-based financial transactions. Universal banks seem to show some advantages over more focused banks but they are complex organizations from a managerial perspective. According to the author, European banks have to tackle the challenge of closing the performance gap in relation to US banks if they want to make sure that they have the control of their own destiny in their hands. They must renew their strategies. Organic growth requires innovation, marketing capabilities and customer service, qualities that many European banks do not excel at. European banks must also rethink their international strategy and modernize their organizational design. Control systems and risk management, conflicts of interest within universal banks and other governance issues must be dealt with.

Chapter 2 is the keynote speech given by Jaime Caruana, Governor of Banco de España and Chairman of the Basel Committee on Banking Supervision. According to the governor, there is broad consensus among economists that financial systems have become more vulnerable to financial instability in recent years. This is due to the increased sophistication and complexity of business structures and of the products offered, the greater degree of internationalization and a strong increase in competition. In its work on Basel II, the Committee has taken into consideration the need of a broad approach to foster financial stability. Implementation of appropriate macroeconomic policies is important. So is an appropriate institutional framework including a solid legal structure. The 'Core Principles for Effective Banking Supervision' (1997) establishes a sound foundation of supervisory, legal and accounting systems. Commercial banks carry responsibility for the development of measures linking the risks they face with the appropriate level of capital they should maintain. Supervisors should design and implement incentives-based systems to promote sound and prudent management. Basel II is a major step forward. Traditional banking supervision must be complemented by a more risk-focused analysis. Risk management must be based on a strong foundation of corporate governance. Capital and provisioning policies should be set with an appropriate time horizon that allows at least a full business cycle to be considered. Counter-cyclical elements should be introduced. Banks should be advised to build up capital and provisions during good times in order to be well prepared to face times of difficulty. Basel II provides an appropriate comprehensive framework for managing financial stability.

The keynote speech by Malcolm Knight, General Manager of the Bank for International Settlements (BIS) is presented in Chapter 3. The author argues that the fundamental transformation of the financial industry over the past three decades has driven a significant transformation in the nature of financial risk. The financial industry has gained enormously in richness, depth and variety. Financial activity now represents a much larger share of aggregate economic activity than it did twenty or thirty years ago. At the same time, financial markets have become much more tightly interconnected. Consequently, the management of financial risk has become a more important aspect of economic activity. The new financial instruments have enhanced our ability to dissect a complex risk into its simpler components. Risks can be transferred easily among the market participants. The roles of financial markets and financial institutions have become more complementary. The endogenous component of risk has become more prominent. Firms should therefore develop techniques that uncover vulnerabilities which emerge from the endogeneity of risk. Supervisory authorities should aim at more consistency in their treatment of financial risk across sectors. Macroprudential analysis should supplement the more traditional microprudential focus. Authorities should support the application of a common set of reporting standards focused not only on the profitability of firms but also on their risk profiles.

Chapter 4 is the keynote speech by Josef Christl, Executive Director of the Oesterreichische Nationalbank. The author looks at financial regulation in the spirit of 'regulatory skepticism'. One cannot assume from the outset that financial stability is something that can be delivered by just switching the right regulatory buttons. It should be made clear what financial regulation is trying to achieve. The nature of market failures should be clearly understood. Since financial crises have often been caused by macroeconomic shocks, macroeconomic aspects should be given more consideration. Imbalances that may trigger a crisis may build up under booming economic conditions. Risks may therefore to a large extent be endogenous. Regulators should monitor the build up of imbalances. Capital adequacy rules can limit excessive risk taking by banks and act as a buffer against insolvency crises. Financial stability reviews published by central banks can contribute to a coordination of expectations. Correlated bank exposures and credit interlinkages lie at the heart of systemic risk. Quantitative models of risk assessment should be adapted to the financial system as a whole.

Chapter 5 is the 2004 Marjolin Lecture, given by Anthony M. Santomero, President of the Federal Reserve Bank of Philadelphia. The author describes the differences in the origins and evolution of payment structures between the United States and Europe. Europeans use cash roughly twice as much as do Americans. In Europe, half of all non-cash retail payments are made through a Giro system and only about 15 per cent by check. In the United States, it is almost exactly the reverse. Payment cards account for the remainder of retail payments. European central banks encouraged the use of Giro systems. In the early 1970s, the Fed introduced the Automated Clearing House (ACH), but unlike the European Giro, ACH has not developed into the dominant form of electronic payment. It was the credit card that proved most instrumental in moving US payments from paper to electronics. The author expects retail payments in the United States to continue moving away from paper cheques towards electronic instruments, including credit cards, debit cards, ACH and emerging vehicles such as prepaid cards. The American Central Bank is committed to working to improve the reliability and efficiency of the current generation of payment vehicles. At the same time, it works to foster innovation and to support the next generation of payment vehicles. There seems to be an emerging trend for the US and the European Union (EU) payment systems to converge. The United States and Europe will look more alike, although the two continents will get there from very different starting points.

In Chapter 6, Marko Košak and Peter Zajc (University of Ljubljana) estimate the East/West banking efficiency gap and its dynamics in the 1996–2003 period. They compare the cost efficiency of banks in the 10 new EU member countries and 5 old EU member countries. The authors apply a stochastic cost frontier approach. Data is drawn from the financial statements of individual banks provided by the FITCH/IBCA BankScope Database. In their model, bank production depends on labour, funds and physical capital as inputs. Banking services provided are proxied by total loans, other earning assets and total deposits. Results are presented as average efficiency scores for individual countries and groups of countries that form sub-regions within the EU. It turns out that the average efficiency score is the highest for Cyprus and Malta and the lowest for Central and Eastern Europe (CEE) and the Baltic countries. The dynamic part of the analysis shows that the East/West efficiency gap has been gradually narrowing.

In Chapter 7, Martin T. Bohl and Olena Havrylchyk (European University Viadrina Frankfurt an der Oder) together with Dirk Schiereck (European Business School, Oestrich-Winkel, Germany) look at the wealth effects of fifty-one Polish bank acquisitions by foreign investors between 1996 and 2002. In 1998, a new act on banking came into force that removed all restrictions for the entry of foreign banks. The following transformation of the ownership of Polish banks has been dramatic. At the end of 2002, 14 out of 15 banks listed on the Warsaw Stock Exchange had foreign majority shareholders. The authors apply Thomson Financial SDC Mergers and Acquisitions Database for an event study. They find that the shareholders of target banks experienced positive abnormal returns over the event window. Also shareholders of non/participating banks experienced some positive returns.

In Chapter 8, David B. Humphrey (Florida State University) and Santiago Carbó Valverde and Rafael Lopez del Paso (University of Granada) study the impact of the increasing use of electronic payments and automatic teller machines (ATMs) on cost efficiency in banking. They demonstrate that the shift to new technology has been associated with significant reductions in operating cost as a per cent of bank asset value during the 1990s. The share of non-cash transactions that are electronic rose from 1992 to 2000 and the number of bank employees per 10,000 inhabitants declined in most of the European countries. They perform an empirical analysis of the operating costs at Spanish savings and commercial banks over the period 1992–2000. The new technology has significantly contributed to a reduction of operating costs in the Spanish banking system.

In Chapter 9, Santiago Carbó Valverde and Francisco Rodríguez Fernández (University of Granada and FUNCAS) analyse the effects of changes in bank specialization and diversification on pricing strategies and the evolution of bank margins. They study a sample of 19,322 European banks during 1994–2001. Financial innovation and changes in financial intermediation activities have altered the income structure of European banks significantly. Interest margins have declined while the importance of fees has increased. The authors apply a multi-product framework to study the determinants of bank margins. They incorporate the effects of specialization-diversification options beyond lending and deposit taking. The authors find that both market power and risk parameters alter bank margins when introducing financial innovations. Specialization and bank margins are significantly related. Output diversification permits banks to increase their revenues and obtain higher market power. Fee income may com-pensate, somehow, lower interest margins that result from stronger competition in traditional markets.

Chapter 10 by Michael Koetter (Utrecht School of Economics) on bank efficiency and mis-specified input prices was awarded the 2004 Marjolin Prize for the best contribution to the Colloquium by an author below the age of forty.

The author applies stochastic frontier analysis and compares the effects of alternative input price specifications on the measurement of bank efficiency. In his models, banks produce loans, securities and off/balance sheet activities by means of borrowed funds, labour and fixed assets. Banks are assumed to minimize costs when producing a given output bundle conditional on available equity. The empirical analysis is based on data concerning German banks. Numbers are obtained from the FITCH/IBCD BankScope Database. He estimates cost and profit efficiency with several different model specifications. It is shown that efficiency estimates are affected by alternative input price specifications. The influence is higher on cost efficiency than on profit efficiency. A certain East-effect is documented. There are significant efficiency differences between banks in East and West Germany but the differences are declining through time. Regional information is, however, still important.

In Chapter 11, Wim Boonstra and Johannes M. Groeneveld (Rabobank) study the competitive conditions in the highly concentrated Dutch banking sector. Analyses based on the so-called Structure–Conduct–Performance (SCP) paradigm try to establish a link between market structure, behaviour of banks and profitability. Concentration is seen as a market situation that makes superior bank performance possible. In contrast, the efficiency hypothesis postulates that efficient banks are able to increase their market share due to their higher profitability. As a consequence of superior performance, the degree of concentration increases. The authors find existing studies on competition and concentration in European banking typically based on concentration figures at the macro level unsatisfactory. Instead, they look at C5-ratios and Herfindahl–Hirschman indices (HHI) in individual sub-markets and argue that competition may be more intense than the macro figures suggest. One should also include the competitive implications of structural developments in the distribution of financial services, entrance of new independent intermediaries and new technology. Due to improved internet access, bank customers are increasingly shopping for the best bargains for each product and service. Increasing transparency makes it difficult for banks to cross-subsidize individual products. They conclude that the degree of concentration in a specific banking market is not a reliable proxy for the intensity of competition. The key issue in banking has little to do with 'too big to fail' but with 'too small to survive' instead.

In Chapter 12, Jean Dermine (INSEAD) argues for a balanced view in the sense that strategic management in banking should define both short-term and long-term financial goals and ensure an acceptable degree of diversification. Value-based management should achieve the maximization of both short-term and long-term economic profits. The difficulty of finding a delicate balance is illustrated by the Lloyds TSB (Trustees Savings Bank) case. In the years after 1983, Lloyds TSB demonstrated brilliant performance. After 1999, a more difficult environment and an increasing focus on cost cutting contributed to a share price decline as the market seemed to be questioning the sources of future growth. The company's diversification policy seemed to work well in the early 1990s. Nordea AB is also analysed in the chapter as an interesting example of a cross-border merger in which the management plan to move to a single corporate structure as a 'European Company'. At the end of the chapter, the author returns to the trade-off between short- and long-term corporate objectives and between focus versus diversification. In both respects, the 'in medio virtus' is to be highly recommended.

Chapter 13 is a paper by Javier Delgado, Ignacio Hernando and Maria J. Nieto (Banco de España). The authors analyse what they call 'primarily internet banks' compared to traditional banks. Most banks use a combination of branches and the internet for delivery of services to their customers. The number of bank customers using online facilities is increasing worldwide. The authors attempt to identify and estimate the magnitude of technology based scale and learning effects of banks that heavily rely on new technology in their business model. Primarily Internet banks show significant technology based scale economies arising from their ability to control operational expenses more efficiently than the new traditional banks. Internet banking penetration varies across countries. The Scandinavian countries have the highest levels of Internet banking use. The profitability of European Internet banks was negative on average over the period 1994–2002 due to high costs of website development and promotion. The authors apply data from BankScope. In the empirical analysis they distinguish between primarily Internet banks, small established traditional banks and newly chartered banks. The profitability of primarily Internet banks is so far significantly lower than that of newly chartered traditional banks. Primarily Internet banks show, however, significant scale economies in terms of Return on Assets (ROA) and Return on Equity (ROE).

In Chapter 14, Rudi Vander Vennet and Olivier De Jonghe (Ghent University) and Lieven Baele (Tilburg University) look at the relationship between business cycles and bank risks. They investigate how bank health is related to the economic conditions in which they operate. After a review of theories concerning asymmetric information, agency costs, changing incentives and monetary policy transmission channels, the authors carry out an empirical study based on a sample of 280 listed European banks. Together, the banks in the sample account for more than 80 per cent of the total assets in the European banking industry. Accounting data is retrieved from the BankScope database maintained by FITCH/IBCA/Bureau Van Dijk. Capital adequacy, degree of diversification, type of institution and other characteristics are used to reveal specific strengths or weaknesses of banks when they are confronted with an economic slowdown. The authors find that bank returns and risks differ considerably across countries, that commercial banks and financial conglomerates fare less well in the economic downturn (2000–2003) than traditional intermediaries such as savings banks. Market-based return and risk measures support the conjecture that diversified banks were hit much harder in the economic slowdown than their more specialized peers. The stock market does not view diversification as universally better than focused banking. Capital adequacy, on the other hand, clearly has a positive effect on the risk profile of banks.

Chapter 15 is a paper by John P. Calverley (American Express Bank). The author explores the implications of housing bubbles and high household debt for monetary policy and for bank profitability. It is documented that rapid rises in house prices are a widespread phenomenon among the industrial countries. Analysis based on 1974–2002 data suggests that house prices have become unusually high compared with historical levels, in relation to both earnings and rents. Alongside the rise in house prices there has been a rise in household debt. The household debt-income ratio has risen. The rise in household debt burdens suggests that consumers may be more sensitive to higher interest rates than in the past. The sensitivity depends, however, on the relative importance of respectively floating rate mortgages (the rule in the United Kingdom) and fixed rate mortgages (the rule in the United States). The author discusses imposition of loan-to-value ratios, property exposure limits on bank lending and counter-cyclical provisioning rules as alternatives to monetary policy. All in all, he expects that handling of housing pricing problems will play a major role in monetary policy and the course of the economy in the years to come.

In Chapter 16, Philipp Hartmann, Simone Manganelli and Cyril Monnet (European Central Bank (ECB)) report on the scope, the findings and initiatives of the ECB-CFS (Centre for Financial Studies) Research Network on 'Capital Markets and Financial Integration in Europe'. The Network aims at measuring and monitoring the degree of European integration in each financial market and at stimulating policy-relevant research concerning the current and future structure and integration of the financial system in Europe and its international linkages with the United States and Japan. High priority topics are bank competition and the geographical scope of banking, international portfolio choices and asset market linkages between Europe, the United States and Japan, European bond markets and securities settlement systems. A crucial research theme is the effects of the implementation of the Financial Services Action Plan from 1999 on the development and integration of financial markets. Other important topics on the research agenda of the Network are the enlargement of the EU and the impact that financial integration and financial system development may have on financial stability and economic growth.

1 Strategic and organizational challenges in European banking

Jordi Canals

In the early 1990s, European banks seemed to be in big trouble. The creation of the European Single Market in 1992, the collapse of the European Monetary System, the economic slowdown, the deregulation in financial markets and the emergence of new competitors were factors that created a sense of uncertainty – in some cases, even panic – among many European banks. However, most banks have survived, banking restructuring has been implemented in several countries and most banks are in a stronger position than in the early 1990s.

Many European banks have reinvented themselves by redefining their strategy, designing new organizational forms, launching innovative services and entering into new businesses. We have also seen in Europe the emergence of new universal banks, with a strong diversification strategy away from traditional retail banking, like Deutsche Bank or HSBC, and the creation of stronger regional banks, like Barclays, BBVA or Santander Group.

Nevertheless, the future of European banking looks uncertain. The implementation of the European single market in financial services is still far from being completed, which means that, in some segments of the financial services industry, national markets are still isolated, fragmented and somehow protected from external competitors.

Although the competitive positioning of many European banks has improved over the past few years, their comparison with the financial performance of US banks does not look particularly good. US banks, on average, are more efficient and profitable in using capital than European banks. On top of this, their market value is not only bigger, but also price–earning ratios are higher in US banking. One may argue that because European banks are not very profitable, US banks will not want to increase their business or acquire banks in Europe. But the right argument may be the opposite: precisely because many European banks underperform US banks, there is room for efficiency gains in this industry if better managed and financially stronger banks – in this case, US banks – take over less efficient ones.

The banking system depends very heavily on the state of the economy. With economic prospects in Europe so gloomy and no perspectives of acceleration in the growth rate, banks may have a hard time in generating revenue growth over the next few years. Moreover, Japanese banks seem to be back and we will see in the near future the emergence of banking giants in China. Certainly, scale is not the key factor for long-term survival in banking, but many European banks may be in the brink of being absorbed, unless they think about consolidation and, more important, change the way of running the business which today has become somehow obsolete.

Retail banking in several European countries is still organized the old way (Belaisch *et al.*, 2001), with a heavy cost structure, not very intense price competition, slow innovation and poor customer service. In many ways, European banking does have the same competitive shape as some other European industries about ten years ago. The difference is that the pace of change in banking has been slower than in other industries. Regulation mixed up with political interference and the slow process of implementing the European single market are important explanations for the slow transformation of banking in Europe. But many US and a few European banks have been changing very quickly (see Canals, 2003), showing a possible way out. It seems clear that efficiency will drive the worst performers out of the market.

This paper discusses some strategic and organizational challenges that European banks are facing today. It is structured as follows: we will offer first an overview of some features of the European banking industry; next, we will analyse some major challenges that European banks will face in the next few years: closing the performance gap with US banks, fostering strategic renewal, managing organizational complexity and improving corporate governance.

1.1 Banking: the European landscape

1.1.1 Profitability

Table 1.1 offers an overview of the evolution of net interest margins between 1999 and 2003 for the United States, Japan and some key European countries. Financial margins have fallen since 1999 in all the countries considered. The US banking system still outperforms the rest of countries by far. In Europe, only Spain gets close to the US banking system. France and Germany are left behind and seem unable to offer products innovative enough to maintain the financial margin.

Table 1.1 Banks' profitability as a percentage of total average assets (net interest margin %)

	1999	2000	2001	2002	2003
United States	3.34	3.22	3.11	3.11	2.99
Japan	1.14	1.07	1.01	1.00	0.55
UK	2.30	2.21	2.04	1.96	1.82
Germany	0.95	0.82	0.90	0.82	0.79
France	1.14	0.94	0.65	0.75	0.91
Spain	2.62	2.63	2.92	2.72	2.38

Source: Bank for International Settlements.

The profitability measured on average assets has also declined in all countries except in Spain, as shown in Table 1.2. Nevertheless, the US banking system shows a return on assets far above any other country. Spain and the United Kingdom, the next countries after the United States, show a return on assets 40% smaller than US banks. The case of German and Japanese banks is really bad, although Japanese banks seem to be slowly recovering.

The efficiency ratio – or cost–income ratio (CI) – is another way of looking at the efficiency of the banking industry. Table 1.3 shows the change in this ratio between 2003 and 1998 for the top twenty banks in terms of market capitalization at the end of 2003. US banks are the most efficient ones, with ratios of about 50% or less. The superior performance of US banks has to do not only with their cost

Table 1.2 Banks'profitability as a percentage of total average assets (pre-tax profits %)

	1999	2000	2001	2002	2003
United States	2.17	1.79	1.52	1.71	2.04
Japan	0.42	0.37	−0.69	−0.45	0.07
UK	1.43	1.53	1.24	1.08	1.22
Germany	0.43	0.55	0.14	0.05	−0.20
France	0.69	0.83	0.67	0.46	0.58
Spain	1.21	1.33	1.20	1.05	1.27

Source: Bank for International Settlements.

Table 1.3 Top 20 world banks cost/income ratio (%)

	1998	2003
1 Citigroup	76.79	52.50
2 Bank of America	67.36	53.13
3 HSBC Holdings	54.87	47.93
4 Wells Fargo & Co.	70.04	60.16
5 Royal Bank of Scotland	50.65	55.07
6 UBS	78.43	75.43
7 JP Morgan Chase & Co.	80.98	68.03
8 Wachovia	55.78	66.41
9 Barclays	65.47	58.44
10 Mitsubishi Tokyo Financial Group	102.14	72.44
11 Bank One	67.86	60.31
12 BNP Paribas	68.14	62.90
13 US Bancorp	53.78	44.77
14 Banco Santander Central Hispano	69.58	63.10
15 Mizuho Financial Group	129.48	64.02
16 HBOS	40.40	45.69
17 Deutsche Bank	78.10	81.81
18 Banco Bilbao Vizcaya Argentaria	62.44	56.77
19 Lloyds TSB	46.32	52.21
20 Credit Suisse	72.89	70.46

Source: *The Banker.*

efficiency, but also with their ability to generate higher absolute revenue, stronger than the ability of European banks.

Market valuation highlights how different US and European banks perform and the gap in scale that is dividing banks on both sides of the Atlantic. Table 1.4 shows the top twenty banks in the world in terms of market capitalization (December 2003), with Citigroup far away from the rest of banks and only one European bank, HSBC, getting close to the second US bank, Bank of America.

Table 1.4 Top 20 world banks market capitalization (December 2003, $M)

		2003
1	Citigroup	243,473
2	Bank of America	170,586
3	HSBC Holdings	163,667
4	Wells Fargo & Co.	98,570
5	Royal Bank of Scotland	95,759
6	UBS	86,663
7	JP Morgan Chase & Co.	77,716
8	Wachovia	61,694
9	Barclays	57,471
10	Mitsubishi Tokyo Financial Group	57,225
11	Bank One	54,889
12	BNP Paribas	54,562
13	US Bancorp	52,880
14	Banco Santander Central Hispano	51,362
15	Mizuho Financial Group	50,496
16	HBOS	50,351
17	Deutsche Bank	46,217
18	Banco Bilbao Vizcaya Argentaria	45,583
19	Lloyds TSB	45,013
20	Credit Suisse	42,194

Source: *The Banker*.

Table 1.5 Market concentration (%)[a]

	1997	*2003*
United states	21	24
Japan	39	42
Germany	17	22
France	38	45
United Kingdom	47	41
Italy	25	27
Spain	47	55

Source: Bank for International Settlements.

Note

a Top five banks' assets as a percentage of all banks' assets.

Moreover, the potential for market concentration in the United States is still high, which means that the average scale of top banks in the United States can become bigger. Table 1.5 shows the market concentration index for seven countries in 1997 and 2003. The increase in the concentration levels is generalized. But Germany, the United States and Italy are the laggards. It is more difficult to see more European banks buying US banks than US banks entering more aggressively into Europe. Both trends – further consolidation in the United States and the opening up of European banking to the rest of the world – are good opportunities for US banks and a threat for European banks.

1.1.2   Growth and diversification

The average scale of banks has substantially increased over the past years in Europe and the United States (see Berger *et al.*, 1999). Table 1.6 shows the top twenty banks in terms of total assets in 2003 and their size in 1999. This increase is remarkable. Banking growth has been driven mainly by mergers and acquisitions (M&As), and the diversification process of banks away from retail activities to corporate banking, asset management, capital markets transactions and advisory services.

The increasing importance of financial markets in the Western world has attracted many retail banks to capital markets, setting up new advisory, investment banking, trading and research units or acquiring other firms. The anecdotal evidence of this trend is clear. Deustche Bank acquired Bankers Trust; Dresdner

Table 1.6 Top 20 world banks total assets ($M)

		1999	2003
1	Citigroup	716,937	1,264,032
2	Crédit Agricole Groupe	441,524	1,105,378
3	HSBC Holdings	569,139	1,034,216
4	Bank of America Corp	632,574	736,445
5	JP Morgan Chase & Co	406,105	770,912
6	Mizuho Financial Group	428,804	1,285,471
7	Mitsubishi Tokyo Financial Group	678,244	974,950
8	Royal Bank of Scotland	146,307	806,207
9	Sumitomo Mitsui Financial Group	507,959	950,448
10	BNP Paribas	701,853	988,982
11	HBOS	222,795	650,721
12	Deutsche Bank	843,761	1,014,845
13	Barclays Bank	398,825	791,292
14	Wells Fargo & Co	218,102	387,798
15	Rabobank Group	282,514	509,352
16	Bank One Corp	269,425	326,563
17	ING Bank	351,211	684,004
18	UBS	613,637	1,120,543
19	Wachovia Corporation	67,353	401,032
20	ABN AMRO Bank	459,994	667,636

Source: *The Banker.*

Bank acquired Kleinwort Bentson; Citigroup acquired Schroders; ING acquired Barings; Crédit Suisse acquired Donaldson Lufkin and Jenrette; UBS and SBC merged; Chase Manhattan acquired JP Morgan. The evolution of non-interest income as a percentage of gross income in the European Union (EU) is clear. In the 1980s, this ratio was less than 25% in most EU countries; in 2000, it was about 40% in the Eurozone countries (Canals, 2003). This ratio is not the only indicator of diversification, but shows in a simple way how much banks are going away from traditional intermediation and interest-based transactions to fees-based financial transactions. This means that banks are not only changing the nature of their activities as financial intermediaries, but also the type of capability they need to develop to bolster their competitive advantage.

Moreover, this diversification process of many European banks is not only a reaction against low revenue growth in some traditional banking activities, but also the belief that the universal banking model, with a holding company and several business units competing in different segments of the financial services industry, is the pathway to the future.

Universal banks seem to show some advantages over more focused banks (see Saunders and Walter, 1994; Canals, 1997). The first is the potential to exploit linkages among the bank's business units and, in particular, the advantage of cross-selling of financial services. The opportunities for cross-selling seem to be important in retail banking, asset management, investment funds and insurance. Nevertheless, the volume of cross-selling does not increase as quickly as some banks would wish, for a variety of reasons. First, a bank may not offer the best set of financial services and its competitive advantage in cross-selling may be weak. Second, rivalry in each segment makes competition very tough for universal banks, and specialists may be more efficient. Third, the universal banks' internal organization does not always create an efficient coordination between the business units selling different types of financial services from the clients' point of view. Fourth, the distribution system of universal banks has become increasingly specialized and segmented; the creation of special branches for high-income individuals or special networks for serving the corporate market reflect this trend. This means that fragmentation of distribution channels may play against the integration of financial services that cross selling requires.

The second potential advantage for universal banks is the diversification of the sources of earnings and the prevention of the risk of substitution. This risk consists of the threat of innovation that comes from new financial services or alternative distribution channels. The emergence of new products such as investment funds or new distribution channels, such as Internet banking, makes this threat evident. Some banks' senior managers also argue that the diversification of earnings may increase earnings' stability. This may be true only in those activities in which earnings tend to be stable themselves – for example, they come from recurrent activities – but not in the cases of those activities – like capital markets – which are not. However, from a strategic point of view, what really reduces the risk of substitution is innovation. In this respect, universal banks do not have in fact a clear advantage over specialized banks.

Universal banks may enjoy another advantage: the offer of 'a one-stop shop' by becoming exclusive providers of a wide range of financial services to individuals, families and firms. Firms may be edging towards dealing with a smaller number of banks. However, it is less obvious that a single bank can be superior to others in providing all of the financial services that companies might require. In Europe, some universal banks with a strong corporate banking presence have a leading role in lending. However, it is more difficult for them to compete with US investment banks in advisory functions, mergers or acquisitions. Their problem lies not so much in the size of the market, as in the fact that US banks have an extensive experience and developed unique capabilities in deal-making.

However appealing the advantages of universal banks might be, the problems and challenges that they involve are also relevant. These are extremely complex organizations from a managerial perspective, with specific coordination and compensations problems stemming from the fact that they are the umbrella under which sometimes very different business units operate. Universal banks also generate conflicts of interests, with different business units – investment banking, lending, advisory services, etc. – fighting for their sources of revenue.

From a profitability viewpoint, there is no evidence that universal banks – diversified financial services firms – are more profitable than focused banks. On the contrary, profitable banks may be big and small ones, depending also on the industry conditions in each country and, eventually, on the quality of management of each bank.

Nevertheless, even if the evidence does not fully support the vision of universal banks, there is no doubt that they are shaping financial institutions today in the European landscape.

1.2   European banks: main challenges and risks

Taking into account the competitive and financial position of European banks in the beginning of the 1990s, their evolution over the past ten years has been a reasonable success for many of them. Nevertheless, this industry is clouded by internal challenges and competitive threats. It is difficult to predict which specific pathway its evolution will follow, but it is true that this industry has not gone through a strong restructuring process as other European industries, and the room for efficiency improvement is still significant.

In this section, we will discuss four major challenges that European banks will have to tackle over the next few years, because their survival depends very much on their success in overcoming more intense competition for clients and markets: closing the performance gap with US banks, fostering strategic renewal, managing organization complexity and improving corporate governance.

1.2.1   Closing the performance gap

As seen in the previous section, European banks' profitability has declined over the past few years – see Tables 1.1 and 1.2 – with some notable exceptions. And US banks are, by far, still more profitable than European banks. This generates a performance gap, an asymmetry between banks on both sides of the Atlantic as highlighted earlier. European banks have to tackle the challenge of closing this gap as they want to make sure that they have control of their destiny in their hands.

A deeper explanation for financial performance in European banking is the lack of economic growth and the low potential for growth revenue in many areas of financial services. Slow growth plays into the hands of cost cutting, which becomes the undisputable tool to improve performance in Europe, since European banking has still higher fixed costs and CI ratios. However important it may be, cost cutting is neither a guarantee of long-term survival and success, nor a signal of revitalizing banks' strategies which is what many banks actually need.

Investment in technology has declined over the past three years, but it will come back in banking and will give those banks that invest smartly in technology a more effective weapon to lower operational costs. Unfortunately, many banks have turned their back on technology after the bubble burst in 2001–2002, but there are many successful examples of how technology can help manage banking operations more efficiently.

A direct outcome of the lower banking profitability in Europe is that the European banks' market value is smaller than that of US banks. This lower valuation, in combination with the sheer size of some US banks, transforms them into potential and powerful bidders in European banking. European banks will not be in control of their future unless they can reduce this performance gap.

What are the generic options for European banks in order to close this gap? Three generic approaches have been followed. The first is looking for more efficiency through cost restructuring (Berger and Mester, 1997). The second is downsizing and assets sell-off of those units, which the current management cannot run well and that absorb too much capital in an inefficient way. Finally, a restructuring of the portfolio that include both asset disposal and investment in new business.

These generic approaches could be useful in some instances, but do not resolve the underlying problems of European banks. The reason is simple. The return on assets of any company is the difference between revenue and expenses, over total assets. The problem with the three approaches described previously is that they may be good at cutting costs and refocusing banks away from marginal business, but not good enough for the real challenge that banks have to go through in order to improve long-term performance.

Figure 1.1 shows the arguments. Banks can reduce expenses and improve their return on equity; or sell assets, in order to improve their rate of return on assets. Nevertheless, these are not sustainable policies in the long term, since there is a limit to cutting expenses or how far a bank can proceed with asset disposal. Unless banks make an effort to boost revenue growth in the long term and use capital more efficiently, it will be impossible to close the performance gap that separates US banks from European banks. The growth challenge is the next issue to be discussed.

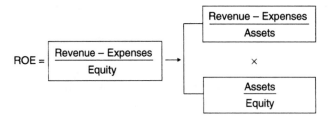

Figure 1.1 Return on equity (ROE).

1.2.2   Strategic renewal

Concern about banks' market value has focused the attention of senior managers inside and outside the banking industry. Nevertheless, this approach is essentially flawed, since the share price should be the outcome, not the driver, of a good business strategy. There is a sense of despair about the market value of some European banks, with a significant asset size, in particular, when they compare their valuation *vis-à-vis* US banks' valuations. However, this uneasiness is useless because there is not the same sense of urgency about rethinking banking strategies, or considering the deeper, underlying factors that drive market value in the long term. Rediscovering the meaning of strategy in banking is critical if banks want to focus on long-term growth.

And the banking landscape for growth will become more difficult in the following years. Revenues in some traditional business segments are flat. Rivalry will become more intense, with savings banks and other financial services firms different from banks offering new, innovative savings products and advisory services. Many indicators seem to suggest that customers in banking are not particularly loyal to their banks and switching costs are more of an unwanted chain around customers than the outcome of excellent bank service. Finally, in Europe economic growth has been disappointing over the past decade and, unfortunately, it does not seem that its prospects may change in the near future. In this landscape, financial services will not grow dramatically unless banks offer some innovative services.

Strategic renewal in banking includes several dimensions. The first is the conviction about the importance of generating organic growth as opposed to acquisitions. The reason is that acquisitions generate instant growth, but not necessarily sustainable growth. Moreover, acquisitions absorb the focus of top managers for too long, at the expense of customer service and product innovation (Houston *et al.*, 2001). And organic growth requires innovation, marketing capabilities and customer service, qualities that many European banks do not excel at. Moreover, they have very rarely been the first priority among senior managers of banks.

The second dimension is commercial execution. Banks are not the best customer-friendly firms. The levels of customer retention are not extremely high in banking. At a time when all types of companies in a variety of industries – including retailing or airlines – are fighting for customer loyalty in different ways, many banks seem to be way behind this effort to captivate the minds, hearts and wallets of their customers.

The third dimension for strategy renewal in banking is rethinking international strategy. Banking in Europe, with some exceptions, is still a national industry. Even banks that have a strong presence outside the home country do not have a clear international strategy. Many banks have been opportunistic in international strategy in the sense of capturing good opportunities, rather than thinking what international strategy could make sense for them in the long term. The question about which countries a bank should operate in to improve its positioning and guarantee long-term success has been replaced by whether a target could fit into the bank's current portfolio of business. There is nothing wrong in using opportunities well. The wrong approach consists of focusing only on opportunities and disdaining strategic thinking. Some questions like the countries where a bank can compete in, which competitive advantages it should have in each country or how to transfer resources or capabilities from the centre to the national subsidiaries are key questions to be answered by a solid international strategy.

Another key strategic issue for banks is how much diversification they can afford to achieve. In the past few years, the trend towards diversification in banking has been inexorable, driven by the slow growth in some traditional areas and the attractiveness of bigger growth potential in others. Nevertheless, there is a limit to what a bank can efficiently accomplish in its diversification process.

The lack of focus in a diversified bank is real and the risk of losing or diluting its competitive advantage over too many activities if a bank does not have the right managerial capabilities may be too high. Herding behaviour is not only a driving factor in financial markets, but also in business strategy, and the banking industry has shown many examples of cloned strategies. The trend towards diversification in banking has been very strong, but the performance of some diversified banks has also been disappointing. And it is far from clear that diversified banks are more profitable than focused, specialized banks.

1.2.3 *Organizational complexity*

Many industries have gone through dramatic changes in their organizational design over the past decades. The automobile industry has adopted the lean manufacturing system first developed by Toyota, a new revolutionary approach to assembling cars. Retailing has also experienced a dramatic change, with new formats and outlets emerging and old ones decaying. Is the organizational change in banking over the past few years enough to cope with future challenges?

The answer is no. Many European banks are still organized as they were ten or twenty years ago, while their business has changed dramatically and they have also been trying to change their strategy. However, a new strategy should be supported by a new organizational design. Otherwise, the new strategy will fail.

There are four basic reasons to foster thinking on how banks have to approach their organizational design in the next few years. The first is that there is not yet an integrated European market for financial services at the retail level. Banks have to deal with customers who have different needs, show different patterns of behaviour and different financial cultures regarding payments systems or specific products. And regulation in Europe is still a national affair. The need to have local strategies for each country is more demanding than in other industries. And, at the same time, banks need to have an international strategy. Moreover, they have to profit from international strategies, by developing synergies, sharing some resources, deploying some capabilities and capturing new learning opportunities. Organizing banks around this diversity of dimensions is particularly complex, and few banks are pleased with what they have in place today.

The second reason is that even those banks with clear international strategies have an organizational design that does not reflect their international scope. International activities are not integrated in the banks' structure and systems in a coherent way. Still, many banks display organizational charts showing the different business units – retail, corporate, advisory services, etc. – and the international division. The latter also reproduces many of the domestic business units. Coordination problems between different areas arise systematically.

The third reason is that banks are diversified organizations with different business units. Each unit has different competitive dynamics, requires different professional profiles, involves different performance assessment processes and needs different resources. The return on investment is also different, which creates problems in terms of resource allocation, performance assessment and compensation systems.

The fourth reason is outsourcing. The integration of new countries into the world economy, with a highly educated population and lower salaries, will open up new possibilities for the relocation of certain activities from Europe to Latin America and Asia. This is a trend that manufacturing firms have been trying to shape and adapt to, but is still a recent challenge for European banks. Only technology and back office work have been outsourced over the past few years. Nevertheless, we will see a more intense shift of activities, towards emerging countries with sophisticated professional skills in the next few years, including activities such as financial analysis, research and advisory services.

There are no simple solutions to those challenges. Nevertheless, it is clear that banks are today multi-business firms and they need to adopt a corporate strategy which is consistent with this reality. Business strategy deals with how a firm competes in an industry. Corporate strategy deals with how a diversified firm with several business units creates advantages for each unit, allocates and shares resources among units, coordinates policies and activities and develops synergies. In a nutshell, corporate strategy must show unequivocally that diversified banks make sense and have a higher value than the mere sum of their parts.

In general, European banks have been good at developing new business strategies, but they have to face the transformation into multi-business firms and develop an integrated, coherent corporate strategy. This includes the design of policies that could enhance revenues across units by sharing resources, best practices or people, or become more efficient by using joint resources better. And it requires the definition of the role of the corporate centre in managing the diversified bank.

1.2.4 Governance challenges

Change in banks' management requires boards of directors that are ready to exert a leadership role in steering banks towards the future and making their long-term survival possible. Banks' boards face today some of the same challenges as boards in other industries. But banking presents some specific issues that make their governance particular.

The first is control systems and risk management. Any company can be afflicted by bad risk management. In the case of banking, this is a particularly serious threat, since risk is not only at the heart of the long-term survival of banks, but is also a basic pillar of financial stability for a country.

The discussion on risk management highlights the complexity of managing in an industry with a strong regulatory framework that, at the same time, no longer enjoys the protection of regulated prices or limited competition. On the contrary, the strong and cold winds of rivalry are blowing in the banking industry and creating new threats to established banks. The pressure to generate revenue growth may push some banks over the border of prudent lending operations, hence making risk management more complex (see Canals, 2003). In this context delineated by clear regulatory rules and stronger rivalry, boards of directors need new competencies to understand the technical issues about regulation and, at the same time, to manage innovation in a prudent way, but also need to get ahead of competitors.

The second specific governance issue is conflicts of interest within universal banks. Some universal banks have an advantage over investment banks because they can advise customers on some operations such as mergers, acquisitions, alliances or initial public offerings (IPOs), and lend them money as well. However, there is a conflict of interest for any universal bank: how much risk in lending money to a customer should be taken up with the prospect of a lucrative fee-based income from advisory services offered to the same customer. Even if universal banks may not be covering corporate lending losses through their investment banking operations, it is certainly a situation where a conflict of interest may arise.

Banks' boards need to be not only prudent but also very transparent about the relationship between advisory services and lending. This means dismantling one of the strong arguments in support of the cross-selling hypothesis. Otherwise, customers, investors and regulators may view this strategy suspiciously.

The third governance area for banks' boards of directors is the relationship between the board and the executive committee. A superficial approach would suggest that this is not a special case in banking, since other companies in other industries face the same challenge. Nevertheless, in industries more intensive in knowledge and sophisticated concepts and techniques – and banking is one of them, particularly in capital markets and risk management operations – boards run the risk of being overshadowed by executive committees that not only know more about the firm and its specific technical issues, but also know how to handle financial tools, concepts and valuation techniques really difficult to grasp by non-experts. As banks become more sophisticated financial institutions, developing more specialized and complex financial instruments and products, boards of directors should have the technical knowledge and competence to be able to use those concepts properly and provide a contrasting view to the proposals of the executive committee. In a nutshell, the board should supervise those operations in an efficient way, but it will not be up to this challenge unless its members do have the right technical background to exert supervision in a competent way.

A final governance issue is that banks are becoming more international, with operations in different countries and continents. But it seems that many boards in European banks are still dominated by members from the same country of origin as the bank. This observation leads to two implications. The first is that boards of directors should increasingly reflect international diversity if they want to be ready to provide a useful supervisory role and help project the bank into the future. The second dimension is that regulation in Europe is still a national affair. This explains why banks need to have board members with a deep knowledge of financial services, but also aware of the specific dimensions of the business and regulation in the different countries where banks operate.

As we pointed out earlier, European banks are more international than ever. Their international strategy may be a sound way to face the challenge of increased competition at home. Nevertheless, it should be supported by an organizational design that takes into account the role of each national subsidiary and the corporate centre, and how they complement each other by sharing resources and transferring competencies. And a solid international strategy should be supervised by a board that understands and can make a good judgement about complex financial operations and the specific risk attached to those operations in some particular countries.

1.3   Some final reflections

European banks today are in much better shape than they were ten years ago. Their transformation has been remarkable, not only adapting to the new realities of the European single market, but also transforming themselves into more sophisticated firms, with better management and the aspiration to operate in different countries outside the home market.

Nevertheless, European banks face a serious threat: their financial performance is poorer than US banks' performance, their scale is smaller and the European single market for financial services is still plagued with many barriers that make the goal of pan-European banking a distant objective. This threat gets more intense because it operates simultaneously with two other important forces: the emergence of new Asian financial giants and the gloomy state of the European economy which does not expect spectacular growth over the next few years. In this complex context, European banks run the risk of being overtaken by US banks or becoming less attractive to investors in the financial services industry. It is true that European banking has a few very strong performers, like Royal Bank of Scotland, BBVA, Santander or HSBC. Nevertheless, the laggards outnumber them.

Banks' long-term survival in Europe requires that their boards of directors and top managers tackle, simultaneously, four basic challenges: closing the performance gap with US banks, developing strategies that foster revenue growth, designing organizations that make sense amid the increasing complexity of banking operations – in particularly, international operations and, finally, putting in place boards of directors with the knowledge, wisdom and experience to understand the complexities of banking operations and the specific realities of banking in the different countries and regions where the banks operate.

None of the previous challenges is specific to the banking industry. But it is true that banking has become more complex and the combination of increasing financial innovation in sophisticated products, geographical diversity and tougher regulatory contexts makes the job of board members and senior managers more demanding. There are several European banks that are already tackling – and apparently, successfully – those challenges. Europe needs a strong banking industry and it is in the interest of Europe to have solid banks that are able to stave off the competitive, financial and organizational risks that banking faces in the twenty-first century.

References

The Banker, London: Financial Times Group.

Belaisch, A, Kodres, L., Levy, J. and Ubide, A. (2001). 'Euro-Area banking at the cross-roads', Working Paper 01/28, IMF.

Berger, A. N. and Mester, L. J. (1997). 'Inside the black box: what explains differences in the efficiencies of financial institutions?', *Journal of Banking and Finance*, 21, 895–947.

Berger, A. N., Demsetz, R. S. and Straman, P. E. (1999). 'The consolidation of the financial services industry: causes, consequences and implications for the future', *Journal of Banking and Finance*, 23, 135–194.

Canals, J. (1997). *Universal Banking*, Oxford: Oxford University Press.

Canals, J. (2003). 'Financial institutions and financial markets: the emergence of a new class of universal banks', in P. C. Padoan, P. A. Breton and G. Boyd, *The Structural Foundations of International Finance*, Cheltenham: Edward Elgar.

Houston, J. F., James, C. M. and Ryngaert, M. D. (2001). 'Where do merger gains come from? Bank mergers from the perspective of insiders and outsiders', *Journal of Financial Economics*, 60, 285–331.

Saunders, A. and Walter, I. (1994). *Universal Banking in the United States*, New York: Oxford University Press.

2 Regulatory capital requirements and financial stability

Jaime Caruana

2.1 Introduction

It is a pleasure for me to be here with you today. The Bank of Spain is also proud to participate in this 25th SUERF Colloquium and to support the IESE Business School in its organization.

One of the main missions of SUERF is to foster an appropriate climate for the analysis and study of monetary and financial issues. At its twenty-fifth gathering, the SUERF Colloquium will once again contribute to this. The success of this meeting is largely ensured thanks to the participation of top academics and researchers from various universities, central banks and other institutions from around the world.

A look at the proposed programme shows that the studies to be submitted to the three working Commissions will be of great interest, and the fact that these have been pre-selected and reviewed guarantees their high quality. The areas on which the Commissions will focus are very important for the banking industry. Perhaps more in line with the subject of the third area (macro-policy and financial stability), I will be setting out my views on the role that capital regulation and, more broadly, prudential regulation play in promoting financial stability.

As you all know, The Basel Committee on Banking Supervision published the text of Basel II in June 2004. The text is the result of the Committee's work over the past six years, during which time it has benefited greatly from the support of industry, supervisors, central banks and academics from around the globe.

The driver of this effort has been the well-documented changes in the environment in which banks, particularly the most sophisticated ones, now operate. These changes have meant that the 1988 Accord is no longer fully satisfactory. Under the leadership of my predecessor as Chairman of the Committee, Bill McDonough, we initiated a process of change which goes beyond the mere reformulation of a rule to maintain a specific level of capital. As a result, together with leading institutions worldwide, supervisors began exploring ways to incorporate more sensitive measures of risk into the capital framework, the final objective being to promote financial stability.

In the presentation of the new capital framework, in June 2004, Jean-Claude Trichet, Chairman of the G10 group of central bank governors and President of the European Central Bank (ECB), stressed this objective when he underlined that Basel II 'will enhance banks' safety and soundness, strengthen the stability of the financial system as a whole, and improve the financial sector's ability to serve as a source for sustainable growth for the broader economy'.

Questions that naturally arise from this statement are how will Basel II foster financial stability? In what way is Basel II different? My intention today is to offer you an answer to these questions.

In a nutshell, I think that the new capital framework represents a significant step towards achieving a more comprehensive and risk sensitive supervisory approach.

Basel II is much more than just setting better minimum quantitative capital requirements. It is about establishing incentive-based approaches to risk and capital adequacy management, within a comprehensive framework of three mutually supporting pillars. In my view, the combination of better risk management, a stronger capital structure and improved transparency standards in the banking system can significantly improve financial stability.

From a different perspective, Basel II represents the recognition of the progress made by banks in recent times to develop and improve their risk management and measurement systems. It is also an encouragement to continue this work. It represents an unparalleled opportunity for banks to improve their capital strategies and risk management systems. Likewise, it offers supervisors an opportunity to enhance co-operation and implementation consistency, to align supervision more closely with sound current industry practices and to foster the dialogue with the industry.

I would like to develop and organize these ideas around ten points. Through them I will summarize some of the elements that are incorporated into Basel II. Thanks to these elements, Basel II will be a more efficient regulation than its predecessor, the 1988 Accord, and will contribute to bringing about a stronger and more stable financial system. Nevertheless, I would like to begin my reflections by sharing with you a prior consideration, that is the need to think about financial stability in a broad sense.

2.2 Prior consideration, financial stability: a broad concept

In recent years, central banks, supervisors, international agencies and academics from all over the world have paid particular attention to financial stability. Increasingly, policymakers are recognizing that financial stability is a public good much like price stability. All of us have long understood the benefits of price stability and the need for sound monetary policy in the pursuit of sustained economic growth.

Even if we do not have as comprehensive a framework for financial stability as we do for price stability, in recent years, we have learned more about the concurrent need for a stable financial system. That includes the need for businesses and consumers to have access to credit on fair and reasonable terms through all stages of the business cycle so that they can build and grow. We need an efficient and resilient payments system to maintain the flow of funds through the economy at all times. We need financial markets that remain active, liquid and trusted regardless of events in the economy.

Given the unique positions of banks at the crossroads of businesses and consumers in every economy – and their special role as intermediaries of credit to both – nothing threatens financial stability more than the presence of poorly managed and poorly capitalized banking institutions.

The crises that a large number of countries have undergone in recent years have highlighted the complex linkages between the real sector and the financial sector and the risk that the latter may amplify the imbalances or shocks generated in other sectors of the economy. This is becoming even more important due to the evolution of financial systems over recent decades, characterized – against a background of technological progress – by the increasing sophistication and complexity of business structures and of the products offered, by a greater degree of internationalization and by a strong increase in competition, among other factors. While this evolution has been beneficial for the development of more efficient financial systems capable of providing greater benefits to the economy as a whole, it is no less true that new risks have arisen and that the probability of contagion has increased.

As a result of the increasing interest in financial stability, important contributions in this area have been achieved. For instance, the work made by the Bank for International Settlements (BIS) and its Managing Director, Malcolm D. Knight has been notable. These studies reveal some important facts about financial stability that must be taken into account.

Financial instability may reveal itself, first, via excessive volatility in asset prices, which can move substantially away from the value which, in principle, their fundamentals would warrant. In such cases, the correction of these deviations in some markets may occur abruptly and significantly disturb the real economy. To be sure, a certain degree of volatility in asset prices is simply the reflection of the normal workings of markets. Likewise, poor results posted by a specific financial institution, and even its bankruptcy, may simply be a consequence of its poor management, without systemic implications. However, financial instability can be very costly if it is on such a scale as to cause harm to the real economy.

Studies concur in pointing to a set of factors which may prompt instability: inflationary processes, currency crises, sharp corrections in financial or real-estate asset prices, payment-system failures and the malfunctioning of financial intermediaries, among others.

All these considerations allow us to draw a conclusion which, while obvious, is nonetheless relevant: the achievement of financial stability must be based on a broad range of tools which we should all seek to strengthen.

Furthermore, in my view, regulation and prudential supervision, in addition to their initial aim of avoiding systemic crisis and safeguarding the solvency of individual institutions, should pay increasing attention to a combination of micro and macro factors to achieve greater financial stability. This latter concept is undoubtedly wider, and includes resilience in the face of external shocks and the capacity to contribute to the proper functioning of the economy in various circumstances.

The New Basel Accord will seek greater financial stability through several mechanisms. Some of these mechanisms were already present in the 1988 Accord – such as setting minimum quantitative capital requirements and a level playing field. But in my presentation of the ten points, I want to focus on what I see as innovations of the new Accord. Let me mention two of the most important ones: to encourage improvements in banks' internal risk-management processes and to promote greater co-operation and co-ordination among supervisors across jurisdictions.

2.3 Elements constituting Basel II

2.3.1 Basel II builds on existing arrangements, preconditions and foundations

Before analysing the key elements which will allow Basel II to promote a more resilient financial system, the central topic of my speech today, I should stress the fact that the Committee has developed its work by taking into consideration the need for a broad approach to fostering financial stability. In fact, the Committee has stressed that if Basel II aims to be a successful framework, it must be built on a series of preconditions and on the foundations of a sound supervisory system. To achieve the benefits, we must ensure that the foundation for Basel II is ready first.

With respect to preconditions, there is a set of issues that should be considered. First, I think there is a broad consensus among all of us about the importance of promoting the implementation of appropriate macroeconomic policies. Nobody has any doubts today about the need to promote price stability. However, this is not a sufficient condition for ensuring financial stability, and even from the macroeconomic standpoint, other measures are needed to strengthen it.

These include, for instance, fiscal discipline, and the design of exchange rate policies that ensure the consistency of the chosen exchange rate system with domestic policies, and that restrict vulnerabilities associated with exchange rate instability in the different sectors of the economy. Macroeconomic policies must also be consistent and sustainable over time. Indeed, unstable macroeconomic settings are one of the main causes of excessive volatility on securities markets.

Second, an appropriate institutional framework is also needed. In particular, a set of mercantile and civil laws must be in place to safeguard agents' property rights, along with a legal and judicial structure that provides legal certainty.

Moreover, it will be necessary to consider microeconomic aspects related to payment-system and market structures.

For example, in designing payment-systems it is possible to pursue different strategies so as to reduce the inherent risks. The options range from systems based on the gross settlement of transactions in real-time to others entailing net multilateral settlement. In any event, avoiding the risks associated with payment-systems entails introducing incentives so that agents operating via such systems control their exposures more effectively, and reducing, through different mechanisms, the risk of a failed operation spreading through and endangering the whole system. On the securities markets, institutional developments seeking to limit situations of instability are also important.

Allow me to conclude this brief review, which is not intended to be exhaustive, of the preconditions on which Basel II must be built, with just a word about the so-called safety net. As banking business depends essentially on agents' trust in intermediaries, and given that the latter are highly sensitive to contagion processes, various institutional arrangements have been put in place in numerous countries in an attempt to limit this risk.

The role of central banks as lenders of last resort is a good example of this, inasmuch as they act as guardians when extremely serious liquidity problems with potentially systemic effects occur. Another example of this type of institutional arrangement is deposit insurance, which offers depositors a certain degree of coverage, so as to avoid the sudden withdrawal of their funds.

Both mechanisms, however, have a serious drawback: they increase moral hazard problems. The solution most countries have adopted is to introduce formulas capable of mitigating the associated moral hazard problem. For instance, central banks may operate under a certain degree of constructive ambiguity, and deposits are not usually guaranteed in their entirety.

As stated earlier, there is also a need for a sound supervisory system. This includes having the 'Core Principles for Effective Banking Supervision' published by the Basel Committee in 1997. These principles are based on the best banking practices identified around the world, and they play a key role in the Financial Sector Assessment Programs (FSAP) of international agencies.

The core principles include the provisions on operational autonomy of the supervisory authority, adequate supervisory resources, regulatory and remedial powers, and a sufficient legal framework. Likewise, sound accounting and provisioning standards are critical to ensure that the capital ratios – however calculated – reflect the bank's ability to absorb losses. Establishing a solid foundation of sound supervisory, legal and accounting systems is an essential requirement for the successful implementation of Basel II.

2.3.2   *Incentives-based system*

Let me now turn to two of the key innovations of Basel II, that are very much interrelated. The new capital framework is an incentives-based system and it is a risk-based framework. By creating the right set of market-friendly incentives to improve risk management, Basel II offers the opportunity to ensure that supervision and regulation take a forward-looking view on risk, that they remain up-to-date with sound practices in the industry and that our supervisory framework motivates responsible risk-taking and prudent behaviour in our markets.

Over the past sixteen years, the methodologies for measuring and managing risk have evolved in ways that the architects of the 1988 Accord could not have anticipated. Improvements in technology and telecommunications have changed the speed at which banks collect and analyse data on their exposures. The explosive growth in the markets for securitized assets and credit derivatives have offered banks new ways to manage and transfer credit risk. And a new discipline in risk management is emerging – namely, operational risk management – through which banks are quantifying in an increasingly reliable manner the risk of losses stemming from failures in internal processes or systems, or from damage caused by an external disruption.

I am convinced that, by creating incentives for banks to understand both their risks and rewards, and to improve their processes for managing both, Basel II will help to promote banks' efficiency and resilience, thereby strengthening the stability of the financial sector.

In fact, Basel II introduces a wide range of incentives which are incorporated through a broad set of elements. Indeed, these elements are an integral part of each of the three pillars on which Basel II is structured.

Pillar 1, to the extent that it promotes a closer link between capital requirements and risk, creates explicit incentives for banks to move ahead in improving their risk measurement techniques. What is more, it allows banks to use their own measurement models, making for a closer approximation to the practices they actually use. Undoubtedly, this is an added incentive to improve risk measurement methods.

Regarding the incentives introduced by Pillar 1, in addition to capital-related incentives, I should like to stress that banks are encouraged to make the provisions that are appropriate for them. To achieve this, banks will have to compare their measurement of expected losses, based on their Internal Ratings Based (IRB) models, with the specific and general provisions they have made. If this comparison shows that provisions are lower than the estimated expected losses, there will be a deduction from capital. If, on the contrary, the provisions are greater than the estimated expected losses, the surplus will be recognized as Tier 2 capital.

Pillar 1 also includes an explicit obligation relating to capital requirements for operational risk. This confirms the importance of the type of risk which, though it was only marginally considered until relatively recently, has proved to be the cause of substantial problems for banks on more than one occasion. Accordingly, the inclusion of capital requirements for operational risk introduces the appropriate incentives so that banks may move – as some started to do some time ago – towards improving the methods available for measuring this type of risk. The Committee is aware that much remains to be done in this area, and that is why it has opted for a flexible approach with room for the in-house models developed by banks.

Pillar 2, namely supervisory review, also includes incentive systems which contribute to promoting better risk management. First, it places the responsibility for considering all other risks not explicitly envisaged in Pillar 1 with banks themselves. As a result, clear incentives are set so that, on determining the overall level of capital to be maintained, this set of additional risks may be identified and taken into consideration.

In my view, however, Pillar 2 introduces the biggest incentives for prudent behaviour by banks, since it is conducive to a frank dialogue between banks and supervisors. This is possible because it entrusts supervisors not only with review of the bank's calculation methods, but also of whether the bank's level of solvency is adequate in terms of the risks assumed and of the systems in place for their management.

Finally, Pillar 3 also introduces incentives for bank managers to act prudently. It is through this pillar that Basel II recognizes the necessary role of market discipline. Insofar as the markets reward well-managed banks, and punish those acting imprudently, incentives for proper conduct will be reinforced.

On the basis of this acknowledgement, Basel II seeks to ensure that transparency regarding the risk profile of a bank is conducive to more effective market discipline. Under Pillar 3, then, banks are responsible for publishing, within a reasonable timeframe, quantitative and qualitative information to enable financial market participants to make these assessments. The information reported by banks must not only be reliable, but also relevant and based on generally accepted valuation principles.

2.3.3   *Risk-based framework*

Today, banks can assume risk positions or incorporate new, complex products that may dramatically and rapidly alter their financial position much more quickly than in the past. This means that it is necessary for supervisors to place a greater emphasis on anticipating problems.

For this reason, traditional banking supervision must be complemented by a more risk-focused analysis. I say complemented, because this type of review still has an important role to play, particularly in assessing asset quality and ensuring proper provisioning and risk-concentration policies.

Traditional analysis should therefore be supplemented by an approach that focuses on identification of the risks to which the bank is exposed and assessment of its capacity to manage them. That requires deeper knowledge of the governance, the organization, the strategies and policies applied by managers, and the risk control and management systems implemented. Also, the relationship with the supervised bank should be increasingly based on a close dialogue. In this setting, on-site inspections will continue to play a key role, but the supervisory review will involve much more than simply checking the bank's accounts. Basel II clearly opts for a risk-based supervisory approach.

2.3.4 *Corporate governance*

I have mentioned throughout my speech today that Basel II will improve risk measurement techniques, but it is much more than numbers. In fact, it provides the correct incentives for banks to strengthen the structures and processes through which they assess and manage their risk exposures.

Despite the significant progress made in the banking industry in the use of models and new technologies, banks still depend largely on risk managers' expert judgement. Quantifying risk involves making assumptions and judgements. And no model, and no software package, no matter how sophisticated, can ever replace the skills of a trained, experienced and conscientious risk manager. Such judgement should be reinforced, however, with the best possible information, techniques and tools for processing that information. To the extent that risk assessment and control methods become more formalized and rigorous, this will lessen the likelihood of bad decisions being made. It will also contribute to the prompt detection of errors and deviations from targets, allowing banks to implement corrective measures at an early stage.

Risk management, as the Committee has long recognized, must be based on a strong foundation of corporate governance. For this reason, the Committee has stressed the importance of bank managers' commitment to the development and implementation of high corporate governance standards.

All these considerations justified the inclusion in Basel II of a wide range of elements that reinforce effective implementation of solid corporate governance standards. We have included provisions on the need for boards and senior management to understand the nature and level of the risks that their banks are exposed to, to set the bank's tolerance to these risks, to ensure that strong risk management and internal controls are adopted throughout the organization, and to ensure that they themselves continue to be appropriately informed about the risks being taken on.

To ensure that the designed structure is appropriate to achieve the aforementioned goals, Basel II also stresses the need for external controls. It is the Board's responsibility to decide on the most suitable connection between external and internal control systems.

2.3.5 *Clear bank and supervisory responsibilities*

Basel II's focus on strong process controls re-affirms that the onus for responsible risk-taking lies with a bank's management. Banks are responsible for the implementation of more professional and transparent risk management and measurement systems. This includes, among other things, the establishment of strategies, policies and procedures that allow banks to identify and understand the risks they face, and to assess their exposures.

Banks' responsibilities also include the development of measures linking the risks they face with the appropriate level of capital they should maintain. In other words, banks should design an appropriate capital policy, including the need to adopt a strategy that allows them to keep the appropriate amount of capital over time.

Supervisory responsibilities are also well defined. Perhaps the main mission facing regulators and supervisors today is to design measures that induce healthy and prudent behaviour by managers. These incentives should be capable not only of complementing those provided by markets, but also of reinforcing them. This task should not involve imposing an unnecessary burden. An excessive degree of interventionism introducing organizational barriers that hamper financial innovation must also be avoided. Furthermore, supervisors should evaluate policies considering not only their benefits but also their costs.

It is for supervisors to determine whether the bank's assessment of the risks associated with its operations and the level of solvency is appropriate. To do this, it is necessary to consider the validity of the processes used to determine the capital needed and the appropriateness of the models employed. Further, supervisors must consider whether the level of solvency is reviewed and controlled by the bank's senior staff, whether management is conducted in a sufficiently able and professional manner, and whether the systems in place for measuring and controlling risks are appropriate.

The responsibility of supervisors also includes promoting a level playing field. That is to say, in the application of capital rules there should be a sufficient degree of consistency across different jurisdictions. This requires, as you can imagine, co-operation, information exchange and co-ordination among supervisors all around the world.

2.3.6   *Appropriate time horizon and counter-cyclical elements*

The sound and stable functioning of banks requires an additional consideration. Namely, risk-management decisions, capital and provisioning policies should be set with an appropriate time horizon that allows at least a full business cycle to be considered and avoids excessive emphasis on the short term when assessing risks. The aim is not to promote the uniformity of time horizons, a rather undesirable characteristic in a financial system, but to encourage managers to consider how risk determinants alter over the cycle and in conditions of stress.

One of the fundamental tenets of risk management is that banks need to create provisions to absorb expected losses and to have sufficient capital to absorb unexpected losses. Accordingly, capital and provisions are an essential part of any supervisory framework. I believe Basel II reinforces the need to implement sound policies in both areas. Moreover, the design of Basel II has also included various instruments that help promote the consideration of an appropriate time horizon by bank managers. This has been achieved through different elements.

In Pillar 1, for example, certain risk factors on which the models for calculating requirements are based draw on long-term averages (the Probability of Default (PD), Loss Given Default (LGD) and Exposure at Default (EAD)). Also, in the design of internal rating systems, it is required that these use relatively long-time horizons. Pillar 2, for its part, incorporates stress test analyses. Hence, when banks assess the capital they need, they must consider a whole range of scenarios taking into account past experience and current conditions, with an emphasis on stress scenarios.

A final general remark on this point is that, in designing any kind of regulations that affect the behaviour of financial institutions, there is a lot of merit in considering how to introduce counter-cyclical elements, compatible with good risk-management practices, which could limit, to some extent, bank managers' typically pro-cyclical behaviour. That is to say, from the standpoint of prudential policy it seems reasonable that banks be advised to build up capital and provisions during good times in order to be well prepared to face times of difficulty. In my view, this argument is fully consistent with the fact that, as experience shows, risks actually increase during cyclical upturns, but materialize in hard times.

2.3.7 Comprehensive approach

A supervisory approach that seeks to meet the demands imposed by modern circumstances must be comprehensive, drawing on the different tools which are available and combining them in an optimal way. In particular, the collaboration of the markets is enormously important today. Minority shareholders, depositors and debt-holders should have the capacity to evaluate banks, rewarding those that are well managed.

All the elements mentioned, along with additional ones, are held together by the three pillars. Basel II has been designed with a markedly comprehensive character and, in this respect, the three pillars are expected to act in conjunction, reinforcing and complementing one another.

I have sometimes explained this joint action using a simile related to portfolio selection theory. Pillar 1 can be understood as emphasizing the adoption of rules. Pillar 2 relies to a greater extent on discretion when determining the requirements of a bank. Pillar 3 adopts a market discipline approach. Each of these approaches to regulation: rules, discretion and market discipline, individually has merits, but also limitations. One might say that Basel II seeks a kind of 'efficient frontier' of policy approaches through the three pillars. Each pillar provides something that the other two cannot. Each is essential to achieving our overall objective of financial stability. The combination of the three approaches provides greater benefits than the sole consideration of any one of the three.

The comprehensive nature of Basel II, however, goes beyond the combined action of the three pillars. As I have indicated, a broad range of risks is covered, not only due to the inclusion of operational risk, but also to the need to consider all those not explicitly taken into account in Pillar 1. Moreover, special consideration has been given to the fact that there are increasingly complex transactions which need to be appropriately included. Perhaps the most illustrative example here is the treatment of asset securitization. Nor should one fail to mention that numerous risk-mitigation techniques have been incorporated with a view to achieving a greater approximation between economic and regulatory capital.

2.3.8   *Evolutionary approach*

I have referred throughout my speech to the notable evolution of banking systems in recent decades. All of us will agree that today it is possible to observe, among other things, greater business sophistication, a greater degree of internationalization and stronger competition in financial markets. This situation of permanent change will continue in the near future, since the industry we seek to regulate and supervise is essentially dynamic. Accordingly, the supervisory model must be flexible and must have the capacity to evolve with time.

The new framework is intended to be a more forward-looking approach to capital supervision, and certainly the Committee intends to keep Basel II up-to-date with changes in risk management in the industry. We must continue to monitor industry developments to make sure that Basel II reflects sound practices. Banking supervisors face the challenge of responding meaningfully to these trends without curbing financial innovation. We intend to do so in part by continuing to cultivate a dialogue with industry participants, other supervisors, academics and researchers in the coming months and years.

In fact, the Committee has already begun its work in various areas. One concerns the treatment of 'double default', the situation that arises when a borrower and a guarantor both default on the same obligation. We are likewise undertaking similar work on another technical area, namely a joint project with the International Organization of Securities Commissions (IOSCO) on various issues related to trading activities.

Over the longer term, the Committee intends to discuss risk-management practices that aim to quantify measures of risk and economic capital, the so-called full credit risk models. Leading institutions have invested substantial resources in modelling credit risk, something that Basel II stops short of recognizing for regulatory capital requirements. We recognize the need to continue discussing such practices with banks and we intend to use Basel II as a means of developing experience in the performance of models.

The Committee will continue this discussion with a view to potentially allowing the greater use of credit risk modelling for regulatory capital purposes in the future and working towards the recognition of diversification effects. These discussions will focus on addressing concerns such as those regarding the reliability, comparability, validation and competitive equity that might arise when greater recognition of full credit risk modelling is permitted.

2.3.9   *Consistency through co-operation*

Finally, one of the main changes that financial systems have undergone has been their growing internationalization. The increasing scope and complexity of banking groups and financial markets are additional challenges that all of us must take into account. This is why it is necessary today to increase the degree of co-operation between the supervisors of different jurisdictions. Combining the necessary supervision at the local level in the host country with effective supervision at the consolidated level in the home country effectively requires greater co-operation, more thorough information-exchange, and better knowledge of financial instruments and links within financial groups.

Basel II is intended to promote a more level playing field for internationally active banks. We want banks to focus on managing their risks rather than managing the demands of different supervisors. The task is extremely difficult because there are differences in legal systems, market practices and business environments in each country. In fact, we cannot and should not expect to create perfect uniformity across all jurisdictions. One of the most important principles underpinning Basel II is the recognition of diversity.

All the foregoing is recognized in Basel II. Moreover, the successful implementation of Basel II requires the promotion of co-operation among supervisors, in order to prevent them adopting very different sets of expectations for banks and interpretations of the minimum requirements.

The Committee set up the so-called Accord Implementation Group (AIG) in late 2001, which seeks to identify and strengthen the mechanisms that may help further international co-operation between banking supervisors. The role of the AIG has become even more important now that the Basel II implementation phase has begun.

I do not intend to enter into the details of the work of the AIG, but let me remind you that we have published a set of high-level principles on cross-border implementation. In addition to these principles, the AIG is currently undertaking a number of 'real case' studies. Such studies have proven to be an important means for improving our understanding of the kind of practical enhanced arrangements and supervisory plans of home and host jurisdictions that are crucial to the effective implementation of Basel II.

2.3.10 Conclusions: the necessary mix of macro and micro perspectives

To conclude, let me insist on an additional general principle that I think supervision should be built on, which I mentioned earlier. Supervision needs to consider a broader analysis of the vulnerabilities internal and external to the banking sector, including the necessary macroeconomic and institutional elements, and those relating to the stability of the financial markets on which banks operate. Basel II recognizes the importance of a combination of micro and macro factors for achieving greater financial stability.

Macro factors must be taken into account because many financial crises have not stemmed from shocks arising in the financial sector, but rather from macroeconomic causes.

Equally important, the Basel Committee believes that if banks are adequately capitalized, well managed and risks are correctly assessed within the appropriate time horizon, their behaviour will be more stable and they will be better equipped to face periods of financial difficulty.

What is more, when banks have the proper incentives to manage risks appropriately and maintain sufficient capital based on such risks, the financial sector will become more resilient and better able to promote sustainable growth.

I am absolutely convinced that Basel II is an important step forward in this direction. Indeed, I think that it appropriately recognizes and promotes macro and micro elements as the proper means of fostering financial stability.

Thank you very much for your attention.

3 Markets and institutions

Managing the evolving financial risk

Malcolm D. Knight

I am very pleased to address this Colloquium. The relationship between the BIS and SUERF goes far back in time and has been a very fruitful one. For many years now SUERF has promoted research in money and finance, topics that – not surprisingly – are close to our hearts at the BIS. Moreover SUERF, inspired by its pan-European charter, has adopted an international point of view in approaching these issues – one that is attentive to both the similarities and the differences in national experiences. This has made SUERF's contribution particularly appealing to an organisation such as the BIS, because our mandate is to promote international cooperation and mutual understanding among national policymakers, especially within the central banking and supervisory communities.

The theme of this Colloquium is competition in financial services. Sometimes this is interpreted narrowly, as having to do with the interactions of players within a single sector of the financial industry. Today, I would like to take a broader perspective and explore the implications of changes in the financial industry as a whole for the nature of financial risk and for how to deal with it. My focus will be very much on the interactions between the various segments of the industry in general, and between markets and financial institutions in particular.

I will argue that the fundamental transformation of the financial industry over the past three decades, of which we are all keenly aware, has driven a significant transformation in the nature of financial risk. I will stress, in particular, how this transformation has resulted in a tighter interaction between different types of risk and the increased prominence of what has been called the 'endogenous' component of financial risk, namely the component that is associated with the impact of the collective actions of market participants on the underlying determinants of risk itself. And although market participants and prudential authorities have been adjusting admirably to these fundamental changes, there is still considerable scope for improvement, and a number of questions remain unanswered.

The structure of my remarks is the following. First, I will briefly recall the main features of the transformation of the financial industry and explore in more detail the associated profound transformation that has been occurring in the nature of financial risk itself. I will then consider the implications of these deep changes in the financial system for market participants and for prudential authorities, tracing the progress made and the areas that call for greater attention.

3.1 A transformed financial landscape alters the nature of risk

By now it is well known that the financial system has undergone a profound transformation over the past three decades, driven by the combined impact of liberalisation and technological innovation. The result has been what might be termed the 'let-a-thousand-flowers-bloom' phenomenon. Long gone is the excessive segmentation of different compartments of the financial system that was induced by extensive regulation. And the industry has gained enormously in richness, depth and variety. Just think of the myriad of new financial instruments that has developed, partly in the wake of breakthroughs in pricing theory and advances in computing technologies.

The impact of these trends on the financial landscape has been profound and multifaceted. For present purposes, however, let me focus on just two aspects: size and interconnectedness.

First, the size of the financial sphere of our economies has increased tremendously along different dimensions. Financial activity now represents a much larger share of aggregate economic activity than it did 20 or 30 years ago, regardless of how it is measured. This is true in terms of inputs, such as employment and capital, in terms of outputs, such as the ratio of credit to GDP, and above all in terms of turnover. As you know, monthly global turnover in the main asset classes far exceeds yearly global GDP. Within financial services, traded instruments have greatly outgrown traditional non-traded ones, such as loans or deposits. This is sometimes described, somewhat misleadingly, as financial markets having grown at the expense of financial institutions. Think, for instance, of the extraordinary expansion of derivatives, including more recently credit derivatives, and of asset-backed securities. Furthermore, individual financial institutions have also grown impressively in size. In the industrial countries, successive waves of consolidation have been creating a small group of dominant firms domestically and, more importantly, at a global level.

My second observation is that the different facets of financial activity have become much more tightly interconnected, as evident in two complementary trends. On the one hand, we have witnessed a broadening of the range of players engaged in the same type of financial activity. And on the other hand, the surge in cross-border activity has heightened the role of non-residents in domestic markets in many countries. With securitisation and the development of secondary markets, portfolio investors, such as insurance companies and pension funds, have diversified into areas that used to be the exclusive domain of credit originators, notably banks. Likewise, there are few substantive differences between the activities of the proprietary desks of the larger commercial and investment banks and those of smaller, independent institutional investors such as hedge funds and private equity financiers. We have also witnessed a broadening of the range of activities performed by any given player. Think, for instance, of the growth of conglomerates, or of the much more diversified investment portfolios of some institutional investors and, via mutual funds, of households themselves.

Another way of describing some of these changes is to say that, somewhat paradoxically, even as the financial system has become more diverse, we have witnessed greater convergence: between financial institutions and capital markets; among different types of financial institutions; and among different national jurisdictions.

What are the implications of these structural trends for the transformation of financial risk? Let me focus on four of them: the nexus with the real economy, the interaction between different types of risk, the relative roles of markets and institutions, and the link between the measurement of value and the measurement of risk.

First, uncontroversially, the management of financial risk has become a more important aspect of economic activity. This also means that problems in the financial system, if and when they emerge, can have larger consequences for the real economy than they did in the past. The message has been hammered home by the costs of the financial crises that have occurred in both industrial and emerging market countries over the past two decades. Not surprisingly, addressing financial instability has become a major policy concern, both nationally and internationally.

Second, more subtly, there is a sense in which the nature of financial risk has become at once purer and more complex. Financial risk has become purer because the myriad of new financial instruments, tailored to the needs of a broader set of investors, has enhanced our ability to dissect a complex risk into its simpler components. Derivatives, for instance, target specific forms of risk; first market risk and, more recently, credit risk. Likewise, collateralised debt obligations (CDOs) slice and dice the risks in the underlying portfolios so as to make them more attractive to particular investors. As a result, more efficient risk transfer mechanisms allow a closer matching between the risk-bearing capacity of players and the types of risk they take on. By the same token, the old analysis of risk that was structured around traditional business lines has become increasingly irrelevant. In other words, the similarities in underlying risks are becoming more apparent, regardless of the type of financial firm incurring them.

In this changed environment, financial risk has become more complex, for several reasons. For one, the deconstruction process does not eliminate risk, it simply transforms it and transfers it among economic agents. Risk is deconstructed to be reassembled in different packages and distributed among different holders. For instance, derivative instruments that originally targeted market risk resulted, as a by-product, in a pyramiding of counterparty risk that required separate management. More fundamentally, we now realise that as the management of risk increasingly comes to depend on mitigation techniques based on instruments that are traded in markets, elements that are extraneous to the parties directly involved in a transaction have a stronger influence on the risks incurred through it. For example, in an ordinary bank loan, credit risk depends exclusively on the financial standing of the borrower. By contrast, counterparty risk in a market transaction depends fundamentally on market conditions, such as liquidity and volatility, which are well beyond the control of the two parties to the contract. In this way, the vast development of risk transfer markets in recent years has strengthened the nexus between the different types of risk and the prices charged for bearing these risks. But the opaque layering of direct and indirect links through the markets also profoundly complicates the assessment of the true underlying risks.

Third, for much the same reasons and contrary to conventional wisdom, the roles of financial markets and financial institutions have become more complementary. At first sight this may appear counterintuitive. After all, the conventional classification of financial systems distinguishes between those where intermediation takes place mostly on the balance sheet of institutions and those where financing through capital market transactions is more pervasive. Institution-based systems put more emphasis on the ability of intermediaries to extract and utilise information about borrowers by leveraging close and long-term relationships. Transactions-based systems are founded on the ability of the market mechanism to distil the diversity in investors' views into a single price; they emphasise transparency of information and arm's-length relationships. Clearly, there are large benefits for economies that combine effectively both intermediation channels. The ability to switch smoothly between balance sheet financing and market-based financing contributes to the robustness of a financial system and improves its ability to deal with strain. Think, for instance, of the resilience exhibited by the US financial system in the early 1990s as one of the two channels of finance – commercial banks – experienced difficulties.

At the same time, the greater complementarity between these two forms of intermediation should not be overlooked. On the one hand, institutions rely more and more on markets for their funding, for their investments and, crucially, for the management of risks. Continued market liquidity is essential in this context. On the other hand, markets rely more and more on institutions for their liquidity, drawing on market-making services and backstop credit lines. Globally, the ongoing consolidation in the financial sector has created a smaller number of very large financial firms that are engaged in both types of intermediation. But financial conglomerates that combine commercial and investment banking operations, insurance and brokering services raise potential concentration risks for the financial system, despite apparent diversification of intermediation channels. In these large, internationally active financial institutions, a common capital base underpins on-balance sheet intermediation, capital market services and market-making functions. By the same token, losses in one activity can put pressure on the entire firm, affecting its activities in other areas.

Fourth, arguably the interaction between the determination of value and the drivers of risk has become tighter, or at least more clearly visible. This is not simply because market participants, in determining valuations, have become more operationally aware of the importance of risk assessments and the willingness to take on risk. Think, for instance, of the growing use of risk-adjusted returns as a basis for evaluating performance and allocating capital. More fundamentally, what is sometimes referred to as the 'endogenous' component of risk has become more prominent. This is the component that reflects the impact of the collective actions of market participants on the ultimate drivers of risk themselves, such as asset prices and system-wide leverage. While this endogenous component of risk has always existed, it has arguably become more visible as a result of several factors. One is the relaxation of aggregate financing constraints associated with financial liberalisation. Another is the much larger role played by markets, with prices telescoping the impact of the changing collective assessments and attitudes towards risk. A third is the increasing common component of asset prices that results from the greater interconnectedness of the financial system, as exemplified by the closer co-movement of returns across different asset classes, especially in times of stress.

This endogeneity is natural – it is part of the physiology of the financial system. At times, though, it may have undesirable side effects and result in financial distress. For example, lending booms can boost economic activity and asset prices to unsustainable levels, sowing the seeds of subsequent instability. Likewise, if a large number of financial market participants assume that markets will remain liquid even under collective selling pressure, they could be induced to overextend their position-taking, thus generating the very pressures that would cause markets to become illiquid. From this perspective, financial distress reflects the unwinding of financial imbalances that have gradually built up over time.

This type of behaviour can be collectively dysfunctional. And it is especially hard to address because it can be fully consistent with individually rational behaviour. It is, for instance, consistent with the short horizons that are inherent in contractual arrangements designed to address informational asymmetries between providers and users of funds, such as arrangements for the frequent and regular assessment of third-party asset managers' performance. Concerns with underperformance in the short term may numb the contrarian instincts of investors and push them to seek safety in numbers. Likewise, the impact of the rational retrenchment of individual investors and market-makers in reaction to spikes in market volatility or losses can trigger a self-propelling spiral of selling, market price declines and evaporating liquidity. Tighter financing constraints at those times can exacerbate distress further. These mechanisms were quite prominent, for instance, in the market turbulence following the Russian default and the long-term capital management (LTCM) crisis of 1998.

3.2   Implications for market participants

The structural changes I have just discussed have had a profound impact on the way market participants measure and manage financial risk. Risk management has now become a core activity for financial firms, with much more resources devoted to it at all levels of an enterprise. More specifically, its transformation has largely mirrored that of the broader environment. Let me briefly review three changes and highlight areas where further work is desirable.

First, companies have increasingly focused on the management of risk on a firm-wide basis. The general principle is that similar risks should be measured and managed in a similar way across the firm, irrespective of their location. This process has been encouraged by the gradual emergence of a 'common risk language', cutting across traditional distinctions along functional lines. In the process, the financial industry is reconciling differences in methods and frameworks reflecting historical and institutional factors. After all, the value-at-risk measures that are common in banking and the stochastic asset-liability techniques that are common in insurance are, conceptually, the same sort of tool; they differ primarily with respect to the instruments that are included in the analysis and the horizon used for assessing risk. As a recent Joint Forum report has concluded, this natural and welcome trend is unmistakable, although it still has a long way to go.

Second, firms have adopted a more holistic approach to risk management, taking into account the interactions between different types of risk. The long-term ideal would be a fully integrated treatment of risk, based on a common metric. Here again, the trend is unmistakable but the challenge is truly daunting. Current measurement technology is just not sufficiently advanced. In line with trends in the development of markets, the process has advanced furthest in the integration of market risk and credit risk; it is at best incipient for other categories of risk, not least for liquidity risk. Arguably, stress testing is the only concrete tool available that allows firms to analyse the joint impact of the broader set of risks in a meaningful way. This practice should be encouraged and developed further. Indeed, investors should be demanding more information about the outcomes of firms' stress tests as part of their due diligence analysis.

Third, the area that remains largely unexplored is the treatment of the 'endogenous' component of risk. This raises questions with regard to both risk measurement and risk management.

As regards measurement, stress tests can of course help here too: they are a way of describing scenarios where the interaction between market participants' responses to risk and the evolution of that risk can be mapped out, however crudely. I would argue, nevertheless, that firms should devote more resources to two additional tasks. One is developing techniques that uncover vulnerabilities which emerge from the endogeneity of risk. Of course here I am referring to the signs of overextension that can herald subsequent distress. Work in this area, including at the Bank for International Settlements (BIS), has met with some success in identifying leading indicators of banking crises at business cycle frequencies, on the basis of simple proxies for 'excessive' credit and asset price expansion. One may wonder whether similar indicators might also be possible for signs of pending market distress, as occurred during autumn 1998. Perhaps such indicators could be based on measures of excessive compression of spreads and some indirect measures of market leverage. Another task is to seek to disentangle more purposefully the impact of changes in risk assessments from that of changes in the market's risk appetite when evaluating risk using the information embedded in asset prices. Many commonly used measures of risk, such as those derived from equity prices and credit spreads, are likely to be contaminated by time-varying risk appetite. This introduces an extraneous element that can lull participants into a false sense of security, because it is precisely high risk appetite that can sow the seeds of subsequent problems.

As regards risk management, the challenge is even more daunting. Addressing it clashes with the incentive structures that are at the root of the problem. Admittedly, even here some progress seems to have been made. For instance, a recent survey conducted by the BIS-based Committee on the Global Financial System (CGFS) suggests that, since the events of autumn 1998, some key market participants have become less inclined to respond automatically to risk-limit violations because they now have a better awareness and understanding of the strategic interdependencies among players, and the impacts on market prices. This is an area that, by its very nature, falls naturally within the remit of prudential authorities, whose task is precisely that of internalising such externalities.

3.3 Implications for prudential authorities and standard setters

To a considerable extent, the implications of the changing nature of financial risk for prudential authorities mirror those for the private sector. In the limited time that remains, let me briefly highlight four points: the need for consistency in the treatment of risk across sectors; the need to strengthen the macroprudential orientation of prudential frameworks; the need to improve their incentive compatibility; and the need to promote a financial reporting framework that is fully consistent with best practice in risk management.

First, the wide-ranging convergence process in the financial industry naturally calls for greater consistency in the supervisory treatment of financial risk across sectors, be they geographical jurisdictions or functional segments of the industry. Greater consistency of prudential rules enhances the efficiency of the financial system by removing any distortions embedded in the policy framework, notably by promoting a level playing field and reducing the scope for regulatory arbitrage. As you are well aware, substantial progress has been made here.

Across geographical jurisdictions, progress is most advanced in banking, less so in insurance. Across functional lines, it has clearly proceeded much further within national jurisdictions, not least helped by the increasingly common practice of consolidating financial sector supervision into a single agency. At the same time, some steps have also been taken internationally. Witness the work of the Joint Forum, which brings together representatives of the international regulatory authorities in banking, securities and insurance. Increasingly, the benefits to prudential authorities from developing a common view are becoming evident.

Second, improving the safeguards against instability for a financial system that is larger and more interconnected, and where the endogenous component of risk is more prominent, naturally calls for a strengthening of the macroprudential orientation of prudential frameworks. After all, it is now well accepted that a system-wide perspective and a focus on the endogenous component of risk are precisely the distinguishing features of such an approach. This 'macro' orientation requires a shift away from the notion that the stability of the system is simply a consequence of the soundness of its individual components. It involves the same shift in focus that a stock analyst is required to make in order to become a portfolio manager. In evaluating financial system vulnerabilities, a macroprudential approach would focus on the commonality in the risk exposures of the different segments of the financial system. In calibrating policy instruments, it would stress the need to establish cushions as financial imbalances build up, in order to give more scope to run them down as the imbalances unwind. This would act as a kind of self-equilibrating mechanism. The logic is analogous to that of calling for fiscal consolidation in good times to allow an effective counter-cyclical fiscal policy in bad times.

By now, the importance of the macroprudential perspective as a complement to the more traditional microprudential focus is widely recognised. As a result, steps have been taken to put it into practice. For instance, as regards the task of identifying vulnerabilities, macroprudential analysis is now routinely carried out in various forums, including the IMF and the World Bank, the Financial Stability Forum and the CGFS; and, of course, in many national jurisdictions. As regards the calibration of policy instruments, too, there are signs of a keener awareness. In banking, for instance, one such illustration is the various adjustments that were made to Basel II, at least partly with a view to addressing concerns about procyclicality. And banking supervisors here in Spain have gone one step further, by adopting statistical provisioning in loan accounting. This provides a long-term anchor to loan provisioning that is independent of the state of the business cycle. Efforts to strengthen the macroprudential perspective should be pursued further, but they may well need to await the development of additional analytical tools to help measurement and calibration.

Third, in a highly interconnected and innovative financial system the prudential framework should work as far as possible with private incentives. This means empowering, rather than numbing, the natural incentive of market participants to instil discipline. And it means avoiding the imposition of rules that do not meet the 'use test' by firms. An excessively prescriptive approach is an invitation for regulatory arbitrage and for practices that respect the letter of the standards but violate their spirit. Hence the major efforts by regulators to develop standards in close cooperation and consultation with the regulated communities in the private sector, to stress the adequacy of risk management processes and to strengthen disclosures. These are all welcome trends that should be encouraged further.

Fourth, the financial convergence process has put a premium on a common set of financial reporting standards; hence the current efforts of international accounting standard setters to put one in place. This is a worthy goal that has profound implications for the financial system and for financial risk. The measurement of value for accounting purposes has a first-order effect on the behaviour of financial institutions and their risk management, given the intimate link between valuations and risk. The stakes are high. And at the same time, the process of establishing such standards has brought to the fore significant differences of views between accounting standard setters on the one hand, and prudential authorities on the other. It is important that these differences be reconciled.

I wanted to flag this issue because of its importance, although I know full well that I cannot do it justice in my remarks today. In a recent speech to the International Conference of Banking Supervisors, I have discussed the key ingredients of the debate and offered a sketch of a possible solution. Here, let me simply make three points. First, it seems desirable to think of the ultimate goal of any such reconciliation as establishing a set of accounting rules that seek to portray the best approximation to an 'unbiased' and comprehensive picture of the financial condition of firms while prudential regulators seek to instil the desired degree of prudence in their behaviour on the basis of that portrayal. This would mean avoiding reliance on deliberately conservative estimates of value as a means of establishing safety cushions. Second, the portrayal of the financial condition of a firm should cover not just its profitability, cash flows and balance sheet, as it does today, but also its risk profile, including some indication of the margin of error surrounding point estimates. This is an area where prudential authorities have taken the lead, by encouraging greater risk disclosure by regulated firms. Finally, it is essential that at all stages during the transition towards this long-run goal, the prudential authorities are in a position to redress any adverse implications which changes in accounting standards that are desirable in the long term may have for the safety and soundness of regulated financial intermediaries over the near to medium term. In other words, the transition should be properly coordinated. It is my hope, and my expectation, that the dialogue between prudential supervisors and accounting authorities will intensify and become more institutionalised.

* * *

In closing, let me summarise the key message. I have argued that the trends in the financial system have brought about a transformation in the nature of financial risk. These trends have put a premium on the links and interactions between different types of risk, largely reflecting a tighter relationship between financial institutions and financial markets. This transformation requires adapting risk management both at the level of individual firms and in the financial system as a whole. Essential dimensions of this adaptation are greater consistency in the treatment of similar types of risk, greater analysis of the interaction between different types of risk and a keener recognition of the endogenous component of risk. Progress has been made in many of these dimensions, but there is clearly scope for further improvements.

The academic community can play an important role in supporting and shaping this adaptation. More research is needed in understanding the interactions between different types of risk and the way they, in turn, are shaped by the structure of markets and institutions. The same is true for the analysis of the mechanisms that underpin the endogeneity of financial risk. And ways need to be found to turn this greater understanding into operational solutions. These are not easy questions and they often require skills that transcend disciplinary boundaries. Policymakers are eagerly awaiting the answers. I certainly hope that researchers' inquiring and agile minds will seek to provide them.

Thank you.

4 Macroeconomic consequences of financial regulation

Josef Christl

4.1 Introduction

Many economic policy debates during the past two decades have been guided by a principle that could be characterized as "regulatory skepticism." This skepticism has its roots in historic experience with the limits of economic policy and the daily experience with tight constraints policymakers have to face in a globalized world. This general skepticism has affected some areas in economics more than others. Financial regulation is an issue that has been relatively unaffected. It is a widely held conventional wisdom that the financial system has to be firmly embedded in quite an extensive regulatory framework, and debates seem to revolve around details of this framework rather than focus on the principle itself.

This general attitude to financial regulation is of course rooted in historic experience of episodes of financial crises and the difficulties to deal with them as well as in insights from a huge body of research in economics and finance. We know that the costs of financial instability can be huge and affect a large number of people.

Nevertheless it might be worthwhile to take the occasion of this lecture to have a look at financial regulation in the spirit of regulatory skepticism. Regulators always have to be careful not to represent special interests and to devise policies that promote these special interests in the name of the common goal "financial stability."

For these reasons, clear ideas about what exactly financial regulation aims to achieve and the analysis of the exact mechanisms by which certain regulatory policies are supposed to work are essential. In particular, this requires pinning down as precisely as possible the nature of market failures which regulatory intervention tries to correct. Furthermore, it is important to consider not only the direct but also the indirect consequences of financial regulation.

Given the fundamental role of the financial system in directing funds from households to productive investments of firms and in allocating and sharing risks, the indirect consequences of regulation are most likely to occur in the form of repercussions for the economy as a whole. These repercussions have to be carefully considered when we assess the benefits and costs of financial regulation.

To be honest, I will not be able to provide a definite – sometimes not even a preliminary – answer. I will raise some issues concerning financial regulation that deserve consideration and perhaps further critical assessment. In particular, I want to argue by way of examples that macroeconomic aspects should be given more consideration in the design and the practice of financial regulation.

Having said this I should point out that the regulatory community and academia have recently discussed numerous arguments and thoughts in this direction. I am therefore not raising new issues but rather trying to contribute to an ongoing discussion. I hope that this discussion will ultimately result in a better understanding of the possibilities as well as the limits of financial regulation.

4.2 What is the problem?

When we look at financial crises we experienced in the past, nearly all of them were caused by large macroeconomic shocks: huge hikes in interest rates, extreme exchange rate and stock market movements or recessionary dynamics in general. This observation is important because it suggests that the exposure to these risk factors lies at the heart of the problem of financial instability and systemic crises.

Emphasizing the link between financial instability and adverse macro-economic developments might seem obvious to most of you. However, it is worthwhile to point out that much of the economic literature on banking crises and bank runs drawing on an influential paper by Diamond and Dybvig (1983) has taken a different perspective. The focus in this literature has been on the dynamics of an event that starts somewhere in the banking system with the failure of a single institution and then affects other institutions through various contagion channels, such as information effects, or through direct interbank credit links.

The macroeconomic perspective suggested earlier hints to the other source of financial instability. Financial institutions may have correlated exposures, and an adverse economic shock may directly result in simultaneous failures. Research recently undertaken at the Oesterreichische Nationalbank and the Bank of England has shown that quantitatively correlated exposures dominate the contagion problem by a huge margin as a source of systemic risk, providing evidence for the casual observation made previously.

Looking at the problem from this perspective does, of course, not provide us with an answer to the question how these exposures to macroeconomic risk factors are built up and whether this is something that regulatory policy can and should deal with. Here the story has to be augmented by further considerations in particular by a time dimension.

Borio (2003) described a stylized pattern of a financial cycle as it had repeatedly been observed in the past, notwithstanding the many differences between individual crises with respect to the different patterns of vulnerability as well as with respect to the triggering events. The build-up of imbalances that trigger a crisis usually starts under booming economic conditions. This boom is accompanied by a climate of overly optimistic risk assessment, the gradual weakening of financing and credit constraints and rising asset prices – in particular those of property and real estate. In this climate financial and real imbalances build up. At some point an essentially unpredictable trigger like an asset price drop or the interruption of an investment boom causes a sudden rundown of financial buffers, and once these buffers are exhausted and the contraction exceeds a certain threshold, a full-scale financial crisis occurs.

This stylized story has some essential features which are worthwhile to emphasize here. First we see a dynamic interaction between the financial system and the real economy over time during the build-up of the crises. Therefore, rather than the cross-section perspective, the intertemporal perspective, which looks at a set of institutions at a single point in time, is essential. Common exposures to interest rate risk, exchange rate risk, and the business cycle in general play a dominant role. Much of the build-up of the crises occurs on the asset side of a bank's balance sheet, whereas the liability side plays its main role in the unfolding and triggering of the crises.

Maybe less obvious but nevertheless important is the fact that the build-up of a crisis through the dynamic, intertemporal interaction between the financial system and the real economy suggests that the risks are to a large extent endogenous. They both influence and are themselves influenced by the behavior of people in the financial system. This feedback mechanism should be taken into account when policy measures are designed. Again, it may be obvious to most of you familiar with the day-to-day reality of the financial system. I emphasize it because many of the quantitative state-of-the-art risk assessment models we use in analyzing financial risks rely on the assumption that financial risks are driven by an exogenous random process, which influences the behavior of financial market participants but itself is not influenced by their behavior. These models therefore assume away the feedback mechanism between behavior and risk, which plays such an important role in the reality of financial markets, in particular in situations of crises and distress.

Having sketched a stylized picture of financial instability and having pointed out the main features characterizing it, we may ask what the role of a regulator in all of this is. We have learned from the past that the triggering event is essentially unpredictable and diverse. It is furthermore beyond the control of any particular individual, even of such institutions as financial regulators and central banks. Their potential role seems to be connected to the dynamic problem of the build-up of imbalances and the monitoring and early understanding of the emergence of a crisis situation rather than to the triggering event itself.

Still the question is what the exact nature of the problem in the build-up of crises is. I think we can identify two different problems. One is a fairly straight-forward externality problem. Financial market participants may have an incentive to take more risks than a socially optimal risk allocation would require because in their plans they take into account only the individual costs of their decisions but not the social costs that occur in a situation of financial distress. Yet it is of course not fully clear what the exact reason may be that market prices do not reflect the full costs of taking risky decisions. Given one believes the externality story the problem of the regulator is to implement an optimal risk allocation by suitable policy instruments. In practice, this is of course not exactly a neat textbook problem and requires considerable judgment and practical expertise. The second problem seems to be a coordination problem. The feedback from behavior to the build-up of risk and back to behavior can lead to a coordination problem: it is individually rational to act on the overly optimistic risk assessment as long as everybody else does but again the social optimum might lie elsewhere. Many such situations are discussed abstractly in game theory. Here the role of the regulator becomes one of supporting coordination on a sustainable equilibrium of behavior.

The challenging problem in all cases is to deal with the characteristic feedback loop where actions of financial market participants influence financial risks and these risks feed back on actions and so on. This feedback loop lies at the heart of the problem why regulatory instruments may have macroeconomic consequences.

4.3 Regulatory policy and macroeconomic consequences

Financial regulation encompasses both markets and financial institutions, most importantly banks. In the area of markets, financial regulation mainly concentrates on providing a legal framework (a set of rules) that facilitates the market exchange of financial instruments. From an abstract viewpoint, financial contracts are promises to exchange goods or money between different points in time and across different possible future states of the world. This very nature of financial contracts brings along a host of incentive, enforcement, and information problems, which create a direct need for this legal infrastructure. If we pass on to financial institutions, regulation often interferes directly with the decisions that can be taken by economic agents, like restrictions on asset holdings and competition or restrictions on the capital structure of banks. Thus, these regulatory measures interfere with the feedback loop between behavior and financial risks discussed earlier and are therefore notoriously hard to assess.

The regulatory instrument that has been given most attention during the past decade, certainly, is capital adequacy for banks. It is the regulatory instrument most frequently discussed in the context of financial stability as well as concerning its macroeconomic consequences. It thus perhaps serves as a good example to discuss some of the more general issues that I want to raise here.

Usually, the following two arguments are given in favor of capital adequacy: first, it is seen as an instrument limiting excessive risk taking by bank owners with limited liability and, thus, promoting optimal risk sharing between bank owners and depositors. Second, capital adequacy regulation is often viewed as a buffer against insolvency crises, limiting the costs of financial distress by reducing the probability of insolvency of banks. It is the hope of regulators that capital adequacy provides a safeguard against a systemic crisis, the widespread breakdown of financial intermediation.

In the context of the stylized facts of the build-up of crises and the given dynamics, these arguments focus on the cross-sectional rather than on the intertemporal aspect of risk. The idea that a bank that holds more equity has larger buffers against the risks it is exposed to does not relate directly to the dynamic story of how equity may be optimally adjusted over time.

The cross-sectional view has also shaped the big recent changes to capital adequacy in the Basel II framework. In an effort to improve risk sensitivity, the new framework stipulates that minimum capital for a given portfolio changes with its perceived riskiness as measured by external or internal ratings. This is a big reform step that leads to a much better relative risk assessment across institutions at a given point in time. Without doubt, this reform is a milestone that will substantially improve risk management and risk awareness.

One of the discussions in the run-up to the New Basel Capital Accord concerned the macroeconomic implications of capital requirements if they are set independently of macroeconomic conditions. The arguments that have been raised have been based mostly on an intertemporal perspective and mainly concerned the endogenous nature of financial risks.

The basic argument is plain and straightforward. When the economy is hit by a recession enterprises' debt service is impaired. The reduction in bank profits – in absence of compensating issues of outside equity or reduction in dividends – leads to a reduction in bank equity. No matter how sophisticated the cross-sectional capital regulation is calibrated this decline in bank equity must result in reductions in bank lending. This in turn reduces business investments and exacerbates the shock to aggregate demand. Thus, in an intertemporal context the regulation that boosts individual buffers at the bank level acts as a potential crises amplifier at the system level through the macroeconomic consequences of the regulatory instrument. Clearly, if we take the stylized story of financial crises and crisis dynamics seriously the intertemporal aspects of risk are perhaps not yet sufficiently taken into account. The previous analysis of crisis dynamics implies that the adjustment of capital over time requires as much attention as the cross-sectional aspects that are now taken into account in a very detailed and sophisticated way.

Let me now – as a second example – turn to the problem of coordinating expectations. The coordination problem arises when in a climate of overly optimistic risk assessment it might be optimal for each individual to respond by equally overly optimistic assessments as long as everybody else holds excessively optimistic views about the economic environment. Here the dynamics of expectations have a potentially huge impact on financial cycles with repercussions for the macroeconomic environment. Expert risk assessments by institutions in charge of financial stability, such as central banks and supervisors, act as potentially important coordination devices and can contribute to coordinating expectations to realistic and well-founded risk assessments. Exactly these aspects are the motivation for many central banks to publish financial stability reports.

We have seen that led by the Basel process, impressive progress in quantitative risk assessment models and in the skillful use of these techniques by supervisors and regulatory institutions in charge of financial stability has been taking place. The difficulty of many of these techniques so far is that they are devised for individual banking institutions and not for the system as a whole. To capture systemic risk, it is however, decisive to take a system perspective. Elsinger *et al.* (2002) and, in a recent paper, Elsinger *et al.* (2005) demonstrate that an individual institution approach that ignores correlations and interlinkages – as many quantitative risk assessment models do – does indeed underestimate systemic events of bank insolvencies by a considerable margin.

I think that regulatory institutions in charge of maintaining financial stability can contribute a great deal to coordinate expectations on realistic risk assessments by devising credible and good quantitative models that are able to capture risk at the level of the banking system. Such contributions can establish a beneficial link between regulatory supervision and financial stability. If they smoothen expectation-driven financial cycles, a positive impact on macroeconomic stabilization can be established. If such models can be run at regular intervals with a continuous updating of information risk assessment over time may also be improved.

4.4 Conclusions

So let me conclude. I have taken the viewpoint of a regulatory skeptic to point out some of the particular challenges financial regulation has to face. In an attempt to pin down the major reasons why we might want regulatory intervention in the first place I have identified an externality problem and a coordination problem. Both problems are intimately connected to the dynamic nature of financial instability. Both problems mainly materialize in the dynamics and the build-up of financial and real imbalances, which then suddenly unfold, triggered by an essentially unpredictable event. The dynamics are so intricate because the major risks are endogenously driven by a feedback from macroeconomic conditions to behavior and back to macroeconomic conditions.

I have argued using the example of capital adequacy regulation that this instrument is very finely tuned to considerations of relative risk at a particular point in time and less so to the intertemporal aspects, which is where the externality problem kicks in. Thus further explorations to include the intertemporal aspects and therefore to design the instrument with a stronger focus on its macroeconomic consequences may be useful.

I have also pointed out the usefulness of quantitative models of risk assessment for coordinating expectations about financial developments. A shortcoming of many of these models is that they are geared very much toward individual institutions rather than to the system as a whole and may therefore perform poorly in the assessment of systemic events. If these improvements can be successfully accomplished a reform of supervisory monitoring may be achieved that has a beneficial role in coordinating expectations and in supporting financial and macroeconomic stability.

Overall I think we have to strive for progress with respect to both the regulatory instruments that we use as well as the quantitative models we rely on in making our assessments. Thus with respect to financial stability we have to aspire to a state that has already been reached by monetary analysis. Here the policy instrument is clearly defined. The decisions are supported by a host of canonical quantitative models, which are built on a combination of theory, practical relevance, and empirical fit. The impact and feedback mechanisms of policy are fairly well understood and relatively uncontroversial.

There is no principal reason to assume that financial stability analysis and financial regulation will not arrive at a similar state of theoretical and practical knowledge in the future. The tremendous progress that has been made in the past two decades gives reason for such optimism. To foster this progress we will however need considerable further effort in research and a constant attempt to review current policy practice. I think that this conference and the activities of SUERF provide an excellent and valuable contribution to this ambitious goal.

Acknowledgment

I want to thank Martin Summer for helpful discussions and comments.

References

Borio, C. (2003). "Towards a macroprudential framework for financial market regulation and supervision," BIS Working Paper No. 128.

Diamond, D. and Dybvig, P. (1983). "Bank runs, deposit insurance and liquidity," *Journal of Political Economy*, 91(3), 401–419.

Elsinger, H., Lehar, A. and Summer, M. (2002). "Risk assessment for banking systems," OeNB Working Paper No. 79.

Elsinger, H., Lehar, A., Summer, M. and Wells, S. (2005). "Using market information for banking system risk assessment," *International Journal of Central Banking*, forthcoming.

5 The changing pattern of payments in the United States

Anthony M. Santomero

5.1 Introduction

Good morning. It is a pleasure to be here and a great honor to present this year's Marjolin lecture and prize. I thank you for the invitation and the opportunity to share some of my perspectives with you today.

As we bring the colloquium to a close this morning, we can reflect on the many ideas and challenges presented by the changing landscape of European financial services that have been discussed during our sessions. In preparing my lecture for the colloquium, I thought I could best contribute to the events of the past several days by offering you my commentary – as a career academic and current US central banker – on some changes taking place in the financial services industry "across the pond." Specifically, I thought I might use my time with you today to discuss what is happening in the US payments system. I believe you will find the changes occurring there interesting in their own right and as a point of comparison and contrast with what is happening in the European payments arena.

As anyone who knows the sector would readily admit, the origins and evolution of payments structures on our two continents could not be more different. Now, however, we are beginning to see signs that our two systems are starting to converge. We are both moving toward more electronic payment services through a number of vehicles. What we are experiencing is two systems that started out quite differently converging toward similar future systems. On the United States side, the pattern of payments is indeed evolving – some might say it is experiencing a radical change. America's paper-based payments system is giving way to a new realm of electronic payments vehicles – a transition that has already occurred in Europe. Indeed, there has been quite a bit of diversity in the forms of payments used in the United States. However, as is typical in this area, change has been, and will be, greatly affected by our financial history and its legacy systems.

This presents our central bank with many challenges, because unlike most central banks in Europe, the Federal Reserve is not only a regulator but also a service provider. We have been a vital part of the retail payments system since our founding over ninety years ago. From its inception, the Federal Reserve has had a dual role as the central bank charged with ensuring the integrity of the payments system and as a participant in its evolution.

Over time, the Fed's role in payments and that of European central banks are likely to converge as well. It is expected that the Fed's role in paper processing will diminish over time as checks recede in both absolute volume and relative importance in our retail payments system. As this occurs, it will further our resemblance to the central banks of Europe. Over time, both the Fed and European central banks will concentrate more of their efforts on their services on large dollar gross settlement, with TARGET 2 likely following the evolution of Fedwire.

So, with that prologue, I would like to spend my time with you today sharing my thoughts on payments concentrating on three issues:

- the current status of the US payments infrastructure *vis à vis* Europe's,
- how the roots and evolution of the US payment system differ from that of Europe,
- and finally, the likely future path of the US payment system and the Fed's role in it, with an emphasis on how we are likely to resemble Europe and how we will be different.

5.2   The current state of payments technology in the United States

Historically, Americans and Europeans have long relied on an entirely different mix of payments vehicles. For example, Europeans use cash roughly twice as much as Americans.

However, looking at our noncash transactions gives evidence of where our differences truly lie. In Europe, half of all noncash retail payments are made through a Giro system and only about 15 percent are made by check. In the United States, it is almost exactly the reverse. Half of all noncash retail payments are made by paper check and less than 10 percent are made through our automated clearing house (ACH), which is the American version of a Giro system.[1]

The dominance of the Giro in Europe and of the check in the United States is a long-standing feature of our respective payment systems. The history of how this dominance evolved is interesting and instructive, as I will elaborate in just a minute.

Payment cards account for the remainder of retail payments. Here there are similarities and differences between Europe and the United States. The similarities are in our use of debit cards. Debit cards, a relatively recent innovation, have caught on quickly both in Europe and in the United States, and now account for about a quarter of noncash retail payments in both places. The differences are in our use of credit cards. Credit cards have long been an important payment vehicle in the United States, and at present account for about a quarter of noncash retail payments there. In Europe, credit cards are used less frequently – in fewer than 10 percent of transactions, though I would note that Europeans' use of credit cards has picked up in recent years.[2]

The long-standing success of the credit card in the United States, and the rapid rise of the debit card in both Europe and the United States, are also interesting and instructive stories.

But first, let's begin with the story of the Giro and the check.

5.2.1 The European structure

To understand the dominance of the Giro in Europe and the check in the United States we have to go back about 100 years to the late nineteenth and early twentieth century. At that time, European banks did not provide routine payment services. They served primarily as merchant banks and as private banks for wealthy individuals.

In the late 1800s, local post offices began establishing postal Giro systems as a convenient way for common people to deposit savings and later evolved to allow them to remit and receive payments. The system was successful in that it allowed every post office savings account holder to make and receive payments both locally and nationally. This revolutionary achievement rendered noncash payment transactions accessible to large sectors of the population.

Later, in the 1950s and 1960s, European banks sought to broaden their business lines to encompass the mass market as a way to expand their deposit base to fund loans. This meant providing routine payments services to customers, and so bank Giro systems were created to handle the volume.

This evolution occurred relatively smoothly and rapidly as a result of Europe's concentrated banking industry – a few banks operating nationwide, cooperating closely with each other.

At the same time, European governments wanted to establish payment systems that minimized costs and maximized access. The advent of technological advances created such opportunities through electronification. When technology made it economical to replace paper Giros with electronic Giros, European governments pushed for the transition, and the concentration of the payments system in the hands of the postal service and a few national banks made it relatively easy to accomplish. Because of its Giro system, Europe had, or could easily set up, centralized accounts for credit transfers. In short, European central banks encouraged – and in some cases, mandated – the use of electronic Giro systems.

5.2.2 The US structure

In contrast, the US payments system evolved quite differently from Europe's. Historically, US banks tended to provide services – including payments services – to the broad spectrum of people and businesses. On the loan side, commercial banks focused on commercial and industrial lending, but they took deposit balances from all economic strata.

In early America, the geographical expanse of the country encouraged a fragmented system where state banks issued their own notes. Entry into the banking business was relatively easy, but bank branching was very restricted. Banks were prohibited from branching outside their home state, and in many states, branching was restricted still further. As a consequence, a region would be served by a relatively large number of banks, but there were no banks operating nationwide.

To effect transactions, people paid one another with paper checks drawn on their bank or paper currency notes issued by their bank. The banks would then clear these checks and notes among themselves.

With so many individual banks spread out across such a big country, and banks clearing paper instruments among themselves, effecting transactions outside the local area was cumbersome. When someone received a bank check or a bank note as payment and deposited it at his bank, the bank would discount the instrument's value based on the cost of presenting it to the "drawn on" bank for payment and some assessment of the creditworthiness of the "drawn on" bank. The farther away the bank, the less familiar its financial condition and the greater the transportation cost associated with clearing the instrument, and so the greater the discount tended to be. So a merchant in Kansas City, Missouri, accepting as payment a check drawn on a bank in Allentown, Pennsylvania, knew he would be credited with less than the face or par value of the check and would have to consult with his bank to find out how much less. Obviously, this was a payment system inimical to the growth of national commerce.

By the turn of the twentieth century, it was clear that the United States needed a more well-integrated national payment system. Indeed, one of the main reasons Congress established the Federal Reserve System back in 1913 was to create a national clearing system in which checks could exchange at par value. To achieve this, the Federal Reserve offered check clearing services free of charge to banks that joined the Fed System.

However, the Fed did not become the sole provider of check clearing services, despite offering its services for free. First of all, not all banks chose to join the Fed System, primarily because of some of the regulatory implications. In addition, large correspondent banks offered smaller respondent banks an array of "bankers' bank services" including check clearing, and banks could take advantage of local and national clearing house arrangements.

Nonetheless, the Fed established a large market presence, providing a baseline level of national check clearing services accessible to all banks, large and small, anywhere in the country. Thus, the Fed contributed to the viability of both the paper check and the small community bank.

In the 1960s and 1970s, US banks and the Fed applied advances in computing technology to check processing, increasing the efficiency of their operations. Banks found the paper check payments business to be profitable, and consumers were quite comfortable and confident in the use of checks.

In short, checks were the dominant form of noncash payment, and there was little momentum for change in the US payments system. One might argue that bank Giro systems, which were arising in Europe at the time, would have increased the efficiency of the payments system even more. Yet with so many banks in the United States – all serving local markets – developing the legal framework, industry standards, and institutional arrangements necessary to establish such a payments network nationally would have been a daunting task. And in any case, American banks are forbidden under antitrust law to work together.

The Fed itself introduced its version of an electronic Giro system in the early 1970s. We call it our automated clearing house, or Fed ACH. Fed ACH has met with some success.

However, unlike the European Giro, ACH has not developed into the dominant form of electronic payment, in part, because, traditionally, only banks – not individuals – could initiate ACH payments. This made the ACH practical only for companies engaged in batch-processing a large number of payments, such as payroll disbursement.

In a typical transaction, a firm would forward to its bank an electronic file containing payments to be made from the firm's account. The bank would then initiate the ACH transactions by sending the file to the Fed, which would transfer funds from the bank's account to the accounts of the various payees' banks, and then notify them of the account holders to be credited.

I will add that a relatively recent variant allows large organizations to collect regular payments using the ACH. A typical transaction of this nature would involve individual customers' authorizing their bank to make ACH payments directly to a firm – perhaps their utility company or mortgage company – on a recurring basis.

5.3 Cards drive changes in US payments

While Fed ACH saw some success as a means to effect electronic payments, it was the credit card that proved most instrumental in moving US payments from paper to electronics. The credit card actually was the first electronic payments instrument to emerge in the United States. Credit cards were introduced in the 1950s, and their use grew rapidly over the next three decades.

5.3.1 Credit cards

Not coincidentally, the US credit card infrastructure looks a lot like the European banking system. There are relatively few major card associations. They operate nationwide. And they are not subject to the antitrust laws that prohibited collaboration among US banks. In fact, the credit card associations benefited from some early antitrust rulings against banks.

In the 1990s, when the tech boom made information processing and telecommunications more powerful and less expensive, the credit card associations were well positioned to take full advantage of these developments. Low-cost telecom has made real-time, point-of-service verification of cardholders and their credit status widespread, speeding transactions and curtailing fraud. Of significance for the future, this technology has made the credit card a viable means of payment for e-commerce.

5.3.2   Debit cards

After the credit card, the debit card is the second most popular electronic instrument for making retail payments in the United States today. The debit card arrived on the scene relatively recently – during the 1980s – in both the United States and Europe. But since its arrival, growth in usage has been dramatic.

In Europe, the debit card emerged as an evolution of banks' automatic teller machine (ATM) systems. Instead of using their card to withdraw cash from an ATM to pay merchants, bank customers simply present their card to the merchants and their bank account is debited directly.

This same progression occurred in the United States, too. But in the United States, the credit card networks responded with debit card products of their own. Visa and MasterCard already had an infrastructure in place for processing credit card transactions at the point of sale. They leveraged this infrastructure to establish offline debit card networks. Indeed, in the United States, these so-called "signature" debit cards are proving at least as popular as ATM, or "PIN-based," debit cards.

Signature debit cards now account for about two-thirds of the total of debit transactions at the moment, so it could be said that they are even more popular than their PIN counterparts. However, PIN-based debits are growing a bit faster than signature.

In any case, debit cards in general seem to be leading the migration away from cash and checks and toward electronic payments in the United States. This trend is substantiated by the Survey of Consumer Finances, sponsored by the Federal Reserve Board of Governors and compiled by the Research Department at the Philadelphia Fed.

The survey indicates that fewer than 18 percent of households used debit cards in 1995. But by 2001, nearly half of all households were using them. Not coincidentally, the survey also divulged a substantial reduction in the use of cash over the same period.

The growing popularity of debit cards in the United States seems to be part of a broader phenomenon. As mentioned earlier, debit cards have caught on just as quickly in Europe. In fact, recently, for the first time ever, Visa's global debit sales volume surpassed its credit sales volume.[3]

5.4   The future of the US retail payments system

By now, I hope I have given you some perspective on the current state of US retail payments and the evolutionary process that brought Americans there.

Looking ahead, retail payments in the United States will continue moving away from cash and paper checks toward electronic instruments, including credit cards, debit cards, ACH, and emerging vehicles such as prepaid cards.

Though roughly half of our noncash payments are still being made by paper check, the tide has turned. In fact, recent research by the Federal Reserve shows check usage peaked in the mid-1990s and has been declining steadily ever since. So paper checks are not only losing market share, they are actually declining in volume and have been for about a decade.

The share of retail transactions handled by cards will continue to grow in the United States, particularly at the point of sale. Debit cards have made particularly deep inroads in the realm of "micropayments" – purchases under $20. According to a survey by MasterCard International, debit cards now account for about one-third of all micropayments, a 61 percent increase over 2001.[4] And Visa claims to have authorized 82 percent more payments at quick-service restaurants between January and July of this year than during the same time period last year.[5] Here we see debit transactions replacing cash, since the survey indicated a substantial drop in cash micropayments.

Several big-name fast-food chains are promoting greater use of payment cards at their restaurants. (It undoubtedly has not escaped their attention that customers spend, on average, over 50 percent more when they pay with a card rather than cash.[6]) This movement has tremendous upside potential. Last year, consumers used their cards to make purchases of $6.5 billion at fast-food restaurants, and that was with only 10 percent of such restaurants accepting cards.[7]

Into the future, organizations other than banks will expand their role in the payments system, especially retailers themselves. As a result of recent legal action brought by WalMart against US card companies, retailers now appreciate the costs and benefits associated with alternative payment processing arrangements and will weigh in to protect their interests going forward. As you may know, WalMart, the largest retailer in the United States, along with other merchants, balked at the idea of accepting signature debit cards – and their associated fees – without the right to negotiation. They sued US bank credit card associations, prevailing in a good portion of their efforts. Their settlement eliminated the "honor all cards" rule, effectively allowing merchants to decline signature debit products without jeopardizing their ability to accept credit products or PIN debit cards.

In short, I expect keen competition among card providers, and aggressive marketing by both card providers and merchants, to increase the speed with which cards replace paper for point-of-sale transactions in the United States.

How quickly US consumers move from paper to electronics, when it comes to bill paying, is an interesting question. The speed and scope of that transition depend on the evolution of our payments system.

As I mentioned earlier, our ACH system has not been as successful as your Giro systems. But things may be changing. Financial institutions are finding innovative new uses for ACH, spanning a broad range of retail transactions and shifting substantial volumes to this system, primarily at the expense of check volume.

The most important of these innovations is accounts receivable check (ARC) conversion. Large organizations that receive paper checks from customers as remittance for retail payments are now scanning the checks to digitally capture their relevant payment information. The companies can then use this information to create an electronic file, which is then transmitted to an ACH payments provider – usually the Fed – for processing. In some cases, even individual merchants who accept customer checks at the point-of-sale can use the information on the check to generate an electronic file. That file is then sent to the merchant's bank for processing through the ACH.

Conversion to ACH is helping to streamline payments initiated by check, even when the paper check would follow. It is also being used to process one-time payments initiated via the Internet.

As the owner/operator of the Fed ACH system, the Federal Reserve has been working to ensure its ACH system is equipped to accommodate changes in volumes and the nature of payments, even as these applications proliferate. As in check processing, the Fed is not the sole provider of ACH. Though the Federal Reserve network currently originates about two-thirds of all ACH payments volume, we are also seeing growth among private-sector ACH networks. Indeed, as ACH continues to gain acceptance as a payment vehicle, its products and marketing will evolve so as to make it more attractive and accessible to individuals and businesses.

5.5   Managing the transition

So, the private sector is shifting retail payments in the United States away from paper-based instruments and toward electronic ones. But history tells us that people's payment habits change only gradually. When people are comfortable with, and confident in, a payment structure, they are reluctant to give it up. As a result, the paper check is likely to be with us for some time.

In the meantime, the Fed has been trying to take full advantage of the efficiencies afforded by electronic processing of payments initiated by paper check in the interest of maximizing the efficiency of the payment system. Thus, the Fed is doing what it can to foster check truncation and electronification at as early a stage as possible in the payment process.

The Fed is now well positioned to pursue this objective. Two pieces of legislation have set the stage. One is a law that has been on the books for nearly twenty-five years now: the Monetary Control Act of 1980. The second was passed just a year ago and goes into effect this month: The Check Clearing for the 21st Century Act, commonly called Check 21. Let me explain the significance of each.

Recall that when the Fed began its check processing operations, it provided the service at no charge to its member banks. The Monetary Control Act of 1980 changed all that. It required the Fed to offer its payments services to all banks at prices fully reflecting the Fed's costs of production including imputed profits. This change established a marketplace incentive for the Fed and its private-sector competitors in check processing to maximize the efficiency of their check processing operations.

The second piece of legislation, Check 21, adds an important new dimension to the competitive drive for greater efficiency in check processing. The essence of the new law is that it makes the facsimile of a check created from an electronic image serve as the legal equivalent of the check itself. In doing so, it eliminates a significant legal barrier to check truncation and electronification of the check processing. A collecting bank can soon create an electronic image of a check, transmit the image to the paying bank's location, and then present the paying bank with a paper reproduction or with the electronic image itself. The hope and expectation is that gradually more and more paying banks will prefer the image itself.

Accepting images for both deposit and presentment eliminates back office capture of the check as well as the inconvenience of physical transportation. Indeed, under the new Check 21 legislation, it will become even easier to move toward a more electronic check process because banks will be provided with additional options for processing image-based payments.

As a provider of financial services, we have been actively engaged in bringing a whole array of image products to market to take advantage of the capability of image clearing. We have established an image archive for electronic items; we have enhanced our ability to produce facsimile checks; and we have extended clearing times to encourage the use of the new image technology that the act allows. In short, the Fed is introducing new services that will enable banks to take full advantage of Check 21.

How fast will the transition occur? It is our best guess that the industry will be slow to embrace the new capabilities that the law permits. We must also consider the possibility that making check processing more efficient will actually extend the life of the waning check. In any case, the Federal Reserve Banks' financial services division is committed to working with the industry to ensure a smooth transition.

5.6 The challenge to the Fed

With the evolution of the payments system in the United States accelerating, the Federal Reserve must make some major adjustments to its payments services as the changing payments system alters its role. Nonetheless, the Fed is committed to working to improve the reliability and efficiency of the current generation of payments vehicles, even as it works to foster innovation and to support the next generation of payments vehicles. Both commitments are equally important during this period of transition.

With this dual commitment in mind, we continue to fulfill our traditional role as payments processor even while we support the move to our new electronic clearing environment. Striking the right balance between these two seemingly divergent goals is a challenge. Nonetheless, the Fed has begun implementing a strategy that includes key elements to help us successfully meet both commitments.

The Fed has recently announced a program of "aggressive electronification" of retail payments in the United States. This push toward electronics will help facilitate Check 21 and quicken the transition to an all-electronic world. The Fed is also investing heavily in technologies that enable electronification. In addition, as check volumes decline the pressure has been on to find new processing efficiencies. The transition will not be easy, particularly for the Federal Reserve System.

The Fed currently clears about one-third of all checks written in the United States. As check volumes have declined, the Fed has had to consolidate its operations, closing down processing sites where appropriate. Nonetheless, it has attempted to maintain reasonable service levels nationally by re-routing checks to nearby sites.

So that you can see the scale of this effort, I will note that two years ago the Fed had forty-five check processing sites. By early 2006 we will be down to twenty-three. This downsizing to match costs and revenues helps us fulfill our traditional role of payments processor while at the same time maintaining efficiency in this new environment.

Such a radical transformation within our financial services division is made necessary by law. As I mentioned earlier, the Monetary Control Act mandated that we set prices on our services to fully recover our costs. At the same time, we are required to adjust our portfolio of services to correspond to the clearing needs of the industry. As such, the aggregate decline in volume in this volume-based service creates a substantial challenge to the System. And achieving full cost recovery will become more challenging for us as the volume of check usage continues to decline.

Nonetheless, by setting prices that reflect the low cost of electronic check processing relative to paper the Fed will allow, indeed encourage, the market to drive checks toward electronics. In addition, we will continue to develop our capabilities and expand our electronics capacity to respond to the market's evolution and consumers' needs. The impact of these changes and those that follow will ultimately transform the US payments system and enable a radical restructuring of its service capabilities.

5.7   A word about wholesale payments

Before closing, let me say just a few words about our wholesale payments operation. Aside from its role in supporting retail payments, or small-dollar transactions systems, the Fed has long had a role in facilitating wholesale, or large dollar, transactions. As you are no doubt aware, Fedwire is the Fed's real-time wholesale payments operation. It is used to transfer both funds and securities. Fedwire transactions typically involve large value, time-critical payments, such as payments for the settlement of interbank purchases and sales of federal funds, or securities or real estate transactions.

Fedwire first went into operation back in 1918. Its operations have evolved with advances in technology and the integration of financial markets. The Fed has recently centralized Fedwire operations from all twelve Reserve Banks to our New York Bank – with both a hot and a cold backup.

Now, a parallel process seems to be in motion in Europe. The initiative known as TARGET 2 will likely consolidate European central banks' wire transfer operations. As in the case of Fedwire, this standardized processing platform will reduce costs through economies of scale and improve flexibility of wholesale payments.

5.8 Conclusion

By way of summary, let me suggest that my discussion today had several goals. First among them was to review and explain the state of payments technology in the United States to you, my colleagues who come from a different tradition and institutional structure. There is a reason for most things, and the roots of our payment systems are found in our different banking structures and different perceptions of appropriate regulation.

Yours is a system of few large banks that can easily be regulated into a centralized world – first with near-universal Giro accounts and soon with an electronic world of more centralized clearing.

In the United States, markets and consumers led us to a multiplicity of banks and a payments system that has been paper intensive. In the United States this is changing, as cards are replacing checks, and electronic clearing is truncating the maze of paper that fills our post offices. Indeed, it seems the US payments system is moving toward convergence with the European model. Our progress, while promising, occurs largely in fits and starts. The United States is a large nation with many providers, much complexity, and a philosophy of market-based solutions.

This has presented challenges for the Federal Reserve as a provider of financial services. It has necessitated restructurings, plant closings, and difficult decisions that most central banks in Europe have been spared. Yet, by law, we are charged with the dual role of a regulator seeking to maintain the stability and efficiency of the payments system and a provider of payment services. At times, these roles present different challenges. This is one of those times.

Nonetheless, as payments technology moves forward in the United States, our payments system will continue to change as evolutionary forces generate new innovations in payments and new ways to deliver them. In some ways we will look more like the European system even as our two payments systems move to the next generation of payments. We will look more alike, although we will get there from a very different starting point.

Thank you.

Notes

1 Data from Bank for International Settlements, cited in *Statistics on Payment and Settlement Systems in Selected Countries*, March 2004 (Figures for 2002), prepared by the Committee on Payment and Settlement Systems of the Group of Ten Countries.

2 Data from source cited in Note 1.
3 Press release, "Visa Global Debit Card Sales Volume Surpasses Credit," Visa International, April 20, 2004.
4 David Breitkopf, "MasterCard, Pulse report wider use of debit cards," *American Banker*, May 17, 2004.
5 W. A. Lee, "CEO confident as Visa posts more records," *American Banker*, August 5, 2004.
6 Data from source cited in Note 5.
7 "Cards…at participating restaurants," *Electronic Payments International*, August 19, 2004.

6 The East–West efficiency gap in European banking

Marko Košak and Peter Zajc

6.1 Introduction

The processes of liberalisation, globalisation and integration have dramatically changed the banking landscape around the world. In Europe, two key developments have affected and altered the banking environment. First, in the European Union (EU) the Second Banking Directive opened up the banking sectors of all EU member-countries to other EU banks. The introduction of the Economic and Monetary Union in 1999 contributed to a large and transparent common banking sector. Second, the transition of Central and Eastern European (CEE) countries from centrally planned economies to market economies, which commenced in the late 1980s, crucially changed the banking sectors of these countries. In fact, one could argue that in the pre-transition period they did not have a banking system at all, or at least it was a monobank system in which the central banks performed some commercial banking functions. Consequently, the efficiency of banks in CEE countries was initially very poor and had to be improved so that the banking sector could perform its role adequately.

Emerging from these developments is the question of the efficiency discrepancy between banks in EU-14 banking sectors and banks in CEE countries. Very little research has been done (e.g. Weill, 2003) to investigate the size of the efficiency gap between Western and Eastern European banking sectors in the 1990s, when the transition processes in CEE countries were at full speed, and in the run-up to the EU enlargement in 2004. Along these lines, the objective of this chapter is to estimate the cost efficiency of banks in ten new EU member-countries (Czech Republic, Cyprus, Estonia, Hungary, Lithuania, Latvia, Malta, Poland, Slovakia and Slovenia) and four old EU member-countries (Austria, Belgium, Germany, Italy) during the 1996–2003 period.[1] Cost efficiency provides information on how close (or far) a bank's costs are from a best-practice bank's costs. It is estimated using a common frontier, thus allowing us to compare efficiency estimates across countries and to examine the development of the East-West efficiency gap over the sample period.

The rest of this chapter is structured as follows. First, we give an overview of the literature. The discussion of the latter is organised along two lines: bank efficiency studies for CEE countries and cross-country studies of bank efficiency.

The next section sketches out the theory of efficiency measurement. This is followed by a discussion of the theoretical foundations and design of the empirical estimation used in our analysis. Finally, our estimation results for cost efficiency are presented. The chapter concludes with a comment on the results.

6.2   Overview of bank efficiency studies

Some studies on the performance of banks focus on a presentation of financial ratios and an analysis of scale and scope economies.[2] Molyneux *et al.* (1996) noted that there are other aspects of efficiency such as technical and allocative efficiency. These two components of efficiency were first identified by Farrell (1957). The concept of X-efficiency encompasses both allocative and technical efficiency.[3] X-efficiency was introduced by Leibenstein (1966) and basically reflects the differences in managerial ability to control costs or maximise profits (Molyneux *et al.*, 1996).

The dominance of X-inefficiency over scale and scope inefficiency in banking has been recognised for quite some time, but researchers have only recently turned their attention to studying X-inefficiency. This new area or direction of research has brought about several approaches and methods of analysis. Molyneux *et al.* (1996) indicated that there is no agreement on how to measure and model X-inefficiency. The key issue is how to measure or determine the efficiency frontier. Farrell (1957) proposed that the efficiency frontier can be estimated from sample data applying either a non-parametric or a parametric approach. The most widely used non-parametric estimation technique is the data envelopment analysis (DEA), while the stochastic frontier approach (SFA) and the distribution-free approach (DFA) are the most commonly used parametric techniques.

Berger and Mester (1997) in their article 'Inside the black box: what explains differences in the efficiencies of financial institutions?' give a very informative synopsis of the elements of efficiency measurement (efficiency concept, measurement technique and functional form) and analyse the sources of differences in efficiencies across banks. They find that, in general, the choice of measurement technique and functional form does not make a substantial difference when determining the average efficiency of the banking sector or the ranking of individual banks.

Although the body of literature on bank efficiency is substantial, it is heavily geared towards studies of US banks, followed by European banks in a distant second place. There are only a few studies on bank efficiency in less developed countries. CEE countries have so far not received much attention. Another area of bank efficiency research that still has not been intensively explored is bank efficiency across countries. In their survey, Berger and Humphrey (1997) merely list five inter-country comparisons at the time of their study. They note that cross-country studies are difficult to perform and interpret because: (1) regulatory and economic environments differ between countries; and (2) there are differences in the quality of banking services between countries that are difficult to account for. The first cross-country study was the 1993 comparative analysis of bank efficiency in Finland, Norway and Sweden by Berg *et al.* (1993). They found Swedish banks to be the most efficient within the pooled sample.

As to CEE economies, at least four studies need to be mentioned here. The first is the 2002 working paper 'Determinants of Commercial Bank Performance in Transition: An Application of Data Envelopment Analysis' by Grigorian and Manole (2002). They estimate bank efficiency using the DEA technique. Their sample is quite heterogeneous, that is, it includes countries at substantially different development levels. They divide the countries included in the study into three groups: Central Europe, South-East Europe and the Commonwealth of Independent States. Overall, banks from Central Europe are found to be the most efficient.

The second study is the recent working paper *Efficiency of Banks: Recent Evidence From the Transition Economies of Europe 1993–2000* by Yildirim and Philippatos (2002). They use both the SFA and the DFA approach to estimate bank efficiency for twelve CEE countries, as well as efficiency correlates for the banking sectors in this group of countries. The estimated inefficiencies were found to be significant, with respective average cost-efficiency levels for 12 countries of 72 and 76 per cent according to the DFA and SFA. However, the relatively large number of countries in the sample suggests the sample is quite heterogeneous, meaning it encompasses more advanced economies which recently obtained EU membership as well as economies that still need to make significant progress in order to draw near development levels that are common in the EU.

Third, a recent paper by Bonin *et al.* (2004) focuses on evaluating bank efficiency and identifying relevant efficiency correlates in transition countries, with focus on the efficiency-ownership relationship. The authors applied stochastic frontier estimation procedures to banks in 11 transition countries. The results provided by Bonin *et al.* (2004) indicate that private ownership is, by itself, insufficient to ensure bank efficiency in transition countries because no statistically significant evidence of an adverse effect of government ownership relative to private domestic ownership was found. Foreign-owned banks turn out to be more cost efficient than other banks and they also provide better services, particularly if they have a strategic foreign owner.

A study by Weill (2003) represents an attempt of a direct comparison of the banking efficiency in Western and Eastern European countries. Weill's research provides evidence on the existence of an efficiency gap between Western and Eastern banks, which is mainly caused by differences in managerial performance, whereas environmental and risk preference effects did not turn to be important. As indicated by the author, further research in this area is needed, not only on the existence of the efficiency gap but also on the evolution of efficiency and its explanations. In that sense this chapter can be considered as work in that direction, since we extend the investigation period for three more years, and include in the analysis the entire set of transition countries that entered EU in 2004.

6.3   Methodology

The concept of efficiency measurement assumes that the production function of the fully efficient firm or firms is known. Since this is not the case in practice, one has to estimate the production function. A number of different techniques are used to estimate efficiency. Farrell (1957) proposed that the production function can be estimated from sample data applying either a non-parametric (mathematical programming) or a parametric (econometric) approach.[4]

The two most commonly used non-parametric efficiency estimation techniques are the DEA and the free disposable hull (FDH), the latter being a special case of DEA. DEA is a linear programming technique where the DEA frontier is constructed as piecewise linear combinations connecting a set of best-practice observations (Berger and Humphrey, 1997). Non-parametric techniques have some drawbacks. They focus on technological optimisation rather than economic optimisation. Since they ignore prices, they only provide information on technical efficiency and ignore allocative efficiency. Non-parametric techniques generally do not allow for random error in the data, that is, they do not consider measurement error and luck as factors affecting efficiency estimates (Berger and Mester, 1997). Thus, any deviation from the frontier is assumed to reflect inefficiency. If there were any measurement errors, they would be reflected in a change of measured efficiency. Moreover, as pointed out by Berger and Humphrey (1997) any of these errors in one of the banks on the efficient frontier may change the measured efficiency of all banks. On the other hand, DEA does not require an explicit specification of the functional form of the underlying production function and thus imposes less structure on the frontier.

The three main parametric techniques are the SFA, the DFA and the thick frontier approach (TFA). These methods focus on the difference or distance from the best-practice bank (efficient frontier), that is, this distance reflects the inefficiency effect u_i. For example, if costs are higher than those of the best-practice bank, then the bank is cost inefficient. The key characteristic of parametric techniques is that they a priori impose a rule (assumption) for how random errors can be separated from inefficiency. Thus, they make an arbitrary distinction between randomness and inefficiency, which is the main drawback and criticism of parametric techniques (Schure and Wagenvoort, 1999). Estimation techniques differ in the way they handle the composite error term $v_i + u_i$, that is, in the way they disentangle the inefficiency term u_i from the random error term v_i. In the empirical part given here we apply the SFA technique, which is based on the assumption that the random error v_i is symmetrically distributed (normal distribution) and that the inefficiency term u_i follows an asymmetric (one-sided) distribution (truncated normal distribution).

6.4   Stochastic frontier estimation technique

There is a general distinction between deterministic and stochastic frontier production functions (Kaparakis *et al.*, 1994). The main drawback of the deterministic frontier is that it does not account for measurement errors and statistical noise problems, thus all deviations from the frontier are assumed to reflect inefficiency (Coelli *et al.*, 1998). This can seriously distort the measurement of efficiency. The stochastic frontier production function avoids some of the problems associated with the deterministic frontier. Aigner *et al.* (1977), and Meeusen and van den Broeck (1977) independently proposed a stochastic frontier function with a composite error term, which allows the production function to vary stochastically:

$$y_i = x_i \beta + e_i \quad i = 1, \ldots, N \tag{6.1}$$

where y_i is the logarithm of the maximum output obtainable from x_i, x_i is a vector of logarithms of inputs used by the i-th firm, β is the unknown parameter vector to be estimated and e_i is the error term.

The error term e_i is composed of two parts:

$$e_i = v_i - u_i \quad i = 1, \ldots, N \tag{6.2}$$

where v_i is the measurement error and other random factors, u_i is the inefficiency component. The v_i component captures the statistical noise, that is, measurement error and other random or uncontrollable factors. Aigner *et al.* (1977) assumed that v_i is independently and identically distributed normal random variable with mean zero and a constant variance, that is, $v_i \sim$ i.i.d. $N(0, \sigma_v^2)$. The u_i component is a non-negative random variable accounting for technical inefficiency in the production of firms. It measures technical inefficiency in the sense that it measures the shortfall of output from its maximal possible value given by the stochastic frontier $x_i \beta + v_i$ (Jondrow *et al.*, 1982). This shortfall or, more generally, these deviations from the frontier are due to factors that are under the control of management, as opposed to v_i, which is not under management control (Chang *et al.*, 1998). u_i is distributed either i.i.d exponential or half-normal.

The main shortcoming of the SFA is the a priori distributional assumption of u_i. This assumption is necessary in order to use the maximum likelihood method to solve for the parameters. In general, the stochastic frontier model can be estimated by using corrected ordinary least squares (OLS), but maximum likelihood is asymptotically more efficient. In our estimation, we apply the maximum likelihood method.

The mean of the distribution of the u_i (the mean technical inefficiency) is easy to compute. One simply calculates the average of e_i estimates, and the statistical noise component v_i averages out. Computing technical inefficiency for individual firms is more demanding. The decomposition of the error term into its two components, v_i and u_i, remained unresolved until Jondrow *et al.* (1982) proposed how to calculate the observation (bank) specific estimates of inefficiency conditional on the estimate of the error term e_i. The best predictor for u_i is the conditional expectation of u_i given the value of $e_i = v_i - u_i$. The predictor for efficiency is obtained by subtracting the inefficiency from one.

Battese and Coelli (1988) showed that the best predictor of technical efficiency, $\exp(-u_i)$, is obtained by using

$$E[\exp(-u_i)|\varepsilon_i] = \frac{1 - \Phi(\sigma_A + \gamma\varepsilon_i/\sigma_A)}{1 - \Phi(\gamma\varepsilon_i/\sigma_A)} \exp\left(\gamma\varepsilon_i + \frac{\sigma_A^2}{2}\right) \tag{6.3}$$

where $\Phi(.)$ is the cumulative density function of a standard normal random variable, σ_A is the $\sqrt{\gamma(1 - \gamma)\sigma_S^2}$, $\gamma \equiv \sigma^2/\sigma_S^2$, $\sigma_S^2 \equiv \sigma^2 + \sigma_V^2$, σ^2 is the variance of u_i and σ_v^2 is the variance of v_i.

6.5   Cost efficiency model

The technical efficiency concept based on a production function is easily modified and extended to measure bank cost efficiency. Cost efficiency is derived from the cost function. It provides information on how close (or far) a bank's costs are from a best-practice bank's costs, producing the same output in the same conditions. In other words, cost efficiency reflects the position of a particular bank relative to the cost frontier. A stochastic cost frontier is presented here, where $C(.)$ is a suitable functional form.

$$\ln c_i = C(y_i, w_i; \beta) + v_i + u_i \quad i = 1, 2, \ldots, N$$

where c_i is the observed cost of production for the ith firm, y_i is the logarithm of the output quantity, w_i is a vector of logarithms of input prices, β is a vector of unknown parameters to be estimated, v_i is the random error and u_i is the non-negative cost inefficiency effect.

Note that the inefficiency factor u_i is added because the cost frontier represents minimum costs (Coelli *et al.*, 1998).[5] The random error v_i accounts for measurement errors and other random factors. The inefficiency factor incorporates both technical inefficiency (i.e. employing too many of the inputs) and allocative inefficiency (i.e. failures to react optimally to changes in relative prices of inputs) (Berger and Mester, 1997). The random error and the inefficiency term are assumed to be multiplicatively separable from the cost frontier. Efficiency measurement techniques differ in how they separate the composite error term $v_i + u_i$, that is, how they distinguish the inefficiency term from the random error.

We use panel data on banks from Central and Eastern Europe and the model by Battese and Coelli (1992) to estimate cost efficiency. They proposed a stochastic frontier model with time-varying inefficiency effects. The model can be written as

$$\ln (y_{it}) = x_{it}\beta + v_{it} + u_{it} \quad i = 1, 2, \ldots, N; \ t = 1, 2, \ldots, T \tag{6.4}$$

where y_{it} is the output of ith firm in the tth time period, x_{it} is a K-vector of values of logarithms of inputs and other appropriate variables associated with the suitable functional form, β is a K-vector of unknown parameters to be estimated, v_{it} are random errors assumed to be i.i.d. $N(0, \sigma_v^2)$ independent of u_{it} and u_{it} are technical inefficiency effects.

Different distributions of u_{it} have been assumed for this panel data model (see Coelli *et al.*, 1998, for a short overview of the evolution of this model). The model permits unbalanced panel data and u_{it} is assumed to be an exponential function of time, involving only one unknown parameter,

$$u_{it} = \{\exp[-\eta(t-T)]\}u_i \quad i = 1, 2, \ldots, N; \quad t = 1, 2, \ldots, T \tag{6.5}$$

where u_i is assumed to be i.i.d. generalised truncated normal random variable and η eta is an unknown scalar parameter to be estimated.

In period T (i.e. $t = T$), the exponential function $\exp[-\eta(t-T)]$ has a value of one and thus the u_i is the technical inefficiency for the *i*th firm in the last period of the panel. Inefficiency effects in all previous periods of the panel are the product of the technical inefficiency for the *i*th firm in the last period of the panel and the value of the exponential function $\exp[-\eta(t-T)]$. The value of the exponential function is determined by the parameter eta (η) and the number of periods in the panel. Inefficiency effects can decrease, remain constant or increase as time increases, that is, $\eta > 0$, $\eta = 0$ and $\eta < 0$, respectively. This specification of inefficiency effects implies that the ranking of firms according to the magnitude of their technical inefficiency effects is the same in all time periods. Thus, this model cannot accommodate the situation where an initially relatively inefficient firm becomes relatively more efficient (a change in relative ranking) in subsequent periods (Coelli *et al.*, 1998).

6.6 Data

The analysis covers eight CEE countries: Czech Republic, Estonia, Hungary, Latvia, Lithuania, Poland, Slovakia and Slovenia – advanced transition countries – and Malta and Cyprus, all being new EU members. We also included four old EU countries (Austria, Belgium, Germany, Italy). Although there are differences between the banking sectors of these countries, they nevertheless form a relatively homogeneous group. In particular, preparations for EU membership and membership itself saw the installation of the common EU legislative framework and common regulation standards. This allows us to perform an efficiency analysis and compare estimated efficiencies across countries.

To construct the sample, we used information drawn from the financial statements of individual banks provided by the Fitch/IBCA's BankScope Database. Fitch/IBCA collects data from balance sheets, income statements and other relevant notes in audited annual reports. To ensure consistency, only data for commercial banks in the unconsolidated format were used. Data, expressed in euros, were collected for the 1996–2003 period and corrected for inflation in order to ensure comparability (see Table 6.2 for descriptive statistics of the data).

Mathieson and Roldos (2001) indicated three important characteristics of the BankScope Database. First, its comprehensive coverage as BankScope has data on banks accounting for around 90 per cent of total bank assets in each country. Second, comparability – the data-collection process is based on separate data templates for each country to accommodate different reporting and accounting standards. Fitch/IBCA adjusts the collected data for country specificities and presents them in a so-called global format, that is, a globally standardised form for presenting bank data. Thus, BankScope Database is comparable across banks and across countries, that is, it allows cross-country comparisons (Claessens *et al.*, 2001). Third, BankScope provides balance sheet data for individual banks, which are usually not available from other sources.

In specifying input prices and outputs of the cost function, we follow the intermediation approach as suggested by Sealey and Lindley (1977). Three inputs (labour, funds and physical capital) are used to produce three outputs (loans, other earning assets and deposits) (Table 6.1). The three inputs reflect the three key groups of inputs in the bank production process: bank personnel and the management expertise necessary for the provision of bank services (*labour*), funds collected on the liabilities side (*funds*), and offices, branches and computer hardware (*physical capital*).

BankScope does not provide data on the *price of labour* (w_1) directly, that is, there is no information on the number of employees to enable the construction of the ratio of personnel expenses to the number of employees as the unit price of labour. Instead, we use the ratio of personnel expenses over total assets, which is a common approach in bank efficiency studies based on BankScope (Yildirim and Philippatos, 2002). *Price of funds* (w_2) was constructed as the ratio of interest expenses over funding. *Price of physical capital* (w_3) also cannot be directly taken from BankScope and was constructed as depreciation over fixed assets. The three

Table 6.1 Input and output variables

	Variable	Name	Description
Dependent variables	C	Total cost	Sum of labour, interest, physical capital and other costs
Input prices	w_1	Price of labour	Personnel expenses over total assets
	w_2	Price of funds	Interest expenses over the sum of deposits, other funding
	w_3	Price of physical capital	Depreciation over fixed assets
Output quantities	y_1	Total loans	Sum of short- and long-term loans, mortgages and other
	y_2	Other earning assets	Sum of total securities, deposits with banks and equity investments
	y_3	Total deposits	Sum of demand and savings deposits, deposited by bank and non-bank depositors
Other variables	z	Equity capital	Total amount of equity capital

Source: Authors.

outputs, loans, other earning assets and deposits are proxies for banking services provided. *Total loans* (y_1) is the total customer loans item from BankScope. *Other earning assets* (y_2) is the sum of total securities, deposits with banks and equity investments. *Total deposits* (y_3) is the sum of demand and savings deposits held by bank and non-bank depositors. The dependent variable, *total cost* (C), is the sum of total operating expenses and interest expenses. *Equity capital* (z) is the amount of bank equity that reflects both the size and riskiness of banking operations. Table 6.2 presents descriptive statistics of dependent variables, inputs and output for cost.

Following Berger and Mester (1997), cost and input prices were normalised by the price of labour in order to impose homogeneity. Cost and output quantities were normalised by equity to control for potential heteroscedasticity. Large banks have much larger costs (and profits) than smaller banks, thus their random errors would have substantially larger variances if no normalisation were performed. However, ratios of costs to equity vary much less across banks of different sizes. As the inefficiency terms are derived from the (composite) random error, the variance of the inefficiency term might be strongly influenced by bank size if it were not for the normalisation by equity. Normalisation also allows the model a more economic interpretation.

The sample of banks is not constant, that is, we do not require a bank to have existed throughout the sample period for it to be included in the sample. Thus, in the unbalanced panel the number of banks across years varies for all countries. In Table 6.3 we summarise the number of banks included in the sample in specific years and across sub-regions. The largest group represent banks from the EU-4 countries and the smallest one banks from Cyprus and Malta, but we decided for this type of segmentation in order to assure the homogeneity across groups. For the last year of the observation period (2003) the number of banks drops substantially in all sub-regions due to data incompleteness in BankScope Database. This might be also reflected in the efficiency estimates for year 2003, so results for this year should be interpreted cautiously.

Table 6.2 Descriptive statistics of dependent variables, inputs and outputs for cost

Variable	Units	Mean	SD	CV
Total assets	EUR mil	6,350	32,190	5.07
Total loans	EUR mil	3,194	15,767	4.94
Total other earning assets	EUR mil	2,746	14,904	5.43
Total deposits	EUR mil	4,385	23,021	5.25
Price of labour	%	1.85	2.58	1.40
Price of funds	%	13.18	245.07	18.59
Price of physical capital	%	2.70	38.78	14.38
Total cost	EUR mil	380	1,666	4.38
Total equity	EUR mil	323	1,334	4.13

Source: Authors' calculations.

Note
Figures in EUR million are in 2003 prices.

Table 6.3 Number of banks across sub-regions

Region	1996	1997	1998	1999	2000	2001	2002	2003
EU-4 countries	458	475	464	457	447	453	417	206
CEE-5 countries	126	128	110	113	117	103	91	29
Baltic countries	36	39	33	33	34	34	34	25
Cyprus and Malta	16	19	22	19	21	20	19	7
Total	636	661	629	622	619	610	561	267

Source: Authors' calculations.

6.7   Results

In order to be able to make a cross-country comparison of cost efficiency, we employ a common frontier function by pooling the data set of all banks comprising all countries included in the analysis. The cross-country frontier function in the form of a translog function was estimated for the 1996–2003 period by using an unbalanced panel data set on an annual basis.

The translog functional form was specified as follows:

$$
\begin{aligned}
\ln(C/w_3z) = {} & \alpha_0 + \sum_{i=1}^{2} \alpha_i \ln(w_i/w_3) + \frac{1}{2}\sum_{i=1}^{2}\sum_{j=1}^{2} \alpha_{ij} \ln(w_i/w_3)\ln(w_j/w_3) \\
& + \sum_{k=1}^{3} \beta_k \ln(y_kz) + \frac{1}{2}\sum_{k=1}^{3}\sum_{m=1}^{3} \beta_{km} \ln(y_k/z)\ln(y_m/z) \\
& + \sum_{k=1}^{3}\sum_{i=1}^{2} \delta_{ki} \ln(y_k/z)\ln(w_i/w_3) + \kappa_1 \ln z + \frac{1}{2}\kappa_2(\ln z^2) \\
& + \sum_{i=1}^{2} \rho_i \ln(w_i/w_3) \ln z + \sum_{k=1}^{3} \tau_k \ln(y_k/z)\ln z + \ln v + \ln u
\end{aligned}
$$

(6.6)

where C is total cost, y_k is the kth output, w_i is the ith input price, z is the equity capital, v is measurement error term and u is the inefficiency term.

The duality theorem requires the cost function to be linearly homogeneous in input prices and for the second-order parameters to be symmetric (Altunbas *et al.*, 2001).[6] Therefore, the following restrictions apply to the parameters of the cost function:

$$
\sum_i \alpha_i = 1 \qquad \sum_i \alpha_{ij} = 0, \text{ for all } i \qquad \sum_k \delta_{ki} = 0, \text{ for all } k
$$
$$
\alpha_{ij} = \alpha_{ji}, \text{ for all } i,j \quad \beta_{km} = \beta_{mk}, \text{ for all } k, m
$$

The maximum likelihood method was applied for estimation. The inefficiency effects are incorporated in the error term. The error term in a stochastic cost frontier model is assumed to have two components. One component is assumed to have a symmetric distribution (measurement error, v_{it}) and the other is assumed to have a strictly non-negative distribution (inefficiency term, u_{it}). The estimation technique we use is based on the Battese and Coelli (1992) parameterisation of time effects in the inefficiency term and accordingly the inefficiency term is modelled as a truncated-normal random variable multiplied by a specific function of time. The idiosyncratic error term is assumed to have a normal distribution. As is always the case when implementing frontier estimation techniques, the efficiency score acquired from the frontier function measures the efficiency of a specific bank relative to the best-practice or most efficient bank.[7]

Since the aim of our work is not to investigate the reasons underlying cost efficiencies within individual banks but to find evidence of the existence or inexistence of a cost-efficiency gap in EU banking markets, we present the results as average efficiency scores for individual countries and groups of countries that form sub-regions within the EU.

In the process of constructing the cost function, when we were altering the normalisation of cost and input prices (normalisation with personnel cost vs. normalisation with other operating costs) and when we were assessing specifications with three vs. four product variables, we ended up with a three-product cost frontier function (loans, other earning assets, deposits), normalised with personnel cost as a preferred cost function. The inclusion of off-balance-sheet items as a fourth product variable turned out to significantly reduce the total number of observations, whereas the normalisations with personnel costs increased the number of statistically significant coefficients.

We report selected summary statistics of the estimated translog function in Table 6.4. The parameters μ and σ_u^2 represent the distributions parameters of the inefficiency effects, parameter η is the decay parameter in modelling the inefficiency effects $u_{it} = \exp\{-\eta[t - T_i]\}u_i$ as in Battese and Coelli (1992) and indicates the time dynamics of measured inefficiencies. Parameter γ indicates the proportion of the variance in disturbance that is due to inefficiency, $\gamma = \sigma_u^2/(\sigma_v^2 + \sigma_u^2)$. The γ value is high and shows that inefficiency variation is more important than any stochastic variation in the frontier itself.

The average efficiency scores calculated for the entire sample of countries/banks and for three EU sub-regions (the EU-4 group, the CEE and

Table 6.4 Selected estimation results for the translog cost function specification

	Coefficient	SE
$\text{Ln}(\sigma^2)$	4.974	0.0020
μ	-450.603	
η	-0.002	0.0047
Log likelihood	-72.998	
σ_u	12.025	0.2915
σ_v	0.198	0.0011
$\gamma = \sigma_u^2/(\sigma_v^2 + \sigma_u^2)$	0.999	0.0000

Source: Authors' calculations.

Table 6.5 Average efficiency scores for the entire sample of banks, EU-4 countries, CEE and Baltic countries, and Cyprus and Malta in the 1996–2003 period

Year	Entire sample		EU-4		CEE and Baltic		Cyprus and Malta	
	Mean efficiency score	Std. err. of mean	Mean efficiency score	Std. err. of mean	Mean efficiency score	Std. err. of mean	Mean efficiency score	Std. err. of mean
1996	0.830	0.0065	0.832	0.0077	0.763	0.0108	0.939	0.0055
1997	0.825	0.0065	0.826	0.0078	0.768	0.0100	0.933	0.0087
1998	0.841	0.0072	0.844	0.0088	0.760	0.0114	0.933	0.0077
1999	0.834	0.0075	0.835	0.0091	0.792	0.0110	0.929	0.0048
2000	0.813	0.0075	0.813	0.0095	0.807	0.0099	0.918	0.0137
2001	0.812	0.0076	0.813	0.0093	0.784	0.0110	0.915	0.0158
2002	0.830	0.0080	0.831	0.0098	0.794	0.0105	0.905	0.0243
2003	0.795	0.0158	0.793	0.0199	0.813	0.0112	0.908	0.0390
Total	0.824	0.0028	0.826	0.0034	0.786	0.0039	0.918	0.0061
Variability measures	*SD*	*CV*	*SD*	*CV*	*SD*	*CV*	*SD*	*CV*
1996/2003	0.150	0.182	0.152	0.184	0.111	0.141	0.062	0.067

Source: Authors' calculations.

Baltic countries group and Cyprus and Malta) are reported in Table 6.5. The average efficiency score for every specific group of countries for each year is obtained as a weighted average of individual banks' efficiency scores, where the relative importance of the total assets of specific banks is used as a weight for the bank. We consider the weighting approach to be essential for the correct interpretation of the average efficiency results for specific sub-regions.

The calculated average efficiency scores indicate that the average efficiency of the entire sample of banks for the entire period was 0.824, meaning that banks were, on average, only 82.4 per cent efficient and could reduce their costs by 21 per cent. As one can see in Table 6.5 the average efficiency score differs among regions, the highest being for Cyprus and Malta (91.8 per cent efficient banks) and the lowest for CEE and Baltic countries (78.6 per cent). The differences in efficiency scores proved to be statistically significant at $p < 0.05$. Although the efficiency scores vary in time the rankings between all three regions remain unchanged. Time dynamics statistics are reported later in this section.

The measured variability reported in Table 6.5 demonstrates the differing variability of efficiency scores in specific regions. While the coefficient of variation (CV) for the entire sample amounts to 0.182 (standard deviation SD = 0.15), the CV statistics for CEE and Baltic countries do not exceed 0.15 (SD = 0.111). The CV statistics for Cyprus and Malta even lie below 0.10 (SD = 0.067). The highest efficiency variability among all three regions is estimated for the EU-4 group (CV = 0.184 and SD = 0.152) which might, at least partially, also be a consequence of the large number and great diversity of banks from that region included in the analysis.

As shown in Table 6.6, the variability of efficiency scores differs widely among the countries included in the sample. The lowest efficiency variability was recorded for Cyprus (CV = 0.033) and the highest, somewhat surprisingly, in the case of Austria (CV = 0.229). The latter could be a result of greater diversity of Austrian commercial banks in terms of their size and variety of operations. However, it seems that efficiency levels are not strongly related to efficiency variability.

The average efficiency results for other countries do not reveal any surprising findings. In the EU-4 group only Italian banks (efficiency = 0.777) turned out to be substantially less efficient than most banks in other EU-4 peer countries. Among fourteen banking sectors included in the analysis, the banking sectors of Cyprus and Malta clearly stand out by their superior efficiency since their average efficiency reaches 91.5 per cent in the case of Cyprus and 92.1 per cent in the case of Malta. Obviously, these two countries have banking sectors that are more advanced than the banking sectors of CEE and Baltic countries even though they joined the EU together. However, a more detailed analysis would be necessary in order to isolate the factors making these two countries' banking sectors superior in cost efficiency, both in comparison with CEE and Baltic countries, and relative to old EU members.

Another important aspect of bank efficiency studies that needs to be addressed is the time dynamics of banking efficiency. The time varying decay model developed by Battese and Coelli (1992) models inefficiency effects as: $u_{it} = \exp\{[-\eta(t - T_i)]\}u_i$. The estimated η coefficient provides information on the time dynamics of inefficiency effects. When $\eta > 0$, the degree of inefficiency is decreasing over time and when $\eta < 0$, the degree of inefficiency is increasing over time. For the purpose of η coefficients estimations for specific regions, we estimated a cost frontier function for each region separately. The estimated η coefficients are presented in Table 6.7. The η coefficients for the entire sample,

Table 6.6 Average efficiency scores and statistics for individual countries

Region	Country	Mean efficiency	SD	Std. err. of mean	N	Max.	Min.	CV
Baltic	Estonia	0.751	0.0424	0.0065	47	0.899	0.500	0.0564
	Latvia	0.747	0.0552	0.0068	67	0.935	0.502	0.0738
	Lithuania	0.675	0.0761	0.0064	147	0.962	0.521	0.1126
CEE-5	Czech R.	0.659	0.0766	0.0070	127	0.915	0.352	0.1162
	Hungary	0.788	0.0923	0.0106	77	0.950	0.615	0.1171
	Poland	0.877	0.0385	0.0026	236	0.973	0.570	0.0439
	Slovenia	0.830	0.0542	0.0061	84	0.969	0.622	0.0653
	Slovakia	0.765	0.1132	0.0117	98	0.905	0.036	0.1479
CY&MT	Cyprus	0.915	0.0306	0.0043	54	0.967	0.798	0.0335
	Malta	0.921	0.0782	0.0107	54	0.955	0.427	0.0848
EU-4	Austria	0.835	0.1909	0.0135	214	0.956	0.073	0.2286
	Belgium	0.853	0.1424	0.0102	225	0.963	0.213	0.1669
	Germany	0.840	0.1412	0.0045	1,061	0.970	0.163	0.1681
	Italy	0.777	0.1597	0.0063	713	0.971	0.196	0.2055

Source: Authors' calculations.

Table 6.7 Time dynamics of banking efficiency in the entire sample and three sub-regions within the EU for the 1996–2003 period

Region	η coefficient	SE	z	p>|z|	Log likelihood
EU-4	−0.0041	0.0048	−0.84	0.40	89.8495
CEE & Baltic	0.0535	0.0128	4.18	0.00	−5.5397
Cyprus & Malta	−0.3132	0.2016	−1.55	0.12	63.4700
Entire sample	−0.0023	0.0047	−0.49	0.62	−72.9981

Source: Authors' calculations.

for EU-4 countries and for Cyprus and Malta are negative, indicating increasing average bank inefficiencies for the entire sample and both sub-regions. However, none of the estimated coefficients turns out to be statistically significant, meaning that any conclusions about time dynamics are unreliable. On the contrary, the estimated coefficient for CEE and Baltic countries proved to be positive and statistically significant at $p < 0.01$, indicating that average banking efficiency in this group of countries improved in the 1996–2003 period. Keeping in mind that we estimated separate efficiency frontiers for each region separately, that is, a positive η indicates increasing cost efficiency in the respective region and does not *per se* allow a comparison to another region, the results might suggest that the improved average cost efficiency in CEE and Baltic countries, as a result of profound banking reforms and the adoption of the EU banking regulation, has contributed to the narrowing of the East–West efficiency gap.

6.8   Conclusions

The banking sectors of new EU members, that is, countries in Central and Eastern Europe, have undergone a remarkable transformation over the last 15 years. They have adopted the common EU legislation and regulation, and become integrated into the EU's banking sector. Banks in Central and Eastern Europe benefited from their extensive privatisation and restructuring processes. Nevertheless, keeping in mind their starting point in the late 1980s it remains unclear how successful banks from the new EU member-countries have been in closing the efficiency gap *vis-à-vis* the old EU states.

This paper's aim was to shed light on the dynamics of the East-West bank efficiency gap. We applied the standard efficiency measurement methodology to estimate the average cost efficiency for selected countries and geographical regions. We used the stochastic frontier approach and the Battese and Coelli (1992) specification of the technical efficiency model with a truncated-normal distribution of efficiency effects and a time varying decay model. Data was obtained from the BankScope Database for 10 new and 4 old EU member-countries. The unbalanced panel covers the 1996–2003 period. As expected, the results confirm the existence of an East–West efficiency gap since banks in the old EU countries proved, on average, to be significantly more cost efficient (82.6 per cent efficient) than their counterparts in CEE and Baltic countries (78.6 per cent efficient). The analysis of time dynamics showed that average bank inefficiency in CEE and Baltic countries decreased over the entire period ($\eta = 0.0535$ at $p < 0.01$), whereas statistically significant changes in the time dynamics of the average efficiency of EU-4 banks were not confirmed. This seems to indicate that the East-West efficiency gap has been gradually narrowing. It is likely that this process will continue in the future until a complete or at least a high degree of convergence in average bank efficiency is achieved.

Our results provide an interesting insight into the efficiency gap in the enlarged EU. Nevertheless, there is still ample scope for further research. The robustness of the results could be checked by applying other parametric and/or non-parametric methodologies. One could include a set of correlates to help explain the different factors driving changes in bank efficiency. In particular, it would be interesting to explore the role of foreign ownership and its impact on cost efficiency across countries in the sample. Finally, one could extend the analysis to include profit efficiency.

Acknowledgement

The views expressed are those of the authors and do not reflect those of the institutions with which the authors are affiliated.

Notes

1 The expression 'New EU member-countries' refers to those countries which joined the EU on 1 May 2004, while the expression 'Old EU member-countries' refers to all the other EU countries.
2 DeYoung (1997, p. 21) noted that 'accounting-based expense ratios can be misleading and that statistics-based efficient cost frontier approaches, although far from flawless, often provide more accurate estimates of cost efficiency'.
3 The terms *X-efficiency* and simply *efficiency* are not used consistently in the literature, nor in this paper. They both refer to frontier efficiency.
4 See Bauer *et al.* (1998) for a discussion of parametric and non-parametric estimation techniques.
5 The production frontier represents maximum output and u_i is subtracted from it.
6 The duality theorem states that any concept defined in terms of the properties of the production function has a dual definition in terms of the properties of the cost function and vice versa. See Varian (1992) for more details.
7 Cost efficiency can take values between zero and one. For example, a bank with cost efficiency of 0.80 is 80 per cent efficient. In other words, the bank could improve its cost efficiency, that is, reduce its costs, by 25 per cent. The bank's cost inefficiency is $1 - 0.80 = 0.20$.

References

Aigner, D., Lovell, C. A. K. and Schmidt, P. (1977). 'Formulation and estimation of stochastic frontier production function models', *Journal of Econometrics*, Vol. 6, pp. 21–37.

Altunbas, Y., Gardener, E. P., Molyneux, P. and Moore, B. (2001). 'Efficiency in European Banking', *European Economic Review*, Vol. 45, No. 10, pp. 1931–1955.

Battese, G. E. and Coelli, T. J. (1988). 'Prediction of firm-level technical efficiencies with a generalised frontier production function and panel data', *Journal of Econometrics*, Vol. 38, pp. 387–399.

Battese, G. E. and Coelli, T. J. (1992). 'Frontier production functions, technical efficiency and panel data with application to paddy farmers in India', *Journal of Productivity Analysis*, Vol. 3, pp. 153–169.

Bauer, P. W., Berger, A. N., Ferrier, G. D. and Humphrey, D. B. (1998). 'Consistency conditions for regulatory analysis of financial institutions: a comparison of frontier efficiency methods', *Journal of Economics and Business*, Vol. 50, No. 2, pp. 85–114.

Berg, S. A., Forsund, F. R., Hjalmarsson, L. and Suominen, M. (1993). 'Banking efficiency in the Nordic countries', *Journal of Banking and Finance*, Vol. 17, pp. 371–388.

Berger, A. N. and Humphrey, D. B. (1997). 'Efficiency of financial institutions: international survey and directions for future research', *European Journal of Operational Research*, Vol. 98, pp. 175–212.

Berger, A. N. and Mester, L. J. (1997). 'Inside the black box: what explains differences in the efficiencies of financial institutions?', *Journal of Banking and Finance*, Vol. 21, pp. 895–947.

Bonin J. P., Hasan I. and Wachtel P. (2004). 'Bank performance, efficiency and ownership in transition countries', *Journal of Banking and Finance*, Vol. 29, No. 1, pp. 31–53.

Chang, E. C., Hasan, I. and Hunter, W. C. (1998). 'Efficiency of multinational banks: an empirical investigation', *Journal Applied Financial Economics*, Vol. 8, pp. 689–696.

Claessens, S., Demirguc-Kunt, A. and Huizinga, H. (2001). 'How does foreign entry affect domestic banking markets?', *Journal of Banking and Finance*, Vol. 25, pp. 891–911.

Coelli, T. J., Rao, D. S. P. and Battese, G. E. (1998). *An Introduction to Efficiency and Productivity Analysis*. Boston, MA: Kluwer Academic Publishers.

DeYoung, R. (1997). 'Measuring bank cost efficiency: don't count on accounting ratios', *Financial Practice and Education*, Vol. 7, No. 1, pp. 20–31.

Farrell, M. J. (1957). 'The measurement of productive efficiency', *Journal of the Royal Statistical Society*, Vol. 120, pp. 253–281.

Grigorian, D. A. and Manole, V. (2002). 'Determinants of commercial bank performance in transition: an application of data envelopment analysis', IMF Working Paper No. 146. International Monetary Fund.

Jondrow, J., Knox Lovell, C. A., Materov, I. S. and Schmidt, P. (1982). 'On the estimation of the technical inefficiency in the stochastic frontier production function model', *Journal of Econometrics*, Vol. 19, pp. 233–238.

Kaparakis, E. I., Miller, S. M. and Noulas, A. G. (1994). 'Short-run cost inefficiency of commercial banks: a flexible stochastic frontier approach', *Journal of Money, Credit, and Banking*, Vol. 26, No. 4, pp. 875–893.

Leibenstein, H. (1966). 'Allocative efficiency vs. "X-Efficiency" ', *American Economic Review*, Vol. 56, No. 2, pp. 392–415.

Mathieson, D. J. and Roldos, J. (2001). 'Foreign banks in emerging markets', in Litan, R. E., Masson, P. and Pomerleano, M. (eds), *Open Doors – Foreign Participation in Financial Systems in Developing Countries*, Washington, DC: Brookings Institution Press, pp. 15–55.

Meeusen, W. and van den Broeck, J. (1977). 'Efficiency estimation from Cobb-Douglas production functions with composed Error', *International Economic Review*, Vol. 18, No. 2, pp. 435–444.

Molyneux, P., Altunbas, Y. and Gardener, E. (1996). *Efficiency in European Banking.* Chichester: John Wiley & Sons Ltd.

Schure, P. and Wagenvoort, R. (1999). *Economies of Scale and Efficiency in European Banking: New Evidence.* Economic and Financial Reports 99/01. Luxembourg: EIB.

Sealey, Jr. C. W. and Lindley, J. T. (1977). 'Inputs, outputs, and a theory of production and cost at depository financial institutions', *Journal of Finance*, Vol. 32, No. 4, pp. 1251–1266.

Varian, H. R. (1992). *Microeconomic Analysis.* 3rd edition. New York: W. W. Northon & Co.

Weill, L. (2003). 'Is there a lasting gap in bank efficiency between Eastern and Western European countries?', Working Paper, LARGE, Université Robert Schuman, Institut d'Etudes Politiques.

Yildirim, H. S. and Philippatos, G. C. (2002). 'Efficiency of banks: recent evidence from the transition economies of Europe – 1993–2000', University of Tennessee, EFMA 2002 London Meetings. http://ssrn.com/abstract=314894

7 Foreign acquisitions and industry wealth effects of privatization

Evidence from the Polish banking industry

Martin T. Bohl, Olena Havrylchyk and Dirk Schiereck

7.1 Introduction

Similar to other transition countries in Central and Eastern Europe (CEE), Poland opened its banking market for foreign participants in 1998. The removal of entry barriers has caused a 53 per cent increase in assets controlled by foreign banks in just two years, with about 70 per cent of total banking assets under foreign ownership in 2000. At the end of 2002, 14 out of 15 banks listed on the Warsaw Stock Exchange had foreign majority shareholders. This rapid transfer of ownership rights lets us focus on the benefits of allowing foreign banks' entry into transition countries.

Despite the profound changes in the Eastern European banking sector, there has been little empirical research in this field so far. Only three capital markets oriented studies shed any light on (Western) European banking mergers and acquisitions (Tourani-Rad and Van Beek (1999); Cybo-Ottone and Murgia (2000); Beitel *et al.* (2004)), together with some efficiency- and performance-oriented analyses (e.g. Altunbas *et al.* (1996); Molyneux *et al.* (1996); Vander Vennet (1996)). However, the empirical evidence presented in these studies faces two important differences to our sample. First, we focus on a transition country where the banking industry is by far not as developed as in Western Europe, the home countries of the acquiring banks. Second, the transactions are privatization deals. Contrary to all other studies cited earlier the main seller of bank stocks in Poland is the Polish state who could interfere in the privatization process itself and even exert influence on the governance of already privatized banks, decreasing the benefits of foreign ownership.

Privatizing banks via trade sales to foreign investors might not only effect the value of the acquired bank targets but also influence the shareholder wealth of rival bank owners in the same market. Especially, the announcement effects on rival returns are not clear. On the one hand, negative returns might occur because rivals can loose market shares to more efficient foreign banks. On the other hand, there is a probability of efficiency spill-over effects with possible improvements of the cost–income ratios for domestic banks and also an anticipation of future takeover premia.

To uncover the effects of privatization to foreign investors, we study a new data set of fifty-one acquisitions of foreign banks between 1996 and 2002 relying on robust event study methodology that includes very recent data. First, we analyse the shareholder wealth effects of the Polish bank targets around the announcement date of acquisitions. Next, we look for shareholder wealth effects for the non-participating rival banks in the Polish bank market and present wealth effects for the remaining domestic banks (Bessler and Murtagh (2002)). Poland is the most interesting country to look for capital market reactions because the Warsaw Stock Exchange hosts the largest number of listed banks in CEE.[1]

The remainder of the chapter is structured as follows. Section 7.2 describes potential costs and benefits for the banks acquired by foreign investors and for the non-participating banks. In Section 7.3 we describe the trends in foreign bank ownership on the Polish banking market. These sections should serve as a background for the discussion that follows. Section 7.4 presents the data and the methodology, and Section 7.5 provides empirical results of the investigation. Finally, Section 7.6 draws some conclusions.

7.2 Potential wealth effects from foreign bank ownership

Recently, some studies analyse the value generated to target companies' shareholders by the announcement of acquisitions involving foreign European firms. For example, Danbolt (2004) and Goergen and Renneboog (2004) present evidence for positive share price reactions of acquisition targets being higher for cross-border transactions than for domestic ones, however, the differences are either not significant or disappear when other factors are controlled for. Additionally, a few studies that measure the stock price reaction of target banks to foreign acquisitions in Europe (Tourani-Rad and Van Beek (1999), Cybo-Ottone and Murgia (2000), Beitel *et al.* (2004)) report evidence in favour of wealth effects that are higher for targets in cross-border deals.

These studies rely on the traditional merger framework. The seller is assumed to be a diffuse shareholder group and unable to influence the behaviour after acquisition. However, the results might be different when the seller is the government, as it is the case in Poland. Governments can influence the company after privatization through economic policy, retaining some ownership or by setting privatization conditions, such as limiting post-privatization lay-offs (Uhlenbruck and de Castro (2000)). Campa and Hernando (2004) show that acquisitions in industries that had previously been under government control or that are still heavily regulated generate lower value than Mergers and Acquisitions (M&As) announcements in unregulated industries. Additionally, their findings indicate that this difference is significant when the acquirer is a foreign firm and when the merger takes place in a financial industry.

The literature discussed earlier focuses on developed countries in Europe, but we are not aware of any event study that analyses the capital market reaction to foreign acquisitions in CEE. However, we can rely on the findings of X-efficiency studies that identify a number of advantages of foreign ownership for banking institutions in transition countries where it replaces state ownership.[2] In this case foreign owners enhance banks' efficiency by reducing the importance of directed credit and introducing better risk management practices, bringing access to cheaper resources and streamlining banking operations. A number of authors measure relative efficiency of foreign and domestic banks in transition countries and find that foreign banks enjoy higher efficiency than their domestic peers (Bhattacharyya *et al.* (1997), Grigorian and Manole (2002), Isik and Hassan (2002), Hasan and Marton (2003)). Claessens *et al.* (2001) find that foreign banks in transition countries tend to have lower overhead costs and loan loss provisions and higher profits than domestic banks.

The impact of foreign banks' entry on the remaining domestic banks is even less clear. It is usually assumed that foreign banks spur competition and thus render domestic banking markets more efficient. Claessens *et al.* (2001) demonstrate that for most countries higher foreign ownership is associated with a reduction of costs and net interest margins for domestically owned banks. Domestic banks also benefit from spill-over effects by copying from foreign banks' new financial practices and modern techniques. There is also evidence that foreign banks positively improve regulation and supervision of banking markets in their host countries.

However, the benefits from higher foreign bank ownership for the remaining domestic banks might not materialize immediately. In fact, Claessens *et al.* (2001) find that profitability of domestic bank falls after the entry of foreign banks. This highlights the risks for domestic banks, which can suffer from the lower charter value and be forced to pursue riskier activities in order to compete with their foreign counterparts. Lensink and Hermes (2004) show that after the entry of foreign banks, domestic banks in developing countries with inefficient banking systems experience initially higher costs because they have to invest in modern technology, training personnel, etc.

Additionally, we can also expect positive abnormal returns for the non-participating banks that would be consistent with the market power hypothesis, which states that the consolidation of the banking market gives the remaining banks more market power in setting prices on retail financial services (Berger *et al.* (2000)). This is very relevant for the Polish banking market, because foreign bank ownership spurred its consolidation. The number of banks in Poland decreased from 83 institutions in 1997 to 59 in 2002, which happened mainly due to 28 mergers that took place during this period. Consolidation was often directly caused by foreign ownership because foreign owners decided to merge two institutions that were under their control. Additionally, many domestic banks chose to merge in response to the growing competition pressure from foreign banks.

Alternatively, the positive reaction of non-participating banks could be driven by the stock behaviour of the remaining domestic banks. When Polish authorities agreed to liberalize foreign banks' entry, there was a great interest from foreign investors in acquiring domestic banks. Thus, the announcements of foreign acquisitions were good news also for non-participating domestic bank shareholders, because they could anticipate the interest of foreign investors in their institutions as well.

7.3 The Polish banking system

Foreign banks were allowed to purchase controlling stakes in Polish banks relatively late in comparison to other CEE countries. When privatization started in 1993, foreign banks were entitled only to minority shares whereas controlling stakes remained with the treasury. In 1998 a new Act on Banking came into force, which removed all restrictions for foreign banks. The concept of privatization changed as well and the government started to seek reputable foreign banks in order to collect large privatization revenues. The high minimum capital requirement of five million European Currency Units (ECUs) accelerated the involvement of foreign banks, since domestic banks could not raise such large amounts of money on the local market.

In Section 7.2 we argued that state involvement in governance of privatized banks could diminish wealth effects for shareholders of target banks. Bonin and Wachtel (1999) describe the privatization process in Poland and conclude that multiple policy objectives delayed the transfer of control to independent investors. In certain cases, even when the government retained only a minority share of a bank, it was able to exert pressure. To illustrate this, we can consider the privatization of Bank Handlowy, where the sale contract included a number of restrictions, such as a limit on the disposal of shares by core investors. Moreover, in 1999 the government decided to use its 25 per cent non-voting share to recapitalize the Polish state insurance company, but did not inform the bank management before the transaction was reported in the press.

Despite these difficulties, the importance of foreign banks in the Polish banking market increased as can be seen from the measures in Table 7.1. The year 1998 was the turning point in terms of foreign ownership of Polish banks. Even though the share of assets and capital controlled by foreign investors has not changed significantly during this year, the value of foreign acquisitions grew ten times in comparison with the previous year. Just two years later, in 2000, 15 out of 16 banks listed on the Warsaw Stock Exchange had already foreign majority ownership and the share of assets controlled by foreigners grew from about 17 per cent in 1998 to about 70 per cent in 2000.

Foreign banks pursued two strategies in acquiring Polish banks during the privatization process. A number of banks (Citibank, Bank Austria Creditanstalt, Bayerische Hypovereinsbank) first established Greenfield Operations in the form of subsidiaries, then acquired Polish institutions and finally merged subsidiaries with the domestic banks they controlled. Other institutes (Commerzbank, KBC, Allied Irish Bank) acquired Polish banks without prior presence on the Polish banking market.

Since our methodology allows us to analyse the impact of foreign ownership only on listed banks, it is necessary to consider the role that they play in the Polish banking industry. As can be seen from Table 7.1, the number of listed institutions and their share in total banking assets, loans and deposits increased almost continuously since 1996 and in 2002 fourteen listed banks accounted for about 66 per cent of total assets. It is noteworthy that listed institutions differ significantly

Table 7.1 Summary statistics of the Polish banking structure

	1996	1997	1998	1999	2000	2001	2002
Number of commercial banks	81	83	83	77	74	71	59
of which foreign-owned banks	25	29	31	39	47	48	45
Number of listed banks	11	14	16	16	16	16	15
of which foreign	5	5	5	9	15	15	14
Assets controlled by foreign banks (in %)	13.7	15.3	16.6	47.2	69.5	69.2	67.4
Capital controlled by foreign banks (in %)	20.9	24	24.7	50.2	77.6	80.2	77.8
Share of listed banks in the total banking market in terms of							
Loans	22.9	39.5	54.2	58.8	58.5	67.2	68.4
Total assets	20.0	35.3	52.1	55.1	58.1	65.6	65.8
Deposits	19.0	31.9	48.4	52.7	56.3	65.3	64.5
Value of analysed acquisition deals in mil. US$	68.7	123.4	1,229.4	1,588.1	1,173.2	786.9	148.7

Notes
The number of commercial banks does not include banks declared bankrupt or under liquidation. Cooperative banks are also excluded. The numbers were sourced from National Bank of Poland (1998, 1999, 2000, 2001, 2002).

from unlisted banks in terms of shares controlled by foreign and small investors, as well as by the Treasury. For example, in 2002 foreign investors owned about 75.1 per cent of listed banks stocks, whereas only about 63.2 per cent of unlisted banks stocks were owned by foreigners. Small investors and the Treasury controlled 19.5 per cent and 1.9 per cent of listed banks stocks, as well as 10.0 per cent and 17.3 per cent of the stocks of unlisted institutions.

7.4   Data and methodology

To identify foreign bank acquisitions in Poland between 1996 and 2002 we use Thomson Financial SDC (Securities Data Company – M&A Database). Bloomberg only provides data for deals back to 1997. To verify data we use additional press research in the *Financial Times*. Data on returns on individual equities, market capitalization and the WIG index are directly provided by the Warsaw Stock Exchange. Transactions are selected according to the following criteria: first, the transaction was announced between 1 January 1996 and 31 December 2002. Second, the bidder was a non-Polish bank.[3] Third, the target was an exchange listed Polish bank. Fourth, the transaction had been closed (the deal status is 'completed'). Both, the target firms and the rivals were listed on the Warsaw Stock Exchange for at least 170 trading days prior to the announcement and 20 days (i.e. one month) after the announcement of a transaction. The data are summarized in Table 7.2.

Table 7.2 shows the fifty-one transactions. The total volume exceeds US$5 billions. The average transaction value is worth about US$160 millions,

Table 7.2 Summary of cross-border M&A transactions

Target name	Acquirer name	Value (mil. US$)	Number of deals
Bank Handlowy SA	Commerzbank AG	n.a.	2
Bank Handlowy SA	Citibank NA	1,023.34	5
Bank Przemyslowo-Handlowy SA	AIB Group	65.95	1
Bank Przemyslowo Handlowy SA	Bayerische Hypovereinsbank	1,420.22	6
Bank Rozwoju Eksportu SA	Commerzbank AG	n.a.	3
Wielkopolski Bank Kredytowy SA	Allied Irish Bank	179.22	3
Bank Polska Kasa Opieki SA	Investor Group	1,047.58	3
Bank Inicjatyw Gospodarczych SA	Merrill Lynch International	n.a.	1
Bank Komunalny SA	Nordbanken AB	8.93	1
Bank Ochrony Srodowiska SA	Skandinaviska Enskilda Banken	73.18	3
Bank Amerykanski w Polsce SA	Banque Bruxelles Lambert SA	n.a.	1
Bank Amerykanski w Polsce SA	Bayerische Landesbank	2.32	1
Bank Amerykanski w Polsce SA	DG Bank	67.12	1
Bank Amerykanski w Polsce SA	DZ Bank AG	11.54	1
Bank Wspolpracy Regionalnej SA	Deutsche Bank AG	59.58	2
Pierwszy Polko-Amerykanski Bank SA	Generale de Banque SA	3.5	1
Pierwszy Polko-Amerykanski Bank SA	Fortis AG	89.11	2
Kredyt Bank SA	EBRD	5.35	1
Kredyt Bank SA	Kredietbank NV	3.94	2
Kredyt Bank PBI SA	KBC Bancassurance Holding NV	575.09	5
Kredyt Bank PBI SA	Banco Espirito Santo	n.a.	1
Powszechny Bank Kredytowy SA	Bank Austria AG	111.25	3
Powszechny Bank Kredytowy SA	Bayerische Hypovereinsbank	340.25	2
Total		5,087.47	51
Average		159.94	
Median		67.77	
Maximum		1,047.58	
Minimum		0.23	

Source: Thomson Financial SDC Mergers and Acquisitions Database.

ranging from US$2.3 millions to US$1.4 billions.[4] The average share that was acquired by foreign investors is about 55 per cent and the median about 31 per cent. Therefore, we are able to analyse whether the size of a transaction has any additional wealth effect. We can assume that the target stock price reaction would be more significant when a larger share is acquired and thus a foreign bank assumes control over the target.

In order to estimate the wealth effect of foreign acquisitions for shareholders of Polish banks we perform an event study. Due to the fact that some stocks were infrequently traded on the Warsaw Stock Exchange, the traditional market model would produce beta coefficients, which would be biased downwards. Therefore, following Dimson (1979) we rely on the aggregated coefficient method and regress observed bank stock returns on preceding, synchronous and subsequent market returns:

$$R_{it} = \alpha_i + \sum_{k=-3}^{1} \beta_{ik} M_{t+k} + w_{it}, \tag{7.1}$$

where R_{it} is the return for the bank stock i at date t, and M_{t+k} is the market return on the benchmark for the day $t + k$. The model parameters α_i and β_{ik} are estimated for each stock separately with ordinary least squares (OLS). As market benchmark we employ the WIG index. We have chosen 150 days prior to the event window as our estimation period.[5]

As can be seen from formula (7.1), the traditional market model is augmented by lagged and leading terms of the market return. At first, we included five lagged and five leading market terms, however, only the three lagged and one leading term turned out to be statistically significant and produced the highest $\bar{R}^2$. Hence, we have decided on this specification. It is noteworthy that when we add non-synchronous market terms, the $\bar{R}^2$ rises from 22 per cent to 31 per cent showing that Dimson's method has higher explanatory power than the conventional market model.

Abnormal returns are computed using the following formula:

$$AR_{it} = R_{it} - \hat{\alpha}_i - \sum_{k=-3}^{1} \hat{\beta}_{ik} M_{t+k}. \tag{7.2}$$

We calculate cumulative abnormal returns (CARs) for each stock over the following event windows: $[-20, 0]$, $[-10, 0]$, $[-5, 0]$, $[-2, 0]$, $[-1, 0]$, $[0, 0]$, $[-1, 1]$, $[-2, 2]$, $[-5, 5]$, $[-10, 10]$, $[-20, 20]$. Further, we average the CARs for all stocks and test whether CAR is different from zero using the J_1 test statistic suggested by Campbell *et al.* (1997). We estimate the long-term impact of announcements by relying on CARs for the $[-100, 100]$ event window.

In addition to the analysis of the impact of foreign acquisition announcements on target banks, we apply the same methodology to investigate the effect of increased foreign participation on the banking industry as a whole. For this purpose, we study CARs around announcement dates for the two bank indexes. An index consisting of all institutions (domestic and foreign) that do not participate in crossborder M&As at this moment, and an index consisting of the remaining domestic banks. Of course, the number of domestic banks included in the index declined during the analysed period since almost all listed banks were acquired by foreign owners.[6]

After estimating the cumulative abnormal returns, we take our analysis a step further and investigate which factors have an effect on them. First, we expect that abnormal returns will be higher when foreign investors gain control over a bank, allowing them to embark on the necessary reorganization. Second, large institutions may be more difficult to restructure and thus their size, measured by the market capitalization, would have a negative impact on abnormal returns. To test these two hypotheses, we estimate the following regression:

$$\text{CAR}_i = \alpha_i + \beta_1 \text{Share}_i + \beta_2 \text{Capitalization}_i + \beta_{3t} D_t + \varepsilon_i, \tag{7.3}$$

where CAR_i is the cumulative abnormal returns of a bank i, Share_i the share of a transaction's value in the capitalization of a bank i and Capitalization_i the logarithm of the capitalization of a bank stock i on the Warsaw Stock Exchange on the last day of the month prior to foreign acquisition. D_t, $t = 1996, \ldots, 2002$ are year dummies.

7.5   Empirical findings

7.5.1   Stock market's reaction to announcements

Figure 7.1 reports CARs for 41 days surrounding the announcement of foreign acquisition and Table 7.3 the corresponding estimation results. The findings are reported separately for three groups of banks, namely (1) for target banks, (2) all other banks that have not participated in acquisitions and (3) the remaining domestic banks. As can be seen from Figure 7.1 and Table 7.3 the shareholders of target banks experienced positive abnormal returns of 3.64 per cent over the 41 days event window. The results are consistent with other studies that analyse cross-border M&As and find a positive reaction of targets to foreign acquisitions.

However, the magnitude of our results is smaller than those reported by other studies. For example, Beitel *et al.* (2004) show that the average CARs over the 3 days event period $[-1, 1]$ equals 7.22 per cent (compared to our 2.84 per cent) for international target banks acquired by West European banks. This difference may result from different corporate governance structures in our data set, namely

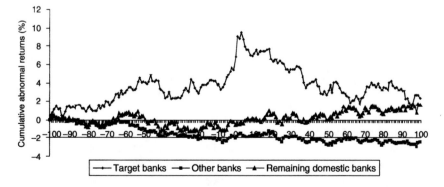

Figure 7.1 Cumulative abnormal returns for target and other banks (201 days event window).

Table 7.3 Estimation results on cumulative abnormal returns (41 days event window)

	CAR in %	J_1	SD in %	Positive	Negative
A. Target banks					
[−20, 0]	4.05***	13.71	12.15	32	19
[−10, 0]	2.81***	17.83	8.94	30	21
[−5, 0]	3.17***	35.95	7.79	31	20
[−2, 0]	1.76***	41.51	5.86	31	20
[−1, 0]	1.15***	20.68	5.25	29	22
[0, 0]	1.40***	29.93	4.61	28	23
[−1, 1]	2.84***	46.72	7.69	31	20
[−2, 2]	3.23***	33.74	10.22	30	21
[−5, 5]	3.86***	21.91	11.62	31	20
[−10, 10]	3.05***	6.57	14.90	31	20
[−20, 20]	3.64***	5.05	18.21	32	19
B. All other banks					
[−20, 0]	0.47***	7.03	0.59	27	24
[−10, 0]	0.04***	−8.66	0.29	24	27
[−5, 0]	−0.04***	−15.13	0.15	22	29
[−2, 0]	−0.01***	−43.23	0.08	19	32
[−1, 0]	−0.16***	−70.89	0.05	22	29
[0, 0]	−0.13***	−110.74	0.02	22	29
[−1, 1]	−0.24***	−80.59	0.07	21	30
[−2, 2]	−0.07***	−48.72	0.13	20	31
[−5, 5]	−0.08***	−13.49	0.29	26	25
[−10, 10]	−0.33***	−9.77	0.60	25	26
[−20, 20]	0.92***	4.14	1.30	28	23
C. Remaining domestic banks					
[−20, 0]	0.66**	2.62	0.70	25	17
[−10, 0]	−0.10	0.52	0.34	22	20
[−5, 0]	0.64***	33.92	0.18	22	20
[−2, 0]	−0.32***	−17.98	0.09	18	24
[−1, 0]	−0.38***	−57.65	0.06	21	21
[0, 0]	−0.24***	−51.23	0.03	21	19
[−1, 1]	−0.48***	−64.13	0.09	20	22
[−2, 2]	−0.43***	−17.31	0.15	20	21
[−5, 5]	0.82***	26.43	0.34	26	15
[−10, 10]	0.56***	10.00	0.70	25	15
[−20, 20]	2.08***	9.07	1.52	28	14

Notes

This table shows the results for the regression equations (7.1) and (7.2). The table reports cumulative abnormal returns, J_1 statistics, SD of returns, and the number of positive and negative abnormal returns. To calculate abnormal returns we relied on the aggregated coefficient method which we applied to the estimation period of 150 days prior to the 41 days event window. **, *** denote results are significant at the 95% and 99% level, respectively.

from the fact that we have the state as one remaining (minority) shareholder after the transaction and that we included all deals in our analysis regardless of their size and the acquired share. We can assume that deals that involve the transfer of control to foreign owners should be greeted by higher abnormal returns. We will investigate this issue further in the second subsection.

Our results show that the announcements were already anticipated by the market. The CARs for 20 days prior to acquisitions [−20, 0] are about 4 per cent and are higher than those for the [−20, 20] event period. Figure 7.1 shows that CARs of target banks increase by 6 per cent, then fall by approximately 2 per cent and stabilize at around 4 per cent. The anticipation of acquisitions is a common finding in the literature and was reported by numerous other M&A studies (e.g. Cybo-Ottone and Murgia (2000)).

In the next step following Bessler and Murtagh (2002), we estimate CARs for the non-participating banks for the 41 days surrounding the announcement date. The results are presented in Panel B of Table 7.3. We find that the shareholders of non-participating banks also experience positive abnormal returns that equal about 1 per cent, which is consistent with the market power hypothesis. To test whether the remaining domestic banks might anticipate the acquisitions, we separately investigate their reaction and the results are presented in Panel C of Table 7.3. As expected, we observe positive and significant CARs of around 2 per cent in the 41 days event window, which is higher than the results for all other non-participating banks. Interestingly, abnormal returns calculated for smaller event windows are often negative.

With respect to political and legal changes we study whether the market reactions changed significantly since 1998, when restrictions on foreign ownership were repealed. At an early stage of transition many privatization deals were characterized by delays and a persistent involvement of the State Treasury in the governance of privatized banks (Abarbanell and Bonin (1997)). Therefore, we would expect that earlier transactions created less value for shareholders. To investigate this aspect, we calculate CARs separately for deals conducted before and after 1998 and test the hypothesis whether the differences between them equal zero. The results are presented in Table 7.4. When looking at the test statistics no definite conclusions can be drawn from the results. The findings are mixed and are highly sensitive to the chosen event window.

To analyse the long-term wealth effects of foreign acquisitions, we calculate abnormal returns for 201 days surrounding the announcement date. The findings are reported in Figure 7.1 and Table 7.5. CARs for the target banks peaked at 10 per cent just following the announcement, but have shown only 2.3 per cent increase in the long-run. The shareholders of all non-participating banks have observed negative CARs. However, these results are driven by rival foreign banks since the remaining domestic banks exhibit slightly positive abnormal returns over the long time period. Because none of the long-term results are statistically significant, they should be treated with caution.

7.5.2 *Regression analysis*

Table 7.6 documents the results of the regression equation (7.3) to investigate the determinants of the CARs. Using CARs over different event windows as the dependent variable we provide a check of robustness. The regressions are run with and without year dummies in order to reflect the changes during the analysed time period.

Table 7.4 CARs for transactions announced before 1998 and after 1998

	Before 1998	After 1998	t-statistics
A. Target banks			
[−20, 0]	2.38	4.46	−0.74
[−10, 0]	2.65	2.85	−0.14
[−5, 0]	1.56	3.56	−2.71***
[−2, 0]	0.77	2.01	−3.32***
[−1, 0]	−0.17	1.48	−6.43***
[0, 0]	1.10	1.47	−2.99***
[−1, 1]	2.42	2.95	−1.30
[−2, 2]	4.12	3.02	1.65
[−5, 5]	4.48	3.71	0.53
[−10, 10]	7.50	1.97	1.95*
[−20, 20]	4.76	3.37	0.23
B. All other banks			
[−20, 0]	2.34	−0.03	2.63***
[−10, 0]	1.38	−0.22	3.59***
[−5, 0]	0.50	−0.13	2.72***
[−2, 0]	0.12	−0.01	1.11
[−1, 0]	−0.35	−0.10	−3.34***
[0, 0]	−0.77	0.03	−21.07***
[−1, 1]	−0.01	−0.29	2.44**
[−2, 2]	0.99	−0.30	6.66***
[−5, 5]	1.13	−0.34	3.28***
[−10, 10]	0.73	−0.50	1.35
[−20, 20]	3.43	0.34	1.54
C. Remaining domestic banks			
[−20, 0]	−0.05	0.88	−1.03
[−10, 0]	0.34	−0.24	1.33
[−5, 0]	0.34	0.73	−1.69*
[−2, 0]	−0.76	−0.19	−5.14***
[−1, 0]	−1.02	−0.18	−11.36***
[0, 0]	−0.65	−0.12	−14.54***
[−1, 1]	−0.89	−0.36	−4.74***
[−2, 2]	−0.72	−0.34	−1.97*
[−5, 5]	1.30	0.66	1.45
[−10, 10]	2.25	0.03	2.45**
[−20, 20]	3.59	1.62	1.02

Notes

This table shows the results for the regression equations (7.1) and (7.2). The table reports cumulative abnormal returns separately for transactions that took place before and after 1998. To calculate abnormal returns we relied on the aggregated coefficient method which we applied to the estimation period of 150 days prior to the 41 days event window. The third column presents *t*-statistics for the null hypothesis that the difference between cumulative abnormal returns before and after 1998 equals zero. *, **, *** denote results are significant at the 90%, 95% and 99% level, respectively.

The results show that the larger the share of the acquired capital, the higher the wealth effect enjoyed by shareholders of target banks. The results are statistically significant at least at the 10 per cent confidence level for the event windows [−5, 5], [−2, 2], [−1, 1], [−5, 0], [−2, 0], [0, 0] and insignificant for the other event

Table 7.5 Estimation results on cumulative abnormal returns (201 days event window)

	CAR in %	J_1	SD in %	Positive	Negative
Target banks [−100, 100]	2.30	0.81	39.65	22	26
Other banks [−100, 100]	−2.82	−0.95	19.38	23	28
Remaining domestic banks [−100, 100]	1.60	−1.15	26.37	20	21

Notes
This table shows the results of an event study analysing the reaction of forty-eight Polish banks to being acquired by foreign investors. Three banks were excluded from the analysis because their stocks were not listed on the Warsaw Stock Exchange 351 days prior to the event day. Additionally, the reaction of other banks and the remaining domestic banks is reported. The table reports cumulative abnormal returns, J_1 statistics, SD of returns, and the number of positive and negative abnormal returns. To calculate abnormal returns we relied on the aggregated coefficient method which we applied to the estimation period of 150 days prior to the 201 days event window.

windows. This finding confirms the expectation that the benefits of foreign ownership can only materialize when a foreign bank has full control over an acquired institution. Very large banks, on the other hand, can be very difficult to restructure and thus we can anticipate smaller wealth enhancements for large institutions. As can be observed from the findings in Table 7.6, the size of a target bank, measured by its market capitalization, is negatively related to market valuation of the deal, confirming this prediction.

7.6 Conclusions

In 1998, the regulation of financial markets in Poland was liberalized allowing foreign banks to enter without any restrictions. In this paper, we investigate the stock market valuation of foreign acquisitions of Polish banks between 1996 and 2002. In our study, the focus lies not only on the reaction of target bank stocks, but we also measure abnormal returns for the non-participating banks. The novel aspect of this study is the focus on the reaction of the remaining domestic banks to foreign acquisitions of their peers.

Our results as shown in Figure 7.3 indicate that foreign acquisitions created wealth for participating banks in the short-run. The shareholders of target banks experienced an almost 4 per cent increase in the stock value during 41 days surrounding the announcement date. It is noteworthy that deals where large shares had been transferred into foreign control exhibited significantly higher abnormal returns. The long-term effects were also positive albeit not significant. Thus, the shareholders of target banks anticipated that foreign owners would render acquired banks more profitable, confirming the hypothesis that foreign bank ownership in transition countries adds value. This finding is in line with the results produced by numerous studies employing other methodologies

Table 7.6 Summary of the regression results

Capitalization	[−20, 20]	[−20, 20]	[−10, 10]	[−10, 10]	[−5, 5]	[−5, 5]	[−2, 2]	[−2, 2]	[−1, 1]	[−1, 1]
Share	0.00	−0.03	0.02	0.00	0.06**	0.06*	0.07***	0.07**	0.06***	0.05**
Capitalization	−0.05**	−0.06*	−0.06***	−0.06**	−0.03***	−0.04**	−0.03***	−0.03**	−0.02**	−0.02*
D_{1996}		0.45**		0.45***		0.31***		0.26***		0.16**
D_{1997}		0.41*		0.42**		0.22**		0.18*		0.14*
D_{1998}		0.37		0.37*		0.27**		0.23**		0.16**
D_{1999}		0.57**		0.53***		0.31**		0.25**		0.19**
D_{2000}		0.49*		0.47**		0.32**		0.23**		0.14*
D_{2001}		0.46		0.47**		0.28*		0.19*		0.11
D_{2002}		0.34		0.40**		0.24**		0.17*		0.09
F	2.78*	1.31	6.79***	2.06*	11.51***	3.88***	18.43***	5.65***	15.76***	6.02***
R^2	17.07	36.03	33.46	46.93	46.03	62.44	57.72	70.76	53.85	72.07
$\bar{R}^2$	10.92	8.62	28.53	24.18	42.03	46.34	54.59	58.23	50.44	60.10

Capitalization	[−20, 0]	[−20, 0]	[−10, 0]	[−10, 0]	[−5, 0]	[−5, 0]	[−2, 0]	[−2, 0]	[0, 0]	[0, 0]
Share	−0.00	−0.04	0.01	−0.02	0.04**	0.02	0.05***	0.03**	0.04***	0.03***
Capitalization	−0.03*	−0.04**	−0.02*	−0.03*	−0.01	−0.02	−0.01	−0.01	−0.01**	−0.01**
D_{1996}		0.30**		0.19**		0.12*		0.07		0.08**
D_{1997}		0.20		0.15		0.08		0.01		0.08*
D_{1998}		0.28**		0.18*		0.12		0.05		0.08*
D_{1999}		0.44***		0.30***		0.19**		0.12**		0.13***
D_{2000}		0.38**		0.22**		0.16*		0.06		0.09**
D_{2001}		0.29*		0.20		0.11		0.05		0.07
D_{2002}		0.29*		0.17		0.10		0.05		0.07*
F	1.95	2.16*	2.74*	2.22*	4.39**	3.44***	10.13***	5.18***	17.11***	8.36***
R^2	12.65	48.08	16.86	48.77	24.53	59.57	42.88	68.93	55.89	78.18
$\bar{R}^2$	6.18	25.83	10.70	26.82	18.94	42.24	38.65	55.61	52.62	68.82

Notes

This table reports results on the regression analysis (7.3). The dependent variables are defined as cumulative abnormal returns for the different event windows. Share is the ratio of transaction value to capitalization and Capitalization the logarithm of capitalization of a given bank stock on the Warsaw Stock Exchange on the last day of the month previous to the deal. D_t are year dummies for the years $t = 1996,\ldots,2002$. F denotes the F-test of joint significance of the coefficients. R^2 and $\bar{R}^2$ are the coefficients of determination. *, **, *** denote statistically significant coefficients at the 10%, 5% and 1% level, respectively.

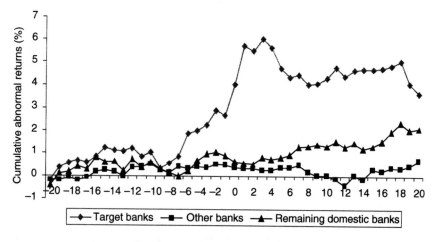

Figure 7.2 Cumulative abnormal returns for target and other banks (41 days event window).

(Bhattacharyya *et al.* (1997), Claessens *et al.* (2001), Grigorian and Manole (2002), Isik and Hassan (2002), Hasan and Marton (2003)).

When foreign acquisitions were announced, the shares of non-participating banks also experienced positive wealth effects in the short-run. The effect was much higher for the non-participating domestic banks, indicating that their share-holders anticipated foreign acquisition of the remaining domestic institutions. This could also explain why there was a significant price increase for the participating banks prior to announcements.

Notes

1 As of April 2004, there were 14 bank stocks listed on the Warsaw Stock Exchange. For comparison, 3 and 10 bank stocks were listed on the stock exchanges in Prague and Budapest, respectively.
2 Interestingly, the efficiency literature on developed countries gives the opposite results. Foreign banks that enter already developed banking markets perform worse than their domestic counterparts due to additional costs of overcoming informational asymmetries.
3 All transactions are included when a Polish bank was acquired by foreign investors, regardless of transaction volume. We cannot compare the results of foreign acquisitions with domestic ones, because only one listed bank was acquired by a domestic investor: Bank Rozwoju Eksportu SA tookover Polski Bank Rozwoju SA in 1998.
4 Beitel *et al.* (2004) and Cybo-Ottone and Murgia (2000) analyse M&As of banks in Europe and observe an average transaction value of US$3.3 and 1.61 billions, respectively. However, they only include transactions that exceed US$100 millions and when a change in control of the target took place. If we exclude from our sample deals that lie below the threshold of US$100 millions, the average transaction value rises from about US$160 to 390 millions.
5 We tried a number of longer estimation windows as well. The results do not change substantially. However, the fit of the model is better when shorter estimation windows are used.
6 The only Polish listed bank that is still domestically owned is Bank Ochrony Srodowiska SA. The bank is controlled by the National Fund for Environmental Protection and

regional environmental funds, but even it has a foreign investor, Sweden's Skandinaviska Enskilda Banken AB, which bought 32.1 per cent of bank's shares in 2000.

References

Abarbanell, J. and J. P. Bonin (1997). 'Bank privatization in Poland: case of bank Slaski', *Journal of Comparative Economics*, 25, 31–61.

Altunbas, Y., E. P. M. Gardener and P. Molyneux (1996). 'Economies of scale, cost sub-additivity and x-efficiencies in European banking', Bangor: University College of North Wales.

Beitel, P., D. Schiereck and M. Wahrenburg (2004). 'Explaining M&A success in European Banks', *European Financial Management*, 10, 109–139.

Berger, A. N., R. DeYoung, H. Genay and G. F. Udell (2000). 'Globalization of financial institutions: evidence from cross-border banking performance', *Brookings-Wharton Papers on Financial Services*, 3, 23–158.

Bessler, W. and J. P. Murtagh (2002). 'The stock market reaction to cross-border acquisitions of financial services firms: an analysis of Canadian banks', *Journal of International Financial Markets, Institutions and Money*, 12, 419–440.

Bhattacharyya, A., C. A. K. Lovell and P. Sahay (1997). 'The impact of liberalization on the productive efficiency of Indian commercial banks', *European Journal of Operational Research*, 98, 332–345.

Bonin, J. P. and P. Wachtel (1999). 'Lessons from bank privatization in Central and Eastern Europe', William Davidson Working Paper No. 245.

Campa, J. M. and I. Hernando (2004). 'Shareholder wealth creation in European M&As', *European Financial Management*, 10, 47–81.

Campbell, J. Y., A. W. Lo and A. G. MacKinlay (1997). *The Econometrics of Financial Markets*, Princeton, NJ: Princeton University Press.

Claessens, S., A. Demirgüc-Kunt and H. Huizinga (2001). 'How does foreign entry effect domestic banking markets?', *Journal of Banking and Finance*, 25, 891–911.

Cybo-Ottone, A. and M. Murgia (2000). 'Mergers and shareholder wealth in European banking', *Journal of Banking and Finance*, 24, 831–859.

Danbolt, J. (2004). 'Target company cross-border effects in acquisitions into the UK', *European Financial Management*, 10, 83–108.

Dimson, E. (1979). 'Risk management when shares are subject to infrequent trading', *Journal of Financial Economics*, 7, 197–226.

Goergen, M. and L. Renneboog (2004). 'Shareholder wealth effects of European domestic and cross-border takeover bids', *European Financial Management*, 10, 9–45.

Grigorian, D. A. and V. Manole (2002). 'Determinants of commercial bank performance in transition: an application of data envelopment analysis', IMF Working Paper No. 02/146.

Hasan, I. and K. Marton (2003). 'Development and efficiency of the banking sector in a transitional economy: Hungarian experience', *Journal of Banking and Finance*, 27, 2249–2271.

Isik, I. and M. K. Hassan (2002). 'Technical, scale and allocative efficiencies of Turkish banking industry', *Journal of Banking and Finance*, 26, 719–766.

Lensink, R. and N. Hermes (2004). 'The short-term effects of foreign bank entry on domestic bank behaviour: does economic development matter?', *Journal of Banking and Finance*, 28, 553–568.

Molyneux, P., Y. Altunbas and E. Gardener (1996). *Efficiency in European Banking*. New York: John Wiley & Sons.

National Bank of Poland (1998, 1999, 2000, 2001, 2002). *Summary Evaluation of the Financial Situation of Polish Banks*. Poland: NBP.

Tourani-Rad, A. and L. Van Beek (1999). 'Market valuation of European bank mergers', *European Management Journal*, 17, 532–540.

Uhlenbruck, K. and J. O. de Castro (2000). 'Foreign acquisitions in Central and Eastern Europe: outcomes of privatization in transitional economies', *Academy of Management Journal*, 43, 381–402.

Vander Vennet, R. (1996). 'The effect of mergers and acquisitions on the efficiency and profitability of EC credit institutions', *Journal of Banking and Finance*, 20, S. 1531–1558.

8 Electronic payments and ATMs

Changing technology and cost efficiency in banking

Santiago Carbó Valverde, David B. Humphrey and Rafael Lopez del Paso

8.1 Introduction

Of the numerous technical changes in banking, two stand out as having a large impact on operating costs. These are the expanded use of automatic teller machines (ATMs) to supplement and replace expensive branch offices in delivering an important subset of depositor services and the concurrent substitution of lower cost electronic payments for paper-based transactions. Both of these newer banking technologies intensively use computers and telecommunication facilities and have benefited from cost reductions and efficiency improvements in these important inputs. Our purpose is to quantify the overall effect these newer banking technologies in service delivery and payment method have had on banking costs. We also illustrate the portion of the overall cost change attributed to expanded ATM use versus the shift to electronic payments. This is implemented using a statistical model relating operating costs to certain physical characteristics of service delivery and payment levels and mix for Spanish savings and commercial banks over 1992–2000.

The usual approach for identifying cost savings from technical change in banking has been to specify a time-specific indicator variable or, less often, tie technical change to the use of certain inputs (e.g. less labor and more capital). Our approach is quite different. Instead of relying on a time dummy or presuming that technical advances are embodied in or augment the use of certain inputs, we relate operating expenses to five characteristics of banking service output that reflect known differences in cost. As the service mix shifts to these lower cost characteristics, unit operating expenses should fall and reflect the savings associated with the spread of new technology within the industry. By specifying five output characteristics associated with technical change we are able to not only provide an overall estimate of the cost savings from new technology versus scale effects, but also show more clearly how these various components have contributed to this change.

In what follows, Section 8.2 provides background on how service delivery methods and use of different payment instruments have changed over the past decade in eleven Euro-using countries (which include Spain) plus the United Kingdom. Our cost model is specified in Section 8.3. Although we rely on a composite cost function for our analysis (Pulley and Braunstein, 1992; Pulley and Humphrey, 1993), we demonstrate the robustness of our results by specifying and estimating the more commonly used translog and Fourier cost models.

Section 8.4 presents and discusses our estimates of the cost effect of new technology for both savings and commercial banks in Spain. We find that banks have apparently saved 37 percent in unit (or average) operating cost between 1992 and 2000 which translates into 4.5 billion euros for the banking system as a whole. As larger institutions have progressed further in shifting from branch offices to ATMs for dispensing cash and also process higher volumes of lower cost electronic payments, these institutions have benefited the most from the reduction in unit operating expenses. Section 8.5 notes our translog and Fourier cost function results, illustrating the robustness of our composite cost model, while Section 8.6 summarizes our main conclusions. Since the same service delivery and payment trends shown to have benefited Spain are observed for other European countries, it is likely that similar gains may have occurred in these countries as well.

8.2 Changes in service delivery and payment mix

All European countries (including Spain) deliver banking services using ATMs as well as branch offices and have provided electronic as well as paper-based payment methods. While the mix of these delivery and payment methods often differs markedly among countries, all have consistently expanded the supply of ATMs relative to branches and have increased the share of non-cash transactions which are electronic. For the services they deliver, ATMs are considerably cheaper than branches and an electronic payment only costs about one-third to one-half as much as a paper-based transaction. Thus it is not surprising to find that the shift to ATMs and electronic payments appears to be associated with significant reductions in operating cost as a percent of bank asset value during the 1990s. Indeed, Table 8.1 suggests that this has been the case for eleven Euro-using countries in Europe plus the United Kingdom.[1]

ATMs and branch offices generate labor and capital costs associated with service delivery or front office expenses. The rapid expansion of ATMs in Europe indicates that, for the range of services provided (cash withdrawal, account transfer, balance inquiry), ATMs have replaced the traditional banking office for a large and growing segment of depositors. Evidence of this shift can be seen in Table 8.1 (row 1) which shows that the ratio of ATMs to branch offices rose by 110 percent during the 1990s.[2] While the number of branch offices used to deliver banking services can differ considerably across countries, this primarily reflects differences in the average size of banking offices in a country.[3] Regardless of the number of branches or their average size, the number of bank employees per 10,000 inhabitants fell in all but Germany and the United Kingdom during the

Table 8.1 Service delivery, payment, and operating cost in Euroland + UK (1992–1999)

	1992	1994	1996	1998	2000	% change
ATM/branch office	0.62	0.76	0.93	1.12	1.30	110
Non-cash/POP	97	105	112	125	136	40
Ele/non-cash	0.56	0.63	0.68	0.75	0.79	41
OC/TA	0.020	0.018	0.017	0.016	0.016	−21
Spain OC/TA	0.030	0.027	0.024	0.022	0.019	−37

Sources: OECD, European Central Bank (ECB), Bank of Spain, and own calculations.

Note
Ele Electronic payments; POP per person.

1990s, suggest that ATM use has conserved on bank labor costs as well as capital.[4] Another major contributor to banking costs is associated with the number and mix of payment transactions. Payments have to be processed and debited/credited to accounts and so generate the vast majority of back office capital (including computer) and labor expenses. As seen in Table 8.1 (row 2), the number of non-cash (check, giro, card) transactions per person (POP) per year has risen from 97 in 1992 to 136 in 2000, a 40 percent increase.[5] Importantly, it is also seen that the share of non-cash transactions that are electronic, and thus cheaper to process, has also risen by 41 percent so that by 2000 fully 79 percent of all non-cash transactions were electronic. Electronic debit card or giro payments for point-of-sale transactions, consumer bill payments, and employee disbursement are typically cheaper than their paper-based alternatives (a check or paper giro transaction). For these types of transactions survey information and cost estimates suggest that an electronic payment costs only one-third to one-half as much as a comparable paper-based transaction (Flatraaker and Robinson, 1995; Wells, 1996; Humphrey *et al.*, 2001; Humphrey *et al.*, 2003).[6] The large expansion of ATMs relative to branch offices combined with the shift to electronic payments would be expected to lower bank unit operating costs. As shown in the fourth row of Table 8.1, this seems to be the case. Operating costs as a percent of asset value fell by 21 percent over 1992–2000 for the eleven Euro-using countries plus the United Kingdom.[7] For Spain, the operating cost ratio reduction has been 37 percent.[8] In what follows, we attempt to determine the effect on operating cost of the shift to electronic payments and ATM use in Spain. This requires a statistical analysis which relates savings and commercial bank operating costs to bank-specific information on ATMs, branch offices, labor, and capital input prices, as well as national information on the transaction volume of different types of payment instruments.

8.3 Using output characteristics to determine cost effects of technical change and scale

Costs in banking are primarily incurred by providing payment processing, deposit safekeeping, cash access, and loan initiation and monitoring services through a geographically diversified set of general and specialized branch offices as well as ATMs. While deposit safekeeping and loan services are specific to branch offices, ATMs substitute with branches for cash withdrawal, balance inquiry, and account transfer services. Some initial payment processing may occur at branch offices but most is incurred in separate dedicated facilities associated with the bank or outsourced to non-bank processors.[9] All of these services involve labor, physical capital, and materials operating expenses and our purpose is to determine statistically the association of operating costs to the processing of check, giro, and card payment transactions as well as the use of ATMs and branch offices. Interest rates on deposits and loans do not really affect the production of payment services and ATMs but can influence the tradeoff between the use of branch offices to collect (lower cost) deposit funds and sell/service mutual funds relative to (more expensive) interbank purchased monies over the interest rate cycle. For Spain, this effect is minor: the aggregate ratio of produced deposits plus mutual funds to assets was very stable over 1992–2000 consistent with little substitution.

The common approach taken in academic studies regarding technical change does not directly measure the actual flow of payment or other banking services as we try to do here. Rather, it is assumed that this service flow is proportional to the value of the stock of bank deposits, securities, and loans in the balance sheet. Inferences on how costs may vary from changing technology and scale of operation are obtained by relating total operating and interest expenses across banks and over time to the value of their deposits, loans, and security holdings (or some other combination of balance sheet positions). As information does not normally exist regarding the adoption of specific technical and other cost-saving innovations in banking, the default is to assume that unknown technical change occurs linearly (or quadratically) with the passage of time and/or is somehow associated with (embodied in) the value of particular inputs.

Our approach directly relates bank operating (not interest) costs to measurable physical characteristics of banking output associated with service delivery and payment processing levels and mix.[10] This achieves two goals. First, the number of bank branches (BR) and ATMs – but not necessarily their mix – is directly associated with the size of a bank and its capital and materials operating cost as is the number – but not necessarily the mix – of transactions being processed on behalf of bank customers. When mix is constant and technology is not improved, levels of these activities reflect bank size and hence scale economies.[11] Second, changes in the mix of ATMs to branches or in the mix of electronic to paper-based transactions over time, along with improvements in their associated technology, represent an alternative and more specific way to identify the cost effect of technical change in banking.[12]

8.3.1 A composite cost function

Our data consist of an unbalanced panel of ninety-three commercial and savings banks over 1992–2000 in Spain observed at six-month intervals (giving 1,541 observations).[13] Bank-specific information on operating cost, numbers of ATMs, branch offices, and labor and capital input prices were combined with aggregate (national) data on the number of check, giro, and card payments and used in a non-linear, functionally separable, composite cost function.[14] The composite model can approximate better the scope-type joint cost effects that are associated with altering how banking services are delivered and how payments are processed. This is because the level of banking output in a composite function is not in logs, although input prices are. By keeping output in absolutes, we specify a direct relationship between output and operating costs that is likely more accurate – for prediction purposes when one or more outputs are small – than if the log of output is related to the log of operating cost.[15] As well, by specifying the log of input prices, it is possible to impose the theoretical condition of linear homogeneity in input prices in estimation.[16]

The composite cost function (8.1), in its output/input price separable quadratic form, is estimated jointly with $n-1$ cost share equations. The Box-Cox (1964) transformation is represented by a superscripted parameter in parenthesis (ϕ) where

$$OC^{(\phi)} = (OC^{\phi} - 1) / \phi \text{ for } \phi \neq 0 \quad \text{and} \quad OC^{(\phi)} = \ln OC \text{ for } \phi = 0 \text{ in:}$$
$$OC^{(\phi)} = f^{(\phi)}(Q, \ln P)$$

$$= \left\{ \left[\alpha_0 + \sum_{i=1}^{5} \alpha_i Q_i' + \frac{1}{2} \sum_{i=1}^{5} \sum_{j=1}^{5} \alpha_{ij} Q_i' Q_j' \right] \cdot exp \left[\beta_0 \right. \right.$$

$$\left. \left. + \sum_{k=1}^{2} \beta_k \ln P_k + \frac{1}{2} \sum_{k=1}^{2} \sum_{m=1}^{2} \beta_{k,m} \ln P_k \ln P_m \right] \right\}^{(\phi)}$$

$$S_k = \beta_k + \sum_{m=1}^{2} \beta_{k,m} \ln P_m \tag{8.1}$$

where OC is the total operating expenses, composed of labor, capital, and materials costs;[17] $Q_{i,j}'$ i, j are the five output characteristics composed of two service delivery alternatives – ATM and BR – along with three payment processing alternatives – the number of checks (CHECK), giro payments (GIRO), and debit and credit card transactions (CARD).[18] Service delivery data are available by bank but payment transactions data are not (so data for all banks are used instead). In (8.1), $Q' = Q - 1$; P_{km} k, m are the two input prices referring to the average labor cost per employee and an approximation to the price of physical capital and materials represented by capital depreciation expenditures divided by the value of physical capital; and S_k is the cost shares for the labor input (the capital/materials input share is deleted to avoid singularity).

It is expected that operating costs not directly associated with the mode of service delivery or type of payment will be represented in the intercept term. The composite function is non-linear and is estimated iteratively. Following Pulley and Braunstein (1992), let $D = 0$ and $GM^{\phi - 1}$ be the geometric mean of operating cost OC, then the separable quadratic form of the composite model is estimated from the pseudo model (8.2):[19]

$$D = [-(OC^{(\phi)}/GM^{\phi-1}) + f^{(\phi)}(Q, \ln P)/GM^{\phi-1}]$$

$$= \left\{ -\left[\left(OC^\phi - 1\right)\Big/\phi GM^{\phi-1}\right] + \left\{\left[\left(\alpha_0 + \sum_{i=1}^{5}\alpha_i Q_i'\right.\right.\right.$$

$$+ \frac{1}{2}\sum_{i=1}^{5}\sum_{j=1}^{5}\alpha_{ij}Q_i'Q_j'\right) \cdot \exp\left(\beta_0 + \sum_{k=1}^{2}\beta_k \ln P_k\right.$$

$$+ \frac{1}{2}\sum_{k=1}^{2}\sum_{m=1}^{2}\beta_{k,m}\ln P_k \ln P_m\right)\Big]^\phi - 1\Big)\Big/\phi GM^{\phi-1}\right\}$$

$$S_k = \beta_k + \sum_{m=1}^{2}\beta_{k,m}\ln P_m \qquad (8.2)$$

8.3.2 *Alternative translog and Fourier cost functions*

To illustrate the robustness of our results, we also estimate translog and Fourier cost functions. A translog function may generate biased results, compared to the composite form, when levels of some outputs are small and outputs are specified in logs. Even so, as these two additional functions are often used in cost analyses, it is useful to compare their results with those from our composite form.

The translog cost function (8.3) is estimated jointly with $n-1$ cost share equations:

$$\ln OC = \alpha_0 \sum_{i=1}^{5}\alpha_i \ln Q_i + \frac{1}{2}\sum_{i=1}^{5}\sum_{j=1}^{5}\alpha_{ij}\ln Q_i \ln Q_j + \sum_{i=1}^{5}\sum_{k=1}^{2}\delta_{i,k}\ln Q_i \ln P_k$$

$$+ \sum_{k=1}^{2}\beta_k \ln P_k + \frac{1}{2}\sum_{k=1}^{2}\sum_{m=1}^{2}\beta_{k,m}\ln P_k \ln P_m$$

$$S_k = \beta_k + \sum_{m=1}^{2}\beta_{k,m}\ln P_m + \sum_{i=1}^{5}\delta_{i,k}\ln Q_i \qquad (8.3)$$

where the variables have been defined.

The Fourier form we use adds sin and cos terms to the translog cost function. As our main concern is to allow for greater flexibility in the local identification of output effects on operating costs, the sin and cos terms are applied to the output (Q) measure. The Fourier form is a globally flexible approximation since the respective sin and cos terms are mutually orthogonal over the $[0, 2\pi]$ interval.

The Fourier function (8.4) is estimated jointly with the cost shares:

$\ln \text{TC} = $ Translog cost function

$$+ \sum_{n=1}^{5} \left[\tau_n \cos(\ln Q_n^*) + \omega_n \sin(\ln Q_n^*) \right]$$

$$+ \sum_{n=1}^{5} \sum_{q=n}^{5} \left[\tau_{nq} \cos(\ln Q_n^* + \ln Q_q^*) + \omega_{nq} \sin(\ln Q_n^* + \ln Q_q^*) \right]$$

$$+ \sum_{n=1}^{5} \left[\tau_{nnn} \cos(\ln Q_n^* + \ln Q_n^* + \ln Q_n^*) \right.$$

$$\left. + \omega_{nnn} \sin(\ln Q_n^* + \ln Q_n^* + \ln Q_n^*) \right]$$

$$S_k = \beta_k + \sum_{m=1}^{2} \beta_{k,m} \ln P_m + \sum_{i=1}^{5} \delta_{i,k} \ln Q_i \qquad (8.4)$$

The new terms are $\ln Q^* = \ln Q \cdot \text{YQ} + \text{ZQ}$, $\text{YQ} = (0.8 \cdot 2\pi)/(\max \ln Q - \min \ln Q)$, $\text{ZQ} = 0.2\pi - \min \ln Q \cdot \text{YQ}$, and $\pi = 3.141593\ldots$, so that $\ln Q^*$ is essentially expressed in radians.[20]

8.4 Cost effects from changes in service delivery and payment levels and mix

8.4.1 *Composite function results*

Predicted unit operating cost from the composite function for ninety-three savings and commercial banks over 1992–2000 is shown in Figure 8.1.[21] While the levels and mix of ATMs, branch offices, and check, giro, and card payment volumes are allowed to vary, input prices are held constant at their mean values. As ϕ in the composite form is 0.20, the estimated model is closer to a specification which includes the log of output as well as input prices (when $\phi = 0.0$) than it is to a specification with output in absolutes and prices in logs (when $\phi = 1.0$).[22] Even so, the estimated model is significantly different from either of these alternatives since ϕ is significantly different from zero or one.[23]

The curve fitted to the scattergram in Figure 8.1 is a cubic spline and illustrates how unit operating cost generally varies by bank asset size over time.[24] This figure combines both technical change (time-series) and scale (cross-section) effects associated with front office service delivery and back office payment processing cost changes. The distinction between technical change (a shift in the unit operating cost curve between years) and scale effects (moving along a unit operating cost curve for a single year) is illustrated in Figure 8.2. Here separate predicted unit operating cost curves are shown for 1992, 1996, and 2000. Scale economies exist since unit cost falls as (the log of) asset size increases on the X-axis. As well, the operating cost curves shift down over time showing that unit operating

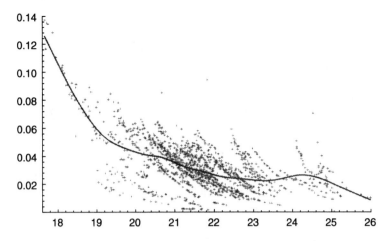

Figure 8.1 Predicted unit operating cost by log of asset value: 1992–2000 in euros (composite function – input prices held constant at the mean value).

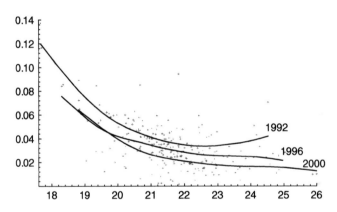

Figure 8.2 Predicted unit operating cost by log of asset value: three separate years – 1992, 1996, 2000 in euros (composite function – input prices held constant at their mean value).

expenses are falling as technical change progresses with the substitution of ATMs for branch offices, the replacement of checks (and cash) with giro and card electronic payments, and technological improvements associated with all five of these output characteristics.

Looking at all banks together where unit operating cost reflects the ratio of the sum of predicted operating expense across all banks divided by the sum of observed asset values, this aggregate ratio is 0.033, 0.023, and 0.018, respectively, for 1992, 1996, and 2000 in Figure 8.2 indicating a predicted 45 percent reduction.[25] This is very similar to the observed ratios in Table 8.1 for Spain (0.030, 0.024, and 0.019) which indicated that for the Spanish banking system as a whole, unit operating cost has fallen by 37 percent over 1992–2000.[26] Since total bank operating cost in 1992 was 12.1 billion euros, this suggests that operating expenses would have been 4.5 billion euros (0.37 times 12.1 billion euros) higher in 2000 than they were if there were no technical change or scale effects to reduce operating costs from their ratio to assets in 1992. This savings equals 0.7 percent of GDP in 2000 and is equivalent to having unit operating cost at banks fall by 4 percent a year due to changes in service delivery and payment costs.[27]

8.4.2 Service delivery costs: ATMs and branch offices

Predicted service delivery costs represent operating expenses associated with installed ATMs and branch offices, holding check, giro, and card payment volumes and input prices constant at their mean values. These predicted delivery expenses, expressed as a ratio to total assets for each bank, fell by 45 percent between 1992 and 2000.[28] Internal estimates from a confidential industry source indicate that an additional ATM costs around 27,500 euros whereas an additional branch costs 112,500 euros. In our sample, the number of ATMs expanded by 142 percent (rising from 17,300 in 1992 to 41,800 in 2000) while the number of branch offices grew by 22 percent (expanding from 28,200 to 34,300). Thus most of the reduction in the service delivery cost to asset ratio is due to using more ATMs relative to branches.

The extent to which this cost ratio falls as the ratio of ATMs to branch offices rises is shown in Figure 8.3. The average ATM/branch ratio rose from 0.6 in 1992 to 1.2 in 2000. Reference to Figure 8.3 indicates that unit costs may continue to fall up to the point where the ATM/branch ratio approaches 2.0. Thus there seems to be additional scope for further operating cost to asset ratio reductions with a higher ratio of ATMs to branch offices in the future.

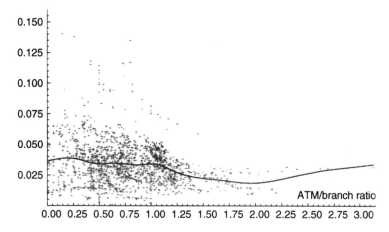

Figure 8.3 Predicted delivery cost to asset ratio by ATM/branch ratio: 1992–2000 (composite function – input prices and all payment volumes held constant at their mean values).

The relative importance of changes in delivery costs versus payment expenses over 1992–2000 can be illustrated by looking at the level of operating cost, rather than its ratio to assets. If only ATMs and branch offices had changed from 1992 going forward to 2000 (i.e. holding payment transactions and input prices at their 1992 levels), then the rise in predicted operating cost from delivery expenses alone is 2.7 billion euros. However, doing the same for payment transactions (i.e. holding ATMs, branches, and input prices at their 1992 levels), results in a fall in predicted operating cost from payment activities alone of 1.9 billion euros. Finally, letting only input prices change after 1992 raises operating costs by 2.4 billion euros.[29] Overall, this suggests that the observed rise in total operating expenses was pretty much equally driven by the rise in input prices (where the average price of labor rose by 40 percent) as it was from the expansion of ATMs and branch offices. Although the volume of our three payment instruments rose by 64 percent, the joint effect of payment scale economies and the shift to cheaper electronic payments seemingly led to an absolute reduction in total payment costs.[30]

8.4.3   Processing costs: check, giro, and card transactions

Predicted payment processing costs represent operating expenses associated with the level and composition of check, giro, and card transactions, holding ATMs, branch offices, and input prices constant at their mean values. These predicted payment costs, divided by the total number of check, giro, and card transactions made each year, give unit payment costs that fall both over time (top of Figure 8.4) and by total payment volume (bottom of Figure 8.4). Predicted unit payment cost fell by

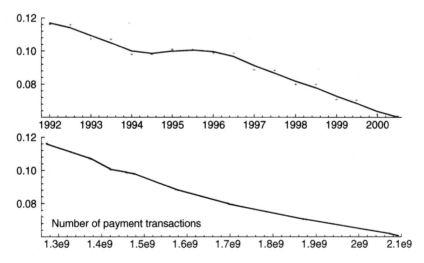

Figure 8.4 Predicted unit payment costs by year: 1992–2000 in euros (composite function – input prices, ATMs, and branch offices held constant at their mean values) and predicted unit payment costs by payment volume (composite function – same variables held constant).

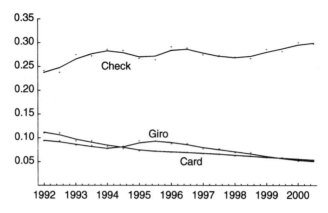

Figure 8.5 Approximate check, card, and giro average cost in euros: per transaction over 1992–2000.

48 percent between 1992 and 2000.[31] Not all payment costs are falling. Indeed, the reduction in unit payment expense seen in Figure 8.4 is composed of rising check average costs and falling giro and card average costs over time. These changes are seen in Figure 8.5 where the level of predicted unit cost for check, giro, and card transactions have been "normalized" at their mean to reflect internal industry estimates of the level of average cost for each of these payment instruments. As a result, and only in this case, both the levels and the changes shown in Figure 8.5 are likely good approximations to cost accounting values – if such values existed – for these three payment instruments. According to confidential industry sources, the average cost of a check is 0.275 euros, a giro transaction is 0.0775 euros, and a card payment is 0.075 euros. These values were used to adjust or normalize the level of the curves shown in Figure 8.5 and suggest that an electronic giro (card) payment costs 28 percent (27 percent) as much as a check. This corresponds to limited survey information available for other countries (Humphrey *et al.*, 2003) and to more detailed cost information available for Norway (Gresvik and Øwre, 2002).

Over 1992–2000, giro and card payments expanded by 85 percent and 81 percent, respectively, while checks fell by 17 percent. As a result, the share of checks in all non-cash payment transactions fell from 0.19 in 1992 to only 0.10 in 2000. Giro transactions accounted for a 0.56 share in 2000 while cards were 0.34. Scale economies in the processing of electronic giro and debit card payments help explain the reduction in the average per transaction payment expenses in Figures 8.4 and 8.5 while the scale benefit works in reverse (to offset some of this benefit) as the number of checks processed falls.

8.5   Translog and Fourier function results

The operating cost results using the easier to estimate translog model (8.3) are very close to those presented earlier for the composite cost function. Indeed,

Figures 8.1 and 8.2 for the composite form – showing predicted unit operating cost over 1992–2000 by bank asset size and for three years separately – are so close to those using the translog that it is difficult to tell them apart. Consequently, the predicted change in the operating cost to asset ratio between 1992 and 2000 was −45 percent for the composite form and −37 percent with the translog. Changes in predicted unit delivery and payment expenses over 1992–2000 were also within a few percentage points of each other.[32]

The Fourier cost model (8.4) adds sin and cos terms for the five output characteristics to the standard translog form. The purpose is to capture more than just the quadratic nonlinearity which would be captured with the translog specification. Since bank-specific data are available for ATM and branch offices in our panel data set, so that for these two output characteristics we have both cross-section and time-series variation, the Fourier form may improve the fit compared to the translog form. However, no country has publicly available bank-specific data on the volumes of check, giro, and card transactions. Thus our payment data have no cross-section variation, only time-series variation at the national level. As payment volumes experience low variance over time, it turns out that the quadratic specification in the translog portion of the Fourier form is sufficient to locally identify all of the nonlinearity in these data. For this reason, all the parameters specified in the full Fourier model in (8.4) could not be estimated and the cos and sin terms in the final estimated model only refer to two (ATMs and branch offices) rather than the full five output characteristics.[33]

The main differences in our results for the Fourier form, compared to the composite, are for the smallest and largest banks, not for the average bank. The simplest way to see this is to compare Figure 8.6, which illustrates predicted unit operating cost for 1992, 1996, and 2000 using the Fourier form, with Figure 8.2, which shows the same three cost curves for the composite function. While the middle segments of these two figures which reflect the average bank are largely congruent, the large operating cost scale economies for the smallest banks shown

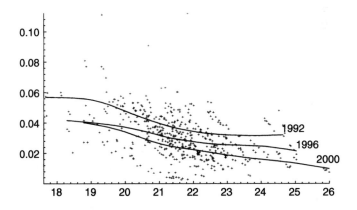

Figure 8.6 Predicted unit operating cost by log of asset value: three separate years – 1992, 1996, 2000 in euros (Fourier function – input prices held constant at their mean values).

for the composite (or translog) form are considerably smaller when the Fourier form is used. As well, the slight scale diseconomies evident for the largest banks in 1992 with the composite (or translog) form are shown as constant unit cost with the Fourier form in that year. Even so, these differences have little effect on the predicted changes in unit operating cost between 1992 and 2000. With the composite form, the change in the predicted operating cost to asset ratio was −45 percent while with the Fourier model it was −46 percent, with similarly close correspondence for changes in unit delivery and payment costs. In sum, the results presented here for the composite function seem to be robust to the use of alternative cost function forms.

8.6   Summary and conclusions

Two common trends among banking systems in developed countries have had a large impact on operating cost, and hence on service level and price, to users. One trend has been the expansion of lower cost and more convenient ATMs, relative to branch offices, to deliver cash, account transfer, and balance inquiry services to depositors. A second trend has been the ongoing replacement of paper-based payment instruments (checks and paper giro payments) with lower cost electronic alternatives (debit cards and electronic giro payments). Indeed, these five banking output characteristics related to service delivery and payment (and deposit account) processing make up the bulk of bank operating costs.[34]

The effect on cost from these five activities incorporates both changing technology and scale influences. A statistical model based on these output characteristics relates operating cost to service delivery and payment levels and mix to determine how changes in these characteristics have affected operating costs at Spanish savings and commercial banks over 1992–2000. We find that the average Spanish bank has apparently saved 37 percent in unit (or average) operating cost between 1992 and 2000, or about 4.5 billion euros for the banking system as a whole (0.7 percent of GDP in 2000). As larger institutions have progressed further in shifting from branch offices to ATMs for dispensing cash and also process higher volumes of lower cost electronic payments, these institutions have benefited the most from the associated reduction in unit operating expenses. In determining the average effect on operating cost from changes in service delivery methods and the level and mix of payment volumes, it does not matter much whether a composite, translog, or Fourier cost model is used (although for very small and very large banks there are some differences).

With respect to the future, it appears that if ATMs were expanded further (relative to branch offices) additional operating cost could be saved. At present, the ATM/branch ratio is 1.2 but costs appear to continue to fall for institutions with ratios up to around 2.0. It is also evident that additional operating expense could be saved with a further shift to electronic payments since they generally only cost one-third to one-half as much as its paper-based non-cash alternative. It would not be surprising if similar savings in operating cost were found in other European countries (or even the United States) as these countries have often experienced similar changes in service delivery and payment composition.

8A.1 Appendix: parameter estimates for the composite cost function

Number of observations = 1541. Log likelihood = 1552.14. Standard Errors computed from heteroscedastic-consistent matrix (Robust-White). Durbin-Watson = 1.953. Likelihood ratio tests of setting the eleven parameters associated with ATM and branch variables, or the fifteen parameters associated with check, giro, and card payment transactions, equal to zero were $-2\ln \lambda$ = 3873 and 25.7, respectively. The ATM and branch variables varied by bank and over time and were significant at the 0.01 level while the three payment transaction variables were significant at the 0.05 level. Payment data by bank are not available in any country so these data only vary over time, which accounts for their lower significance level.

Parameter	Estimate	t-statistic
ϕ	0.2023	8.92
α_0	-50038	-0.40
α_1	0.376E-03	0.42
α_2	-0.400E-04	-0.34
α_3	0.792E-04	0.37
α_4	-24.60	-0.32
α_5	164.0	2.48
α_{11}	-0.164E-11	-0.46
α_{22}	0.313E-13	0.48
α_{33}	-0.342E-14	-0.01
α_{44}	0.0574	3.84
α_{55}	0.1133	8.10
α_{12}	0.361E-12	0.46
α_{13}	-0.479E-12	-0.45
α_{14}	0.473E-06	0.84
α_{15}	-0.662E-06	-1.39
α_{23}	-0.705E-12	-0.25
α_{24}	0.199E-07	0.45
α_{25}	-0.516E-07	-1.23
α_{34}	-0.317E-07	-0.36
α_{35}	-0.360E-07	-0.47
α_{45}	-0.1517	-5.12
β_1	0.4144	37.30
β_{11}	0.0415	17.11

Acknowledgment

Support for this research was provided by the Fundacion de las Cajas de Ahorros Confederadas para la Investigacion Económica y Social.

Notes

1 All ratios in Table 8.1 treat the twelve countries as if they were a single entity (i.e. they are the sum of the numerator divided by the sum of the denominator). To make the

value data in the table comparable across countries, the OECD translated domestic currency values into euros using exchange rates so that changes over time here can differ from national data in domestic currency units. Due to insufficient data, Greece – a more recent Euro-using country – could not be included.

2 During this period, the number of branch offices per 10,000 inhabitants in different Euro-using countries and the United Kingdom either grew slowly or fell. Since any reduction in the number of banking offices was slight, the primary reason for the rise in the ATM/branch ratio was the rapid rise in ATMs.

3 For example, Spain provides 9 to 10 offices per 10,000 inhabitants while Germany, France, Italy, and Portugal provide only 4 to 5. The offset to providing many offices is that there were only around 6 workers per banking office in Spain, which is less than half the 12 to 13 workers per office in Portugal and Italy and about a third as many workers in France (15) or Germany (18).

4 The reduction in workers per 10,000 of population over 1992–2000 was around 5 percent for Spain, Italy, and Portugal with 12 percent for France, and 39 percent for Finland.

5 While the trend is upward, the levels of non-cash use across countries can be quite different. The total number of non-cash transactions per person ranges at the lower end from 42 to 84 payments a year for Italy, Spain, and Portugal while at the higher end it is 156–178 annually for the United Kingdom Finland, Germany, and France.

6 This is largely due to the fact that electronic payments experience greater scale economies than paper-based transactions (since the fixed cost component is much more important than the variable one). In addition, advances in computer and telecommunications technology have lowered the absolute cost of processing electronic payments at all scales of operation.

7 Specifically, the reductions were 17 percent for Italy, 19 percent for Germany, 38 percent for the United Kingdom and 42 percent for Finland. Reductions close to 25 percent were experienced for France and Portugal.

8 OECD data would show a smaller change in this ratio due to the variation in the peseta/ecu exchange rate used to translate earlier data in domestic currency units into euros and because of coverage differences (i.e. OECD data includes credit co-operatives, leasing companies, and other credit institutions). Our values in pesetas prior to the adoption of the euro were translated into euros using the fixed conversion rate of 1.0 euro = Pta 166.386 and so are unbiased from changes in exchange rates before the adoption of the euro.

9 The initial contact for consumer and some business loans typically involves a customer's local branch office but further processing of loan documents, loan origination, and monitoring services are often handled by larger and more specialized branches or dedicated loan production offices in centralized locations in larger cities.

10 The service delivery and payment functions are largely separable. The primary interaction would be consumers and businesses depositing (a declining number of) checks at a BR and, on a one-time basis, filling out documents to pay recurring bills by electronic giro or applying for a debit/credit card. After establishing a giro account, bill payments occur automatically, as do all card payments, without branch or ATM intervention unless problems arise.

11 The number of branch offices is a good proxy for the stock of loans outstanding, deposits raised, or value of total assets as the R^2s here all range from 0.78 to 0.79.

12 To circumvent the impossibility of separating technical change from scale effects with only time-series data, it has been common practice to use panel data so that the cross-section component identifies scale while the time-series component identifies technical change. Note that in addition to cross-section and time-series components in our panel data set, we use differences in level and mix to assist in the decomposition between technical change and scale.

13 The panel includes all savings banks, all but the very smallest commercial banks (which were excluded due mostly to missing ATM data), but no co-operative banks

(who also had missing data). This accounts for 77 percent (80 percent) of all assets (operating cost) in the Spanish banking system in 1992 and 92 percent (90 percent) in 2000. The excluded co-operative banks only account for five percentage points of the banking system's operating costs while the excluded commercial banks account for the remaining five percentage points in 2000.

14 Use of a balanced panel by (a) backward aggregation of merging institutions before they actually merge or (b) including only acquiring banks could have biased our results. With (a), combining data on banks before they merge and realize possibly lower costs associated with their larger post-merger size would tend to understate scale benefits in pre-merger years. With (b), the sample would exclude acquired banks before they merged and distort measured cost/payment volume relationships over time. For these reasons we use an unbalanced panel.

15 As illustrated in Pulley and Braunstein (1992), this can occur when one or more outputs are less than 5–10 percent of total output. This occurs for ATMs (as a percent of ATMs plus branches) for some banks early in our sample and for checks (as a percent of check, giro, and card transactions) for some later years.

16 A similar function (Constant Elasticity of Substitution, CES-quadratic) was used by Röller (1990) to determine scope effects of local and long-distance telephone costs for the Bell System while Pulley and Humphrey (1993) used a composite form to assess the cost effects of separating risky loan assets from deposit liabilities into two separate banks, funding the former with uninsured CDs (certificates of deposit) and investing the latter in safe assets.

17 OC is in nominal terms. The specification of bank-specific input prices accounts for inflation effects on costs more accurately than use of standard inflation indicators (e.g. cost-of-living index or GDP deflator).

18 Giro transfers are typically electronic in Spain and debit cards accounted for about 55 per cent of all card transactions (a share that only rises about 1 percentage point a year).

19 Pulley and Braunstein (1992) note that it is generally not feasible to estimate both α_0 and β_0 intercepts. As we are more interested in output than input prices, and on the basis of fit, we set $\beta_0 = 0$ and retain α_0 in estimation.

20 See Mitchell and Onvural (1996) and Berger and Mester (1997). Our Fourier specification follows Berger and Mester.

21 Unit operating cost is the ratio of operating cost to asset value and is a measure of average operating cost.

22 The estimated parameters of the composite function underlying this figure are presented in an Appendix. Likelihood ratio tests of setting the eleven parameters associated with ATM and branch variables, or the fifteen parameters associated with check, giro, and card payment transactions, equal to zero were $-2\ln\lambda = 3873$ and 25.7, respectively. The ATM and branch variables varied by bank and over time and were significant at the 0.01 level while the three payment transaction variables were significant at the 0.05 level. Payment data by bank are not available in any country so these data only vary over time, which accounts for their lower significance level.

23 For more on these two alternative specifications which depend on the value of ϕ, see Pulley and Braunstein (1992) or Pulley and Humphrey (1993).

24 Bank size on the X-axis is indicated by the natural log of asset value. Taking the log improves comparability among the numerous smaller and less numerous very large banks. As ATMs and the production functions for processing payments are essentially identical across types of financial institutions, use of a single cost function covering both savings and commercial banks is justified. This accords well with our purpose of illustrating the efficiency gains from the shift to ATMs and electronic payments for the entire banking sector (rather than a subset of the industry).

25 The aggregate ratio gives a larger weight to larger banks that typically have lower unit operating cost.

26 If some of the decline in the operating cost/asset ratio is due to banks substituting purchased funds (which generate interest costs) for produced deposits or servicing

off-balance sheet mutual funds (which generate operating expenses), then we should see a reduction in the ratio of produced deposits (demand, savings, and time deposits) plus mutual funds to assets over 1992–2000. As this ratio rises slightly from 78.0 percent in 1992 to 79.5 percent in 2000, the reduction in the operating cost/asset ratio is attributed to cost effects.

27 The 12.1 billion euro figure is the sum of operating cost for all banks in Spain in 1992 reported to the Bank of Spain. GDP in 1992 was 609.3 billion euros.

28 If the ratio of delivery expenses to asset value were observed in the raw data (as total operating costs are), this ratio would be similar to a measure of average delivery cost per euro of assets. However, as noted by Baumol *et al.* (1982), in a multiproduct cost function where output characteristics are not fully functionally separable, it is not possible to determine accurately the *level* of average cost. This is because the predicted value of delivery expenses, for example, will include the mean values of input prices as well as check, giro, and card expenses. While this does not affect our ability to determine changes in delivery costs over 1992–2000, it does artificially raise the level of predicted delivery expenses.

29 As these three operating cost categories are not fully functionally separable from one another, they will not add up to the change in actual or predicted overall operating costs over this period when two of the three cost categories are being successively held constant at their level in 1992.

30 Although total observed operating expenses rose by 63 percent, total assets expanded by 161 percent (so the ratio of operating cost to assets fell by 37 percent).

31 Again, the predicted unit cost here is not a standard measure of average cost. In addition to the predicted cost of three payment instruments, the mean cost of ATMs, branch offices, and input prices are also included. This raises the level but does not affect the predicted changes over 1992–2000.

32 The strong correspondence between the translog and composite results is not unexpected since ϕ in the composite form is 0.20, indicating that this estimated model is closer to a translog specification which includes the log of output as well as input prices (as would be the case if $\phi = 0.0$).

33 As the sin and cos terms for three output characteristics (check, giro, and card transactions) could not be estimated, all of the single and double summations shown in (8.4) are over two output characteristics (ATMs and branches), not five.

34 While banks also provide loan origination and monitoring services, asset liquidity management with security holdings, and trust and safekeeping services, these are performed using branch offices (an included variable) and the labor input component is small relative to that associated with deposit service delivery and payment activities.

References

Baumol, W., Panzer, J., and Willig, R. (1982). *Contestable Markets and the Theory of Industrial Structure*, San Diego, CA: Harcourt Brace Jovanovich.

Berger, A. and Mester, L. (1997). "Inside the black box: what explains differences in the efficiencies of financial institutions?," *Journal of Banking and Finance*, 21: 895–947.

Box, G. and Cox, D. (1964). "An analysis of transformations," *Journal of the Royal Statistical Society*, Series B, 26: 211–246.

Flatraaker, D.-I. and Robinson, P. (1995). "Income, costs and pricing in the payment system," Norges Bank, *Economic Bulletin*, 66: 321–332.

Gresvik, O. and Øwre, G. (2002). "Banks' costs and income in the payment system in 2001," Norges Bank, *Economic Bulletin*, 73: 125–133.

Humphrey, D., Kim, M., and Vale, B. (2001). "Realizing the gains from electronic payments: costs, pricing, and payment choice," *Journal of Money, Credit and Banking*, 33: 216–234.

Humphrey, D., Willesson, M., Lindblom, T., and Bergendahl, G. (2003). "What does it cost to make a payment?," *Review of Network Economics*, 2: 159–174.

Mitchell, K. and Onvural, N. (1996). "Economies of scale and scope at large commercial banks: evidence from the Fourier flexible functional form," *Journal of Money, Credit and Banking*, 28: 178–199.

Pulley, L. and Braunstein, Y. (1992). "A composite cost function for multiproduct firms with an application to economies of scope in banking," *Review of Economics and Statistics*, 74: 221–230.

Pulley, L. and Humphrey, D. (1993). "The role of fixed costs and cost complementarities in determining scope economies and the cost of narrow banking proposals," *Journal of Business*, 66: 437–462.

Röller, L.-H. (1990). "Proper quadratic cost functions with an application to the Bell system," *Review of Economics and Statistics*, 72: 202–210.

Wells, K. (1996). "Are checks overused?," *Federal Reserve Bank of Minneapolis Quarterly Review*, 20: 2–12.

9 Pricing strategies in European banking

Specialization, technology and intertemporal smoothing

Santiago Carbó Valverde and
Francisco Rodríguez Fernández

9.1 Introduction

During the last two decades, financial innovation has evolved rapidly and banking systems have experienced substantial changes in both their business and income structure. The banking firm has become more complex and diversification, risk management and higher participation in capital markets have happened to be some of the main pillars of modern financial intermediation. Within this context, it appears to be relevant to study how financial innovation has affected bank strategies and, in particular, bank margins.[1] There are three important factors that should be taken into account in this analysis:

1   Regulation has determined, to a large extent, the importance of the impact of financial innovation on bank margins. There are significant differences across countries in terms of the activities that banks have been permitted to undertake.[2]

2   Changes in both bank production technologies and bank income structure are strongly related and there are various strategies that result from combining multiproduct technologies that may affect bank margins significantly. In this context, Allen and Santomero (2001) suggest that empirical and theoretical models should develop dynamic approaches, which explain both the need and reality of financial innovation, since there has been a fundamental shift in the nature of intermediation that affects competition and bank margins. Moreover, the intertemporal behaviour of bank margins is expected to pose important implications for aggregate risk on financial activities (intertemporal rate smoothing vs. cross-sectional risk sharing hypotheses).

3   The framework of the analysis of bank margins should depart from traditional models that only consider interest margins. There is a need to incorporate a broader definition of bank margins, according to the evolution of financial innovation. The seminal model of Ho and Saunders (1981) has been the reference framework for most empirical analyses on the determinants of bank margins. However, this model relies only on interest margins. Lerner (1981) discussed the Ho–Saunders model and suggests that the insights that arise from recognizing that a (multi-output) production function exists

requires a more comprehensive analysis of bank margins. Several contributions of the so-called 'New Empirical Industrial Organization' (NEIO) suggest that there are potential estimation biases associated with the use of accounting margins and, in particular, when using firm-level data and multi-output production technologies (Bresnahan, 1989, p. 1013; Schmalensee, 1989, p. 961). In this context, Shaffer (2004) indicates that price to marginal costs margins should be employed in order to test bank conduct directly and to compare these with the outcomes obtained using accounting margins. In particular, the use of the Lerner index – defined as '(price-marginal costs)/price' seems to be an appropriate (direct) measure of margins and competitive behaviour.

This paper analyses the relationship between bank margins – using both accounting and NEIO margins – and changes in production technologies related to financial innovations in European banking during 1994–2001. The paper is divided into five sections following this introduction. Section 9.2 offers some background by reviewing the main changes in banks' income structure in Europe. The theoretical setting of the study is presented in Section 9.3, incorporating a multiproduct framework. The results of previous empirical studies investigating the determinants of bank margins are also presented in this section including the effects of specialization/diversification patterns and related changes in intertemporal vs. cross-sectional risk behaviour. Section 9.4 presents the methodology and data of an empirical analysis on the determinants of traditional and non-traditional bank margins on a sample of seven European countries: Germany, Spain, France, Netherlands, Italy, United Kingdom and Sweden. A dynamic panel data approach is employed to account for the endogeneity of bank margins. Additional empirical evidence is provided on the effects of changes in bank margins on the intertemporal smoothing or cross-section nature of risk in financial intermediation activities. Section 9.5 shows the main results of the empirical exercise. The paper ends with a brief summary of the main conclusions and policy implications in Section 9.6.

9.2 Financial innovation and income structure in Europe

Competitive pressures have led to an intense financial innovation process in banking all over the world during the last two decades. First of all, the number of competitors – not only within the banking sector but also from other financial intermediaries – has enlarged considerably. As shown in Table 9.1 – which offers aggregate information for 1997, 2000 and 2002 in the European Union (EU) – the traditional intermediation activities (loans of credit institutions as a percentage of GDP) are still growing rapidly. However, the assets of mutual funds and insurance companies are growing at a faster pace. It should be noted, however, that the so-called 'broad banking' regulatory environment has permitted banks to take control of activities such as mutual and pension funds or insurance in many European countries. At the same time, financial intermediaries have increased their interaction with capital markets and non-financial sector investments.

Table 9.1 Relative importance of credit institutions, mutual fund and insurance companies in the European Union-15 (1997, 2000, 2002) as a ratio of GDP

	1997			2000			2002		
	Loans of credit institutions	Assets of mutual funds	Assets of insurance companies	Loans of credit institutions	Assets of mutual funds	Assets of insurance companies	Loans of credit institutions	Assets of mutual funds	Assets of insurance companies
Belgium	0.95	0.14	0.34	0.99	0.34	0.43	1.04	0.30	0.47
Germany	1.37	NA	0.36	1.42	0.40	0.43	1.47	0.35	0.48
Greece	0.36	0.22	0.04	0.47	0.25	0.06	0.62	0.11	0.06
Spain	0.83	0.33	0.17	0.94	0.27	0.23	1.06	0.21	0.23
France	0.85	0.36	0.45	0.85	0.47	0.56	0.91	0.40	NA
Ireland	1.12	0.61	NA	1.48	NA	0.52	1.67	NA	NA
Italy	0.72	0.18	0.14	0.77	0.38	0.23	0.83	0.26	0.26
Luxemburg	5.49	22.68	0.91	6.58	40.23	1.27	6.89	33.06	NA
Netherlands	1.25	0.19	0.47	1.44	0.29	0.62	1.53	0.21	0.64
Austria	1.17	0.22	0.25	1.20	0.44	0.26	1.27	0.47	0.28
Portugal	0.79	0.24	0.15	1.14	0.22	0.21	1.39	0.20	0.24
Finland	0.48	0.03	0.06	0.54	0.10	0.07	0.60	0.08	0.05
EMU	1.06	NA	0.45	1.12	NA	0.54	NA	NA	NA
Denmark	1.34	0.08	0.46	1.41	0.20	0.59	1.56	0.21	0.57
Sweden	0.97	0.19	0.71	0.96	NA	0.91	NA	NA	0.69
UK	1.18	0.18	1.04	1.21	NA	1.10	1.31	NA	NA
EU	1.03	NA	0.32	1.10	NA	0.40	1.16	NA	NA

Source: European Central Bank (2000).

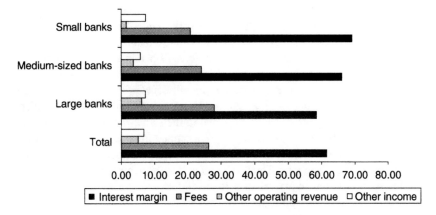

Figure 9.1 EU Banks' income structure as a percentage of total income (December 2002). Source: European Central Bank (2000).

As a result of these trends, changes in financial intermediation activities have also altered EU banks' income structure significantly.[3] As for traditional activities – lending and deposit-taking – the economic and financial integration in the context of a single monetary policy, together with financial liberalization, have resulted in significantly lower average interest rates. As a consequence, interest margins fell as a percentage of total assets. However, the increasing importance of fees and other non-interest income has largely compensated the competitive pressures on interest margins. As shown in Figure 9.1, interest margins still account for more than 60 per cent of total income in 2002 although fees already represented one-third of total European banks' revenues. Specialization patterns of banks will likely determine the scope of these changes in income structure. As observed in Figure 9.1, while small local banks still remain specialized in traditional activities, diversification augments with size and, consequently, income diversification increases too.

9.3 Bank margins and broad banking

9.3.1 A multi-output theoretical setting

The Ho–Saunders model relies on pure intermediation activities (deposits-taking and lending). In order to show the impact of non-traditional activities – fee income and market-based activities – a multi-product framework is employed. The model is adopted from Allen (1988), who applied her analysis to two types of loans. We modify this model to assume that bank portfolio is composed of loans (L) and non-traditional assets (N) – including other earning assets different from loans and other fee income activities – along with deposits (D).

In the Ho–Saunders model, the spread is the difference between lending and deposits rates $(r_L - r_D)$ that equals the provision of immediacy of liquidity services $(a + b)$. In our multi-product framework, banks have two alternatives: (1) they may set prices on loans relative to deposits so that immediacy fees are b_L and a, respectively; (2) they may also set prices on non-traditional activities relative to deposits rates so that non-traditional and immediacy fees are, respectively, b_N and a. Therefore, the interest margin will equal $a + b_L$ and the absolute margin on bank activities will equal $a + b_L + b_N$. As in the Ho–Saunders model, all product transaction sizes are equal to the same transaction size, Q, for all customers and the fees $(a, b_L$ and $b_N)$ are assumed to remain fixed over time. The deposit supply, the loan demand and the non-traditional business demand are assumed to be linear functions. The key element that determines risk in traditional activities is the stochastic arrival of a loan relative to deposits demand. In the multi-output perspective, non-traditional activities are presented as an alternative to loans so that risk (and market power) may be compensated or exacerbated. This should be an empirical hypothesis itself. Considering interactions between loans and non-traditional outputs, the probabilities of selling a loan $(\lambda(b_L))$, receiving a deposit $(\lambda(a))$ or selling a non-traditional output $(\lambda(b_N))$ are, respectively:

$$\lambda(b_L) = \alpha_L - \beta b_L + \delta_N b_N \tag{9.1}$$

$$\lambda(a) = \alpha - \beta a \tag{9.2}$$

$$\lambda(b_N) = \alpha_N - \beta b_N + \delta_L b_L \tag{9.3}$$

where $\alpha, \alpha_L, \alpha_N, \beta, \delta_L, \delta_N > 0$. As shown in equation (9.1) the probability of selling a loan is inversely related to immediacy fees on loans (b_L) and positively related to fees charged in non-traditional activities (b_N). Similarly, the probability of selling a non-traditional product in (9.3) decreases with higher fees in these activities (b_N), although it increases with higher fees on loans (b_L). β is the slope of the deposit supply and output (L or N) demand functions of banks.

In order to analyse the profit-maximizing behaviour of banks in this framework, the Taylor expansion series are applied to obtain the expected utility wealth (w) of the bank conditional on each one of the activities shown earlier:

$$\begin{aligned} EU(w \mid \text{loans}) = {}& u'(w_0)b_L Q + \tfrac{1}{2}u''(w_0)(\sigma_I^2 Q^2 - 2\sigma_I^2 Q I_0) \\ & + u(w_0) + u'(w_0)r_w w_0 \\ & + \tfrac{1}{2}u''(w_0)(\sigma_I^2 I_0^2 + 2\sigma_{IY} I_0 Y_0 + \sigma_Y^2 Y_0^2) \end{aligned} \tag{9.4}$$

$$\begin{aligned} EU(w \mid \text{deposits}) = {}& u'(w_0)aQ + \tfrac{1}{2}u''(w_0)(\sigma_I^2 Q^2 - 2\sigma_I^2 Q I_0) \\ & + u(w_0) + u'(w_0)r_w w_0 \\ & + \tfrac{1}{2}u''(w_0)(\sigma_I^2 I_0^2 + 2\sigma_{IY} I_0 Y_0 + \sigma_Y^2 Y_0^2) \end{aligned} \tag{9.5}$$

$$EU(w \mid \text{non-traditional}) = u'(w_0)b_N Q + \tfrac{1}{2}u''(w_0)(\sigma_I^2 Q^2 - 2\sigma_I^2 Q I_0)$$
$$+ u(w_0) + u'(w_0)r_w w_0$$
$$+ \tfrac{1}{2}u''(w_0)(\sigma_I^2 I_0^2 + 2\sigma_{IY}I_0 Y_0 + \sigma_Y^2 Y_0^2) \qquad (9.6)$$

The end-of-period wealth (Y) is a function of stochastic base wealth $(\tilde{Y})$, stochastic output inventory $\tilde{I} = \tilde{L} + \tilde{N} - \tilde{D})$ and cash (C):

$$Y = \tilde{Y} + \tilde{I} + C \qquad (9.7)$$

$$C = (1 + r)C_0 \qquad (9.8)$$

$$Y = (1 + r_y)Y_0 + \tilde{z}_Y Y_0 \qquad (9.9)$$

where r_y is discount rate of bank wealth, $\tilde{z}_Y$ is the stochastic component of bank wealth during the period and r is the free-risk market rate. Similarly,

$$I = (1 + r_I)I_0 + \tilde{z}_I I_0 \qquad (9.10)$$

where

$$r_I \equiv r_L \frac{L_0}{I_0} + r_N \frac{N_0}{I_0} - r_D \frac{D_0}{I_0} \qquad (9.11)$$

$$\tilde{z}_I \equiv \tilde{z}_L \frac{L_0}{I_0} + \tilde{z}_N \frac{N_0}{I_0} - \tilde{z}_D \frac{D_0}{I_0} \qquad (9.12)$$

Expected utility of bank wealth is a linear combination of equations (9.4) to (9.6):

$$Eu(\tilde{w}) = \lambda(b_L)(9.4) + \lambda(a)(9.5) + \lambda(b_N)(9.6) \qquad (9.13)$$

Solving for the different bank fees, the following first order conditions are found:[4]

$$\frac{\partial Eu(\tilde{w})}{\partial b_L} = -\beta(9.4) + (\alpha - \beta b_L + \delta_N b_N)u'(w_0)Q + \delta_N(9.6) = 0 \qquad (9.14)$$

$$\frac{\partial Eu(\tilde{w})}{\partial a} = -\beta(9.5) + (\alpha - \beta a)u'(w_0)Q = 0 \qquad (9.15)$$

$$\frac{\partial Eu(\tilde{w})}{\partial b_N} = -\beta(9.6) + (\alpha - \beta b_N + \delta_L b_L)u'(w_0)Q + \delta_L(9.4) = 0 \qquad (9.16)$$

Therefore, the interest spread between loans and deposits is:

$$a + b_L = \frac{\alpha}{\beta} + \tfrac{1}{2}R\sigma_I^2 Q + \frac{1}{4\beta}\left[2b_N\left(\frac{\delta_N}{\delta_L} + 1\right) - R\sigma_I^2 Q\right] \qquad (9.17)$$

and the spread between non-traditional outputs and deposits is:

$$a + b_N = \frac{\alpha}{\beta} + \frac{1}{2}R\sigma_I^2 Q + \frac{1}{4\beta}\left[2b_L\left(\frac{\delta_L}{\delta_N} + 1\right) - R\sigma_I^2 Q\right] \qquad (9.18)$$

where $R \equiv -U''/U'$ is the measure of absolute risk aversion of the Ho–Saunders model. As shown by Allen (1988), the only difference between the Ho–Saunders model and the multi-output solution is last term. If $2b_N[(\delta_N/\delta_L) + 1] - R\sigma_I^2 Q < 0$ in (9.17), the introduction of non-traditional activities reduces interest margins. At the same time, if $2b_N[(\delta_L/\delta_N) + 1] - R\sigma_I^2 Q > 0$ in (9.18), the introduction of non-traditional activities along with loans increases bank revenues beyond interest margins. These results will also depend on cross-elasticity of demand across bank products (δ_N and δ_L in equations (9.1) and (9.3)). Therefore, it seems to be convenient to empirically evaluate if diversification towards non-traditional activities may increase or decrease bank margins by altering risk or market power.

9.3.2 Empirical applications: review and reassessment

Two main approaches have been followed in the analysis of bank (interest) margins: the (static) micro-model of the banking firm (Zarruck, 1989; Wong, 1997) and the (dynamic) intermediation/dealership approach (Ho and Saunders, 1981). Both models follow an Industrial Organization (IO) perspective and analyse the effects of risk and market structure on interest margins.

These models are empirically implemented by including variables that proxy competitive conditions and risk. Several studies have also included different sources of (interest, liquidity and credit) risk, as well as the influence of factors such as solvency regulations or operating efficiency (Angbazo, 1997; Saunders and Schumacher, 2000; Maudos and Fernandez de Guevara, 2004). The reduced-form empirical equation that explains interest margins (INTMG) in these models can be described as:

$$\text{INTMG}_{it} = f(S_{it}(.), X_{it}, \varepsilon_{it}) \qquad (9.19)$$

where $S_{it}(.)$ is a vector of the determinants of the pure spread (market power and risk variables), $X_{it}(.)$ is a vector of other bank-specific variables (efficiency, solvency) and ε_{it} is the error term.

Both the intermediation/dealership approach and the micro-model of the banking firm rely solely on INTMG. This assumption implies that the underlying bank business is lending and deposit-taking exclusively. However, the evolution of financial innovation requires a wider framework to study the determinants of bank margins. Additionally, contributions from the NEIO suggest the use of direct tests of firm conduct as the Lerner index for two main reasons. First, this measure avoids potential bias associated with the use of accounting measures, such as the INTMG. Second, since marginal costs in the Lerner index can be estimated directly from the production function, the multi-output nature of banks is then captured.

As opposed to equation (9.19), in the empirical analysis of the determinants of bank margins within a multi-output (broad banking) environment, the issue of specialization/diversification plays an important role. Changes in bank production technologies may affect both the pure spread (market structure and risk) parameters as well as other variables that proxy the competitive behaviour of banks (such as efficiency).

Therefore, we extend the reduced-form empirical equation shown in (9.19) to incorporate the effects of specialization/diversification options beyond lending and deposit-taking:

$$\mathrm{MG}_{it} = f(S_{it}(.), X_{it}, \mathrm{SD}_{it}, \mathrm{OC}_{it}, \varepsilon_{it}) \tag{9.20}$$

MG_{it} is a bank margin definition in a broad sense (not only INTMG but also direct margins such as the Lerner index); $S_{it}(.)$ is a vector of the determinants of the pure spread (market power and risk variables); $X_{it}(.)$ is a vector of other bank-specific variables (efficiency, solvency); SD_{it} is a vector of bank output specialization/diversification strategies showing the structure of bank's assets portfolio; OC_{it} is a vector of other control variables such as changes in economic activity or in regulation; and ε_{it} is the error term.

At this point, we survey the empirical evidence found in previous studies on the various factors that explain bank margins. As for the determinants of the pure spread ($S_{it}(.)$), most of the studies rely on a Herfindahl–Hirschman concentration index (HHI) to analyse the relationship between prices and market power. As opposed to the assumptions of the Structure–Conduct–Performance (SCP) hypothesis, many studies have not supported the hypothesis that prices and market power rise with concentration (i.e. Gilbert, 1984; Hannan, 1991; Berger, 1995).

The multi-output nature of the banking firm brings on a wide range of bundling strategies. With bundling, prices of all products are set jointly considering the competitive conditions on each one of the market segments where the bank operates. This is the case of bank deposits, which are often found as a loss-leader product. Loss-leader behaviour implies that rates and fees on deposits are lower than their implicit price, so that mark-ups on deposits are negative (Vives, 2001). Petersen and Rajan (1995) indicate that loss-leader behaviour may affect not only deposits but also certain types of loans to attract demand to other types of loans. All things considered, the objective appears to be to generate long-term relationships and cross-selling opportunities.

Regarding the different sources of risk, the links between diversification and risk (and its impact on bank margins) have been directly or indirectly considered in recent studies that find a reduction on credit, liquidity and interest risk as a result of output diversification (Gallo *et al.*, 1996; Angbazo, 1997; Siems and Clark, 1997; Wong, 1997; Rogers and Sinkey, 1999; Saunders and Schumacher, 2000).

Other bank-specific factors (X_{it}), such as efficiency and solvency, can also affect banks' income structure significantly. However, the relationship between operating efficiency and margins remain unclear. On the one hand, specialization may imply higher operating efficiency (driven by a reduction in transaction costs). This may result in lower margins if banks reduce prices along with costs (Siems and Clark, 1997; Rogers and Sinkey, 1999). On the other hand, as noted by Maudos and Fernandez de Guevara (2004) for the European banking system, specialized banks exhibit higher unit costs on average so that margins and efficiency may be lower with specialization. Regulatory pressures on capital have been found to represent a premium on bank prices and to widen margins (Angbazo, 1997; Wong, 1997; Saunders and Schumacher, 2000).

The innovative vector in the equation of bank margins is SD_{it}, which states for output technology specialization/diversification variables. As shown earlier, we expect a close relationship between business and income diversification levels.

Finally, the vector OC_{it} refers to other control variables such as economic conditions or regulation. Changes in business cycle and different degrees of liberalization may result in significant differences on bank margins across countries and regions (Jayaratne and Strahan, 1997; Carbo *et al.*, 2003).

9.3.3 Bank margins and aggregate risk behaviour

Changes in banks margins may also have important implications for processes such as changes in households' financial portfolios, the interaction between financial intermediaries and capital markets, or the extent to which differences between bank-based and market-based financial systems still apply. In this context, there are two main macroeconomic hypotheses related to banks' margins that affect aggregate risk in financial markets. The first one is the hypothesis of cross-sectional risk sharing, which states that intermediaries transfer risk from certain agents to others although aggregate risk does not change. The alternative hypothesis is the so-called intertemporal risk smoothing, which states that banks may benefit from long-term relationships when households' portfolios are not so dynamic and most of the financial savings are invested in deposits. Banks may then take advantage of their relatively large liquidity holdings to offer lower rates on loans during downturns and compensate this with higher loan rates – relative to market rates – during upturns. Therefore, aggregate risk decreases with intertemporal smoothing (Allen and Gale, 1994, 1996; Berlin and Mester, 1999). Allen and Santomero (2001) maintain that bank-based financial systems have traditionally benefited from intertemporal smoothing while cross-sectional risk sharing has dominated market-based financial systems.

Regulation and financial structure might then explain differences in bank intermediation across countries. In any event, it should be taken into account that many financial systems labelled as 'bank-based' have experienced a substantial growth of financial markets in recent years along with an increasing interaction between intermediaries and capital market activities. Therefore, differences in the activities undertaken by financial intermediaries across countries are progressively blurring and the distinction between bank-based and market-based models or cross-sectional risk sharing and intertemporal rate smoothing is no longer clear (Scholtens, 1999; Barth *et al.*, 2000).

9.4 Empirical methodology and data

In this section, we undertake the empirical analysis for a representative sample of banks from seven European countries – Germany, Spain, France, Netherlands, Italy, United Kingdom and Sweden – during 1994–2001. The two main empirical aims:

1 To estimate the determinants of bank margins employing a traditional measure of interest margins (the loan to deposits rate spread) and a broader measure of bank margins following the NEIO perspective (the Lerner index).
2 To test the hypothesis of intertemporal rate smoothing vs. the hypothesis of cross-sectional risk sharing by analysing the relationship between the loan to market rate spread and the evolution of the GDP.

9.4.1 The determinants of banks' margins: a dynamic panel data approach

A dynamic panel data approach is employed to study the determinants of bank margins in European banking. At this point, it should be noted that our theoretical model follows a dynamic approach where banks need to match the random deposit supply function and the random demand of lending and non-traditional activities across periods. The maximization of bank wealth considers both initial and end-of-period information. Therefore, endogeneity may affect bank margins significantly. The empirical implementation of the reduced-form equation in (9.20) results in:

$$MG_{it} = MG_{it-1} + S_{it}(.) + X_{it}, + SD_{it} + OC_{it} + \mu_i + \varepsilon_{it} \qquad (9.21)$$

where MG_{it} states, alternatively, for the loan to deposit rate spread (SPREAD) – as a pure intermediation margin – and the Lerner index (LERNER) – as a broader banking margin and a measure of market power. Endogeneity is considered since margins in period $t - 1$ (MG_{it-1}) are expected to affect margins in period t. The vectors of the determinants of the pure spread $S_{it}(.)$; other bank-specific factors (X_{it}); output technology specialization/diversification variables (SD_{it}) and other macroeconomic environment control variables (OC_{it}) are also included, while μ_i is the individual unobservable effect. Endogeneity requires a simultaneous equations estimation framework. In order to avoid estimation bias with panel data and dynamic variables, we follow the Arellano and Bond (1991) Generalized method of moments (GMM) procedure. Two simultaneous equations are estimated, one with first-differenced variables and another one in levels. There are two sets of simultaneous equations to be estimated:

$$\begin{aligned}
SPREAD_{i,t} - SPREAD_{i,t-1} = {} & \alpha(SPREAD_{i,t-1} - SPREAD_{i,t-2}) \\
& + \beta'(S_{i,t} - S_{i,t-1}) + \chi'(X_{i,t} - X_{i,t-1}) \\
& + \delta'(SD_{i,t} - SD_{i,t-1}) \\
& + \lambda'(OC_{i,t} - OC_{i,t-1}) + (\varepsilon_{i,t} - \varepsilon_{i,t-1})
\end{aligned}$$
$$(9.22)$$

$$\text{SPREAD}_{i,t} = \alpha\text{SPREAD}_{i,t-1} + \beta'S_{i,t} + \chi'X_{i,t} + \delta'SD_{i,t}$$
$$+ \gamma'OC_{i,t} + \eta_i + \varepsilon_{i,t} \tag{9.23}$$

$$\text{LERNER}_{i,t} - \text{LERNER}_{i,t-1} = \alpha(\text{LERNER}_{i,t-1} - \text{LERNER}_{i,t-2})$$
$$+ \beta'(S_{i,t} - S_{i,t-1}) + \chi'(X_{i,t} - X_{i,t-1})$$
$$+ \delta'(SD_{i,t} - SD_{i,t-1})$$
$$+ \lambda'(OC_{i,t} - OC_{i,t-1}) + (\varepsilon_{i,t} - \varepsilon_{i,t-1}) \tag{9.24}$$

$$\text{LERNER}_{i,t} = \alpha\text{LERNER}_{i,t-1} + \beta'S_{i,t} + \chi'X_{i,t} + \delta'SD_{i,t}$$
$$+ \gamma'OC_{i,t} + \eta_i + \varepsilon_{i,t} \tag{9.25}$$

The Arellano and Bond (1991) GMM procedure requires the use of appropriate instruments. The instruments for the equations in differences are the one-lagged explanatory (including the lagged dependent) variables. The lagged first-differenced explanatory variables are the appropriate instruments for the equations in levels. Country-specific dummies were also included to account for unobservable effects across countries.

Although there might be correlation between the explanatory variables in levels and the individual effects, these effects are not necessarily correlated with the first-differenced variables, as noted by the following moment conditions of the GMM estimator:

$$E\big[y_{i,t-s} - y_{i,t-s-1}(\eta_i - \varepsilon_{i,t})\big] = 0, \quad s = 1 \tag{9.26}$$

$$E\big[S_{i,t-s} - S_{i,t-s-1}(\eta_i - \varepsilon_{i,t})\big] = 0, \quad s = 1 \tag{9.27}$$

$$E\big[X_{i,t-s} - X_{i,t-s-1}(\eta_i - \varepsilon_{i,t})\big] = 0, \quad s = 1 \tag{9.28}$$

$$E\big[SD_{i,t-s} - SD_{i,t-s-1}(\eta_i - \varepsilon_{i,t})\big] = 0, \quad s = 1 \tag{9.29}$$

$$E\big[OC_{i,t-s} - OC_{i,t-s-1}(\eta_i - \varepsilon_{i,t})\big] = 0, \quad s = 1 \tag{9.30}$$

where y represents any of the dependent variables (SPREAD, LERNER). The consistency of the GMM estimator depends on the validity of the instruments. A Sargan test for restrictions overidentifcation is employed. The null hypothesis in this test is that the instrumental variables and the residuals are not correlated.

9.4.2   An evaluation of aggregate risk behaviour in intermediation activities

We also analyse loan pricing behaviour relative to interbank market interest rates (three-months rate) in order to test the hypothesis of intertemporal rate smoothing vs. the hypothesis of cross-sectional risk sharing. In this context, the loan to (interbank) market rate spread (LMSPR) is related to the evolution of the GDP and the rest of the pure spread and bank-specific variables. Using the same

Arellano-Bond GMM dynamic procedure, the following system of equations is estimated:

$$\text{LMSPR}_{i,t} - \text{LMSPR}_{i,t-1} = \alpha(\text{LMSPR}_{i,t-1} - \text{LMSPR}_{i,t-2})$$
$$+ \beta'(S_{i,t} - S_{i,t-1}) + \chi'(X_{i,t} - X_{i,t-1})$$
$$+ \lambda'(\text{GDP}_{i,t} - \text{GDP}_{i,t-1}) + (\varepsilon_{i,t} - \varepsilon_{i,t-1})$$
$$(9.31)$$

$$\text{LMSPR}_{i,t} = \alpha\text{LMSPR}_{i,t-1} + \beta'S_{i,t} + \chi'X_{i,t} + \gamma'\text{GDP}_{i,t} + \eta_i + \varepsilon_{i,t} \quad (9.32)$$

Two main hypotheses are then tested:

- *Hypothesis H0*: If $\gamma > 0$, the LMSPR increases when GDP grows. Therefore, an intertemporal rate smoothing behaviour will be expected.
- *Hypothesis H1*: If $\gamma > 0$, the LMSPR decreases when GDP grows and a cross-sectional risk sharing behaviour will be expected.

9.4.3 Data

The sample consists of 19,322 European banks (annual observations) from Germany, Spain, France, Netherlands, Italy, United Kingdom and Sweden using Bureau Van Dijk-Bankscope Database information between 1994 and 2001. Sample composition is shown in Table 9.2. The panel is unbalanced due to mergers and acquisitions during the period. Five sets of empirical variables are employed:

1 Dependent variables:

- *SPREAD*: Loan to deposits rate spread. It is the difference between the price of loans – computed as the ratio 'interest income/loans' and the price of deposits – computed as the ratio 'interest expense/deposits'.
- *LERNER*: The ratio '(price of total assets-marginal costs)/price of total assets'. The price of total assets is computed as the ratio 'total (interest and non-interest) revenue/(total assets and off-balance sheet activities'.[5]

Table 9.2 Sample composition by country and year

	Total	France	German	Italy	Netherlands	Spain	Sweden	UK
1994	2,098	345	1,265	216	36	148	14	74
1995	2,284	350	1,372	244	47	153	18	100
1996	2,434	350	1,445	262	51	186	19	121
1997	2,512	345	1,476	296	49	200	17	129
1998	2,549	337	1,508	314	46	191	20	133
1999	2,579	372	1,480	343	48	183	24	129
2000	2,541	361	1,440	362	42	179	25	132
2001	2,325	335	1,288	345	33	181	25	118
Period	19,322	2,795	11,274	2,382	352	1,421	162	936

Marginal costs are estimated using a single output (for the sum of total assets and off-balance sheet activities) translog cost function with three inputs (deposits, labour and physical capital). The functional form of the translog specification is shown in Appendix A.

- *LMSPR:* is the spread between bank loan rates and the interbank market (three months) rate.

2 Determinants of the pure spread $((S_{it}(.))$:

- *HHI:* Herfindhal–Hirschman index computed from banks total assets in national markets. According to the traditional SCP hypothesis, concentration and banks margins will be positively related. However, this relationship may be influenced by third variables and margins can be found to be negatively affected by concentration (see, for example, Cetorelli and Gambera, 2002).
- *Liquidity risk:* As a proxy for liquidity risk we employ the ratio 'liquid assets/short-term funding'. Liquidity risk is expected to affect bank margins positively (Angbazo, 1997).
- *Interest rate risk:* computed as the difference between the interbank market (three months) rate and the interest rate of customer deposits. Interest risk increases bank interest margins (Saunders and Schumacher, 2000).

3 Other bank-specific variables (X_{it}):

- *Inefficiency:* Computed as the ratio 'operating costs/gross income'. Higher operating inefficiency imply higher operating costs. Therefore, we expect that those banks experiencing higher costs will increase prices to a larger extent, so that inefficiency will result in higher margins.
- *Capital to assets ratio:* A proxy of banks' solvency computed as the ratio 'capital and reserves/total assets'. Capital requirements represent a premium on bank margins (Berger, 1995). Therefore, a positive relationship between this variable and bank margins is expected.

4 Specialization/diversification variables (SD_{it}):

- *Lending/total assets:* Customer and interbank loans as a ratio of total assets. As specialization in traditional activities increases, efficiency on these activities may increase and, therefore, banks might offer lower (interest) margins.
- *Deposits/total liabilities:* Total deposits as a ratio of total liabilities. As shown previously, the relationship between deposits-taking specialization and bank margins may be either negative – if deposits are not a loss-leader product – or positive – if deposits are loss-leader products that permit to operate with larger interest margins.
- *Other earning assets/total assets:* Total earning assets different from loans as a ratio of total assets. Contrary to the loan to assets ratio, a higher value of this ratio will imply a higher diversification towards fee-income and/or market-based activities. Therefore, bank margins should

increase as a result of higher income diversification and higher market power.

- *Loan commitments/total assets*: Total loan commitments (credit cards and lines of credit) as a ratio of total assets. Although these activities are considered as non-traditional, they represent an off-balance sheet expansion of lending activities. Therefore, as the level of loan commitments increases, the specialization/efficiency effect on lending activities will be larger and interest margins will be expected to fall.
- *Fee-based activities (Boyd–Gertler estimator as a ratio of total assets)*: The Boyd and Gertler (1994) estimator is a proxy of bank fee-based activities which is directly comparable with balance sheet assets. It is computed as ([fee income/(total revenue − fee income)] · total bank assets). Higher levels of fee-income activities will represent higher income diversification towards non-traditional activities. Higher market power is associated with fee-based activities and, as a result, an increase of bank margins will also be expected.
- *ATMs/branches*: A proxy of technical change in delivery channels. The ratio is computed using national data on banks' ATMs and branches. As this variable grows, banks are expected to reduce their unit operating costs and increase fee-income from the use of these services. As a consequence, bank margins will be expected to enlarge.

5 Other control variables (OC_{it}):[6]

- *GDP*: GDP, in constant 1995 US dollars. The relationship between bank margins and growth will depend on the correlation between prices, costs and the business cycle. Economic growth is negatively related to bank prices and costs although the extent to which these variables can be affected may be significantly different so that the net effect on margins cannot be clearly determined (Carbo *et al.*, 2003).

All the variables were computed using Bureau Van Dijk-Bankscope Database information except interbank market rates (*International Financial Statistics*, International Monetary Fund), ATMs and branches (*Blue Book*, European Central Bank) and GDP (*World Development Indicators*, World Bank).

The summary statistics – mean and standard deviation – of the posited variables are shown in Tables 9.3a (over time) and 9.3b (by country).

9.5 Main results

9.5.1 *Determinants of the loan to deposit rate spread*

The results of the estimations, where the loan to deposits rate spread (SPREAD) is the dependent variable, are shown in Table 9.4. The lagged SPREAD variable in the right-hand-side is positive and significant in all cases, showing the relevance of accounting for endogenity in these equations. As for the determinants of pure

Table 9.3a Summary statistics: means of the posited variables over time

Variable	1994	1995	1996	1997	1998	1999	2000	2001	Period
Loan to deposit rate spread	0.10	0.09	0.09	0.08	0.08	0.07	0.06	0.05	0.08
	(0.16)	(0.22)	(0.20)	(0.17)	(0.38)	(0.20)	(0.29)	(0.41)	(0.72)
Lerner index(−1)	0.32	0.33	0.34	0.35	0.35	0.36	0.36	0.37	0.33
	(0.26)	(0.42)	(0.14)	(0.13)	(0.15)	(0.44)	(0.12)	(0.10)	(0.32)
Loan to market rate spread	0.08	0.10	0.10	0.09	0.08	0.09	0.07	0.07	0.08y
	(0.40)	(0.16)	(0.16)	(0.12)	(0.17)	(0.41)	(0.12)	(0.30)	(0.26)
HHI	0.38	0.39	0.23	0.25	0.31	0.24	0.26	0.25	0.31
	(0.11)	(0.12)	(0.15)	(0.16)	(0.22)	(0.15)	(0.13)	(0.12)	(0.10)
Liquidity risk	0.26	0.28	0.30	0.29	0.28	0.27	0.26	0.27	0.28
	(0.14)	(0.15)	(0.16)	(0.17)	(0.18)	(0.18)	(0.16)	(0.19)	(0.17)
Interest rate risk	0.004	0.003	0.005	0.006	0.006	0.004	0.002	0.001	0.003
	(0.03)	(0.04)	(0.04)	(0.03)	(0.04)	(0.04)	(0.03)	(0.04)	(0.04)
Inefficiency	0.65	0.63	0.62	0.62	0.60	0.59	0.58	0.56	0.60
	(0.21)	(0.12)	(0.10)	(0.12)	(0.08)	(0.07)	(0.09)	(0.07)	(0.10)
Capital/total assets	0.08	0.08	0.09	0.10	0.09	0.11	0.12	0.11	0.09
	(0.03)	(0.05)	(0.09)	(0.07)	(0.05)	(0.06)	(0.04)	(0.07)	(0.08)
Lending/total assets	0.74	0.73	0.72	0.72	0.71	0.71	0.70	0.70	0.72
	(0.16)	(0.16)	(0.16)	(0.16)	(0.16)	(0.16)	(0.17)	(0.16)	(0.16)
Deposits/total liabilities	0.80	0.76	0.80	0.79	0.78	0.80	0.80	0.79	0.79
	(0.14)	(0.14)	(0.14)	(0.14)	(0.14)	(0.14)	(0.14)	(0.15)	(0.14)
Other earning assets/total assets	0.26	0.25	0.24	0.25	0.28	0.27	0.28	0.30	0.28
	(0.14)	(0.15)	(0.14)	(0.17)	(0.13)	(0.18)	(0.15)	(0.14)	(0.17)
Loan commitments/total assets	0.35	0.31	0.31	0.32	0.33	0.34	0.35	0.35	0.34
	(1.06)	(0.88)	(0.84)	(0.76)	(1.13)	(1.25)	(1.38)	(0.90)	(1.07)
Fee-based activities (Boyd–Gertler estimator as a ratio of total assets)	0.025	0.032	0.031	0.037	0.042	0.053	0.051	0.053	0.048
	(0.03)	(0.05)	(0.07)	(0.06)	(0.03)	(0.05)	(0.07)	(0.04)	(0.08)
ATMs/branches	0.76	0.82	0.92	0.98	1.02	1.12	1.22	1.31	1.03
	(0.21)	(0.26)	(0.27)	(0.36)	(0.32)	(0.31)	(0.30)	(0.27)	(0.32)
GDP (€ billion)	1.40	1.45	1.49	1.51	1.55	1.58	1.63	1.79	1.54
	(0.46)	(0.49)	(0.54)	(0.51)	(0.49)	(0.49)	(0.49)	(0.50)	(0.50)

Note
Total sample (Germany, Spain, France, Netherlands, Italy, United Kingdom and Sweden), no. of observations: 19,322, and standard deviation in parenthesis.

Table 9.3b Summary statistics: means of the posited variables by country (Standard deviation in parenthesis)

Variable	Germany	Spain	France	Netherlands	Italy	United Kingdom	Sweden
Loan to deposit rate	0.06	0.10	0.12	0.07	0.09	0.10	0.09
spread	(0.12)	(0.08)	(0.07)	(0.06)	(0.05)	(0.04)	(0.03)
Lerner index(-1)	0.35	0.38	0.27	0.26	0.37	0.33	0.29
	(0.12)	(0.05)	(0.04)	(0.08)	(0.06)	(0.12)	(0.06)
Loan to market rate	0.06	0.10	0.12	0.06	0.09	0.11	0.06
spread	(0.03)	(0.05)	(0.08)	(0.07)	(0.08)	(0.06)	(0.04)
HHI	0.12	0.55	0.47	0.16	0.45	0.24	0.20
	(0.02)	(0.05)	(0.04)	(0.03)	(0.05)	(0.03)	(0.05)
Liquidity risk	0.29	0.21	0.15	0.35	0.41	0.34	0.33
	(0.04)	(0.03)	(0.02)	(0.05)	(0.03)	(0.04)	(0.03)
Interest rate risk	0.002	0.003	0.003	0.005	0.002	0.003	0.002
	(0.03)	(0.02)	(0.02)	(0.04)	(0.02)	(0.03)	(0.02)
Inefficiency	0.58	0.60	0.62	0.56	0.68	0.59	0.62
	(0.08)	(0.09)	(0.09)	(0.10)	(0.08)	(0.11)	(0.07)
Capital/total assets	0.10	0.11	0.11	0.10	0.09	0.10	0.09
	(0.07)	(0.06)	(0.04)	(0.05)	(0.04)	(0.08)	(0.08)
Lending/total assets	0.73	0.73	0.71	0.68	0.70	0.69	0.70
	(0.07)	(0.08)	(0.09)	(0.08)	(0.06)	(0.08)	(0.06)
Deposits/total	0.87	0.85	0.72	0.79	0.69	0.73	0.66
liabilities	(0.04)	(0.04)	(0.05)	(0.05)	(0.08)	(0.09)	(0.06)
Other earning assets/	0.26	0.27	0.29	0.32	0.31	0.31	0.30
total assets	(0.05)	(0.04)	(0.05)	(0.06)	(0.07)	(0.08)	(0.09)
Loan commitments/	0.33	0.30	0.34	0.38	0.30	0.33	0.35
total assets	(0.08)	(0.07)	(0.06)	(0.09)	(0.08)	(0.06)	(0.07)
Fee-based activities	0.047	0.047	0.056	0.053	0.040	0.045	0.049
(Boyd–Gertler	(0.02)	(0.03)	(0.04)	(0.03)	(0.02)	(0.04)	(0.05)
estimator as a ratio							
of total assets)							
ATMs/branches	1.06	1.17	1.10	1.01	1.02	1.01	1.12
	(0.08)	(0.09)	(0.08)	(0.07)	(0.07)	(0.09)	(0.09)
GDP (€ billion)	1.92	0.53	1.28	0.35	1.05	1.18	0.21
	(0.02)	(0.04)	(0.03)	(0.02)	(0.03)	(0.02)	(0.03)

spreads, the HHI is negatively and significantly related to SPREAD, suggesting that higher concentration is related to lower interest margins. This is in line with recent evidence that has found that margins and concentration are not necessarily positively related and that interest margins may be even lower in more concentrated markets (Cetorelli and Gambera, 2002). However, both liquidity and interest rate risk measures are found to augment loan to deposits rate spreads significantly.

Operating inefficiency is also positively and significantly related to the loan to deposits rate spreads, since banks with higher costs apparently tend to operate with higher margins. As predicted, the capital to assets ratio – which is also positively and significantly related to interest margins – represents a premium on bank margins due to pressures of solvency regulations on bank lending activities.

Table 9.4 Determinants of the loan to deposits rate spread in the European banking sectors

Variable	(I)	(II)	(III)	(IV)	(V)	(VI)	(VII)
Constant	0.05961*	−0.01052	0.06547	0.01989*	0.06882*	0.03064	0.00409*
	(0.01)	(0.02)	(0.06)	(0.06)	(0.03)	(0.02)	(0.03)
Loan to deposit rate spread ($t-1$)	0.11538	0.28015*	0.46697*	0.29668*	0.35539*	0.39194*	0.44096*
	(0.11)	(0.09)	(0.14)	(0.12)	(0.12)	(0.13)	(0.11)
HHI	−0.75431*	−0.07247*	−0.11039*	−0.01976	−0.12497*	−0.12277*	−0.11132*
	(0.03)	(0.03)	(0.02)	(0.05)	(0.02)	(0.02)	(0.02)
Liquidity risk	0.08603*	0.11491*	0.13012	−0.15558*	0.23564*	0.11422	0.17004*
	(0.08)	(0.05)	(0.06)	(0.07)	(0.06)	(0.07)	(0.07)
Interest rate risk	0.69357*	0.86325*	0.99932*	1.10406*	0.95792*	1.02309*	0.95955*
	(0.13)	(0.09)	(0.06)	(0.13)	(0.08)	(0.10)	(0.09)
Inefficiency	0.00026*	0.00028*	0.00032*	0.00029*	0.00022*	0.00031*	0.00031*
	(0.01)	(0.01)	(0.01)	(0.01)	(0.01)	(0.01)	(0.01)
Capital/total assets	0.73891	0.65936	0.66273	0.76338	1.00199	0.77423	0.89812
	(0.87)	(0.53)	(0.58)	(0.82)	(0.56)	(0.48)	(0.46)
Lending/total assets	—	−0.21361*	—	—	—	—	—
		(0.05)					
Deposits/total liabilities	—	—	0.12583*	—	—	—	—
			(0.16)				
Other earning assets/ total assets	—	—	—	0.80678*	—	—	—
				(0.25)			
Loan commitments/ total assets	—	—	—	—	−0.02073*	—	—
					(0.05)		
Fee-based activities (Boyd–Gertler estimator)	—	—	—	—	—	0.00001	—
						(0.01)	
ATMs/branches	—	—	—	—	—	—	0.03572
							(0.01)
GDP	−0.21E-06*	−0.15E-06*	−0.48E-07*	−0.19E-06*	0.14E-08	0.50E-07	0.14E-04
	(0.01)	(0.01)	(0.01)	(0.01)	(0.01)	(0.01)	(0.01)
F-test	0.012	0.015	0.014	0.015	0.010	0.009	0.011
Sargan test	0.007	0.009	0.005	0.004	0.006	0.004	0.005

Notes
Total sample (Germany, Spain, France, Netherlands, Italy, United Kingdom and Sweden), no. of observations: 19,322, dynamic panel data analysis (GMM estimator) and standard errors in parenthesis.
* Significantly different from zero at 5 per cent level or lower.

As for the specialization/diversification variables, the coefficient of the ratio 'loans to total assets' is negatively and significantly related to SPREAD, suggesting that those banks specialized in lending can offer lower bank margins (higher efficiency). However, deposit-taking specialization seems to rise spreads. This behaviour supports the hypothesis of a loss-leader behaviour in traditional inter-mediation activities with banks assuming higher costs on deposits and compensating it with higher interest margins or larger loan transactions. Regarding non-traditional activities, the relative weight of other earning assets is found to affect SPREAD positively which, in turn, indicates that more diversified banks operate with higher interest margins in lending/deposit-taking activities compared to specialized banks. However, innovations related to traditional activities – such as loan commitments – are found to be negatively and significantly related to loan to deposits rate spreads, suggesting that lending relationships may permit banks to operate with lower interest margins and compensate this with fees from other activities such as credit cards or loan commitments. As for the effect of the evolution of GDP, banks are found to reduce interest margins during the upturns following the evolution of market interest rates.

For simplicity purposes, the results by country are not shown although they were in line with those in Table 9.4.[7] Additionally, due to the fact that German banks account for almost 60 per cent of the number of observations, we also undertook the same empirical analysis removing the German institutions from the sample for robustness purposes. These results are shown in Appendix B (Table 9B.1) and are clearly in line with those obtained for the entire sample.

9.5.2 Determinants of the Lerner index

The introduction of a direct measure of banks margins – the Lerner index – produces some interesting results (Table 9.5) compared to the outcomes obtained when employing SPREAD as the dependent variable.[8] First of all, neither the concentration variable (HHI) nor the liquidity risk measure are found to affect LERNER significantly, a result that is in line with Maudos and Fernandez de Guevara (2004). However, interest rate risk is significant, since both prices and marginal costs are clearly affected by the evolution of market interest rates. Interestingly, inefficiency is negatively and significantly related to LERNER, suggesting that market power may decrease with higher bank operating inefficiency.

As opposed to the case of SPREAD, a higher ratio of loans to total assets seems to be positively and significantly related to LERNER, while market power decreases with a higher level of deposits over total liabilities. This result supports the hypothesis of loss-leader behaviour in intermediation activities since the negative effect of deposits specialization on bank margins can potentially be compensated with higher market power in lending activities. Other variables such as the weight of other earning assets (different from loans), the variable that relates the Boyd–Gertler estimator to total assets, the level of loan commitments and the

Table 9.5 Determinants of the Lerner index in the European banking sectors

Variable	(I)	(II)	(III)	(IV)	(V)	(VI)	(VII)
Constant	0.01416	0.08026	0.01500	0.01201	0.00690	0.01837	0.00819
	(0.01)	(0.01)	(0.01)	(0.01)	(0.11)	(0.01)	(0.01)
Lerner index(-1)	0.59956*	0.21477*	0.15002*	0.15148	0.50375*	0.67846*	0.55182*
	(0.10)	(0.06)	(0.05)	(0.08)	(0.10)	(0.09)	(0.09)
HHI	0.04473	-0.02925*	-0.09375	0.03003	0.01429	0.05734	-0.00759
	(0.06)	(0.09)	(1.36)	(0.07)	(0.08)	(0.06)	(0.05)
Liquidity risk	-0.01355	0.01486	0.09294	-0.02425*	-0.01142	-0.01582	-0.05867
	(0.01)	(0.01)	(0.01)	(0.01)	(0.01)	(0.01)	(0.01)
Interest rate risk	0.01367*	-0.00442	-0.00389	-0.00817	0.01328*	0.01542*	0.00831
	(0.01)	(0.01)	(0.01)	(0.01)	(0.01)	(0.01)	(0.01)
Inefficiency	-0.00007*	-0.00006*	-0.00006*	-0.00005*	-0.00008*	-0.00007*	-0.00007*
	(0.01)	(0.01)	(0.01)	(0.01)	(0.01)	(0.01)	(0.01)
Capital/total assets	-0.18346	-0.11799	-0.09156	-0.16075	-0.32436*	-0.15474	-0.12985
	(0.10)	(0.09)	(0.07)	(0.10)	(0.12)	(0.09)	(0.08)
Lending/total assets	—	0.04991*	—	—	—	—	—
		(0.01)					
Deposits/total liabilities	—	—	-0.03644*	—	—	—	—
			(0.06)				
Other earning assets/total assets	—	—	—	0.09016*	—	—	—
				(0.01)			
Loan commitments/total assets	—	—	—	—	0.04806*	—	—
					(0.02)		
Fee-based activities (Boyd–Gertler estimator)	—	—	—	—	—	0.00072*	—
						(0.01)	
ATMs/branches	—	—	—	—	—	—	0.00050*
							(0.01)
GDP	0.15E-05*	0.12E-07*	0.86E-08	0.75E-08*	0.10E-07*	0.84E-08	0.17E-07*
	(0.01)	(0.01)	(0.01)	(0.01)	(0.01)	(0.01)	(0.01)
F-test	0.016	0.017	0.012	0.018	0.013	0.014	0.018
Sargan test	0.004	0.005	0.007	0.010	0.007	0.006	0.008

Notes
Total sample (Germany, Spain, France, Netherlands, Italy, United Kingdom and Sweden), no. of observations: 19,322, dynamic panel data analysis (GMM estimator) and standard errors in parenthesis.
* Significantly different from zero at 5 per cent level or lower.

relative substitution of branches for ATMs are also positively and significantly related to LERNER. These results are not surprising, since all these variables represent higher income from fees resulting from innovations. Overall, European banks have apparently found that new sources of market power in fee-earning activities tend to face increasing competition in traditional business. Therefore, as shown in equations (9.17) and (9.18), diversification towards non-traditional products may raise bank margins by increasing market power.

According to the previous results, a tentative interpretation is the existence of, at least, two different playing fields in European banks' margin strategies. First of all, although competition has increased in traditional activities – with interest margins falling in recent years – banks apparently can take advantage of deposits to enjoy higher loan interest margins (loss-leader behaviour). At a second stage, those banks that diversify their assets portfolio to a larger extent may also benefit from the lower level of competition – higher market power – in fee-earning activities.

Although it is difficult to obtain information on prices and costs of fee-earning activities, we can, at least, provide additional evidence on the loss-leader behaviour in traditional activities. Using the same single output translog function used to estimate marginal costs on total assets, we estimate marginal costs of loans and deposits by taking these two activities as the output in the translog functional form. The mark-up of loan (deposits) prices relative to their marginal costs is then computed to explore the evolution of the margins of each one of these activities[9] during 1994–2001. The summary of the results is presented in Figure 9.2 for the whole sample and by country. In all cases, there seems to be evidence of loss-leader behaviour since mark-ups on deposits were found to be negative while mark-ups on loans are positive and higher on average.

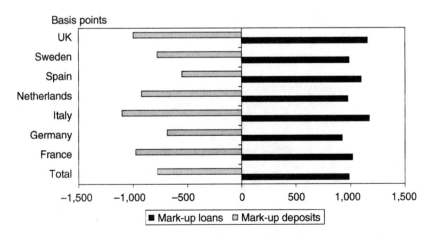

Figure 9.2 Mark-up of loans and deposits in the European banking sectors (1994–2001).
Source: Own estimations.

The results by country when the Lerner index is the dependent variable are not shown for simplicity. These results remain quite similar to those obtained for the whole sample. We also run these tests removing German institutions from the sample for robustness purposes (Appendix B, Table 9B.2) and the results are in line with those obtained for the entire sample.

9.5.3 Intertemporal rate smoothing vs. cross-sectional risk-sharing

The results of the equations, where the LMSPR is the dependent variable, are shown in Table 9.6. At this point, it appears to be convenient to report the results across countries since there are potential differences in banks' aggregate risk behaviour depending on the bank-based or market-based structure of their financial systems (Allen and Santomero, 2001).

The coefficient of the GDP variable is found to be negative and significant for the whole sample as well as in the cases of Germany, Spain, Italy and Sweden. Therefore, intertemporal rate smoothing hypothesis does not seem to apply in European banking during 1994–2001. This result appears to be more in line with the hypothesis that cross-sectional risk sharing seems to dominate in European banking. Banks tend to reduce (increase) the spread between loan and interbank market rates during the upturns (downturns). These results remain quite similar when taking the GDP variable in second- or third-differences, which suggests that cross-sectional risk sharing behaviour persists over time.[10]

9.6 Conclusions

This paper studies the relationship between financial innovation and bank margins in Europe. Using a multi-output model where prices on loans, deposits and other non-traditional activities are set simultaneously, we find that both market power and risk parameters alter bank margins when introducing financial innovations.

Empirical tests are implemented for a sample of 19,322 banks European – from Germany, Spain, France, Netherlands, Italy, United Kingdom and Sweden – to analyse the determinants of bank margins during 1994–2001. Both the loan to deposit rate spread – as the conventional approach to bank margins – and the Lerner index – as a more direct and broader measure of banks margins – are employed as dependent variables. The results suggest that specialization and bank margins are significantly related although these relationships can be only observed when considering a broader definition of bank margins (the Lerner index). Output diversification permits banks to increase their revenues and obtain higher market power. In particular, non-interest (fee) income may 'compensate', somehow, lower interest margins that result from stronger competition in traditional markets.

Table 9.6 Determinants of the loan to interbank market rate spread in the European banking sectors: testing the intertemporal rate smoothing hypothesis

Variable	Total	Germany	Spain	France	Netherlands	Italy	United Kingdom	Sweden
No of observations	19,322	2,795	11,274	2,382	352	1,421	162	936
Constant	0.08089*	0.01233	-0.00541	0.01733	-0.02480	-0.01587	0.01899	0.07887
	(0.03)	(0.01)	(0.02)	(0.03)	(0.04)	(0.02)	(0.09)	(0.01)
Loan to market rate spread ($t-1$)	0.84444*	0.91895*	0.02632	0.49827*	0.31467*	0.75201*	0.29902*	0.10442*
	(0.13)	(0.11)	(0.06)	(0.09)	(0.07)	(0.17)	(0.11)	(0.01)
HHI	-0.12502*	-0.10477	-0.06928*	-0.15534	0.33324	0.12458*	-0.28772*	0.61413
	(0.02)	(0.18)	(0.02)	(0.10)	(0.40)	(0.04)	(0.10)	(0.52)
Liquidity risk	0.29999*	0.01437	-0.00183	0.19301*	-0.01434	0.19317*	0.24323*	0.17213*
	(0.06)	(0.01)	(0.02)	(0.05)	(0.12)	(0.04)	(0.11)	(0.04)
Interest rate risk	-0.03805	-0.05974	-0.20622	-0.05576	-1.07978*	1.12410*	-1.28434*	0.03446*
	(0.07)	(0.12)	(0.22)	(0.05)	(0.35)	(0.22)	(0.55)	(0.01)
Capital/total assets	1.42258	-0.06132	1.71005*	0.62324	-0.04642	-0.06067	2.59771	-2.21123
	(0.77)	(0.28)	(1.11)	(0.40)	(1.40)	(0.13)	(2.19)	(1.22)
Inefficiency	0.00021*	0.00454*	0.08842*	0.00025*	-0.00043	0.00026	-0.00961	-0.00374*
	(0.01)	(0.01)	(0.01)	(0.01)	(0.01)	(0.02)	(0.01)	(0.01)
GDP	-0.61E-07*	-0.33E-08*	-0.88E-07*	0.73E-07	-0.11E-06	-0.13E-06*	0.32E-07	-0.40E-06*
	(0.01)	(0.01)	(0.01)	(0.01)	(0.01)	(0.01)	(0.01)	(0.01)
F-test	0.013	0.009	0.011	0.013	0.015	0.009	0.010	0.014
Sargan test	0.003	0.002	0.003	0.004	0.002	0.005	0.003	0.002

Notes
Total sample (Germany, Spain, France, Netherlands, Italy, United Kingdom and Sweden), no. of observations: 19,322, dynamic panel data analysis (GMM estimator), and standard errors in parenthesis.
* Significantly different from zero at 5 per cent level or lower.

Additional evidence is provided on the effects of these changes in financial innovation on aggregate bank risk behaviour. There appears to be no evidence of intertemporal rate (risk) smoothing advantages, which has been the conventional wisdom hypothesis for European banking for a long time (Allen and Santomero, 2001). Cross-sectional risk sharing has apparently become the most plausible hypothesis in most European banking systems. Recent shifts in household and firms' financial portfolios towards market-based investment products appear to help explain these changes. Banks customers seem to value a broader range of services beyond lending and deposit activities and diversify their financial wealth by investing in shares, mutual or pension funds and insurance products, among other alternatives. In any event, further research is needed in the context of changes in European financial structure, the related transformations in the financial decisions of the private sector and the effects of both on banks' performance.

9A.1   Appendix A

Marginal costs are computed using a single output (for the sum of total assets and off-balance sheet items) translog cost function with two cost share equations over 1994–2001:

$$
\begin{aligned}
\ln TC = {} & \alpha_0\alpha_1 Q + \phi_t t' + \tfrac{1}{2}\delta_{11}Q^2 + \tfrac{1}{2}\phi_{1t}[t']^2 + \eta_{1t}Q\,t' + \rho Q(\ln R_1) \\
& + \rho_{12}Q(\ln R_2) + (-\rho_{12} - \rho_{12})Q(\ln R_3) + \beta_1 \ln R_1 + \beta_2 \ln R_2 \\
& + (1 - \lambda_1 - \lambda_2)(\ln R_3) + \tfrac{1}{2}[\gamma_{11}\ln R_1^2 + \gamma_{22}\ln R_2^2 \\
& + [(\gamma_{11} + \gamma_{12}) + (\gamma_{12} + \gamma_{22})\ln R_3^2]] + \gamma_{12}\ln R_1(\ln R_2) \\
& + (-\gamma_{11} - \gamma_{12})\ln R_1(\ln R_3) + (\gamma_{12} - \gamma_{22})\ln R_2(\ln R_3) \\
& + \mu_{1t}t'\ln R_1 + \mu_{2t}t'\ln R_2 + \mu_{3t}t'\ln R_3 + \varepsilon
\end{aligned}
\tag{9A.33}
$$

$$
SH_1 = \rho_{11}Q + \beta_1 + \gamma_{11}\ln R_1 + \gamma_{12}\ln R_2 + (-\gamma_{11} - \gamma_{12})R_3 + \mu_{1k}t'
\tag{9A.34}
$$

$$
SH_2 = \rho_{12}Q + \beta_2 + \gamma_{22}\ln R_2 + \gamma_{12}\ln R_1 + (-\gamma_{22} - \gamma_{12})R_3 + \mu_{2k}t'
\tag{9A.35}
$$

where the standard symmetry, summation and cross-equation restrictions are imposed and $\ln TC$ is the log of total operating and interest cost; $\ln Q$ is the log of the value of total assets (an indicator of total banking output); $\ln R_i$ is the log of each one of the three input prices (deposit and other funding interest rate, average price of labour and the average price of physical capital); SH_1 and SH_2 are the cost share equations of deposit and other funding interest expense and labour cost share (the cost share of physical capital is excluded); t is a time dummy reflecting the effects of technical change on costs over time.

9B.1 Appendix B

Table 9B.1 Determinants of the loan to deposits rate spread in the European banking sectors (excluding Germany)

Variable	(I)	(II)	(III)	(IV)	(V)	(VI)	(VII)
Constant	0.04327*	−0.02553	0.09265*	0.01258*	0.05489	0.07047	0.08072*
	(0.01)	(0.03)	(0.07)	(0.04)	(0.02)	(0.04)	(0.04)
Loan to deposit rate spread $(t-1)$	0.12489	0.38546*	0.44482*	0.24547*	0.30145*	0.36214*	0.34577*
	(0.12)	(0.09)	(0.13)	(0.11)	(0.11)	(0.11)	(0.13)
HHI	−0.65877*	−0.04722*	−0.10584*	−0.01001*	−0.13289	−0.09110*	−0.05428*
	(0.03)	(0.02)	(0.01)	(0.02)	(0.01)	(0.03)	(0.03)
Liquidity risk	0.07589*	0.09125*	0.13025*	−0.12245	0.17002*	0.14021	0.15428*
	(0.06)	(0.04)	(0.05)	(0.05)	(0.04)	(0.08)	(0.06)
Interest rate risk	0.61112*	0.68223*	0.87992*	0.82420*	0.78243*	1.00547*	0.72187*
	(0.12)	(0.10)	(0.05)	(0.11)	(0.04)	(0.11)	(0.09)
Inefficiency	0.00021*	0.00024*	0.00019*	0.00019*	0.00021*	0.00021*	0.00026*
	(0.01)	(0.01)	(0.01)	(0.01)	(0.01)	(0.01)	(0.01)
Capital/total assets	0.52330	0.64712	0.61124	0.45878	0.99822	0.63524	0.61022
	(0.82)	(0.53)	(0.62)	(0.42)	(0.50)	(0.48)	(0.34)
Lending/total assets	—	−0.20141*	—	—	—	—	—
		(0.04)					
Deposits/total liabilities	—	—	0.10247*	—	—	—	—
			(0.14)				
Other earning assets/total assets	—	—	—	0.75321*	—	—	—
				(0.19)			
Loan commitments/total assets	—	—	—	—	−0.01151*	—	—
					(0.04)		
Fee-based activities (Boyd–Gertler estimator)	—	—	—	—	—	0.00021	—
						(0.01)	
ATMs/branches	—	—	—	—	—	—	0.05224
							(0.01)
GDP	−0.20E-06*	−0.14E-06*	−0.37E-07*	−0.19E-06	0.17E-07	0.42E-07*	0.18E-04
	(0.01)	(0.01)	(0.01)	(0.01)	(0.01)	(0.01)	(0.01)
F-test	0.013	0.015	0.012	0.014	0.012	0.010	0.013
Sargan test	0.008	0.010	0.004	0.006	0.004	0.003	0.003

Notes

Total sample (Spain, France, Netherlands, Italy, United Kingdom and Sweden), no. of observations: 8,048, dynamic panel data analysis (GMM estimator), standard errors in parenthesis.

* Significantly different from zero at 5 per cent level or lower.

Table 9B.2 Determinants of the Lerner index in the European banking sectors (excluding Germany)

Variable	(I)	(II)	(III)	(IV)	(V)	(VI)	(VII)
Constant	0.00963*	0.05200	0.04513	0.05814	0.00528*	0.01421	0.01932
	(0.07)	(0.04)	(0.02)	(0.05)	(0.13)	(0.09)	(0.05)
Lerner index(−1)	0.49512*	0.25480*	0.14532	0.11154*	0.42583*	0.08426*	0.15224*
	(0.08)	(0.07)	(0.06)	(0.04)	(0.06)	(0.09)	(0.07)
HHI	0.02042	−0.02542	−0.05458	0.02038	0.01256	0.00730	−0.00944
	(0.04)	(0.07)	(0.08)	(0.09)	(0.09)	(0.06)	(0.06)
Liquidity risk	−0.00897	0.011526*	0.05654	−0.02264*	−0.00987	−0.01221	−0.04705
	(0.01)	(0.01)	(0.01)	(0.01)	(0.02)	(0.03)	(0.02)
Interest rate risk	0.00985*	−0.00665	−0.00244	−0.00632	0.00910	0.01257	0.01017*
	(0.01)	(0.01)	(0.01)	(0.01)	(0.01)	(0.07)	(0.01)
Inefficiency	−0.00004*	−0.00007*	−0.00004*	−0.00005*	−0.00006*	−0.00006*	−0.00008*
	(0.01)	(0.01)	(0.01)	(0.01)	(0.01)	(0.01)	(0.01)
Capital/total assets	−0.14788	−0.13421	−0.0941	−0.10210	−0.21931*	−0.09444*	−0.15447
	(0.08)	(0.10)	(0.09)	(0.07)	(0.11)	(0.07)	(0.08)
Lending/total assets	—	0.05102*	—	—	—	—	—
		(0.03)					
Deposits/total liabilities	—	—	−0.05102*	—	—	—	—
			(0.04)				
Other earning assets/total assets	—	—	—	0.04565*	—	—	—
				(0.02)			
Loan commitments/total assets	—	—	—	—	0.02647*	—	—
					(0.04)		
Fee-based activities (Boyd–Gertler estimator)	—	—	—	—	—	0.00051*	—
						(0.01)	
ATMs/branches	—	—	—	—	—	—	0.00028*
							(0.01)
GDP	0.12E-05*	0.15E-07*	0.22E-07	0.37E-07*	0.18E-06*	0.44E-08	0.31E-07*
	(0.01)	(0.01)	(0.01)	(0.01)	(0.01)	(0.01)	(0.01)
F-test	0.018	0.015	0.013	0.017	0.015	0.016	0.018
Sargan test	0.005	0.004	0.005	0.011	0.008	0.004	0.009

Notes

Total sample (Spain, France, Netherlands, Italy, United Kingdom and Sweden), no. of observations: 8,048, dynamic panel data analysis (GMM estimator), standard errors in parenthesis.

* Significantly different from zero at 5 per cent level or lower.

Acknowledgement

Support for this research was provided by the Fundacion de las Cajas de Ahorros Confederadas para la Investigacion Economica y Social.

Notes

1 In this chapter, we focus on net prices as pricing behaviour. That is why we analyse bank margins instead of analysing only prices.
2 Barth *et al.* (2000) have shown the existence of multiple restrictions and prohibitions for US banks in activities such as brokerage, distribution of mutual and pension funds or investment in industrial or other bank participations until 1999 with the advent of the Gramm–Leach–Bliley Act and the repeal of the Glass–Steagall Act. Contrarily, many European countries have enjoyed the so-called 'broad banking' during the last two decades. Therefore, these regulatory differences should have important implications for bank margins and competition.
3 See ECB (2000) for a comprehensive analysis of changes in EU banks' income structure.
4 Second order conditions are negligible since Y is an efficient portfolio (Ho and Saunders, 1981).
5 In this estimation, off-balance sheet items include loan commitments and guarantees. These activities are included in order to account for traditional and non-traditional output in the estimation of marginal costs.
6 An additional control (dummy) variable was employed taking the value 0 for bank-based financial systems – France, Germany, Spain, Italy – and 1 for market-based financial systems – Netherlands, Sweden and United Kingdom. However, the distinction between bank-based and market-based financial system was not found to be relevant for any of the tests used in this chapter.
7 These results are available upon request.
8 Additionally, we employed gross income as a broader accounting measure of bank margins. Since gross margin includes revenues from fees and market investments, the mix of activities associated with the production function is wider than in the case of SPREAD. However, estimation bias problems are also likely to be larger when using gross income. Unfortunately, this was true in our case and the results were significantly less robust than in the case of SPREAD. Among the specialization variables, only the Boyd–Gertler fee-income specialization ratio was found to be statistically significant, which, in turn, underlines the logic importance of fees in generating gross income. These results are not shown for simplicity although they are available upon request to the authors.
9 Loan prices are computed as the ratio of interest income to total loans. Estimating the mark-up on deposits is difficult since the price of deposit services is implicit, not explicit. The implicit price that depositors pay is taken to be the difference between the average market interest rate minus the average rate they earned on their deposits which gives the implied price for this period. This implied price approximates what depositors could potentially have earned on their deposits minus what they did actually earn. This difference effectively represents an indirect or implicit price for the depositor services they consume. The alternative would be for banks to pay a market rate on deposits and assess direct fees for the full cost of each depositor service supplied.
10 Financial innovation and changes in regulation have made it more difficult to distinguish between bank-based and market-based financial systems during the 1990s (Scholtens, 1999).

References

Allen, F. and Gale, D. (1994). *Financial Innovation and Risk Sharing*, Cambridge, MA: MIT Press.

Allen, F. and Gale, D. (1996). 'Financial markets, intermediaries and intertemporal smoothing'. WP 96–33. The Wharton School Institutional Center. University of Pennsylvania.

Allen, F. and Santomero, A. M. (2001). 'What do financial intermediaries do?', *Journal of Banking and Finance*, 25: 271–294.

Allen, L. (1988). 'The determinants of bank interest margins: a note', *Journal of Financial and Quantitative Analysis*, 23: 231–235.

Angbazo, L. (1997). 'Commercial Bank net interest margins, default risk, interest rate risk and off balance sheet activities', *Journal of Banking and Finance*, 21: 55–87.

Arellano, M. and Bond, S. (1991). 'Some tests of specification for panel data: Monte-Carlo evidence and an application to employment equation', *Review of Economic Studies*, 58: 277–287.

Barth, J., Brumbaugh, R. D. and Wilcox, J. (2000). *The Repeal of The Glass–Steagall Act and The Advent of a Broad Banking*. Economic Policy Analysis WP 2000–5. Office of the Comptroller of the Currency.

Berger, A. (1995). 'The profit structure relationship in banking. Tests of market-power and efficient-structure hypotheses', *Journal of Money, Credit, and Banking*, 27: 404–431.

Berlin, M. and Mester, L. J. (1999). 'Deposits and relationship lending', *The Review of Financial Studies*, 12: 579–607.

Boyd, J. and Gertler, M. (1994). 'Are banks dead? Or are the reports greatly exaggerated?' *Federal Reserve Bank of Minneapolis Quarterly Review*, 18: 1–27.

Bresnahan, T. (1989). 'Empirical studies of industries with market power', in Schmalensee, R. and Willig, R. D. (eds), *Handbook of Industrial Organisation*, 2, Amsterdam: North-Holland, 1011–1057.

Carbo, S., Humphrey, D. and Rodriguez, F. (2003). 'Deregulation, bank competition and regional growth', *Regional Studies*, 37: 227–237.

Cetorelli, N. and Gambera, M. (2002). 'Banking market structure, financial dependence and growth: international evidence from industry data', *The Journal of Finance*, 56: 617–648.

European Central Bank (2000). EU banks' income structure, Occasional Papers, April.

Gallo, J. G., Apilado, V. P. and Kolari, J. W. (1996). 'Commercial bank mutual fund activities: implications for bank risks and profitability', *Journal of Banking and Finance*, 20: 1775–1791.

Gilbert, A. (1984). 'Bank market structure and competition: a survey', *Journal of Money, Credit, and Banking*, 16: 617–656.

Hannan, T. (1991). 'Foundations of the structure–conduct–performance paradigm in banking', *Journal of Money, Credit, and Banking*, 23: 68–84.

Ho, T. and Saunders, A. (1981). 'The determinants of bank interest margins: theory and empirical evidence', *Journal of Financial and Quantitative Analysis*, 16: 581–600.

Jayaratne, J. and Strahan, P. E. (1997). 'The benefits of branching deregulation', *Economic Policy Review*, Federal Reserve Bank of New York, December: 13–29.

Lerner, E. M. (1981). 'Discussion. The determinants of banks interest margins: theory and empirical evidence', *Journal of Financial and Quantitative Analysis*, 16: 601–602.

Maudos, J. and Fernandez de Guevara, J. (2004). 'Factors explaining the interest margin in the banking sectors of the European Union', *Journal of Banking and Finance*, 28: 2259–2281.

Petersen, M. A. and Rajan, R. (1995). 'The effect of credit market competition on lending realtionship', *The Quarterly Journal of Economics*, 42: 407–444.

Rogers, K. and Sinkey, J. F. (1999). 'An analysis of non-traditional activities at U.S. commercial banks', *Review of Financial Economics*, 8: 25–39.

Saunders, A. and Schumacher, L. (2000). 'The determinants of bank interest rate margins: an international study', *Journal of International Money and Finance*, 19: 813–832.

Schaffer, S. (2004). 'Patterns of competition in banking', *Journal of Economics and Business*, 56: 287–313.

Schmalensee, R. (1989). 'A inter-industry studies of structure and performance', in Schmalensee, R. and Willig, R. D. (eds), *Handbook of Industrial Organisation*, 2, North-Holland, Amsterdam: 951–1009.

Scholtens, B. (1999). 'Bank and market oriented financial systems', *Banca Nazionale del Lavoro Quarterly Review*, 202: 301–323.

Siems, T. F. and Clark, J. A. (1997). 'Rethinking bank efficiency and regulation: how off balance sheet activities make a difference', *Financial Industry Studies*, Federal Reserve Bank of Dallas, December: 1–12.

Vives, X. (2001). 'Competition in the changing world of banking', *Oxford Review of Economic Policy*, 17: 535–547.

Wong, K. P. (1997). 'On the determinants of bank interest margins under credit and interest rate risk', *Journal of Banking and Finance*, 21: 251–271.

Zarruck, E. R. (1989). 'Bank margins with uncertain deposit level and risk aversion', *Journal of Banking and Finance*, 13: 797–810.

10 The magnitude of distortions when measuring bank efficiency with misspecified input prices

Michael Koetter

10.1 Introduction

Since its introduction by Aigner *et al.* (1977), Battese and Corra (1977) and Meeusen and van der Broeck (1977) stochastic frontier analysis (SFA) has received increasing attention in the literature as a methodology to measure a single firm's efficiency. Much of this popularity results from the opportunity offered to the researcher to rank individual firms, to obtain average industry efficiency and to identify best and worst practice (Coelli *et al.*, 1998). From a regulatory perspective, these are appealing features of SFA in order to gather information on bank stability in times when bank industries around the world undergo significant changes. For practitioners, the methodology provides interesting orientation as to which banks might serve as a role model (see, for example, Molyneux *et al.*, 1997).

Already Berger and Humphrey (1997) surveyed 130 studies from more than 20 countries. At the core of most of these applications rests the specification of a cost or profit function under the assumption of perfect input markets. The error term is assumed to be composed of both white noise and inefficiency. By means of maximum-likelihood techniques a best-practise frontier is estimated, relative to which all firms in the sample are compared. For each firm the error term is decomposed. Firms deviate to varying degrees from this frontier according to the estimated inefficiency. Most of these studies examine US banking markets.[1] Owing to the improved availability of bank-level data studies for European countries become increasingly available.[2]

But despite the frequent use of SFA the vast majority of studies share a potential specification error, as noted by Mountain and Thomas (1999). Efficiency is benchmarked against a cost or profit function. Both are derived from a cost minimisation or profit maximisation problem that is based on the assumption of perfect input markets. Hence, the prices a bank faces to purchase inputs should be determined exogenously in the respective market. Instead, most studies employ each bank's price individually. Factor payments are divided by employed production factors.[3] Implicitly, one assumes that banks possess market power.

In our view the assumption of perfect competition does not entail a specification error *per se*. After all, especially in German banks which are numerous, transaction and information cost declined steadily with technological advances, and market concentration is among the lowest in Europe. Alternative theoretical approaches such as oligopoly or even monopoly models do not seem appropriate.

Therefore, we understand the misspecification problem raised by Mountain and Thomas (1999) to be primarily a measurement problem of input prices. The purpose of this Chapter is to assess the magnitude and direction of this measurement error. We suggest to employ alternative market confinements upon which banks compete for inputs.[4] Bank input prices are calculated based according to market definitions. We then compare efficiency estimates using endogenous input prices with results from the employment of exogenously determined prices to gain insight into the relevance of this mis-measurement issue.

To do so the remainder of this Chapter is organised as follows. The next section briefly reviews German efficiency studies and related literature on how to tackle the problem of mis-measured input prices. Section 10.3 introduces the methodology to measure cost and alternative profit efficiency (CE and PE). Section 10.4 elaborates on the data used in this study. Section 10.5 presents and discusses our results. Section 10.6 concludes.

10.2 Literature

We begin this section by introducing the available evidence on German bank efficiency studies. Next, we review studies that approach the pitfalls when measuring input prices.

10.2.1 German efficiency studies

Despite the important role of banks in Germany's financial system (see, for example, ECB (2002), Bikker and Haaf (2002) or Hackethal (2004)) it is somewhat surprising that evidence on German bank efficiency remains scarce. We are aware of four studies, of which only the most recent one by Altunbas *et al.* (2001) employs fairly current data in order to examine PE and CE between 1989 and 1998. Distinguishing between banks of different size and ownership, the authors study systematic differences between efficiency scores. They find that cost inefficiencies are higher for commercial institutes and large banks. In total, inefficiencies amount to 17 per cent for the banking sector as a whole. The ability of banks to realise potential profits is even worse, as average profit inefficiency amounts to 20 per cent.

Three studies focusing on cooperative banks in Bavaria are Lang and Welzel (1996, 1998a,b). The authors use data collected from a non-commercial database. In sum, these three studies find improving CE during the early 1990s, resulting in average CEs of around 7 per cent. Also, their evidence suggests that smaller cooperatives perform better than larger cooperatives and that mergers between low efficiency targets and better performing ones increase overall efficiency. The authors carefully note, however, that their results only apply to the sector of cooperative banks in general and to those located in the state of Bavaria in particular. Apparently, regional and ownership differences prohibit a generalisation of their results.

10.2.2   *Alternative SFA studies*

The results available for German banking suggest that marked efficiency differences exist between banks of different sectors, size and region. However, according to Mountain and Thomas (1999) the heterogeneity in efficiency scores might to some extent also result from the use of wrongly measured input prices. They suggest two possible ways to improve the reliability of results. First, to account for the fact that banks operate in different regional markets and therefore to use additional information about market characteristics when constructing the frontier. Second, to choose alternative ways to specify input prices. Accordingly, two strands developed in the efficiency literature to tackle the issue.

The first approach continues to fit the frontier to bank-specific prices but takes into account market differences by conditioning the efficient frontier on environmental factors, such as demographic or regulatory information. A number of US studies tackled the issue along these lines and compared, for example, state and federal efficiency scores. Mester (1997) finds that average efficiency scores are lower when measured against a federal frontier compared to efficiency measured against state specific frontiers. Berger and Humphrey (1992) control for systematic differences between output demand and input prices across states by developing and applying a thick-frontier approach (TFA). DeYoung (1998) controls for differences between states regarding regulation and environmental differences. All of these studies find that accounting for state specific factors affects efficiency estimates. One might suspect that this is primarily due to different regulatory regimes across US states during the 1990s. Consequently, the relevance for a European banking market with single banking licenses and little differences in regulation would be small. However, a recent study on European banking underlines the importance of economic characteristics other than regulation between different European countries. In a study on CE of European commercial banks, Lozano-Vivas *et al.* (2002) review ten countries. They employ ten different non-regulatory variables in a data envelopment analysis (DEA).[5] The efficiency results from their complete model increase starkly compared to their model excluding the environmental factors. In the case of Germany for example, this increase in performance is around 30 per cent. The authors conclude that accounting for different market characteristics is important and yields improved efficiency scores. Further evidence on the existence of regional markets even within small European countries is provided by a study of Bos and Kool (2004). Another study by Bos and Schmiedel (2003) applies a so-called metafrontier approach to envelope country specific frontiers with a common European frontier to compare efficiency scores across different markets. Their findings also support the conclusion that efficiency scores from a common frontier tend to underestimate individual firm's efficiency. In sum, by correcting for banks operating on different markets efficiency scores tend to improve.

A second approach tackles the problem of how to measure input prices in a perfect competition specification more directly. It follows the suggestion of Mountain and Thomas (1999) to specify input prices per input market. The only study we are aware of that pursues this approach is Berger and Mester (2003). Using data on US banks of three cross-sections in 1984, 1991 and 1997 they derive prices per geographical market. For each bank they calculate the average price faced as an average of all other banks in that particular market, weighted by it's market share. Thereby, they avoid to violate the assumption of perfect markets by using for each bank a price determined exogenously, namely by it's competitors in the respective market. As their study focuses on static and dynamic sources of cost, profit and alternative PE changes, the authors do not provide a comparison with traditionally specified input prices.

This discussion shows that the issue of potentially mis-measured input prices is related to the existence of different markets on which banks operate. Some studies try to adjust the frontier by including additional environmental information. However, only one study seems to exist that extends along the lines suggested by Mountain and Thomas (1999), namely to use input prices on the basis of regional data. We want to fill this gap with our application of SFA to an extended data set created for German banks.

10.3   Methodology

In order to compare the effects of alternative input price specifications we rely to a large extent on standard approaches to efficiency analysis. By altering only one element of the specification we limit changes in efficiency to changes in input price specification and exclude effects for example due to environmental variables. Along these lines this section presents our methodology to measure efficiency against both a cost and alternative profit frontier. We start by defining variables used and briefly introduce the theoretical models underlying most SFA applications. Next, the empirical specification and how to measure CE and alternative PE is presented. Finally, we introduce our measures of input prices according to a benchmark model and three alternative market definitions to measure exogenous input prices.

10.3.1   Theoretical models in SFA

We follow the intermediation approach suggested by Sealy and Lindley (1977) to model bank production. The main task of a bank is to channel funds from savers to investors.[6] We follow the literature and define three outputs. The first output captures total loans, y_1, provided. Next, banks are modelled to produce securities, y_2. Due to the growing importance of off-balance sheet (OBS) business we also specify total OBS activities as a third output, y_3 (see, for example, Jagtiani and Khanthavit (1996) and Clark and Siems (2002)). A bank uses three production factors to produce these outputs, total borrowed funds, x_1, labour, x_2 and fixed assets, x_3. For these input factors the bank faces an input price vector of w_i, where i indexes the input used. In transforming inputs into outputs we account for the role of equity, z, as an alternative source to fund outputs and as an indicator of different risk-preferences among bank managers (Hughes and Mester, 1993). Hence, the transformation function of the banking firm is depicted by $T(y, x, z)$.

In sum, we model a bank to minimise cost to produce a given output bundle conditional on available equity, z. As the dependent variable we employ total operating cost, TOC, for the cost minimisation problem and profits before tax, PBT, in the alternative profit maximisation problem.

Using these definitions the cost minimisation problem is written as

$$C(y,w_i) = \min (w_i^* x_i)$$
$$\text{s.t. } T(y,x,z) \leq 0. \tag{10.1}$$

Taking partial derivatives with respect to each output and setting these equal to zero results in optimal input demand functions, $x_i^*(y, w_i, z)$, conditional on the available level of equity, z, and output vector produced, y. The minimum cost level is then obtained by substituting the optimal input demand functions into the total cost function given by equation (10.1) resulting in

$$C^* = \sum_i w_i^* x_i(y,w,z) = C^*(y,w,z). \tag{10.2}$$

To measure PE, we employ the alternative profit model introduced by Humphrey and Pulley (1997). Their model possesses the interesting feature to allow for market imperfections on the output side. If perfect competition prevails in both input and output markets, optimal input demand from cost minimisation is identical to input demand from profit maximisation (see, for example, Mas-Colell *et al.*, 1995). Banks would choose input and output quantities given prevailing prices in order to maximise profits and, hence, the maximum profit function would depend on input and output prices.

However, as noted by Berger and Mester (1997) banks might possess some market power when selling their products. Under this assumption banks continue to face perfect input markets and therefore choose input quantities at given prices. But on the revenue side they are able to set prices subject to a pricing opportunity set $H(p, y, w, z)$, where p denotes output prices. The profit maximisation problem can then be written as

$$\pi(y,p,w) = \max_{p,x} (p^* y - w_i^* x_i)$$
$$\text{s.t. } T(y, x, z) \leq 0,$$
$$\text{and } H(p, y, w_i, z) \leq 0. \tag{10.3}$$

Solving the maximisation problem yields optimal input demand functions, x_i^* (y, w_i, z) and optimal prices $y^*(y, w_i, z)$. Using these to obtain a maximum profit function results in

$$\pi^* = \left[p^*(y,w_i,z)^* y - \sum_i w_i^* x_i^*(y,w_i,z) \right] = \pi^*(y,w_i,z). \tag{10.4}$$

Note, that this model of a profit frontier does not require the use of output prices. Profits depend on exogenously determined input prices and available equity to produce a given output. Because output prices are, if available at all, frequently subject to substantial measurement problems – this is another appealing feature of the alternative profit model. When measuring alternative PE we are able to evaluate not only banks' performance to convert inputs as cost efficient as possible into outputs, but also their success in realising opportunities in their output markets.

10.3.2 Empirical specification

To estimate reduced forms of equations (10.2) and (10.4) a variety of specifications have been put to use in the literature. For a review and comparison of some of the most popular forms see Bauer *et al.* (1998) and Berger and Humphrey (1997). As noted, we rely on established procedures to address our interest in measuring the effects of mis-measured input prices as directly as possible. For the cost model, we follow Lang and Welzel (1996) and employ a multi-output translog function and amend time trend variables to capture technological change. For a bank k this cost function takes on the form

$$
\begin{aligned}
\ln C_k(w_k, y_k, z_k) = {} & \alpha_0 + \sum_{i=1}^{3} \alpha_i \ln w_{ik} + \sum_{m=1}^{3} \beta_m \ln y_{mk} + \delta_0 \ln z_k \\
& + \frac{1}{2}\sum_{i=1}^{3}\sum_{j=1}^{3} \alpha_{ij} \ln w_{ik} \ln w_{jk} + \sum_{i=1}^{3}\sum_{m=1}^{3} \gamma_{im} \ln w_{ik} \ln y_{mk} \\
& + \frac{1}{2}\sum_{m=1}^{3}\sum_{n=1}^{3} \beta_{mn} \ln y_{mk} \ln y_{nk} + \frac{1}{2}\delta_1 (\ln z_k)^2 \\
& + \sum_{i=1}^{3} \varepsilon_i \ln w_{ik} \ln z_k + \sum_{m=1}^{3} \zeta_m \ln y_{mk} \ln z_k + \eta_0 t + \frac{1}{2}\eta_1(t)^2 \\
& + \sum_{i=1}^{3} \kappa_i \ln w_{ik} t + \sum_{m=1}^{3} \tau_m \ln y_{mk} t + \delta_2 \ln z_k t + \varepsilon_k.
\end{aligned}
$$

(10.5)

As outlined previously, w_i denotes input prices, y_m denotes outputs and z depicts the level of equity capital. As shown here, the model employs endogenous input prices, that is each bank's individual price. This specification is the baseline case, which represents the approach followed most frequently in the literature. We subsequently substitute w_i's from three respective market definitions introduced in the following subsection to investigate the effects on efficiency and robustness of estimation results.

For the alternative profit model the only change refers to the left-hand side variable. Instead of cost we employ ln PBT as dependent variable. Note, however, that this poses a problem when having banks with zero or negative profits. Two approaches exist to curb this problem. One is to add the minimum profit plus one to all banks' profits. Alternatively, one might choose to simply exclude those banks with negative profits. Both approaches bear the risk of leading to biased results. However, our data has relatively few banks with negative profits while the minimum value is an extreme outlier.[7] We feel that the cost of reducing our sample size by only a few observations is less compared to inflating all profits by such an extreme value. We therefore opt to exclude banks with zero and negative profits.

As noted in Coelli *et al.* (1998), certain restrictions have to be imposed before estimation. These are depicted by

$$\sum_{i=1}^{3} \alpha_i = 1, \quad \sum_{i,j=1}^{3} \alpha_{ij} = 0 \quad \text{for all } i \text{ and } j,$$

$$\sum_{i=1}^{3} \gamma_i = 0, \quad \sum_{i=1}^{3} \varepsilon_i = 0, \quad \sum_{i=1}^{3} \kappa_i = 0,$$

$$\alpha_{ij} = \alpha_{ji} \quad \text{and} \quad \beta_{mn} = \beta_{nm} \quad \text{for all } i, j, m \text{ and } n.$$

The first restrictions require linear homogeneity in input prices. An increase in input prices should result in proportionally increased total cost. Put differently, the input mix a bank chooses to produce its outputs is not altered if all prices are inflated identically. Only relative price changes result in different input mixes. We impose these restrictions by normalising all factor price variables and the dependent variable by one factor price. Consequently, only two input price coefficients are estimated and the third one can be recovered from the homogeneity conditions. The second restriction stems from the use of duality when estimating a cost function and refers to the symmetry of cross partial derivatives of the conditional factor demand functions.

To measure inefficiency, SFA assumes a composed error term. The error term ε_k in equation (10.5) consists partly of random noise, v_k, and partly of inefficiency, u_k. In the case of a cost frontier, inefficiency implies above frontier costs incurred. Therefore, it enters the error term with a positive sign, leading to $\varepsilon_k = v_k + u_k$.

For the case of a profit frontier, inefficiency results in below frontier profits and therefore it must be subtracted, leading to $\varepsilon_k = v_k - u_k$. Following Battese and Coelli (1988) we assume the random error term v_k to be i.i.d. with $v_k \sim N(0, \sigma^2_v)$ and independent of the explanatory variables. The inefficiency term is i.i.d. with $u_k \sim |N(0, \sigma^2_u)|$.[8] We use Ordinary Least Squares (OLS) estimates as starting values when maximising in a second step the maximum likelihood function derived by Aigner *et al.* (1977). We employ their re-parameterisation of $\lambda = \sigma_u/\sigma_v$ and $\sigma^2 = \sigma^2_v + \sigma^2_u$. Consequently, λ indicates the ratio of standard deviation attributable to inefficiency relative to the standard deviation due to random noise. An insignificant estimate of λ means that no inefficiency prevails. All of the error is due to random noise and specification of a stochastic frontier model is inappropriate.

Next, we need a way to obtain firm-specific efficiency measures in the case of a cost frontier. For firm-specific efficiency estimates Jondrow *et al.* (1982) found that the conditional expectation of the u_k given ε_k can be used. Following Battese and Coelli (1988), a measure of CE is calculated as

$$CE_k = [\exp(u_k)]^{-1}.$$

This measure takes a value between 0 and 1 where the latter indicates a fully efficient bank. The value indicates which percentage of observed cost would have been enough to produce the observed output if the bank was fully efficient. By obtaining firm-specific efficiency estimates we are able to examine whether alternative input price specifications identify different banks as best or worst performers, that is whether the ranking of firms is sensitive when correcting for mis-measured prices. Similarly, a measure of PE is calculated as

$$PE_k = [\exp(-u_k)].$$

This measure also ranges between 0 and 1 and indicates the percentage of actual profits relative to what the bank could have realised given its input quantity and output price mix. Specification of PE under imperfect output markets allows us also to identify those banks, which are best practice performers on both the cost and the revenue dimension of banking. We turn now to our benchmark definition of input prices and three alternative market definitions, which we employ to measure exogenous prices.

10.3.3 Input prices and markets

Specification errors in efficiency analysis can arise from two major reasons. On the one hand, they can result from the inappropriate use of a production model based on perfect competition. If markets are deviating considerably from the most important characteristics of perfect markets, alternative theoretical models such as monopolistic competition or oligopoly models should serve as a point of departure. On the other hand, specification errors can be the result of data construction, which is only remotely suited to represent the desired variable from the theoretical model. Consider as an example the frequent use of labour expenses over total assets as a measure of the price of labour (see, for example, Altunbas *et al.*, 2001 or Lang and Welzel, 1996). An improved specification to measure the cost of labour might rather use the contractual wage rate and/or distinguish between different kinds of labour, for example high versus low skilled work.

To put our approach into perspective we begin with a motivation of our model choice in Section 10.3.1, which is based on perfect competition. Second, we straighten out which kind of adjustments we conduct to improve the specification of efficient cost and profit frontiers. The first question is therefore whether one is willing to assume that a production model based on the assumptions of perfect competition is appropriate to describe German banking. Therefore, we should be confident that the most basic properties of perfect markets, namely an atomistic market structure, no transaction cost and information transparency, hold to a sufficient degree.

Bikker and Haaf (2001) provide a recent overview of the extensive literature on bank market structure. While the evidence remains mixed, Bikker and Haaf (2002) note that on the basis of concentration measures Germany is among the most atomistic markets compared to other industrialised economies. Regarding transaction cost and the degree of accessibility of information the ECB (2002) notes that both the use of automated services like ATMs and Internet banking and the increasing availability of low-cost and high-quality information continues to spur competition in EU banking markets. In sum, we cannot rule out market imperfections based on results in the literature. But as noted in Hempell (2004) the available evidence leads us to accept that a theoretical model from the realm of perfect competition is superior to imperfect market models in the German case. We are therefore confident that the approach taken in the efficiency literature to build upon models along the lines suggested in Section 10.3.1 is appropriate. Consequently, we focus on measurement errors arising from deficiencies of the employed data to represent model variables. This approach also enables us to compare results from our approach with those from data usually applied and we can assess the importance of this measurement error.

Let us therefore turn now to the clarification of the measurement error we address. In both the cost and alternative profit model the factor prices for inputs, w_i, are exogenous variables. They are assumed to be determined in their respective factor markets and enter the production model in Section 10.3.1 as given. But the input prices employed in most studies are calculated for each bank individually and can thus be regarded as endogenous. Consider as an illustration the production factor of fixed assets (FA). The traditional way to arrive at a price for the input FA relates to the expenses on FA, that is rent, depreciation or other expenses on FA, to the employed quantity of that factor, that is the average value of FA used. This way we arrive at an average price of FA for each bank.

In our empirical investigation we define this specification of input prices as our benchmark model. We refer to it for the cost frontier as model 1.1 and in the alternative profit case we label it as model 2.1, respectively. But under perfect competition we expect the equilibrium price of FA to be determined, for example, in real estate markets.[9] In a simple market model this input price is identical for all banks – the very notion of price taking.

We regard the approach to use individual bank prices versus the use of one identical price for each input across all banks as two polar cases. The former allows each bank to possess extensive pricing power within a model of perfect competition as opposed to the assumption that no bank can influence prices whatsoever. While the shortcoming of the former approach to appropriately reflect the underlying theoretical model is obvious, we also regard the latter approach as suboptimal for two reasons. On a more empirical note the use of one single price for each production factor would prohibit estimation of cross-sectional data completely and reduce all variation in panel estimations to be the result of changes over time. An argument related to theory concerns the evidence presented in Section 10.2.2. A number of bank market studies highlight the existence and importance of different markets within certain geographical regions. The crucial question is then how to define a market.

Studies on German banking suggest that efficiency differences persist between banks of different sector, region and size. The notion of separate markets on the basis of sectors is supported by Edwards and Fischer (1993). They note that regulators and the government continue to favour the 'three-pillar-system'.[10] According to Hempell (2004) the existence of different markets between different sectors is further illustrated by strict demarcation between private and public banks. Most recent tendencies to allow commercial banks to buy savings banks still face massive opposition by the respective lobbies (see, for example, Krosta and Schmid, 2003) and therefore changes cannot be expected soon, if at all. The existence of regional markets within the sector of public banks is underlined by the fact that distinct separation of regional activities for each cooperative and savings bank are enforced.[11] With regard to size as a distinguishing argument, it appears that only bigger institutes, both commercial and public, operate federally. The majority of small and medium sized banks concentrate on certain states, too.[12]

Therefore, we assume that markets can be defined by states and size classes. The price a bank faces to purchase inputs is determined in these markets. For each bank, k, this price is the average of prices paid by all other banks in that market excluding the bank's own price. We start with the benchmark model x.1 introduced earlier. We calculate each bank's own price. It is calculated by taking expenditure over inputs employed to arrive at a price for each input for each bank, w_{ik}, where $k = 1, \ldots, K$ indexes a bank and K is the total number of banks in a market m. This step is illustrated in the example given in Table 10.1 under the heading 'Benchmark model'.

In the benchmark model each bank is treated as if it operated in its own market m. To specify exogenous input prices we start by defining different markets distinguished first by state and second within each state by size classes. The last three columns under the heading 'Market model' illustrate that, first, banks within state 1 are considered and, second, are further distinguished into size classes 1 and 2, respectively. Hence we have two markets m in state 1 as indicated by the last column in Table 10.1 containing three banks, respectively. For a bank k in market m the price it faces is then $w_{il} = \sum_{k=1; l \neq k}^{K} w_{ik}/(K - 1)$. To illustrate this

Table 10.1 Illustration of input price calculation

Bank k	Input level	i = FA expenses	State	Size	Benchmark model			Market model		
					Calculation	w_{ik} (%)	m	Calculation	w_{ik} (%)	m
1	100	20	1	1	20/100	20.0	1	(0.2 + 0.12)/(3–1)	16.0	1
2	1,000	250	1	2	250/1,000	25.0	2		7.5	2
3	2,000	400	1	1	400/2,000	20.0	3	(0.2 + 0.12)/(3–1)	16.0	1
4	500	25	1	2	25/500	5.0	4		17.5	2
5	250	30	1	1	30/250	12.0	5	(0.2 + 0.2)/(3–1)	20.0	1
6	750	75	1	2	75/750	10.0	6		15.0	2
7	1,600	120	2	1	120/1,600	7.5	7		15.0	3
8	900	203	2	2	202.5/900	22.5	8		12.5	4
9	300	53	2	1	52.5/300	17.5	9		10.0	3
10	1,200	180	2	2	180/1,200	15.0	10		16.3	4
11	800	100	2	1	100/1,800	12.5	11		12.5	3
12	400	40	2	2	40/400	10.0	12		18.8	4
Mean						14.8			14.8	
SD						6.28			3.59	

procedure for one market consider the three rightmost columns under the heading, 'Market model'. Within market $m = 1$, the first bank, $k = 1$, faces an input price equal to the average input prices paid by the remaining banks in the market, that is, banks $k = 3, 5$.

Note, that this procedure leaves the average input price paid by all banks unaffected. However, the variation of input prices is reduced as can be seen from the last row in the example discussed earlier. Intuitively, the closer the market resembles perfect competition, the lower the variation, because price differences ultimately approach zero until a single market-clearing price prevails. Additionally, those banks that paid, say, the highest price within their market are now modelled to face substantially lower prices (and vice versa). Put differently, extreme values for input prices are levelled out. This implies that we explain in a specification utilising exogenous input prices actual operating cost on the left-hand side with prices prevailing in the market on the right-hand side. If these exogenous prices are better suited to explain costs and profits the total error ε_k in equation (10.5) becomes smaller. Consequently, the *level of efficiency* would also decrease. However, we do not know a priori which specification is, in an empirical sense, superior as measured by a smaller total error. In addition, we expect that the levelling out of extreme input prices leads to a change in the *distribution of efficiency* scores and, hence, relative rankings. To measure the distortions of efficiency measures due to the outlined specification error is thus one major goal of this chapter.

Summing up, the specification of exogenous input prices should not only affect the level of efficiency but also the distribution of efficiency scores. The decisive question of what defines a market is obviously a critical one. As an alternative to the benchmark model (model x.1) we therefore suggest in this chapter three additional approaches how to define a market as a mean to measure input prices (models x.2 through x.4). We start with comparisons of cost frontiers (models 1.y) and continue with profit frontiers (models 2.y). Let us turn now to these three alternative ways on how to determine input prices.

Throughout, we classify banks with more than €50 billion in total assets as large.[13] We start with market definition x.2. In this model we assume that large banks constitute a market of their own across state borders. Hence, small banks face the prices set by the competition in markets defined according to size classes within their states. In contrast, large banks compete for labour, funds and fixed capital on a federal market and face the prices set by other large banks in this geographically bigger market. In a first step, the price each large bank faces is calculated as the average price of all other large banks. In a second step, the procedure is repeated for small banks within their states and size class. The rationale of this specification is for example illustrated by choice of an office building. Small banks are constrained to choose administration offices in the region of their banking activities. They compete with other banks and perhaps even other firms of similar size for, say, buildings of approximately similar capacity. In contrast, large banks are able to choose between one large office complex anywhere in the republic or splitting up operations into several administrations in different locations.

In our third market definition, model x.3, we allow large banks to possess market power in input markets. We utilise exogenous prices for small banks and employ endogenous prices for banks in the federal market. The motivation of this specification is that large banks might have some power to set for example wages when recruiting employees. This market power could result from the fact that only a few banks can offer a high diversity of tasks, quality of work and strong brand image. On the labour supply side they can draw recruitees from a larger pool of persons willing to move to the location of an interesting employer. In contrast, smaller banks which act only on a regional level might be less attractive for mobile employees and are therefore restricted to recruit from a smaller labour pool around their area of activity.

Our final market definition, model x.4, relaxes the assumption of large banks competing on a federal market. Instead, we assume here that large banks are part of regional state markets and represent merely (part of) one of many size classes within their state. The absence of federal competition could be justified when noting the highly fragmented market structure for Germany as a whole. While concentration ratios for other European countries, for example, the Netherlands, are in the region of 80 per cent for the three biggest institutes, the entire commercial sector accounts for just 23 per cent of total assets in Germany. Thus, a conceivable argument is to assume that large banks are simply not large enough to set prices and do therefore not exert market power.

To illustrate the four different approaches we employ once more the example introduced in Table 10.1. Table 10.2 compares the input prices of our four different models.

At this point we like to point out two potential pitfalls. The first concern is that it would be more desirable to define markets strictly on a geographical basis, as

Table 10.2 Comparison of alternative input prices

Bank k	Input level	i = FA expenses	State	Size	Model x.1		Model x.2		Model x.3		Model x.4	
					w_{ik} (%)	m	w_{ik} (%)	m	w_{ik} (%)	m	w_{ik} (%)	m
1	100	20	1	1	20.0	1	16.0	2	16.0	7	16.0	1
2	1,000	250	1	2	25.0	2	12.5	1	25.0	1	7.5	2
3	2,000	400	1	1	20.0	3	16.0	2	16.0	7	16.0	1
4	500	25	1	2	5.0	4	16.5	1	5.0	2	17.5	2
5	250	30	1	1	12.0	5	20.0	2	20.0	7	20.0	1
6	750	75	1	2	10.0	6	15.5	1	10.0	3	15.0	2
7	1,600	120	2	1	7.5	7	15.0	3	15.0	8	15.0	3
8	900	203	2	2	22.5	8	13.0	1	22.5	4	12.5	4
9	300	53	2	1	17.5	9	10.0	3	10.0	8	10.0	3
10	1,200	180	2	2	15.0	10	14.5	1	15.0	5	16.3	4
11	800	100	2	1	12.5	11	12.5	3	12.5	8	12.5	3
12	400	40	2	2	10.0	12	15.5	1	10.0	6	18.8	4
Mean					14.8		14.8		14.8		14.8	
SD					6.28		2.54		5.75		3.59	

Note
Size class 2 depicts large banks in this example.

is done for example in Berger and Mester (2003) who employ data on a county level for US banks. However, market characteristics and data availability are different in the German case. First, no information on bank activity is readily available on a more detailed level than per state. Second, market barriers are to a substantial degree due to demarcation between and within banking sectors. As banks of the three sectors differ considerably in terms of average total assets we believe that size classes are a good approximation to define bank markets where firms compete for inputs. The second concern is that it would be most desirable to use prices resulting from explicit models of input markets. A superior approach might, for example, use information on different kinds of labour employed in a banking firm and apply a labour market model to determine equilibrium wages.

However, the available data do not allow for such an approach. We therefore consider our methodology as a fruitful start to learn about the relevance of this specification problem. We continue in the following subsection by introducing the data employed in our empirical work.

10.4   Data

In this section we start by discussing the data source, definition of variables and peculiarities of the data generation process. Next, we provide descriptive statistics. In accordance with the previously employed determinants of markets, namely region and size, we also present some information from these two angles, respectively. This sequence will also serve as guideline along which we will discuss later on results from our empirical work.

10.4.1   Data sources and processing

The data used in this study is obtained from the Fitch-IBCD 'Bankscope' database. This database serves as source to the majority of European bank efficiency studies. As laid out in Section 10.3.1 we define next to equity capital, z, three inputs and three outputs. As in Altunbas *et al.* (2001) we measure the cost of funds, w_1, by total interest expense over total borrowed funds. Cost of labour, w_2, is measured by total labour expense over total assets and the cost of physical assets, w_3, is measured by the sum of expenses for premises and depreciation over total fixed assets. All level variables are denoted in deflated millions of euro and all price variables are denoted in percentages. Despite frequent use, Bhattacharya (2003) notes that the Bankscope database also suffers from some substantial deficiencies. For German bank data we note that three caveats deserve particular attention.

First, a substantial share of banks do not provide a detailed split-up of their assets. The problem can be curbed to a certain extent by defining outputs more broadly. Still, we had to make some concessions and exclude some banks on grounds of missing observations for one or more of our variables.

The second caveat refers to a considerable amount of specialised banks. Balance sheet and profit and loss account data for these banks are sometimes differently listed in Bankscope compared to commercial banks. This could be a reason why many studies report observations with 'implausible' values, for example, funding cost beyond 100 per cent. We correct for potentially resulting wrong input prices by taking into account bank sector specific accounting procedures.

A third and major problem is the use of up to three different accounting rules applied by single banking firms.[14] Also, the high number of cross-holdings in German banking frequently poses a problem when selecting a sample of banking firms, which are assumed to be independently operating units pursuing their objectives. In order to ensure a sample of comparable banks we carefully screened our data for double entries of banks due to more than one accounting rule included in Bankscope. Where applicable, we used unconsolidated statements of banks and excluded the according consolidated statement of the parent institute. We only selected those statements reporting data according to the German commercial code (*Handelsgesetzbuch, HGB*).

10.4.2 Full sample

This process left us with 13,923 observations from all sectors during the period between 1994 and 2001.[15] Table 10.3 provides descriptive statistics of all variables employed in SFA and total assets with their mean values in the period 1994–2001.

Table 10.3 illustrates that the most important line of activity in German banking is credit business as exhibited by the substantially higher amount of loans produced compared to OBS and securities. The growing importance of OBS activities for all banks is underlined by a compound annual growth rate of 5.3 per cent for y_2 as opposed to 2.5 per cent for y_1 and 2.7 per cent for y_3 during the eight years of observation. The distribution of outputs, equity and total assets clearly illustrates the heterogeneity of firms in our sample. While some banks only had outstanding loans on the order of some thousand euro, the largest bank recorded a position of outstanding loans worth €220 billion in a single year. The standard deviation of input prices underlines two issues. First, substantial differences

Table 10.3 Descriptive statistics between 1994 and 2001

Variable	Mean	SD	Skew	Kurt	Minimum	Maximum	N
y_1	1,603.70	9,062.04	12.98	211.73	0.1	220,177	13,923
y_2	597.64	3,899.04	16.70	364.38	0.1	140,046	13,923
y_3	425.73	3,956.45	17.08	342.57	0.1	114,277	13,923
w_1	0.0384	0.0098	9.383	253.28	0.0036	0.4267	13,923
w_2	0.0144	0.0064	8.765	181.69	0.0002	0.2009	13,923
w_3	0.1661	0.1129	2.778	12.65	0.0120	0.9624	13,923
z	113.3	731.3	16.5	332.1	0.7	19,620	13,923
TA	3,096.5	19,097.2	13.8	241.9	10.8	566,509	13,923
TOC	47.2	299.8	24.1	808.9	0.4	13,851	13,923
PBT	12.6	96.1	51.4	4,058.6	−937.6	8,289.4	13,923

Note
All level variables measured in millions of €.

among banks and, second, potential measurement problems. The latter becomes apparent from minimum and maximum values for w_is. We therefore believe that accounting for random error due to measurement error is an important feature of our methodology.

As we intend to measure CE and PE with exogenous prices we calculate input prices on the basis of geographically and size-wise determined markets. For this reason we provide subsequently some descriptive statistics from these two perspectives, respectively.

10.4.3   A regional angle

To capture the aspect of regional markets we created a new dataset. We used city information of each bank provided by Bankscope and matched this with a dataset from the federal bureau of statistics to allocate state codes to each bank.[16]

As one might suspect Table 10.4 underpins substantial differences in terms of banking market coverage and mean size of banks across states.

Note, that differences in mean total assets are not limited to an 'East'-effect. Substantial differences exist also among western states. Some states exhibit a local market structure with many, relatively small banks. Examples are Bavaria, Baden-Wuerttemberg and to a lesser extent North Rhine-Westphalia. Other states appear to home only few but large banks, for example Berlin and Hamburg. Contrary to what one might expect, not all large banks concentrate around Frankfurt in Hesse. Only 80 out of 171 large bank observations can be found there

Table 10.4 Mean bank size and input prices per state

State	TA	w_1	w_2	w_3	N
Baden-Wuerttemberg	1,698.6	0.039	0.014	0.140	2,830
Bavaria	2,550.5	0.039	0.015	0.153	2,962
Berlin[a]	14,553.4	0.045	0.010	0.239	138
Brandenburg[a]	1,176.9	0.029	0.013	0.268	169
Bremen	3,826.8	0.042	0.015	0.168	110
Hamburg	6,532.3	0.041	0.015	0.273	218
Hesse	10,267.8	0.042	0.014	0.210	1,405
Mecklenburg-Western Pomerania[a]	588.3	0.029	0.015	0.278	160
Lower Saxony	2,086.1	0.037	0.016	0.149	1,184
North Rhine-Westphalia	2,587.0	0.039	0.015	0.153	2,576
Rhineland-Palatinate	1,261.4	0.038	0.015	0.156	856
Saarland	1,331.4	0.038	0.014	0.156	191
Saxony-Anhalt[a]	687.6	0.028	0.013	0.251	204
Saxony[a]	1,644.5	0.031	0.013	0.219	325
Schleswig-Holstein	2,179.3	0.040	0.015	0.161	417
Thuringia[a]	710.1	0.031	0.013	0.242	178
Federal average	3,096.5	0.038	0.014	0.166	13,923

Note
a Indicates states from the former German Democratic Republic. Total assets in millions of €.

and it appears that some large banks are located elsewhere. This might indicate that even for large banks certain regional boundaries exist as they focus on markets where they are located.

Differences in input prices per state are also illustrated in Table 10.4. As one might expect labour prices differ considerably between states. This is in line with the frequently raised claim that the labour force is relatively immobile in Germany. More surprisingly, the cost of borrowing and especially the cost of fixed assets also differ substantially between regions. We therefore believe that accounting for input prices determined differently per region is necessary when evaluating CE and PE.

10.4.4 A size angle

To highlight the differences between banks of different size consider Table 10.5. It depicts descriptive statistics for the three input prices according to our four market definitions of large banks versus small banks.

The upper panel in Table 10.5 displays the three specified input prices for large banks and the lower panel exhibits input prices for small banks. A comparison illustrates the difference according to size. As the mean is identical across alternative market models it is shown only once for each group and input, respectively. Large banks appear to pay a substantially higher average price for borrowed funds, w_1, and a somewhat higher average price for fixed assets, w_3. In contrast, mean cost of labour, w_2, is substantially lower. While we do not inquire at this stage into possible explanations we take these descriptive statistics as evidence that large banks constitute a group of their own. Consequently, our market definitions take the role of large banks rightfully into account.

In the spirit of the example exhibited in Table 10.2 we also display the different standard deviations per bank group and model. In model x.2 the smoothing effect of the data procedure becomes apparent. For banks of both sizes the standard deviation of all three input prices is reduced substantially. Note, however, that this smoothing effect is largest for the group of large banks in model x.2, where large banks are treated as part of a federal market. In this model, we emphasise the difference between large and small banks by drawing regionally

Table 10.5 Input prices across models

Variable	Mean	SD per model				N
		x.1	*x.2*	*x.3*	*x.4*	
w_1	0.050	0.0086	0.0029	0.0086	0.0070	171
w_2	0.003	0.0032	0.0010	0.0032	0.0025	171
w_3	0.195	0.1371	0.0188	0.1371	0.1041	171
w_1	0.038	0.0097	0.0057	0.0057	0.0061	13,752
w_2	0.015	0.0063	0.0036	0.0036	0.0039	13,752
w_3	0.166	0.1125	0.0600	0.0600	0.0622	13,752

different market boundaries. But within both groups, markets are assumed to be perfect in as much as an individual bank's price is determined by its competitors prices. Hence, a lower variation in prices is in line with utilising data resembling more closely the polar case of one single price for each bank.

In contrast, model x.3 allows for some additional market imperfections on behalf of large banks. We allow large banks to set their own prices and therefore the standard deviation of this group naturally resembles the variation already seen in the benchmark case. For smaller banks we continue to assume operations on nearly perfect markets defined by state and size classes. Thus, their standard deviation equals the results for model x.2. This model displays the largest overall variation of prices among all alternatives employing exogenous input prices because the difference between large and small banks is most pronounced. We expect it therefore to highlight especially efficiency differences between these two groups.

Ultimately, we consider in model x.4 the case when large banks are just part of their local markets. They constitute merely one of the size classes per state. Therefore, the price variation in this model is in-between the ones found in models x.3 and x.2, respectively. Regarding the former, variation of input prices is smaller as the smoothing effect of averaging prices per market decreases the influence of extreme values, which are included in model x.3. With respect to the latter, the variation is higher compared to model x.2 because the number of banks in the large bank size class is in most states very small per year. Hence, the approach of taking averages of the remaining banks does not have such a pronounced smoothing effect.

To see the differences in CE and PE estimates due to alternative input price specifications we turn next to the discussion of our empirical results.

10.5   Empirical findings

We first compare estimation results across cost frontier models 1.1 through 1.4. CE results from the benchmark model are compared with CE estimates according to the three market definitions introduced in Section 10.3.3. Our main findings suggest that, first, CE estimates are most sensitive to the market definition where large banks possess market power. Second, the development over time is fairly stable but efficiency differences across regions vary strongly, depending on the cost model employed. Third, large banks suffer more from cost inefficiencies than small banks.

Next, we provide results from the alternative profit specification. In a nutshell, mean alternative PE appears to be determined mostly by inefficient output mixes and is therefore hardly affected by the specification of alternative input prices. Furthermore, the time pattern exhibits much more volatility than in the cost case. But geographically, results are less dispersed both between states and models. The difference between large and small banks in terms of mean PE confirms the findings from CE – large banks are less efficient.

Finally, we compare CE and PE results from the alternative market definitions with each other. The most important take-away is that only very few banks manage to achieve simultaneous efficiency and we inspect our results as to identify the characteristics of these top performers in terms of size, sector and region.

10.5.1 Cost frontier

In this subsection we start by discussing the estimation results, continue with an inspection of regional and time differences of efficiency and close with a CE comparison between banks of different size.

10.5.1.1 Estimation results and CE

Table 10.6 depicts parameter estimates for cost frontiers estimated with different input price specifications, respectively. Model 1.1 depicts the specification with endogenous prices for each single bank. It therefore represents the benchmark model and resembles the approach usually employed in efficiency studies. The results presented for model 1.2, in contrast, employ input prices determined on several regional markets for small banks and on one federal market for large banks. Model 1.3 only differs as large banks possess market power in input markets. Finally, model 1.4 treats all banks as part of their regional market. Large banks are thus part of one or more size classes within a regional market.

We have employed the cost of borrowed funds, w_1, to impose homogeneity in input prices.[17] All specifications exhibit mostly significant parameter estimates at conventional levels.[18] Unfortunately, interpretation of single coefficients is not straightforward due to interaction terms. We therefore abstain from any conclusions of this kind and focus on the question whether our models support the hypothesis that inefficiency explains indeed some of the deviations from the frontier.

To this end consider the estimate of λ, the ratio of variation attributable to inefficiency relative to random noise. With the exception of model 1.4 this parameter is significant and different from zero. We therefore conclude that inefficiency prevails if we assume that large banks constitute a federal market with or without market power. While λ is insignificant in model 1.4 the estimations of this model are very sensitive to changes of the step lengths. Iterations are already high for a fairly wide grid and quickly ran out of hand when tightening it. We therefore do not have much faith that we reached a global maximum. More importantly, it is not very conceivable from a theoretical viewpoint that no inefficiency prevails in German banking. On these grounds we discard this specification and conclude that large banks are not part of local markets and should be modelled to constitute a market of their own across state borders.

Turning attention to the ratio of variation due to inefficiency relative to random noise, λ, we note a substantial drop for model 1.2 compared to the traditional specification with endogenous prices. At the same time total standard deviation, σ, is virtually identical between the two models. This implies that the explanatory power of our model specifying exogenous prices is as good as usually employed endogenous prices. But a notable result is that fewer banks are deemed

Table 10.6 Cost frontier estimates between 1994 and 2001

Model	Cost 1.1		Cost 1.2		Cost 1.3		Cost 1.4	
N	13,923		13,923		13,923		13,923	
Iterations	43		45		15		63	
σ_v^2	0.0235		0.0728		0.0368		0.0760	
σ_u^2	0.0613		0.0144		0.1359		0.0000	
	Coefficient	p	Coefficient	p	Coefficient	p	Coefficient	p
Variable								
Intercept	2.375	0.000	4.003	0.000	3.356	0.000	3.609	0.985
$\ln y_1$	0.273	0.000	−0.036	0.056	0.041	0.019	0.064	0.000
$\ln y_2$	0.170	0.000	−0.018	0.279	0.028	0.072	0.005	0.746
$\ln y_3$	0.141	0.000	0.033	0.032	0.056	0.000	0.045	0.001
$\ln w_2$	0.576	0.000	0.373	0.000	0.496	0.000	0.341	0.000
$\ln w_3$	−0.144	0.000	−0.856	0.000	−0.830	0.000	−0.560	0.000
$\ln z$	0.256	0.000	0.550	0.000	0.570	0.000	0.453	0.000
$\frac{1}{2}\ln y_1 \ln y_1$	0.112	0.000	0.109	0.000	0.140	0.000	0.115	0.000
$\frac{1}{2}\ln y_1 \ln y_2$	−0.086	0.000	−0.079	0.000	−0.077	0.000	−0.100	0.000
$\frac{1}{2}\ln y_1 \ln y_3$	−0.026	0.000	−0.029	0.000	−0.028	0.000	−0.030	0.000
$\frac{1}{2}\ln y_2 \ln y_2$	0.089	0.000	0.087	0.000	0.082	0.000	0.091	0.000
$\frac{1}{2}\ln y_2 \ln y_3$	−0.013	0.000	0.040	0.000	0.046	0.000	0.030	0.000
$\frac{1}{2}\ln y_3 \ln y_3$	0.033	0.000	0.045	0.000	0.050	0.000	0.042	0.000
$\frac{1}{2}\ln w_2 \ln w_2$	0.030	0.000	−0.706	0.000	−0.555	0.000	−0.584	0.000
$\frac{1}{2}\ln w_2 \ln w_3$	0.125	0.000	0.100	0.104	0.021	0.697	0.130	0.004
$\frac{1}{2}\ln w_3 \ln w_3$	0.059	0.000	0.260	0.000	0.299	0.000	0.170	0.000
$\frac{1}{2}\ln z$	0.015	0.002	0.025	0.000	0.012	0.033	0.013	0.022

$\ln y_1 \ln w_2$	0.010	0.003	-0.044	0.000	-0.056	0.000	0.001	0.937
$\ln y_1 \ln w_3$	-0.001	0.611	0.044	0.000	0.051	0.000	0.017	0.007
$\ln y_2 \ln w_2$	0.056	0.000	0.136	0.000	0.129	0.000	0.100	0.000
$\ln y_2 \ln w_3$	0.018	0.000	0.119	0.000	0.131	0.000	0.106	0.000
$\ln y_3 \ln w_2$	0.006	0.013	-0.129	0.000	-0.117	0.000	-0.118	0.000
$\ln y_3 \ln w_3$	-0.026	0.000	0.000	0.964	-0.012	0.032	-0.003	0.634
$\ln y_1 z$	-0.038	0.000	0.017	0.000	-0.025	0.000	0.018	0.000
$\ln y_2 z$	-0.013	0.000	-0.028	0.000	-0.046	0.000	-0.021	0.000
$\ln y_3 z$	-0.010	0.000	-0.066	0.000	-0.061	0.000	-0.057	0.000
$\ln w_2 z$	-0.048	0.000	0.055	0.000	0.059	0.000	0.039	0.000
$\ln w_3 z$	0.054	0.000	-0.075	0.000	-0.086	0.000	-0.037	0.000
t	-0.118	0.000	-0.141	0.000	-0.081	0.000	-0.123	0.000
t^2	0.010	0.000	0.006	0.000	-0.004	0.000	0.007	0.000
$\ln y_1 t$	0.014	0.000	0.005	0.000	-0.009	0.000	0.004	0.000
$\ln y_2 t$	0.000	0.768	0.005	0.000	0.001	0.400	0.005	0.000
$\ln y_3 t$	-0.002	0.001	-0.001	0.433	0.016	0.000	0.001	0.987
$\ln w_2 t$	0.026	0.000	-0.038	0.000	-0.053	0.000	-0.027	0.000
$\ln w_3 t$	0.014	0.000	0.018	0.000	0.008	0.027	0.012	0.001
λ	1.615	0.000	0.445	0.000	1.921	0.000	0.002	1.000
σ	0.291	0.000	0.295	0.000	0.416	0.000	0.276	0.419

Notes

σ_u^2 – the variance of inefficiency, σ_v^2 – the variance of random noise, $\lambda^2 = \sigma_u / \sigma_v$ – the ratio of standard deviations due to inefficiency over random noise, σ – total standard deviation, where $\sigma^2 = \sigma_u^2 + \sigma_v^2$.

inefficient, as can be seen by the decline of λ. Apparently, specification of endogenous prices overstates inefficiencies. To the extent that this reflects the existence of input prices determined in local markets this result is in line with studies mentioned in Section 10.2.2, which find higher efficiency when accounting for market characteristics.

The results for model 1.3 illustrate that allowing large banks to have some market power in input markets alters results substantially. From a theoretical viewpoint this model is interesting because a number of studies on market structure found monopolistic competition to prevail in Germany (Molyneux *et al.*, 1994; De Bandt and Davis, 2000; Bikker and Haaf, 2002; Hempell, 2004). While total variation measured by σ deteriorates only slightly, the variance due to inefficiency, σ_u^2, almost doubles. According to our results large banks seem to contribute to a large extent to the inefficiency found in many studies. In line with results from Altunbas *et al.* (2001) large German banks suffer stronger from inefficiency compared to smaller competitors. Table 10.7 provides mean efficiency estimates according to the three models under consideration.

The mean efficiency results obtained from our three models reflect the differences in error parameters discussed earlier. Estimates of CE according to model 1.1 are quite in line with the literature and identify potential savings on the order of 19 per cent of actually incurred cost. The standard deviation and skew indicate that many banks are located fairly close to the frontier. But the number of poor performing banks, sometimes located as far as more than 50 per cent of forgone cost savings below the efficient frontier, is still substantial. The diversity of performance is further underlined by a difference between best- and worst-performing banks of 51.6 per cent.

But this spread in efficiency might partly be due to misspecification rather than identified poor performers. The benchmark frontier estimated with each bank's own input prices might be inappropriate. Instead, 'true' input prices determined in local markets should be used to measure efficiency relative to a benchmark considering local market prices. Accordingly, we expect efficiency estimates to change.

This is confirmed by mean CE in model 1.2, which is 9 per cent higher. Note, that the difference between best- and worst-performing banks declines only moderately. This indicates that model 1.2 still identifies extreme performing banks, which are of particular interest to regulators. But at the same time, accounting for exogenous market prices identifies the majority of banks close to mean efficiency.

Table 10.7 Mean cost efficiency estimates, 1994–2001

Model	Mean	SD	Skew	Kurt	Minimum	Maximum	N
CE model 1.1	0.817	0.095	−1.629	5.978	0.463	0.979	13,923
CE model 1.2	0.907	0.027	−4.586	44.057	0.523	0.978	13,923
CE model 1.3	0.730	0.138	−0.879	3.401	0.366	0.973	13,923

Put differently, employing exogenous input prices 'smoothes' performance and highlights extreme performers, especially at the left tail of the CE distribution. A reason could be that in perfect markets healthy banks gravitate to market averages whereas those banks close to market exit stand out more clearly as poor performers.

As noted earlier, other efficiency studies frequently report that large banks are more inefficient than small banks. However, this result could again be due to misspecification if large banks' efficiency should be measured relative to a frontier, which allows them to possess market power whereas the rest of the banks do not. In model 1.3 we therefore allow this group explicitly to have market power in German input markets. Interestingly, mean CE drops to a level of 73 per cent and the efficiency scores are further dispersed. While most banks are still located close to the frontier the extreme performers are situated very far away from it.

The results underline that the assumptions underlying the specification of input prices affect mean efficiency considerably. But they also influence relative efficiency as measured by the banks' respective rankings. To learn more about the changes in rankings when altering input price specifications we present in Table 10.8 rank–order correlations measured by Spearman's ρ for each year. We are most interested in the changes of efficiency relative to the benchmark model. Therefore, we provide only the comparison with results from model 1.1.

Note that both alternative measures are significantly and positively correlated with CE rankings on the basis of model 1.1, that is when employing endogenous input prices. However, as rankings are not perfectly correlated we conclude that our measures of exogenous prices do not identify the same banks as best and worst performers. This is in line with what we would expect from accounting for different markets by employing respective markets' prices. Some banks traditionally identified as poor performers might be outliers due to misspecification. While our measures of efficiency tend to yield by and large similar rankings they seem to contain additional information, especially in the tail of the efficiency distribution. Thus, regulators might find this approach useful when answering the question, which banks deserve heightened attention in order to allocate their resources.

10.5.1.2 CE over time and across regions

To understand more of the dynamics of CE consider Table 10.9. It depicts the differences of mean cost efficiencies for each model over time. In addition,

Table 10.8 Spearman's ρ for CE relative to model 1.1

Model	1994	1995	1996	1997	1998	1999	2000	2001
CE model 1.2	0.519**	0.514**	0.556**	0.568**	0.611**	0.684**	0.636**	0.645**
CE model 1.3	0.447**	0.408**	0.450**	0.492**	0.527**	0.601**	0.581**	0.600**

Note
** Significant at the 1 percent level (two-tailed test).

Table 10.9 Mean CE over time (%)

Year	CE model 1.1	CE model 1.2	CE model 1.3	C–I ratio
1994	80.83	90.56	68.53	79.2
1995	82.55	90.93	72.50	76.8
1996	82.21	90.88	73.16	76.3
1997	81.47	90.70	73.90	77.2
1998	81.93	90.73	75.02	70.0
1999	82.61	90.83	75.55	80.4
2000	80.92	90.33	72.50	83.7
2001	81.11	90.31	71.18	88.2

we provide a simple accounting-based cost performance measure, namely the cost–income ratios (C–I ratios).

In contrast to the traditional key performance C–I ratios the development of CE over time in Table 10.9 exhibits hardly any changes for models 1.1 and 1.2. This indicates that accounting ratios could deliver an incomplete picture of performance. If increasing competition squeezes interest margins for all banks in the market, C–I ratios naturally rise. However, how well a single bank has been able to convert inputs into outputs cannot be assessed. Our results suggest that the ability of banks to perform this task changed little over time. In contrast, the C–I ratio deteriorates overall and fluctuates considerably. This indicates to us that additional information is contained in CE measures from all models.

Regarding geographical differences in CE, the 'smoothing' effect of employing exogenous prices for all banks is clear from Table 10.10.

The difference between the best- and worst-performing states in model 1.2 is a mere 5.5 per cent and only one state, namely Berlin, is out of line. This underlines once more the feature of this model to identify extreme performers as outliers while allowing most banks to be close to average efficiency. The more heterogeneous picture that emerges from CE scores according to model 1.1 is further pronounced by CE results for model 1.3. This could imply that state performance is largely driven by the number of large banks. Note, however, that a state with many large banks is not *per se* deemed inefficient. For example the decline in mean CE for Hesse, with almost half of all large banks, is far less than the decline in Berlin, which hosts only few large banks.

Note also, that to a certain extent an 'East'-effect can be identified. New states are, with very few exceptions, below the federal average. This suggests that structural deficiencies still have an impact and should be considered when specifying a cost frontier. As we focus on the impact of input price specification, we postpone investigation of this issue until further research. From a regional perspective another interesting result is that so-called city states, for example Hamburg, exhibit below average CE. Especially if the share of total assets commanded by large banks is high, as is the case for Berlin, this holds true. This might reflect findings in the US efficiency literature that regional risk-diversification improves the efficiency of banks.

Table 10.10 Mean CE across states (%)

State	CE model 1.1	CE model 1.2	CE model 1.3
Baden-Wuerttemberg	81.18	90.62	74.11
Bavaria	83.75	90.87	74.89
Berlin[a]	68.56	85.83	56.29
Brandenburg[a]	71.92	89.94	66.82
Bremen	82.01	91.41	73.07
Hamburg	78.54	90.57	67.81
Hesse	78.20	90.02	68.61
Mecklenburg-Western Pomerania[a]	77.05	90.66	75.74
Lower Saxony	85.65	91.41	76.20
North Rhine-Westphalia	84.19	91.04	73.48
Rhineland-Palatinate	83.61	90.86	73.85
Saarland	81.93	90.80	72.82
Saxony-Anhalt[a]	73.13	90.07	70.93
Saxony[a]	68.47	89.03	62.66
Schleswig-Holstein	83.11	90.88	72.98
Thuringia[a]	73.58	89.76	68.45
Federal average	81.70	90.70	73.00

Note
a Indicates states from the former German Democratic Republic.

Table 10.11 Cost efficiency differences

Model	Group	Mean (%)	SD	N	t-test[a]
1.1	Large banks	63.5	0.142	171	16.89**
1.1	Small banks	82.0	0.092	13,752	
1.2	Large banks	83.9	0.092	171	9.82**
1.2	Small banks	90.8	0.024	13,752	
1.3	Large banks	37.8	0.037	171	16.07**
1.3	Small banks	73.4	0.133	13,752	

Notes
a Two-tailed.
** Significant at the 1 percent level.

10.5.1.3   CE from the size perspective

When we inspect individual efficiency estimates more closely, we find that bigger banks are still at the lower end of efficiency scores in German banking. Let us therefore turn to some details of efficiency differences between banks of different size. We also suggest a method to assess the implications for foregone cost savings of measured inefficiencies.

Specifically, it appears that large banks contribute to a large extent to measured cost inefficiencies. We therefore investigate the difference in means between large and small banks in all of our three models in Table 10.11.[19]

For all three models the difference in means is significantly different from zero. In our model 1.1 most large banks are located far away from the frontier, while for small banks the opposite holds – the majority is located fairly close to full efficiency. By employing our firm-specific CE results we calculate average potential savings per bank and year of €12 million and total average annual savings of €20.7 billion for all banks in our sample.[20] In line with the distribution of efficiency almost half of these potential savings, namely €10.1 billion, accrue among large banks, owing to below average CE of 63.5 per cent in model 1.1. It follows that the marginal benefits to society are larger when regulators focus on improving the efficiency of relatively few large banks.

However, these efficiency results might be biased due to the use of endogenous prices and, as model 1.2 suggests, overstate the losses due to wasteful employment of inputs. In model 1.2 this difference between large and small banks' performance still exists. But the gap between the two groups declines to 7 per cent as opposed to 18.5 per cent in model 1.1. Consequently, annual average savings per bank amount to only €6.7 million and the total of potential annual savings drops to €11.7 billion. Nevertheless, the share of potential savings for the group of large banks even increases as the total amounts to €6.7 billion and now accounts for more than half of total potential savings. Results from this specification therefore confirm the claim that efficiency estimates might be overstated. But they also confirm the notion that the waste of inputs at large banks deserves more attention both in terms of relative efficiency and in terms of absolute amounts of money wasted.[21]

In model 1.3 the difference in CE between large and small banks is most drastic, amounting to almost 40 per cent difference in means. More importantly, many inefficient banks are large, so that foregone potential savings are highest. Annual average savings are almost twice as high as in model 1.1, reaching the order of €22.6 million. Accordingly, too much total costs spent compared to fully efficient use of inputs sum to €39.4 billion. We note that out of 171 large bank observations only 39 referred to large commercial banks while 83 banks are either central cooperative or central savings banks.[22] Thus, commercial large banks did certainly not excel in terms of efficiency but the lion's share of 'wasteful' banking business on the input side occurred with large public banks. This is in line with conventional wisdom from press reports, for example on spectacular failings of investments and fraud accusations at WestLB, Germany's largest Landesbank. This illustrates the need to account for the distribution of top and flop performers. If, as in our sample, the majority of wasteful resource utilisation occurs at large banks the social cost are substantially higher.

In sum, we conclude that specification of endogenous input prices affects CE estimates. Large banks should be treated as operating on a federal market of their own. The approach to treat this large bank market as perfectly competitive leads to higher mean CE, which exhibits little fluctuation over both time and states. In turn, the alternative to treat the large bank market as imperfect in the sense of possessing pricing power amplifies existing differences between CE in different years and states. We carefully note that some evidence from the literature on bank market structure suggests modelling large banks as having some pricing power. However, a more conservative conclusion is that further theoretical work is needed to make this choice. As opposed to this general result we conclude in all cost model specifications that large banks suffer stronger from cost inefficiency. In particular, the number of inefficient, large public banks is fairly high. Finally, we note that the distribution of inefficiency across size groups drives the absolute euro amount of foregone savings. It simply matters if some small cooperative is wasting 30 per cent of its actual cost or if Deutsche Bank does.

But before we come to a final conclusions on the performance of German banks, we note that the ability to manage costs efficiently is of course only one perspective of evaluation. The second perspective refers to the revenue dimension and we therefore turn now to our results from the specifications of alternative profit models.

10.5.2 *Alternative profit frontier*

With the alternative profit approach we investigate banks' abilities to use input and output quantities as efficiently as possible in order to maximise profits. When discussing the results we follow the order in previous sections. First, we provide an overview of estimation results and overall efficiency. Second, we display the dynamics over time and region. Finally, we provide a comparison of alternative PE between banks of different size.

10.5.2.1 *Estimation results and alternative PE*

Analogous to the cost frontier analysis we specify four different models, model 2.1 through 2.4, to estimate alternative profit frontiers that reflect the market definitions discussed in Section 10.3.3.

Alternative PE depicts the deviation from the efficient frontier due to sub-optimal input quantity and output price choices and indicates the percentage of actually realised profits relative to profits that could have been realised. Table 10.12 presents parameter estimates according to our four models for the efficient frontier, respectively.

While the number of insignificant parameters is higher compared to the cost frontiers all four alternative profit models still yield an acceptable number of parameter estimates significantly different from zero. The inclusion of time trend variables describes our data well and the coefficients for t and t^2 indicate that technological improvement had a marginally decreasing positive effect on profits.[23] Note, however, that the total error is roughly three times larger compared to the cost case. This indicates that our alternative profit model is less suited to explain profits. At the same time, the estimated variation due to inefficiency instead of random noise is substantially higher. This indicates that banks are less successful to generate profits compared to their cost management skills. The adequacy to formulate a frontier is confirmed by a significant estimate of λ.

Table 10.12 Alternative profit frontier estimates between 1994 and 2001

	Profit 2.1		Profit 2.2		Profit 2.3		Profit 2.4	
Model	13,388		13,388		13,388		13,388	
N								
Iterations	44		49		45		45	
σ_v^2	0.0574		0.0577		0.0580		0.0567	
σ_u^2	0.7075		0.6563		0.6543		0.6609	
	Coefficient	p	Coefficient	p	Coefficient	p	Coefficient	p
Variable								
Intercept	1.662	0.000	2.280	0.000	2.320	0.000	2.377	0.000
$\ln y_1$	−0.099	0.000	−0.220	0.000	−0.216	0.000	−0.224	0.000
$\ln y_2$	0.003	0.879	−0.007	0.828	−0.012	0.710	0.080	0.009
$\ln y_3$	0.293	0.000	0.121	0.000	0.126	0.000	0.198	0.000
$\ln w_2$	0.116	0.010	0.126	0.347	0.271	0.013	0.359	0.001
$\ln w_3$	−0.926	0.000	−1.311	0.000	−1.335	0.000	−1.428	0.000
$\ln z$	0.494	0.000	0.700	0.000	0.710	0.000	0.548	0.000
$\frac{1}{2}\ln y_1 \ln y_1$	−0.056	0.000	−0.004	0.310	−0.004	0.334	−0.012	0.008
$\frac{1}{2}\ln y_1 \ln y_2$	−0.007	0.399	−0.033	0.000	−0.032	0.000	−0.044	0.000
$\frac{1}{2}\ln y_1 \ln y_3$	0.006	0.210	−0.018	0.001	−0.019	0.000	−0.004	0.399
$\frac{1}{2}\ln y_2 \ln y_2$	0.076	0.000	0.085	0.000	0.086	0.000	0.086	0.000
$\frac{1}{2}\ln y_2 \ln y_3$	−0.113	0.000	−0.062	0.000	−0.063	0.000	−0.071	0.000
$\frac{1}{2}\ln y_3 \ln y_3$	0.011	0.003	0.020	0.000	0.020	0.000	0.016	0.000
$\frac{1}{2}\ln w_2 \ln w_2$	−0.160	0.000	−0.688	0.000	−0.506	0.000	−0.584	0.000
$\frac{1}{2}\ln w_2 \ln w_3$	0.358	0.000	−0.060	0.615	−0.131	0.145	−0.072	0.370
$\frac{1}{2}\ln w_3 \ln w_3$	0.028	0.068	0.154	0.005	0.161	0.003	0.225	0.000
$\frac{1}{2}\ln z$	−0.072	0.000	0.012	0.389	0.008	0.568	−0.011	0.419

$\ln y_1 \ln w_2$	-0.062	0.000	0.000	0.986	0.007	0.639	-0.040	0.006
$\ln y_1 \ln w_3$	0.094	0.000	0.107	0.000	0.107	0.000	0.121	0.000
$\ln y_2 \ln w_2$	-0.027	0.000	-0.053	0.004	-0.059	0.001	-0.046	0.002
$\ln y_2 \ln w_3$	-0.032	0.000	-0.035	0.024	-0.034	0.029	-0.076	0.000
$\ln y_3 \ln w_2$	0.043	0.000	-0.111	0.000	-0.106	0.000	-0.057	0.000
$\ln y_3 \ln w_3$	-0.069	0.000	-0.004	0.759	-0.004	0.733	-0.042	0.000
$\ln y_1 z$	0.052	0.000	0.057	0.000	0.056	0.000	0.055	0.000
$\ln y_2 z$	0.040	0.000	0.022	0.000	0.023	0.000	0.031	0.000
$\ln y_3 z$	0.012	0.005	-0.031	0.000	-0.029	0.000	-0.023	0.000
$\ln w_2 z$	0.038	0.000	0.202	0.000	0.201	0.000	0.157	0.000
$\ln w_3 z$	0.053	0.000	-0.047	0.020	-0.054	0.007	0.033	0.069
t	0.164	0.000	0.141	0.000	0.146	0.000	0.148	0.000
t^2	-0.037	0.000	-0.039	0.000	-0.039	0.000	-0.040	0.000
$\ln y_1 t$	0.026	0.000	0.034	0.000	0.035	0.000	0.031	0.000
$\ln y_2 t$	-0.004	0.039	-0.008	0.000	-0.008	0.000	-0.008	0.000
$\ln y_3 t$	-0.013	0.000	-0.016	0.000	-0.015	0.000	-0.015	0.000
$\ln w_2 t$	-0.035	0.000	-0.070	0.000	-0.065	0.000	-0.078	0.000
$\ln w_3 t$	-0.021	0.000	-0.032	0.000	-0.034	0.000	-0.031	0.000
λ	3.510	0.000	3.373	0.000	3.359	0.000	3.414	0.000
σ	0.875	0.000	0.845	0.000	0.844	0.000	0.847	0.000

Notes

σ_u^2 – the variance of inefficiency, σ_v^2 – the variance of random noise, $\lambda^2 = \sigma_u/\sigma_v$ – the ratio of standard deviations due to inefficiency over random noise, σ – total standard deviation, where $\sigma^2 = \sigma_u^2 + \sigma_v^2$.

Therefore, an average response function given by OLS estimates is inferior to the formulation of a stochastic frontier for our data.

A striking observation is the stability of results across all four models. Neither total variance, σ, nor the ratio of inefficiency over random noise, λ, varies tremendously. We observe only a minuscule improvement of σ in our three exogenous specifications 2.2 through 2.4 compared to the traditionally used approach, indicating that the explanatory power benefits only marginally from our alternative approaches. This suggests that while inefficiencies measured on the input side are rather sensitive to the measurement of input prices, alternative profit inefficiencies appear to result mainly from poor skills in output markets, that is, in taking advantage of the bank's pricing opportunity set. To get a picture of alternative inefficiency according to our models Table 10.13 presents some descriptive statistics.

As already indicated by parameter estimates for the error term, alternative PE is substantially higher than CE, averaging 42 per cent in all four specifications. This implies that the average bank could have realised almost twice the actually accrued profits if it had chosen optimal input and output mixes. These results suggest that inefficiencies arising on the output side of a bank's business outweigh those occurring on the input side alone. The distribution of inefficiency differs in two respects markedly from that of cost inefficiencies. First of all, most banks are no longer located close to the frontier. Instead, a substantial portion of the entire population is far below best practice behaviour and tails are quite fat. Second, the distribution of alternative PE across our four models does hardly change. This indicates that variation of alternative PE is hardly affected by the specification of exogenous input prices. Consequently, sub-optimal behaviour on the input side is of lesser importance as most of the estimated inefficiencies arise from sub-optimal output choices.

In addition we see that the differences of alternative PE between German banks are much larger. Best- and worst-performing firms differ by as much as 70 per cent. One might hypothesise that the larger difference between good and bad banks is partly due to a higher volatility of earnings compared to the volatility of cost. To illustrate this thought, consider two banks that choose to engage more heavily in riskier production plans, for example, by investing in OBS. More specifically, let the two banks speculate on foreign exchange appreciation and depreciation, respectively. Depending on what 'bet' materialises this could lead to identification of one very profit efficient and one strongly inefficient bank. In contrast, on

Table 10.13 Alternative profit efficiency estimates, 1994–2001

Model	Mean	SD	Skew	Kurt	Minimum	Maximum	N
PE model 2.1	0.574	0.194	−0.225	1.916	0.257	0.964	13,388
PE model 2.2	0.584	0.193	−0.266	1.979	0.257	0.964	13,388
PE model 2.3	0.583	0.194	−0.263	1.982	0.256	0.964	13,388
PE model 2.4	0.583	0.193	−0.246	1.965	0.260	0.964	13,388

the expense side of the income statement interest rates, wages and rents are specified in contracts and are therefore less volatile.

While the different nature of various output choices could potentially help to explain larger spreads in profit compared to CE, we would at the same time expect such "lucky draws" to average out over time. We therefore investigated our results more closely to see if poor performers in one year tended to be good performers in another. It turns out that this is not the case – banks exhibiting a poor ability to realise their chances in output markets do so consistently over time. We therefore infer that the fundamental ability of banks to realise profits is more diverse compared to CE. But note also that, a part of this diversity could represent varying degrees of market power. If market power depends partly on size we would expect to identify small banks as more profit inefficient.

To discuss these thoughts further let us therefore turn to a closer investigation of alternative PE from the perspectives of region and size, respectively.

10.5.2.2 Alternative PE over time and across regions

To examine the time pattern of our estimates consider Table 10.14. PE exhibits a much more volatile development over time compared to mean CEs. The minuscule differences between our four models become apparent as all three specifications employing exogenous input prices result in an almost parallel shift of the frontier, resulting in PE improvements of a mere 1 per cent. However, the steep increase during the first three years and the following downward trend is in line with the development of mean return on equity (ROE). Thus, alternative PE is generally in line with accounting indicators.

Regarding the geographical pattern we refer to Table 10.15. Note, that alternative PE is more stable across specifications compared to the cost case. All states are ranked identically under almost any model. In addition, the 'East'-effect is more pronounced. With the exception of Saxony-Anhalt all eastern states perform poorest in Germany, albeit with lower deviation from the federal average compared to the cost case. Apparently, the ability to generate profits has been lower in these states even after 5–12 years after German unification in 1989. This could

Table 10.14 Mean profit efficiency over time

	PE model 2.1 (%)	PE model 2.2 (%)	PE model 2.3 (%)	PE model 2.4 (%)	ROE (%)
1994	53.60	54.02	54.08	54.07	11.63
1995	59.13	59.73	59.76	59.76	12.16
1996	60.79	61.32	61.42	61.40	12.49
1997	59.39	60.41	60.43	60.32	11.67
1998	56.46	57.57	57.49	57.45	16.79
1999	56.57	57.36	57.34	57.25	9.35
2000	56.97	58.18	58.03	58.04	8.58
2001	55.58	57.58	57.39	57.39	6.51

Table 10.15 Mean profit efficiency across states

State	PE model 2.1 (%)	PE model 2.2 (%)	PE model 2.3 (%)	PE model 2.4 (%)
Baden-Wuerttemberg	55.00	56.28	56.28	56.02
Bavaria	55.89	56.93	56.87	56.85
Berlin[a]	42.33	50.83	48.18	47.80
Brandenburg[a]	54.80	55.94	56.00	55.90
Bremen	56.72	55.42	55.26	55.37
Hamburg	53.31	54.30	54.82	54.11
Hesse	55.13	55.71	55.66	55.41
Mecklenburg-Western Pomerania[a]	54.82	56.96	57.19	57.29
Lower Saxony	62.72	63.20	63.25	63.26
North Rhine-Westphalia	62.79	63.07	63.10	63.46
Rhineland-Palatinate	59.68	60.12	60.10	59.96
Saarland	55.19	55.83	55.77	55.57
Saxony-Anhalt[a]	59.80	61.40	61.55	61.64
Saxony[a]	42.61	44.01	43.94	43.88
Schleswig-Holstein	61.21	63.27	63.27	63.29
Thuringia[a]	51.30	53.56	53.61	53.56
Federal average	57.44	58.37	58.34	58.31

Note
a Indicates states from the former German Democratic Republic.

reflect that the identification of successful investment opportunities, solvent debtors and prospering business continues to be more difficult in the new states.[24] The combination of little knowledge of local market conditions and less experience and, hence, expertise in banking core competencies, such as risk assessment, could then have been the reason for below average performance.

The observed poorer CE performance of banks located in city states does not apply to alternative PE. With the exception of Berlin all other city states seem to perform close to the federal average. This suggests that banks are less restricted as to where to sell their products, thereby suffering from no apparent risk-diversification loss, but incur some efficiency losses due to prevailing restrictions on their input markets.

Let us now turn to the question if an 'East'-effect can be detected. Table 10.16 clearly indicates that independent of the assumed market form the difference between banks in East or West Germany is significant and amounts to approximately 6 per cent.

Accounting for different input markets might capture local market conditions to some degree. But we suspect that some of this efficiency gap is still attributable to more adverse macroeconomic conditions in the new states. When examining the time trend of the efficiency gap, our data exhibits convergence between 'new' and 'old' states. For example in model 2.3 this gap amounts to 16 per cent in 1994 and drops to 5 per cent in 2001. We interpret this decline of the East–West gap as evidence that specifying exogenous input prices alone cannot explain all

Table 10.16 Alternative profit efficiency – East versus West

Model	Group	Mean (%)	SD	N	t-test[a]
2.1	West	58.1	0.189	12,310	10.76**
2.1	East	50.3	0.228	1,078	
2.2	West	58.9	0.188	12,310	8.29**
2.2	East	52.8	0.234	1,078	
2.3	West	58.8	0.189	12,310	8.64**
2.3	East	52.5	0.233	1,078	
2.4	West	58.8	0.189	12,310	8.96**
2.4	East	52.5	0.232	1,078	

Notes
a Two-tailed.
** Significant at the 1 percent level.

Table 10.17 Alternative profit efficiency of large versus small banks

Model	Group	Mean (%)	SD	N	t-test[a]
2.1	Large banks	40.8	0.218	165	9.89**
2.1	Small banks	57.6	0.193	13,223	
2.2	Large banks	59.0	0.269	165	0.29
2.2	Small banks	58.4	0.192	13,223	
2.3	Large banks	64.1	0.311	165	2.42*
2.3	Small banks	58.3	0.191	13,223	
2.4	Large banks	56.0	0.295	165	1.01
2.4	Small banks	58.3	0.192	13,223	

Notes
a Two-tailed.
* Significant at the 5 percent level.
** Significant at the 1 percent level.

efficiency differences. It underlines once more the importance to improve ways to account for regional difference, for example, with respect to macroeconomic variables per region. Moreover, it underlines the importance to use also output prices specified along alternative market definitions in order to test whether market power on the output side of banking business is indeed an appropriate assumption.

10.5.2.3   Alternative PE from the size perspective

We investigate differences in mean alternative PE between banks of different size to examine if these differences in alternative PE can be attributed to large banks possessing more market power. We do so for all of our models to see if any qualitative differences exist between different specifications, which has been absent so far. To this end consider Table 10.17.

While the distributional properties depicted in Table 10.13 do not reveal any particular difference between our models a closer look at alternative PE for large versus small banks yields a slightly different picture. Note that, the benchmark model 2.1 identifies large banks as suffering more from inefficiencies, in particular a marked difference of 17 per cent between mean PE of small versus large banks. While identical to the findings in Section 10.5.1 this result is counterintuitive. Recall that our profit frontier models banks to exert market power on output markets. We hypothesise that large banks enjoy more market power and that smaller banks face a more restrictive pricing opportunity set. Therefore, one would expect that in terms of alternative PE large banks should exhibit better performance. As can be seen from our models utilising exogenous input prices results the difference between large and small banks changes considerably. While model 2.2, assuming perfect competition for all banks, already places the two groups close to each other we cannot reject the hypothesis that their means are equal. Thus, the difference of 0.6 per cent cannot be asserted. However, model 2.3, which allows large banks to possess market power in input markets as well, highlights a moderate and significant difference in performance of 6 per cent. This implies that even if both overall mean efficiency estimates and the distribution of efficiency are left fairly unaffected by specifying exogenous input prices, some groups might still be identified wrongly as culprits or role models.[25]

Let us for this reason examine the absolute waste of profits in model 2.1 and model 2.3, respectively. Average annual profits a bank could have earned in addition to actually realised profits amount to €17 million.[26] Total annual savings sum to €28.4 billion for all banks in the sample with profits above zero. When summing potential additional profits for large banks only, our alternative PE estimates yield an impressive €18.1 billion, thereby leading to a share of wasted profits attributable to large banks of 63 per cent. This is considerably higher compared to the cost case. However, when utilising efficiency estimates from our model 2.3 the picture changes somewhat. Annual average profits per bank that have been left on the road decline to €15.2 million and total annual average savings are reduced to €25.3 billion.

We conclude that while mean industry efficiency, time and geographical pattern do not seem to be strongly distorted, the use of endogenous input prices still yield overstated losses due to sub-optimal output choices. But the observation that the most substantial share of waste, approximately 60 per cent, lies with large banks is still confirmed. Annual savings of this group alone still count for €15.3 billion. Hence, while relative efficiency measures between the two groups lead to a higher mean efficiency of bigger banks, the absolute waste of this group still dominates foregone profits of smaller institutes.

Thus, the inference from CE estimates is confirmed that the public interest should focus on large banks even if they enjoy higher relative efficiency. A final note is rewarded when comparing absolute waste due to too high costs incurred versus potential profits foregone. While the higher importance of alternative PE is reflected also by absolutely higher savings it is important to realise that the dramatic differences between relative efficiency scores are mitigated when examining absolute amounts of potential savings. To obtain a complete picture of performance we therefore note that it is important to examine not only relative efficiency scores but also associated absolute savings.

10.5.3   Comparison of CE and alternative PE

To identify well-managed banking firms we are interested in those banks, which handle their costs and profits simultaneously optimal. We therefore compare our efficiency results in Table 10.18.

The low positive correlation implies that only the minority of banks is able to reach optimal behaviour in both the profit and cost dimension at the same time. It appears that initiatives which focus only on revenue generation, for example by means of acquiring new business lines, or cost reductions, for example by laying off employees, are not sufficient to become a successful player. Banks need to adjust both levers in order to stay ahead of their competitors.

We examine some characteristics of those banks that are simultaneously cost and profit efficient versus those that are both cost and profit inefficient. To this end we construct a combined ranking.[27]

In terms of geographical pattern the distribution of best performers is quite representative for the total sample. Notable exceptions are the two states where the vast majority of cooperative banks are located, namely Bavaria and Baden-Wuerttemberg. But at the same time these two states also only host under-proportionally few worst-performing banks. Hence, we might say that southern German banks do not excel but at the same time provide stable, average banking services to their customers. The states facing a higher number of banks performing badly compared to the federal average are Berlin and Hesse. For the former it is especially the Berliner Bankgesellschaft which contributes to this result. It follows that results from bank efficiency analysis with exogenous prices could assist regulators to identify problem banks earlier and thereby reduce social costs to society.

In terms of size, we find that average total assets for the top 10 per cent of banks in this ranking are close to the sample average, namely €3.2 billion for the former group versus €3.1 billion for the latter. In contrast, the group of simultaneous poor performers commands average total assets of €37.9 billion. Hence, it

Table 10.18 Correlation between CE and alternative PE

PE	CE		
	1.1	1.2	1.3
2.1	0.323	0.266	0.347
2.2	0.322	0.196	0.319
2.3	0.296	0.207	0.298
2.4	0.316	0.215	0.314

appears once more that bigger banks face stronger problems to attain both frontiers at the same time.

In terms of banking sector local public banks dominate the group of successful performers in absolute terms – 94 out of 133 banks are either cooperative or savings banks. But this is below the share of local public banks in the total sample, hence, this group is still under-represented. The sector identified as relatively most successful to manage cost and profits are real estate banks, that is, building societies and mortgage banks.[28] Among the 10 per cent of lowest combined rankings commercial banks are clearly over-represented compared to the sample. While they account for 57 per cent of the low performance group they only represent a mere 7.5 per cent of the total population. Hence, our results confirm previous findings in bank efficiency research for Germany that this group deserves particular attention. The second group of banks identified as loosing out are public central banks. This finding provides evidence that the German system of Landesbanks might not be desirable from the viewpoint of efficiency.

10.6   Conclusion

In this chapter we address a measurement error of input prices that leads to biased bank efficiency analyses. We compare efficiency results from a traditional cost and alternative profit frontier with efficiency results when utilising exogenous input prices for German banks. We suggest three possible approaches to define markets in order to determine exogenous input prices. We define markets according to region and size and assume that banks face prices determined by their competitors in respective markets.

Our results lead us to the primary conclusion that efficiency estimates are affected by alternative input price specifications. Therefore, future efficiency research needs to account for this potential misspecification error. However, the influence on CE is markedly higher compared to the impact on alternative PE.

The measurement of inefficiencies relative to a cost frontier leads us to conclude that large banks operate on a federal market when competing for inputs. The influence on CE depends on whether we allow large banks to possess market power or not. If large banks face a competitive federal market average CE is slightly enhanced. To a certain extent this is in line with findings in the literature that specification of the frontier, taking into account regional market characteristics, leads to higher efficiency compared to benchmarking against a common frontier without regional characteristics. However, we also model large banks to possess market power in input markets as some studies suggest that bigger banks enjoy some price setting opportunities. This approach leads to reduced average efficiency and we conclude that more theoretical work is needed to determine which assumption is appropriate. Independent from the model employed we identify large banks to suffer stronger than small banks from inefficient input use. Within this group central savings and cooperative banks account for the largest number of banks.

In addition, our results suggest that public local banks are superior cost managers compared to commercial banks. From our regional information we are able to conclude that a weak 'East'-effect prevails. New states host banks that are less capable to produce outputs with optimal input usage. This result indicates that specifying input prices on the basis of markets defined by size and region does not capture all relevant information. Instead, specification of an efficient frontier is presumably enhanced further when employing local market characteristics.

We also examine banks' abilities to realise opportunities in their output markets by employing the alternative profit approach. Banks are allowed to set output prices subject to a pricing opportunity set and we find that inefficiencies on the basis of foregone profits dominate those arising from sub-optimal input use. But regarding the impact of different input price specifications we observe that mean PE is hardly affected. We conclude that if banks have market power in output markets, arising inefficiencies are predominantly due to sub-optimal use of the bank's pricing opportunity set rather than inefficient input usage. But while mean PE appears to be largely unchanged at first sight we note that the composition of top and worst performers is affected by the use of our alternative models. More specifically, we find that large banks enjoy higher mean efficiency if measured with exogenously determined input prices. This implies that bigger banks are more efficient in utilising their pricing opportunity set. At the same time our calculations of absolute savings, that is, inefficiency in terms of euro instead of percentages, puts the seemingly drastic dominance of profit inefficiency over cost inefficiency into perspective. While relative mean efficiency of the former type equals 58 per cent for virtually all models, the according mean CE for our model using traditional input prices amounts to 82 per cent. The dominance of the former becomes less spectacular when comparing total average annual savings of €28.4 billion in foregone profits with €20.7 billion of total average annual cost savings. Thus, we point out the importance to examine absolute wastes implied by estimated efficiency scores in order to obtain a complete picture where to focus attention in the German banking landscape.

With respect to a comparison of CE and PE our results indicate that only a few banks manage to be simultaneously cost and profit efficient. We identify especially banks of average size located in western states as successful. While local public banks are represented in this top performer group in line with their sample share, especially specialised banks can be found to be efficient in both dimensions over-proportionately.

In sum, we find that our approach to compare alternatively specified input prices complements findings of other German efficiency studies. Our estimations suggest that regional information is an important ingredient in SFA. Further research using additional and more detailed regional data is needed in order to tighten the grid to identify those banking groups, which require heightened attention by scarce resources of regulatory authorities. A related area for future research refers to the identification of the 'best' model. As the models we employ are not nested we are unfortunately not able to statistically test for the 'correct' model, for example by means of a log–likelihood ratio test. Consequently, we require more research on the market structure of both input and output markets to foot our empirical investigation on theoretically more solid grounds.

Here, we restrict ourselves to pointing out the differences from alternative assumptions on underlying market structures and the effects of employing exogenous input prices. Ideally, we can model input markets in the future explicitly in order to estimate equilibrium prices and combine such results with efficiency research.

Acknowledgements

I greatefully acknowledge financial support from The Boston Consulting Group, Germany. Helpful comments by Clemens Kool and Jaap Bos are appreciated. All remaining errors are my own.

Notes

1 Recent applications include for example Akhigbe and McNulty (2003), focusing on profit efficiency of small banks, DeYoung *et al.* (2001), incorporating risk into efficiency measurement, or Berger and Mester (2003) who decompose erosion of US banks performance into static and dynamic efficiency changes.

2 A review of the earlier efficiency literature for European banking markets can be found in Molyneux *et al.* (1997). Recent country studies are for example focusing on transitional or less developed banking systems (Canhoto and Dermine 2003, Hasan and Marton 2003), particular types of banks such as universal (Rime and Stiroh, 2003) or savings banks (Prior, 2003) or on the influence of new income sources on efficiency (Tortosa-Ausina, 2003).

3 Dividing interest expenses by borrowed funds provides an example found in virtually each study.

4 Due to the lack of factor market data we are not able to estimate equilibrium input prices.

5 Their variables are: income per capita, salary per capita, population density, density of demand, income per branch, deposit per branch, branches per capita, branch density, equity over total assets and return over equity.

6 For an extensive discussion of possible models of bank production see Freixas and Rochet (1997).

7 This extreme outlier exists in all years and reflects the spectacular almost-failure of Berliner Bankgesellschaft.

8 Greene (1993) surveys the majority of alternative distributions used in studies to model inefficiency. In our application we also tested the half-normal model with truncation at μ. We rejected the model as the estimate of μ was not significantly different from zero in all models.

9 Note, that we argue that all factor costs should be the result of such a market clearing process, not only FA.

10 The three pillars are (private) commercial banks (mutual) cooperative banks and (state-owned) savings banks.

11 In addition to this regulatory enforcement some recent studies addressed the existence of regional markets by means of spatial competition models. For example Park and Pennacchi (2004) present a theoretical model with different price finding mechanisms in deposit and loan markets for large and small banks operating in one or more regional markets. While their model cannot readily be used to derive exogenous prices more rigorously, their findings provide further evidence that our approach to define markets on the basis of size and region is a promising start to measure the impact of misspecified input prices on bank efficiency.

12 For private banks this includes especially the group of banks reported by the Bundesbank as 'Kreditbanken' and includes also so-called 'Privatbanken', where regional specialisation is voluntary. As mentioned, the regional demarcation of activities of public banks is enforced.

13 This is approximately equal to the top 1 per cent of banks in terms of total assets.

14 Some banks prepare annual reports according to, first, international standards such as GAAP or IAS, second, a report for tax authorities and third, a report on the basis of the *Handelsgesetzbuch, HGB* for stakeholders.

15 For the alternative profit model the sample size is reduced to 13,388 observations with non-negative profits.

16 Unfortunately, no data are available on a lower level, for example, municipality or county.

17 We tested whether our results are indeed insensitive to the choice of input price to impose homogeneity restrictions. Therefore, we also estimated all models using w_2 and w_3, respectively. In line with what one would expect results are virtually identical.

18 To test each specification's sensitivity to changes in iteration intervals for the function, slope and intercept when maximising the likelihood function we checked results by starting with a step length of 0.01 and decreased the intervals incrementally until a step length of 0.000001. With the exception of model 1.4 results did not change recognisably in terms of significance and coefficients. We are therefore confident that we have reached global maxima, respectively.

19 Due to the high share of public banks in Germany we also examined the differences between central and local public banks versus commercial and specialised banks. It turned out that public banks enjoyed significantly lower mean cost efficiency on the order of 8 per cent.

20 Potential cost savings per bank are calculated according to $TOCSav_{kt} = [(1 - CE_{kt}) * TOC_{kt}]$.

21 Average operating costs for big banks amount to 1,603.7 while they are only around 27.9 for small banks. That is, a 10 basis point improvement in efficiency at an average big bank would approximately require a 6 per cent improvement in efficiency for an average small bank.

22 The remaining 49 observations were specialised institutes.

23 We conduct for all cost and alternative profit models log–likelihood ratio tests whether a specification without time trend variables is more appropriate. In all cases the reduced model is rejected at conventional significance levels.

24 Alternatively, our benchmark might be biased by fitting a frontier through banks operating in both East and West. A remedy could be to include state specific variables reflecting macroeconomic conditions. But as mentioned earlier we postpone this avenue of research and focus for the moment on the effects of input price specification only.

25 Of course, a significant difference in means does not allow any conclusion about the dominance of one model over the other *per se*. Because the alternative profit models are not nested, likelihood ratio tests are inappropriate to identify the 'correct' model. We therefore have to evaluate the theoretical assumptions underlying these models to decide which one most appropriately describes the situation at hand.

26 We calculate average annual profits foregone according to the sum of optimal profits for each bank less the sum of actually realised profits, divided by the number of all banks in the sample, that is, $[\Sigma_{kt} (PBT_{kt} / PE_{kt} - PBT_{kt})]/N$.

27 The combined rank is calculated as the sum of the rank resulting from CE according to model 1.3 and the rank resulting from PE according to model 2.3.

28 While this result could indicate that a higher degree of specialisation leads to improved efficiency we like to caution before drawing such a strong conclusion. The reason is that this performance could also emanate from fitting a frontier with some extreme outliers like specialised banks. An alternative could be to estimate banking sector specific frontiers and envelop these with a metafrontier as done by Bos and Schmiedel (2003) for country specific frontiers.

References

Aigner, D., C. A. K. Lovell and P. Schmidt (1977, July). 'Formulation and Estimation of Stochastic Frontier Production Function Models'. *Journal of Econometrics*, 6(1), 21–37.

Akhigbe, A. and J. E. McNulty (2003, February). 'The Profit Efficiency of Small US Commercial Banks'. *Journal of Banking and Finance*, 27(2), 307–325.

Altunbas, Y., L. Evans and P. Molyneux (2001, November). 'Bank Ownership and Efficiency'. *Journal of Money, Credit, and Banking*, 33(4), 926–954.

Battese, G. E. and T. J. Coelli (1988, July). 'Prediction of Firm-level Technical Efficiencies with a Generalized Frontier Production Function and Panel Data'. *Journal of Econometrics*, 38(3), 387–399.

Battese, G. and G. Corra (1977). 'Estimation of a Production Frontier Model: With Application to the Pastoral Zone of Eastern Australia'. *Australian Journal of Agricultural Economics*, 21, 169–179.

Bauer, P. W., A. N. Berger, G. D. Ferrier and D. B. Humphrey (1998, March–April). 'Consistency Conditions for Regulatory Analysis of Financial Institutions: A Comparison of Frontier Efficiency Methods'. *Journal of Economics and Business*, 50(2), 85–114.

Berger, A. and D. B. Humphrey (1992). 'Measurement and Efficiency Issues in Commercial Banking', in Z. Griliches (ed.), *Output Measurement in the Service Sectors*. Chicago, IL: The University of Chicago Press, pp. 245–279.

Berger, A. N. and D. B. Humphrey (1997, April). 'Efficiency of Financial Institutions: International Survey and Directions for Future Research'. *European Journal of Operational Research*, 98(2), 175–212.

Berger, A. and L. Mester (1997). 'Inside the Black Box: What Explains Differences in the Efficiencies of Financial Institutions'. *Journal of Banking and Finance*, 21(7), 895–947.

Berger, A. N. and L. J. Mester (2003, January). 'Explaining the Dramatic Changes in Performance of US Banks: Technological Change, Deregulation, and Dynamic Changes in Competition'. *Journal of Financial Intermediation*, 12(1), 57–95.

Bhattacharya, K. (2003). 'How Good is the BankScope Database? A Cross-validation Exercise with Correction Factors for Market Concentration Measures'. BIS Working Paper 133, 1–21.

Bikker, J. A. and K. Haaf (2001). 'Measures of Competition and Concentration: A Review of the Literature'. De Nederlandsche Bank. *Directorate Supervision*, Research Series Supervision No. 30.

Bikker, J. A. and K. Haaf (2002). 'Competition, Concentration and their Relationship: An Empirical Analysis of the Banking Industry'. *Journal of Banking and Finance*, 26(11), 2191–2214.

Bos, J. W .B. and C. J. M. Kool (2004). 'Bank Efficiency: The Role of Bank Strategy and Local Market Conditions'. DNB Working Paper Series 2, 1–24.

Bos, J. W. B. and H. Schmiedel (2003, May). 'Comparing Efficiency in European Banking: A Meta Frontier Approach'. DNB Research Series Supervision 57, 1–32.

Canhoto, A. and J. Dermine (2003, November). 'A Note on Banking Efficiency in Portugal, New vs. Old Banks'. *Journal of Banking and Finance*, 27(11), 2087–2098.

Clark, J. A. and T. F. Siems (2002, November). 'X-efficiency in Banking: Looking Beyond the Balance Sheet'. *Journal of Money, Credit, and Banking*, 34(4), 987–1013.

Coelli, T., D. P. Rao and G. E. Battese (1998). *An Introduction to Efficiency Analysis*. Boston/Dordrecht/London: Kluwer Academic Publishers.

De Bandt, O. and E. Davis (2000). 'Competition, Contestability and Market Structure in European Banking Sectors on the Eve of EMU'. *Journal of Banking and Finance*, 24(6), 1045–1066.

DeYoung, R. (1998). 'X-inefficiency and Management Quality in Commercial Banks'. *Journal of Financial Services Research*, 13, 5–22.

DeYoung, R. E., J. P. Hughes and C. G. Moon (2001, March–June). 'Efficient Risk-taking and Regulatory Covenant Enforcement in a Deregulated Banking Industry'. *Journal of Economics and Business*, 53(2–3), 255–282.

ECB (2002). 'Structural Analysis of the EU Banking Sector'. European Central Bank, Frankfurt am Main, 5–65.

Edwards, J. and K. Fischer (1993). *Banks, Finance and Investment in Germany*. Cambridge: Cambridge University Press.

Freixas, X. and J. C. Rochet (1997). *Microeconomics of Banking*. Cambridge: MIT Press.

Greene, W. H. (1993). *The Econometric Approach to Efficiency Analysis*. New York: Oxford University Press, pp. 69–119.

Hackethal, A. (2004). 'German Banks and Banking structure', in J. P. Krahnen and R. H. Schmidt (eds), *The German Financial System*. Oxford: Oxford University Press, pp. 425–449.

Hasan, I. and K. Marton (2003, December). Development and Efficiency of the Banking Sector in a Transitional Economy: Hungarian Experience. *Journal of Banking and Finance*, 27(12), 2249–2271.

Hempell, H. S. (2004). 'Testing for Competition among German Banks'. Discussion Paper Deutsche Bundesbank 04/02, 1–47.

Hughes, J. and L. J. Mester (1993). 'A Quality and Risk Adjusted Cost Function for Banks: Evidence on the "Too-big-to-Fail-Doctrine" '. *Journal of Productivity Analysis*, 4, 292–315.

Humphrey, D. B. and L. B. Pulley (1997, February). 'Banks' Responses to Deregulation: Profits, Technology, and Efficiency'. *Journal of Money, Credit, and Banking*, 29(1), 73–93.

Jagtiani, J. and A. Khanthavit (1996, August). 'Scale and Scope Economies at Large Banks: Including Off-balance Sheet Activities and Regulatory Effects (1984–1991)'. *Journal of Banking and Finance*, 20(7), 1271–1287.

Jondrow, J., C. A. K. Lovell, S. Van Materov and P. Schmidt (1982, August). 'On the Estimation of Technical Inefficiency in the Stochastic Frontier Production Function Model'. *Journal of Econometrics*, 19(2–3), 233–238.

Krosta, A. and F. Schmid (2003). 'Bundesbank ruckelt am Bankensystem'. *Financial Times Deutschland*, 12 December.

Lang, G. and P. Welzel (1996, July). 'Efficiency and Technical Progress in Banking: Empirical Results for a Panel of German Cooperative Banks'. *Journal of Banking and Finance*, 20(6), 1003–1023.

Lang, G. and P. Welzel (1998a, July). 'Technology and Cost Efficiency in Universal Banking a "Thick Frontier" – Analysis of the German Banking Industry'. *Journal of Productivity Analysis*, 10(1), 63–84.

Lang, G. and P. Welzel (1998b, December). 'Mergers among German Cooperative Banks: A Panel-based Stochastic Frontier Analysis'. *Small Business Economics*, 13(4), 273–286.

Lozano-Vivas, A., J. T. Pastor and J. M. Pastor (2002). 'An Efficiency Comparison of European Banking Systems Operating under Different Environmental Conditions'. *Journal of Productivity Analysis*, 18(1), 59–77.

Mas-Colell, A., M. D. Whinston and J. R. Green (1995). *Microeconomic Theory*. New York: Oxford University Press.

Meeusen, W. and J. V. D. Broeck (1977, June). 'Efficiency Estimation for Cobb-Douglas Production Functions with Composed Error'. *International Economic Review*, 18(2), 435–444.

Mester, L. (1997). 'Measuring Efficiency at U.S. Banks'. *European Journal of Operational Research*, 98(2), 230–242.

Molyneux, P., D. Lloyd-Williams and J. Thornton (1994). 'Competitive Conditions in European Banking'. *Journal of Banking and Finance*, 18(3), 445–459.

Molyneux, P., Y. Altunbas and E. Gardener (1997). *Efficiency in European Banking*. New York: John Wiley and Sons.

Mountain, D. C. and H. Thomas (1999, April). 'Factor Price Misspecification in Bank Cost Function Estimation'. *Journal of International Financial Markets, Institutions and Money*, 9(2), 163–182.

Park, K. and G. Pennacchi (2004). 'Harming Depositors and Helping Borrowers: The Disparate Impact of Bank Consolidation' (December). AFA 2005 Philadelphia Meetings Paper.

Prior, D. (2003, April). 'Long- and Short-Run Non-Parametric Cost Frontier Efficiency: An Application to Spanish Savings Banks'. *Journal of Banking and Finance*, 27(4), 655–671.

Rime, B. and K. J. Stiroh (2003, November). 'The Performance of Universal Banks: Evidence from Switzerland'. *Journal of Banking and Finance*, 27(11), 2121–2150.

Sealey, C. W. and J. T. Lindley (1977). 'Inputs, Outputs, and a Theory of Production and Cost for Depository Financial Institutions'. *Journal of Finance*, 32, 1251–1265.

Tortosa-Ausina, E. (2003, July–August). 'Non-Traditional Activities and Bank Efficiency Revisited: A Distributional Analysis for Spanish Financial Institutions'. *Journal of Economics and Business*, 55(4), 371–395.

11 Competition in a highly concentrated banking sector

Theoretical, empirical and practical considerations for the Netherlands

Wim Boonstra and Johannes M. Groeneveld

11.1 Introduction

The Netherlands has one of the world's most concentrated banking sectors. The four largest banks together hold domestic market shares in various financial retail markets between approximately 75% and 80%. Some policymakers and financial analysts regularly point to the alleged detrimental effect of this high level of concentration on competition. It is sometimes also argued that this concentration poses a threat to financial stability, because if one of these large banks were to fail, the implications for the financial system would be disastrous.

In this chapter we seek to make the necessary differentiations to existing studies and opinions on the relationship between concentration and competition in retail banking. First, we feel that the theoretical foundation of the few empirical studies on European banking has methodological shortcomings.

Second, the quality and the availability of the European banking data required for testing the theoretical notions are rather poor. Apart from the questionable theoretical underpinnings, the outcomes of empirical studies must consequently be assessed with great caution. It is therefore unwise to formulate policy conclusions or recommendations based on these questionable findings.

In light of these shortcomings and omissions in the existing literature on European banking, this chapter proposes a much more pragmatic approach. The key point is that the underlying dynamics in banking are neglected in many studies. Theoretical views and empirical studies must be supplemented with a considerable amount of practical knowledge regarding the current state of affairs in banking. While our proposed amendments to the existing literature will be placed in the context of the Netherlands, the considerations we present are equally applicable for other banking systems.

This chapter is structured in the following manner. Section 11.2 provides a brief survey of the theoretical literature on concentration and competition. Section 11.3 presents a critical assessment of the existing empirical research on these topics for European banking industries and highlights the shortcomings of the theoretical concepts and empirical studies. Section 11.4 looks at the practical experience of bankers on these aspects. As will be discussed, existing theoretical and empirical studies cannot take into account the complexity in the banking industry. For instance, banks compete in different retail markets at the same time and it is important to distinguish between the front and back office of banks. Scale in the production and processing is key for banks to afford the mounting investments in information and communication technology (ICT) applications.

This is why banks follow strategies such as multi-distribution, insourcing, outsourcing and co-sourcing. The result is an increasing market share and concentration ratio. Another key development is the breakdown of entry barriers over the last decades. The emergence of many intermediaries and non-banks is a clear reflection of this. Retail banks also aim to distinguish themselves from their competitors by maintaining or creating a different image. Through this diverging behaviour they try to attract different market and/or customer segments. However, if there was a lack of competition, banks would not – be forced to – focus so intensively on strategic positioning issues. Finally, one cannot ignore the most important aspect: The assessment of customers regarding the price and quality of financial services. Our practical extensions also contain messages for policymakers. If competition authorities and supervisors were to pursue policies based on rigid measures of concentration and competition, they would undermine rather than support financial stability.

11.2   Theories and studies of competition and concentration in European banking

The literature on the measurement of competition can be divided into two major strands: (1) structural models (2) nonstructural models.

11.2.1   Structural models

The structural approach to modelling competition consists of the Structure–Conduct–Performance (SCP) paradigm and the efficiency hypothesis, as well as a number of formal approaches that are rooted in Industrial Organisation theory. These models have been frequently applied in empirical estimations, even though they lack a formal theoretical derivation. The difference between the SCP and the efficiency hypothesis is shown in Figure 11.1.

Formally, the difference between the SCP paradigm and the efficiency hypothesis can be demonstrated by the following equation:

$$\Pi_{ij} = \alpha_0 + \alpha_1 CR_j + \alpha_2 MS_{ij} + \Sigma \alpha_i X_i \qquad (11.1)$$

Π_{ij} represents a measure of performance of company i in the j's market. CR_j is a measure of concentration and MS_{ij} is the market share. Both CR_j and MS_{ij} are proxies for the market structure. X_i is a vector of control variables included to account for company as well as market specific characteristics. The traditional SCP relationship holds if $\alpha_1 > 0$ and $\alpha_2 = 0$. The efficiency hypothesis is supported by the data when $\alpha_1 = 0$ and $\alpha_2 > 0$.

The SCP assumes a link between market structure, behaviour of banks and profitability. A highly concentrated market is thought to lead to collusive behaviour

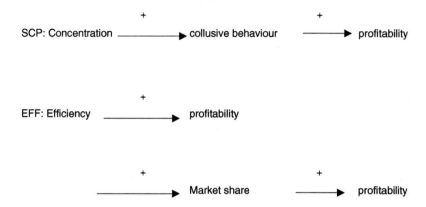

Figure 11.1 Hypothesized relationships in the SCP and efficiency hypothesis.

among larger banks resulting in superior market performance (Goldberg and Rai, 1996). The line of reasoning is that large banks abuse their market power to increase profits. The paradigm states that increased concentration fosters collusion and anti-competitive practices.

This line of reasoning is challenged by two other theoretical strands. The *efficiency hypothesis* (EH) postulates that efficient banks are able to increase their market share due to their higher profitability. Consequently, the degree of concentration increases 'automatically'. A bank with a higher degree of efficiency than its competitors can adopt two different strategies. The first option is to maximise profits by maintaining the present levels of prices and company size. The second alternative is to maximise profits by reducing prices and expanding the size of the company. If the bank chooses the second option, the most efficient banks will gain market share and bank efficiency will be the driving force behind the process of market concentration without necessarily reducing the competitiveness. The *contestability theory* stresses that a concentrated banking industry can behave competitively if the hurdles for new entrants to the market are low (Baumol, 1982). Only the threat of potential entry forces banks with large market shares to price their product competitively under certain conditions. In a perfectly contestable market, entry is absolutely free, exit is completely without cost and the demands for industry outputs are highly price-elastic. Costless exit implies that when a company is planning to enter a new market, it expects to recover fixed costs if it later decides to exit. In fact, salient trends in banking such as deregulation and IT innovations have considerably reduced the entry obstacles and fixed costs for new providers of financial products.[1]

11.2.2   Non-structural models

These types of models include the Bresnahan model and the Panzar and Rosse (PR) model[2], as well as frameworks addressing the dominance in price setting behaviour in retail markets. These models belong to the New Empirical Industrial Organisation approaches. They focus on the competitive conduct of banks without employing explicit information about the structure of the market.

The *Bresnahan model* boils down to a simultaneous estimation of a market demand or supply function and a price setting equation using industry aggregate figures. From this exercise, a parameter indexing the oligopoly solution concept (λ) is identified by standard econometric methods. The comparative static factors of equilibrium, such as price and quantity are moved by exogenous variables and reveal the degree of market power. If λ equals zero, perfect competition exists. If $\lambda = 1$, there is a perfect cartel. Intermediate λ's correspond to other oligopoly solution concepts.

The *PR model* requires company-specific data. This approach leads to the construction of a so-called *H* statistic to make a quantitative assessment of the competitive nature of banking markets and the market power of banks. The *H* statistic is calculated from reduced-form revenue equations and measures the sum of elasticities of the bank's total revenue with respect to the bank's input prices. The PR model shows that this statistic can reflect the structure and conduct of the market in which the bank operates. The testable hypotheses are:

$H \leq 0$:   monopoly
$0 < H < 1$:   monopolistic competition
$H = 1$:   perfect competition

The PR model treats banks as single-product companies, using deposits and other funding costs as inputs to produce merely losans and other interest-earning assets. This reflects the intermediation role of banks.

It should be noted that the optimum size, the size of the market and, on the demand-side, the perception regarding the extent to which the products on offer differ determine the number of viable banks and the natural level of concentration. A natural monopoly will eventually emerge if only one producer is able to produce all products at minimum cost. If, however, there is space for more than one producer, an oligopoly will obviously develop. Moreover, if the banking market is characterised by increasing returns to scale, the optimum size of an individual bank (in terms of an efficient operation) will constantly increase with expanding demand. In this situation, consolidation is the result of a dynamic market process.[3] This natural tendency to concentrate activities would ultimately lead to the survival of only one viable bank and a concentration ratio of one.[4] On the other hand, in the absence of economies of scale and scope for all products and services, it would be possible for numerous banks to operate in a highly competitive market under certain circumstances. There is also room in the market for various banks if customers perceive the products and services offered to be heterogeneous rather than homogeneous.

A third approach is to investigate *the speed of adjustment in pricing behaviour* in retail markets in response to changes in interest rates (see Sterken, 2004). In less competitive markets, it is assumed that banks adjust interest rates more quickly in response to cost increases than to cost decreases. These studies also explore whether the same bank always sets an example for the others in order to test the level of market dominance.

11.2.3 The concept of concentration

As argued, the concept of concentration plays an important role in structural models.[5] Despite the many different approaches to its measurement, there is general agreement regarding the constituting parts of concentration ratios. These are the number of companies (fewness) and the distribution of the company sizes (inequality) in a given industry. However, no systematic classification or concentration measures can be found in the literature. The concentration indices, CI, all display the same general form:

$$CI = \sum_{i}^{n} s_i w_i \qquad (11.2)$$

with s_i being the market share of company i, w_i is the weight that the index attaches to the corresponding market share and n is the number of companies in the market in question. The most commonly used measures are the Herfindahl Index (HI) and the k-firm concentration ratio (CR), respectively.

$$HI = \sum_{i}^{n} s^2 i \qquad (11.3)$$

$$CR_k = \sum_{i=1}^{k} s_i \qquad (11.4)$$

The HI stresses the importance of larger companies by giving them a greater weight than smaller companies.[6] It also incorporates each firm separately and differently in order to avoid arbitrary cut-offs and insensitivity to the share distribution. The k-company concentration ratio (CR_k) gives equal weights to the K leading companines, but neglects the many small companies in the market. However, this measure is often referred to in studies and policy documents.

11.3 An assessment of the existing empirical research

The availability of the required banking data and the length of the series are often limited for European countries.[7] These data are also difficult to compare due to inconsistencies in the definition of the underlying markets across countries. This is why empirical investigations of competitive conditions and concentration in EU banking industries are scarce. The consequence of the poor availability and quality of data is, however, that the outcomes must be assessed with great caution. It is unwise to use the findings for policy conclusions or recommendations. Apart from data problems, we shall now look at methodological and practical shortcomings or omissions of existing studies on competition and concentration in European banking.

11.3.1   Empirical applications of the SCP paradigm and EF

The application of the SCP in the banking literature has been criticised on various occasions (Reid, 1987; Vesala, 1995). The criticism refers to the form of the model rather than to the specification of the various variables. Much criticism is related to the one-way causality from market structure to market performance of the original model as it is still applied in many banking studies. In fact, most studies that apply the SCP framework neglect the – strategic – *conduct* of banks. Banks attempt to distinguish themselves from competitors by following divergent strategies and presenting different corporate images. Furthermore, the empirical results of the scarce studies on the SCP paradigm for European banking markets are equally ambiguous as those obtained from the US banking industry.

The scarcity of European data makes it virtually impossible to define a meaningful and hence relevant market area. Reasonable measures of concentration are also very difficult to construct for universal banks and nation-wide banking conditions because banks operate in many different product markets as well as geographical markets. In addition, national measures of concentration should ideally be adjusted to the size of the market. When one looks at all EU countries, it appears that larger countries generally exhibit lower concentration ratios than smaller countries. This is very logical, because there is room for more viable banks in countries with greater populations. Indeed, if it is assumed that banks have the same optimum size and the same cost function, the number of viable banks grows in tandem with the size of the country.

11.3.2   Studies based on the PR model

The scarce studies on the market structure are predominantly based on the PR model. The findings generally point to monopolistic competition in banking sectors.[8] Interestingly, most European studies already found monopolistic competition in the 1980s (Table 11.1).

It must be stressed that the unclear definition of the relevant market hampers a straightforward interpretation of the estimation results based on the PR model. First, the geographical dimension of banking markets is not adequately taken into consideration. The competitive environment the bank faces abroad is not necessarily identical to the competitive situation prevailing in the country where the bank is located. This is particularly true for large universal banks with sizeable foreign activities. These internationally active banks are obviously confronted with other competitive forces than small regional banks. For countries with relatively closed banking systems, the *H* statistic is thus more indicative of the competitive situation in the domestic banking market. Unfortunately, the high and increasing level of internationalisation has eroded the applicability of the PR model. Although the size of cross-border deposits and loans is still very small,

Table 11.1 PR model results in empirical studies

Authors	Period	Countries considered	Results
Nathan and Neave (1989)	1982–1984	Canada	1982: perfect competition 1983–1984: monopolistic competition
Shaffer (1982)	1979	New York	Monopolistic competition
Lloyd-Williams *et al.* (1991)	1986–1988	Japan	Monopoly
Molyneux *et al.* (1994)	1986–1989	France, Germany, Italy, Spain and UK	Monopoly: Italy; Monopolistic competition: France, Germany, Spain and United Kingdom
Vesala (1995)	1985–1992	Finland	Monopolistic competition for all but two years
Molyneux *et al.* (1996)	1986–1988	Japan	Monopoly
Coccorese (1998)	1988–1996	Italy	Monopolistic competition
De Bandt and Davis (1999)	1992–1996	France, Germany and Italy	Monopolistic competition: large banks in all countries; monopolistic competition: small banks in Italy; monopoly: small banks in France and Germany
Rime (1999)	1987–1994	Switzerland	Monopolistic competition
Bikker and Groeneveld (2000)	1989–1996	Fifteen EU countries	Monopolistic competition

Source: Bikker and Haaf (2000).

the cross-border participations in national banking sectors are considerable in some countries (see Table 11.2). For example, large parts of the Finnish, Irish and Belgian banking sectors are held in foreign hands. Luxemburg is of course a special case. It also makes little sense to perform estimations for different banking sizes to capture different geographic markets (see Bikker and Haaf, 2000). The results of these estimations are not informative. Smaller, more nationally orientated banks feel the competitive pressure from the larger, wealthier and more internationally orientated banks in their country anyway.

Second, the PR approach cannot be applied to separate segments of markets where banks operate. The observed H is an index of the overall competitive conditions in the entire banking market, that is, across product and customer groups. This aspect makes PR not very suitable for most European banking markets. Most banks are part of a financial conglomerate, consisting of many different banking and insurance activities. It is impossible to separate the revenues from these businesses. Besides, one cannot speak of *the* banking market. For instance, one can distinguish between retail, private and corporate banking. All these markets have completely different characteristics and comprise different segments. Regarding retail markets, the savings market cannot be compared with the market for online

Table 11.2 Capital of euro area banks owned by foreign residents

Country of the owners	Country of the participations												
	BE	DE	GR	ES	FR	FI	IE	IT	LU	NL	AT	PT	Average
BE		0.00	0.00	0.00	6.17	0.00	2.88	0.09	18.40	1.23	1.01	0.86	2.79
DK	0.00	0.00	0.00	0.00	0.00	0.00	0.00	0.00	2.17	0.00	0.00	0.00	0.18
DE	1.11		0.00	2.87	2.54	0.00	26.30	1.74	47.30	1.65	9.03	2.02	8.60
GR	0.00	0.00		0.00	0.00	0.00	0.00	0.00	0.32	0.00	0.00	0.73	0.10
ES	0.23	0.66	1.16		1.44	0.00	0.00	1.12	0.00	0.00	0.00	0.99	0.40
FR	0.47	0.38	0.00	1.26		0.00	2.79	2.59	9.80	0.00	0.02	0.78	1.50
IT	0.00	0.86	0.00	1.92	1.09	0.00	0.91		4.28	0.00	0.11	3.19	1.29
LU	0.04	0.06	0.00	0.00	0.19	0.00	5.82	0.28		0.00	0.00	2.82	0.39
NL	27.04	1.98	0.00	0.00	0.58	0.00	0.00	0.67	1.49		0.00	1.83	3.58
PT	0.00	0.00	0.00	1.18	0.02	0.00	0.00	0.00	0.00	0.00			0.11
SE	0.00	0.03	0.00	0.00	0.00	37.64	0.00	0.00	0.27	0.00	0.00	0.00	3.16
UK	0.00	0.00	0.96	2.29	1.56	0.00	1.14	0.11	0.79	0.00	0.00	0.25	0.59
JP	0.00	0.02	0.00	0.00	0.67	0.00	0.00	0.00	0.00	0.59	0.00	0.00	0.11
US	0.24	0.49	1.25	0.00	0.00	2.81	0.01	0.00	0.00	3.10	0.00	3.10	0.92
Other	0.37	0.68	2.72	0.00	0.00	0.22	0.38	3.68	1.02	0.10	0.00	0.10	0.77
Total	29.5	5.2	6.1	9.5	14.3	40.7	40.2	10.3	85.8	6.7	10.2	16.7	22.9

Source: Fitch IBCA Bankscope.

Note
End – 2000, % of total equity capital.

brokerage. One should also discriminate between various customer segments. Loans to private households demand different assessments from those to SMEs.

Third, the relevant market should embrace all suppliers of a certain banking service, which are actual or potential competitors. It is already impossible to include all actual banking competitors in a market in empirical studies, let alone to capture the impact of potential new entrants on the market structure in the underlying data. These – potential – newcomers can have a fundamental impact on the competitive structure in banking, although their market shares are or will remain fairly modest.

11.4 Competition and concentration: practical experiences and extensions

We feel that the existing studies on competition and concentration in European banking have considerable empirical and methodological shortcomings. They fail to capture the dynamics in banking and cannot be used for policy-making purposes. This is particularly true of studies on the possible link between proxies for concentration and competition that are constructed in a questionable way (see Jansen and De Haan, 2002). In this section we offer a counterweight to the existing literature on competition and concentration in banking. We will present other tools and important considerations for competition authorities and banking supervisors to assess the market structure and health of national banking sectors. Although our discussion relates to the Netherlands in particular, we believe that the necessary differentiations are equally relevant for banking systems in other European countries.

11.4.1 Lower aggregation level of analysis

Studies traditionally focus on the degree of concentration on a macro level. They usually take market shares as a percentage of balance sheet total or deposits as a starting point for analysis. Most analyses are also limited to the banking industry, even though other providers of financial services are also active in the market.

These are serious flaws for a number of reasons. The first problem is that analyses at a macro level neglect the impact of smaller niche players. Smaller, more focused financial players can have a major impact on market conditions in their sub-market, even though they tend to be relatively small in terms of balance sheet total. The second problem with traditional approaches is that several companies are significant players in the financial services industry, even though banking is not their core business. Examples include insurance companies, which compete directly with banks in the market for savings and investment products, and supermarket chains that offer payments or savings products.

A first step toward improving the traditional analysis is to examine the degree of concentration and the competition structure in individual sub-markets. Table 11.3 presents calculations of the HI, including some non-banks. The distinction between various markets and the inclusion of two insurance companies

Table 11.3 Ranking major banking institutions and concentration ratios in the Netherlands

	Current accounts	Savings account	Consumer credit	Mortgage loans	Investment funds	Asset management
ABN Amro	3	3	2	3	1	1
Rabobank	2	1	19	1	2	4
ING/Postbank	1	2	1	2	3	3
Fortis	5	5	4	4	4	2
SNS	4	4	3	5	5	
C5-ratio	98	79	75	73	74	66
Herfindahl	3,102	1,990	2,212	1,688	2,242	2,184
Refined Herfindahl				1,393		

Source: Rabobank.

Notes
The calculation of the HI includes insurance companies Achmea and Aegon. The refined Herfindahl is calculated by including the market shares of the thirteen most important players (cumulative market share 97.5%).

already provide a different and more realistic picture. It appears that the degree of concentration is lower for important market segments than the macro analysis excluding insurance companies suggests.

The stories behind individual concentration measures also differ. The high concentration ratio for current accounts is understandable because only a few banks can afford the large investments to offer this service. Moreover, in some sub-markets the HI is strongly influenced by the relatively large market share of the category 'other players'. Further refinement shows that the market for mortgage loans appears to have the lowest degree of concentration, as measured by the HI. The 'refined Herfindahl' in Table 11.3 indicates that competition in this important retail market is more intense than the macro figures suggest.

This conclusion is supported by Sterken (2004). Sterken tested the hypothesis of market dominance in the Dutch market for mortgage loans by analysing price setting behaviour in the market for mortgage loans by the four major banks. While he finds evidence of market leadership, he concludes that there is no evidence of market dominance. It appears that especially the market leader transmits cost increases more quickly than cost decreases, but he also concludes that in the longer run all banks appear to behave competitively.

11.4.2   *Structural developments in the distribution of financial services*

The traditional analysis of competition in banking markets mostly ignores fundamental changes in the distribution of financial services. The role of independent intermediaries has grown impressively in recent decades. As early as the 1980s, more than 30% of mortgage loans were sold via these middlemen, who have positioned themselves between the producers of mortgages and their clients.

In 2002, their market share had risen to approximately 60% (Figure 11.2). The success of intermediaries can be explained by the fact that they have increased the market transparency for the borrower.

This development has undermined the market position of banks in many ways. It means that they are faced with a loss of direct contacts with their customers (Figure 11.3). Customers have become much more aware of differences in prices

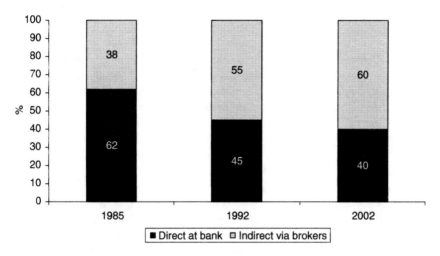

Figure 11.2 Sales of mortgages via banks and brokers.

Source: Rabobank.

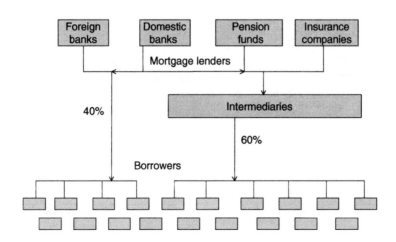

Figure 11.3 Structure of the market for mortgage loans.

Source: Rabobank.

and other terms and conditions. The intermediary helps them to shop around between suppliers of banking products and pick the best offer for each product. Moreover, the presence of intermediaries has helped wealthy insurance companies and pension funds to gain substantial market shares since they usually lack a retail distribution network. This development has forced banks to end the practice of cross-subsidising products, to stop offering loss-making products and to increase their transparency. As a result, price competition has become much more intense and customers have – indirectly – increased their number of banking relationships.

Apart from the increasing importance of intermediaries, technological developments have changed the distribution of banking products. The popularity of direct channels such as automatic teller machines (ATM), electronic funds transfer at point of sale (EFTPOS), telephone banking and more recently Internet Banking has brought about an unpredentic change in the world of financial services. Today, almost every straightforward banking transaction is conducted via one of these direct channels. As a result, the branch outlet has declined in importance (see Figure 11.4). Although the number of 'contact moments' between banks and clients has doubled between 1985 and 2002, the number of visits to the branch offices has dropped by 95%. The branch office network has changed from a necessary outlet into an expensive, but still essential way of contacting the customers. While average banking customers only visit their local banking office less than once a year, they still expect the bank to be located in the neighbourhood just in case they need it. All Dutch banks have responded by reducing the number of branch outlets. They do, however, acknowledge that an overly enthusiastic decrease in the number of branch offices would place their market share under pressure. For example, ING recently re-opened a number of branch offices after it experienced a strong decline in market share.

This trend has considerably altered the character of the banking branch office. When a customer visits the local bank branch office, it is usually because he has

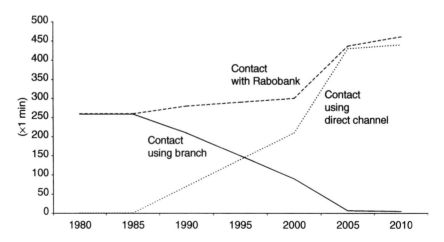

Figure 11.4 Banks' customer contacts.
Source: Rabobank.

a problem (e.g. technical problems with one of the direct channels, incorrect transactions) or a question about a complex product. The traditional bank office is rapidly disappearing and replaced by modern 'financial boutiques' or 'financial advice centres'.

11.4.3 Distribution strategies and the role of (potential) new entrants

The rise of direct channels has opened the market for new – virtual and foreign – competitors. Insurance companies and pension funds have entered the market for banking services via the intermediary channel. We see non-traditional suppliers entering financial retail markets. While the competitive pressures created by all of these – potential – new entrants should not be underestimated, it is scarcely included in empirical studies.

The threat of potential entrants ensures that, even in the case of a highly concentrated sector, existing players act competitively. New players entering into niche markets or focusing on specific client segments give rise to keen price competition in retail markets. Although their market shares may remain modest, their overall impact on competition could be substantial because they force incumbents to respond by offering services at lower cost and/or higher quality (see Llewellyn, 1999). In the Dutch context, the classical example of this phenomenon is provided by the Roparco savings account in the early 1980s. Even though its market share peaked at just 10% some years ago, it has nonetheless fundamentally redefined competition in the market for savings accounts. Today, Royal Bank of Scotland is successfully selling mortgages via Internet with the EUBOS-label and the Turkish Garantibank is offering virtual savings products in the Dutch market.

The emergence of non-traditional suppliers of banking services changes the market structure by enhancing competitive pressures and the degree of contestability. The origin of non-banking lies in the United Kingdom, especially at supermarkets and department stores. Marks&Spencer started offering financial services as far back as 1985 and even went on to establish its own bank. Non-banking has gained a firm foothold in the Netherlands. For example, Vendex KBB[9] introduced BIJfinance to sell insurance products and mortgages. Even trade unions are offering financial products to their union members, mostly employment benefits and insurance services.

Finally, the Internet has boosted competition in banking. Newcomers are able to enter the market for financial services at low costs by using modern technology. Pure internet players can offer cut-rate prices because they do not have to maintain expensive branch networks. They also do not offer the complete range of financial services, but rather concentrate on attractive niches, leaving the less attractive segments of the market to the incumbents. Their arrival challenges incumbents, which usually have large sunk costs in the existing financial infrastructure and cannot permit themselves to operate without a branch network in their home market. Established players have responded by setting up their own internet banking operations. Incumbents must accommodate customer demand by offering internet services at attractive interest rates. As a result even small internet players can really shake up the banking industry by increasing competitive pressures. A good example is Rabobank's experience with launching an internet bank in Belgium. Rabobank.be was able to offer attractive savings interest rates, but within a few weeks the established players brought their interest tariffs in line with those of Rabobank.be. The benefits were clearly passed on to the customers.

11.4.4   Developments on the production side

Economies of scale on the processing and production side are becoming increasingly important in the banking sector. Especially in retail banking, where many products have become commodities and price competition is fierce, scale counts. Not all players realise sufficient scale via their own distribution channels to cover ever-increasing ICT investments or to invent innovative products and services. This explains the emergence of insourcing, outsourcing and co-sourcing.[10] A famous Dutch example is the Interpay payment system. All Dutch banks participate in this system, both as users and as shareholders. It was established in the 1960s as the so-called 'Bankgiro Centrale' (BGC). In the 1990s it was linked with the Postgirosystem into the National Payment Circuit. This system was established under close supervision of the Dutch Central Bank. The system is technically speaking a monopoly, although participating banks are free to set the rates they charge their customers. Given the fact that banking payments in the Netherlands are the cheapest in Europe, if not the world, one can hardly speak of abuse of monopoly power by the banks. If Interpay were to break up, it would certainly lead to higher costs for banking customers. Nevertheless, the system is being closely scrutinised by the competition authorities.

All over Europe, banks are forced to increase efficiency in their operations to survive. In larger countries, such as France or Germany, there is still ample scope for upscaling the back-office activities via consolidation without alarming the competition authorities. In smaller countries, the competition and supervisory authorities should not consider further domestic upscaling as a serious problem. The absolute size of the merged institutions would still be dwarfed by players such as Deutsche Bank or Credit Agricole. In some cases, it is time for competition authorities to abandon their national focus and look at competition and scale issues at the European level. Otherwise, banks in smaller countries would be placed at a disadvantage compared to their counterparts in larger countries, with considerable welfare costs for customers.

11.4.5   Credit availability for SMEs

Some researchers assert that in highly concentrated banking sectors it is more difficult for small and medium enterprises (SMEs) to obtain bank loans at 'reasonable prices'. In the past, several researchers have tried to investigate the financing of SMEs in European countries, but these studies suffered from a lack of available reliable data. Duffhues (2004) finds that Dutch SMEs usually do not encounter problems in obtaining banking credits at reasonable conditions. There are of course exceptions to this rule, but these cases generally stem from the high-risk profile of certain specific sectors. Problems identified by Duffhues are concentrated in the financing of start-ups or young, fast-growing companies.

Similar problems exist in all European countries, irrespective of the degree of concentration. Cogan and McDevitt (2003) have conducted an international study that compares the financing of innovative companies in several European countries. They conclude that 'The Netherlands . . . is a clear leader in the provision of early-phase and growth-phase venture capital to business.' The high degree of concentration in the Dutch financial industry appears to have no negative impact on the availability of credit for SMEs.

11.4.6 *Customer satisfaction as an instrument of analysis*

The examination of competition and concentration cannot be a purely academic exercise. The preceding sections reveal that traditional analyses, based on macro-data and concentration indices, fail to capture many of the dynamic developments in the markets for financial services. At the end of the day it simply comes down to the price and quality of banking products. And customer perceptions of their banks should be included as an important factor when assessing the competitive standing in retail banking. Much more emphasis should be placed on practical experiences and information obtained directly from these end users of banking services. The level of customer satisfaction regarding banks is a key variable and fairly easy to measure. If a highly concentrated banking sector with high entry barriers would lead to non-competitive behaviour, customer satisfaction could be rather low. Not only because the price for banking products could be too high, but also because the quality of the service could be too low.

Recent research by KPMG (2004) indicates that most European banking customers are relatively satisfied with their banks. The most important exception is Italy, where only 56% of banking customers are satisfied with their bank. Apart from Spain and France, all other countries score above 80%. It appears that Dutch customers express the greatest satisfaction with their banks, despite or thanks to the highest level of concentration measured as CK_5 (see Figure 11.5). According to a recent study by KPMG, 86% of Dutch customers are satisfied with their bank. This result reveals that a highly concentrated banking sector is not by definition a bad thing. This finding supports our view that in smaller countries a higher level of concentration is required in order to realise sufficient economies of scale and a certain level of efficiency.

Dutch customers do not feel exploited, which would be visible in low satisfaction levels. This does not come as a surprise given the average price of core banking services in the Netherlands. Figure 11.6 plots the CR_5 against the average annual price of core banking services for eight European countries. The price fluctuates considerably across these countries, ranging from a low of only €31 a year in the Netherlands to a high of €501 in Italy. A study by Cap Gemini Ernst and Young (2004) argues that the impact of the competitive environment on pricing practices in national markets is difficult to assess. It concludes that countries with highly consolidated markets such as the Benelux or countries with

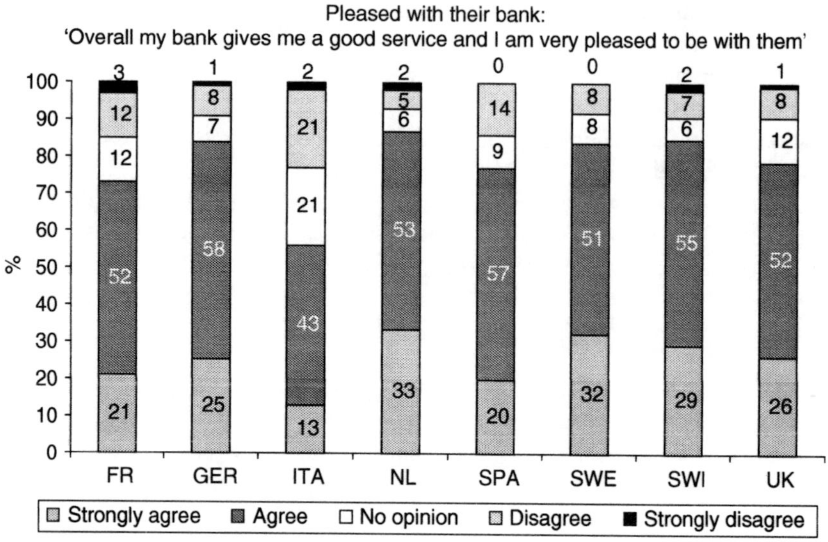

Pleased with their bank:
'Overall my bank gives me a good service and I am very pleased to be with them'

%	FR	GER	ITA	NL	SPA	SWE	SWI	UK
Strongly disagree	3	1	2	2	0	0	2	1
Disagree	12	8	21	5	14	8	7	8
No opinion	12	7	21	6	9	8	6	12
Agree	52	58	43	53	57	51	55	52
Strongly agree	21	25	13	33	20	32	29	26

☐ Strongly agree   ■ Agree   ☐ No opinion   ☐ Disagree   ■ Strongly disagree

Figure 11.5 Customer satisfaction regarding banks.
Source: KPMG (2004).

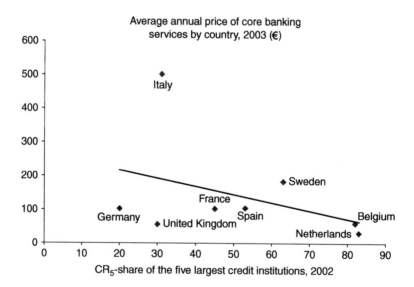

Figure 11.6 Relationship between CR_5 and average price of core banking products.

Source: Own calculations based on data from ECB (2002) and CGE&Y (2003–2004). CR_5 represents the market share of the five largest banks as % of total.

many new entrants such as the United Kingdom offer the lowest prices. The first conclusion is tentatively corroborated in Figure 11.6.

Although customers are generally loyal to their principal bank, most of them also use other financial providers. A 67 percentage of the customers in the countries under review have a relationship with 2–4 providers (see Figure 11.7). In the United Kingdom, 24% of the consumers have a relationship with over five providers. These facts mirror the erosion of the so-called primary financial relationship. While in the past customers obtained most of their banking products from just one provider, today the number of products bought from the main banking relationship has decreased. Due to technological developments and the rise of intermediaries, customers are increasingly shopping for the best buy for each product and service. Increasing transparency makes it rather difficult for banks to cross-subsidise individual products, as any abuse of market power would be punished immediately by customers. They would vote with their feet and turn to different or new players for certain products or services. This is also true for the Netherlands, with its highly concentrated banking sector.[11]

These data underscore the fact that 'hard figures' about customer satisfaction and pricing are much more relevant than questionable proxies for competition and concentration. It is also important to view these analyses from an international perspective. It appears that Dutch banks do not charge high prices and have fairly satisfied customers. The propensity to switch principal banks is one of the lowest in Europe.

11.4.7 Divergent strategies and core values of retail banks

A final point has to do with the changing face of competition and the role of marketing. Banking has been and will always be a 'people business'. Pricing is

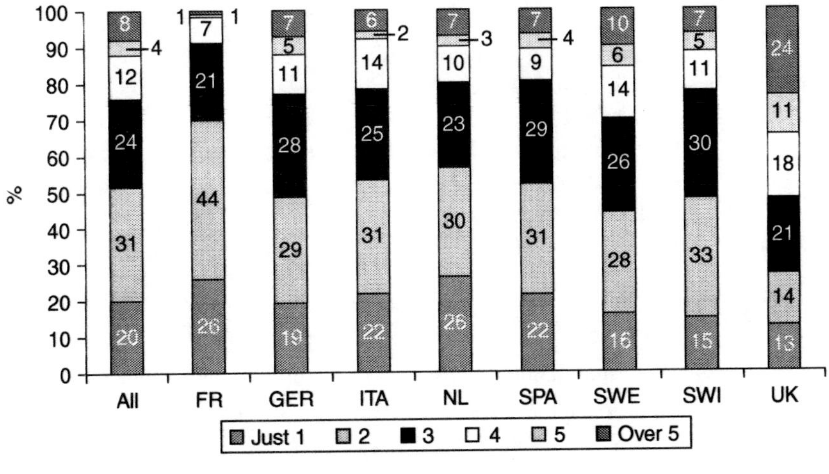

'Including your main bank, how many financial service providers do you have a relationship with (thinking of current accounts, investments, mortgages, insurance etc.)?'

	All	FR	GER	ITA	NL	SPA	SWE	SWI	UK
Over 5	8	1	1	7	6	7	7	10	7	24
5	4	7		5	2		4		5	
4	12	21	11	14	3	9	6	11	11
3	24		28	25	23	29	14	30	18
4 (Just 1)	31	44	29	31	30	31	26	33	21
2							28		14
Just 1	20	26	19	22	26	22	16	15	13

Legend: ▦ Just 1 ▢ 2 ■ 3 □ 4 ▢ 5 ▨ Over 5

Figure 11.7 Number of relationships with providers of financial services.

Source: KPMG (2004).

Table 11.4 Competition: profile of Dutch banks

ABN AMRO	ING Bank	Postbank (ING Group)	Rabobank
Status, up-market	Exclusive, more up-market	Mass market	Cooperative bank 'for everybody'
Arrogant	Distant	Convenience	Social involvement
Trend-setting	Investment	Payments and savings	Market leader in mortgages
Investment	Emphasis on larger SMEs	Simple products	Proximity
International orientation		No nonsense	Sustainability
Large corporates		Proximity	Payment and savings
		Internet banking	Market leader in Internet banking
		Direct Banking	Insurance
		Payments and savings bank	

Source: Rabobank.

important, but there are other reasons why people select and stay with a particular bank. Especially in transparent markets with a high level of price competitiveness, banks try to distinguish themselves by creating their own niches or images. They articulate or emphasise divergent core values to attract certain customer segments. For instance, they emphasise values such as 'sound', 'reliable', 'innovative', 'international', 'close', 'socially responsible' and so on. Of course, these aspects should be mirrored in their actual behaviour. Every bank also tries to capitalise on its specific traditional strengths.

Once people feel attracted to a bank, price becomes less important. For example, proximity is seen as very important by banking clients. They tend to stay with the bank in their neighbourhood, even if they do not always get the best price at the nearest bank. Table 11.4 is based on marketing research and shows the images that the largest Dutch banks have created.

A great deal of effort is put into creating and maintaining these images. Together with the accessibility of financial services, it is one of the most important elements of competition in Dutch retail banking. All banks claim to have intimate knowledge of – the business of – their customers. The intensity of marketing campaigns reflects the fierce competition in the Dutch financial industry.

11.5   Summary and conclusions

We have argued in this chapter that most traditional studies of competition in banking fail to capture the dynamics involved in retail banking. The degree of concentration in a specific banking market is not a reliable proxy for the intensity of competition. The arrival of new entrants, technological developments, the increasing role played by intermediaries and the varying corporate strategies pursued by the suppliers of financial services continuously change the competitive environment of financial retail markets.

We also have argued that that the bottom line should be the opinion of the customer. Customer opinions (measured as customer satisfaction) and behaviour (loyalty) should form the dominant element in assessing the behaviour of banks, together with more objective measures as credit availability and pricing. Therefore, the opinion of competition authorities on the degree of competition in financial services should to a large extent be based on an (international) assessment of these practical issues, instead of theoretical constructions.

A final remark concerns the risk of increasing instability. We have asserted that economies of scale are increasingly important in today's banking markets. The authorities should recognise that if banks are hindered to realise the necessary scale, they will sooner or later encounter problems due to a lack of profitability. Especially in small economies, the necessary scale automatically translates into a high degree of concentration. In relation to these economies, competition authorities should realise that a competition policy based on traditional analyses could easily lead to the wrong conclusions. A fundamental weakening of the domestic banking system and an increasing degree of financial instability would be the highly undesirable result. The key issue in banking for the future has little to do with 'too big to fail' but rather with 'too small to survive'.

Acknowledgements

The views expressed in this chapter are personal and do not necessarily reflect those of Rabobank Nederland. The authors thank their colleagues Wietske Timmermans, Bouke de Vries and Joost Wagemakers for their support in preparing this chapter.

Notes

1 Admittedly, entering banking markets demands considerable investments in terms of sunk costs. Moreover, regulation poses a justifiable entry barrier from a financial stability perspective. However, in contrast to Canoy *et al.* (2001), we expect that the potential negative consequences of a concentrated banking sector will be largely offset by free entry. Incumbents offer a wide range of products and services via various channels at the same time whereas new financial players can easily focus on a particular customer or product market with limited distribution channels. Supermarkets already have a fairly extensive physical distribution network, whereas the entry hurdles for pure internet players are fairly modest (take for instance ING Direct and Rabobank.be in Belgium).

2 See Bresnahan (1982) and Panzar and Rosse (1987).

3 This may provide an explanation as to why the consolidation trend in the banking industry has, in fact, always been present and is likely to continue in the future.

4 Numerous studies have been devoted to this topic (e.g. Berger *et al.*, 1993; Molyneux *et al.*, 1996).

5 See Bikker and Haaf (2000) for a detailed assessment of different measures of concentration.

6 The HI is a statutory measure to evaluate the concentration impact of a proposed merger in the US banking industry.
7 A fairly extensive literature on competition in US banking exists. Lack of data does not appear to be such a problem for US banks.
8 The Bresnahan approach is rarely applied in studies for European banking markets. Bikker and Haaf (2000) tests the Bresnahan model for both the deposit and loan markets in nine European countries. This exercise yields similar results as the outcomes for the markets for all banking activities obtained from most PR models. The hypothesis of perfect competition on these markets cannot be rejected. The pitfalls of the Bresnahan approach are similar to those of the more frequently applied PR model. We will consequently limit ourselves to an evaluation of the PR methodology in the main text.
9 Vendex KBB is the largest Dutch non-food retail trader that operates fifteen shopping formulas including Bijenkorf, V&D and Hema.
10 Due to insufficient scale, Friesland Bank, a relatively small regional bank, has completely outsourced its back-office activities for securities transactions to Rabobank.
11 In this context, it is important to note that the Netherlands is a country with a very high population density. Almost all inhabitants have access to the branch network of several banks within a radius of a few kilometres from their homes.

References

Baumol, W. J. (1982). 'Contestable Markets: An Uprising in the Theory of Industry Structure'. *American Economic Review*, 72, 1–15.

Berger, A. N., D. Hancock and D. B. Humphrey (1993). 'Bank Efficiency Derived from the Profit Function'. *Journal of Banking and Finance*, 17 (2–3), 317–347.

Bikker, J. A. and J. M. Groeneveld (2000). 'Competition and Concentration in the EU Banking Industry'. *Kredit und Kapital*, Heft 1/2000, 62–98.

Bikker, J. A. and K. Haaf (2000). 'Measures of Competition and Concentration, A Review of the Literature'. De Nederlandsche Bank, *Directorate Supervision*, Research Series Supervision No. 30.

Bresnahan, T. F. (1982). 'The Oligopoly Solution Concept is Identified'. *Economic Letters*, 10, 87–92.

Canoy, M., M. van Dijk, J. Lemmen, R. de Mooij and J. Weigand (2001). 'Competition and Stability in Banking'. *CPB Netherlands Bureau for Economic Policy Analysis*, CPB Document No. 15.

Cap Gemini Ernst and Young (2004). *World Retail Banking Report 2004.*

Coccorese, P. (1998). 'Assessing the Competitive Conditions in the Italian Banking System: Some Empirical Evidence'. *BNL Quarterly Review*, No. 205, 171–191.

Cogan, J. and J. McDevitt (2003). *Science, Technology and Innovation Policies in Selected Small Countries.* VATT-Research reports, Helsinki.

De Bandt, O. and E. P. Davis (1999). 'A Cross-Country Comparison of Market Structures in European Banking'. European Central Bank *Working Paper* No. 7.

Duffhues, P. J. W. (2004). *De Financierbaarheid van het MKB. Een analyse van de financiële structuur.* Research report, Center Applied Research, Tilburg University, Tilburg, January.

Goldberg, L. G. and A. Rai (1996). 'The Structure-performance Relationship for European Banking'. *Journal of Banking and Finance*, 20 (4), 745–771.

Jansen, D. J. and J. De Haan (2002). 'Increasing Concentration in European Banking: An Analysis on a Macro Level'. *Maandschrift Economie*, 66, 226–243 (in Dutch).

KPMG (2004). *Banking Beyond Borders: Will European Consumers Buy It?* Financial Services Division, United Kingdom.

Llewellyn, D. T. (1999). *The New Economics of Banking*, SUERF paper, Amsterdam.

Lloyd-Williams, D. M., P. Molyneux, and J. Thornton (1991). 'Competition and Contestability in the Japanese Commercial Banking Market'. Institute of European Finance, *Research Papers in Banking and Finance*, No. 16, Bangor.

Molyneux, P., D. M. Lloyd-Williams and J. Thornton (1994). 'Market Structure and Performance in Spanish Banking'. *Journal of Banking and Finance*, 18(3), 433–443.

Molyneux, P., Y. Altunbas and E. Gardener (1996). *Efficiency in European Banking*. Chichester: John Wiley & Sons Ltd.

Nathan, A. and E. H. Neave (1989). 'Competition and Contestability in Canada's Financial System: Empirical Results'. *Canadian Journal of Economics*, 22, 576–594.

Panzar, J. C. and J. N. Rosse (1987). 'Testing for Monopoly Equilibrium'. *Journal of Industrial Economics*, 35, 443–456.

Reid, G. C. (1987). *Theories of Industrial Organization*, New York and Oxford: Blackwell.

Rime, B. (1999). 'Mesure de degré de concurrence dans le système bancaire Suisse à l'aide du modèle de Panzar Rosse'. *Revue Suisse d'Economie Politique et de Statistique*, 135 (1), 21–40.

Shaffer, S. (1982). 'Competition, Conduct and Demand Elasticity'. *Economic Letters*, 10, 167–171.

Sterken, E. (2004). 'Testing for dominance in the mortgage market'. mimeo. Working Paper, University of Groningen, Groningen, March.

Vesala, J. (1995). 'Testing for Competition in Banking: Behavioral Evidence from Finland', Bank of England, Helsinki, *Bank of Finland Studies*, E:1.

12 Strategic management in banking, *in medio virtus*

Jean Dermine

Casual reading of banks' annual reports reveals the importance of a series of corporate financial goals, such as return on equity (ROE), risk-adjusted return on capital (RAROC), economic profit (EP), growth in earnings-per-share (EPS), or cost–income (C–I) ratio. As all the given measures of performances are based on short-term results, one wonders about the importance of longer term financial goals. Clearly, a balance has to be found between short- and long-term corporate goals.

Moreover, financial analysts seem to follow a pendulum, switching from praise for *focused* institutions to compliment for *diversified* financial services groups. One certainly remembers that Derek Wanless and the management of National Westminster Bank were severely criticized for their efforts to venture into insurance with the (failed) takeover attempt of Legal & General. Recently, both Citigroup and BNP-Paribas have been praised for having a well diversified source of revenue from commercial banking, investment banking, and insurance activities. Focus versus diversification is a second strategic issue.

The purpose of this chapter is to argue for a "balanced view," a need to define both short- and long-term financial goals, and to ensure an acceptable degree of diversification. As philosophers would say: *in medio virtus*.

The chapter is structured into two parts. In the first part, we review the fundamental drivers of share price, economic profit and growth, and discuss the case of the British bank Lloyds TSB over a twenty-year period, 1983–2004. It highlights the need for a balanced approach between short-term performances and long-term growth. In Section 12.2, we review the theoretical benefits of diversification, and present some data on international credit risk diversification. A conclusion follows.

12.1 ROE, RAROC, economic profit, efficiency ratio, growth and value: the case of Lloyds TSB

Over the last twenty years, shareholder value-based management has acquired an almost universal appeal. As the market for corporate control has facilitated takeovers and as institutional shareholders exercise pressure on management, the focus on value creation for the owners of the firm has increased considerably.

Relying on results from welfare economics, M. Jensen (2001) has argued convincingly that, in a competitive economy, this single corporate objective function will increase public welfare.[1] *Enlightened* value maximization, identical to *enlightened* stakeholder theory, specifies long-term value maximization as the firm's objective, while focusing attention on meeting demands of all important corporate constituencies, such as employees, clients, suppliers, and local authorities.

12.1.1 Value-based metrics of bank performance

Shareholder-based measures of performance include the ROE, RAROC, growth in EPS, and EP. According to mainstream finance and common sense, value is created whenever the return on funds invested by shareholders exceeds the opportunity investment return available to them. The opportunity cost of equity is estimated by the current risk-free bond rate plus a risk premium of around 4–5% for commercial banks in OECD countries. To make this performance objective operational, profit centers, now called value centers, are created. They include business units, such as corporate banking or retail branches, large customer relations, or specific products. Profit and equity are allocated to each business unit, so that a risk-adjusted return on capital, RAROC, can be calculated:

$$RAROC = \frac{\text{allocated net income}}{\text{allocated equity}}$$

In essence, the effort is to divide a complex financial institution into a set of small firms, each with its own Profit and Loss (P&L) and balance sheet. Value creation can thus be evaluated at the level of each value center, by comparing the RAROC of a department to the relevant cost of equity. Finally, since the RAROC measure is a percentage measure, which does not take into account the size of operations, a new measure is increasingly being used and reported in annual reports, the EP. It is defined as the difference between the net income allocated to a department and a cost of allocated equity.

$$\text{Economic profit (EP)} = \text{allocated net income} - (\text{allocated equity} \times \text{cost of equity})$$

This measure, which uses the same information as RAROC (allocated income and allocated equity) is a superior measure of performance, as it is an absolute measure of value creation (millions of €, £, $) which takes into account the size of operations.[2] Along with the above measure of shareholder value creation is the efficiency or C–I ratio. This ratio attempts to focus on a specific source of value creation, the control of operating expenses. Defined as operating expenses over gross income, it has become a standard yardstick of cost control.[3] However, if these performance measures are useful indicators of value creation, one should be wary of not sacrificing long-term growth to the benefit of short-term profitability, or, in other words, surrendering to *shortermism*. Indeed, a simple dividend-based model of share prices can show (see Appendix 12A.1) that the capitalized value of shares is equal to the value of current equity plus the present value of future economic profits.

$$\text{Market value of shares} = \text{equity} + \text{discounted value of future}$$
$$\text{economic profits}$$

Value-based management should thus achieve the maximization of both short-term and long-term economic profits. A balance (*in medio virtus*) has to be found between short- and long-term objectives. To illustrate the difficulty of finding a delicate balance, we focus on the case of the British bank, Lloyds TSB, long heralded as the champion of value creation (McTaggart *et al.*, 1994, pp. 37–39; Pitman, 2003).

12.1.2   The case of Lloyds TSB (1983–2004)

In 1983, Brian Pitman became Chief Executive of Lloyds Bank, Sir Jeremy Morse being Chairman of the Board. At a board meeting held in 1983, the members went into a philosophical discussion as to what the relevant corporate objective should be. They finally agreed that the company had to earn a return in excess of the cost of equity, and that the single objective would be: to double the share price every three years (Bose and Morgan, 1998). At the time, the ROE was 12%, when the interest rate on gilt securities was 10%. The ROE was clearly falling short of any measure of the cost of equity, and it was no surprise that the shares of Lloyds TSB were trading at below net asset value.

In the first annual report published under the leadership of Brian Pitman in 1983, appeared the following comments:

- We are committed to the idea that our function is to create shareholder value.
- The key issue for management is: What collection of divestments, acquisitions, and reallocations of capital is necessary to change our return on equity, market value, access to capital, and ability to sustain an appropriate growth?
- A bank's strategy has to start with its customers. A company can only build value for its shareholders if it can create value for its customers.

Although, shareholder value management is now common practice, in those days, it was fairly new thinking, with recommendations of asset disposals, and corporate objectives that seem to have been copied, word for word, from standard corporate finance textbooks.

Many of the significant decisions taken by the management of Lloyds Bank since 1983 are reported in Table 12.1. Comments will be offered on some of these decisions. The first was, in fact, a decision of no-action. At the time of *Big Bang* in 1985, the deregulation of the stock markets in London, Lloyds TSB decided against buying a specialist broker-jobber house, on the ground that they were too expensive. Lloyds Bank was among the very few not to join the herd of European and American banks which paid very high prices to enter this market. To be fair, the second action is a bit outside the strategy. In 1986, Lloyds TSB attempted to

Table 12.1 Lloyds TSB strategy, 1983–2004

Year	Significant decisions taken by Lloyds Bank
1985 (Big Bang)	Did not buy a broker-jobber house in London
1986	Fail in attempt to takeover Standard Chartered
1988	Merge with Abbey Life to create Lloyds Abbey Life
1990	Move retail banking headquarter from London to Bristol
1984–1992	Withdraw from North America, Portugal, Bahrain, Far East (China, Singapore, Korea, Taiwan)
1992	Change pay structure
1992	Conditional bid for Midland (withdrawn)
1994	Buy Cheltenham & Gloucester (C&G)
1995	Merge with TSB
1996	CEO: Peter Ellwood; Chairman: Brian Pitman; close New York treasury operations
1997	Sell Corporate Banking Paris to Crédit Agricole; sell SMH (Germany) to UBS
1999	Buy Scottish Widows
2000	Buy Chartered Trust
2001	Brian Pitman retires
2002	Competition Commission rules out a merger with Abbey National
2003	CEO: Eric Daniels; sell Lloyds Brazil to HSBC and New Zealand operations to ANZ
2004	CFO Hampton resigns; discussion to sell the operations in Argentina

take over Standard Chartered Bank, an institution with significant market shares in various countries of Asia and Africa.[4] This failed, as the wealthy Singaporean Tan Sri Khoo Teck Puat, a white knight, came to the rescue of the bank, with the purchase of a 37% equity stake. The following steps are in line with the strategy announced in 1983. An early move into life insurance with the purchase of Abbey Life in 1988, a move of retail headquarters from expensive London to Bristol in 1990, and a long series of divestments in Canada and USA, Portugal, Bahrain, China, Singapore, Korea, and Taiwan. In 1992, performance-related pay was introduced in the bank. There then followed the start of a series of efforts to acquire domestic financial institutions. A bid to take over the Midland Bank was withdrawn for the fear that it would not be authorized by the British competition authorities.[5] A building society, C&G, was acquired in 1994, one year before the successful merger with TSB (Salomon Brothers, 1995). So, after twelve years under the new management team, had the objective of value creation been met? Figure 12.1 reports the evolution of the share price of Lloyds *vis-à-vis* one of its competitor, Barclays Bank. The figures reported are relative to the Footsie index.

Figure 12.1 is a textbook example of successful value-based management. From 1973 to 1983, one sees both Barclays and Lloyds severely underperforming the index. A turnaround is evident with the arrival of Brian Pitman in 1983, and the series of disposal of assets, domestic mergers, and cost cutting. Barclays continues to underperform the index for a decade, while Lloyds stock performance is brilliant.

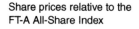

Share prices relative to the
FT-A All-Share Index

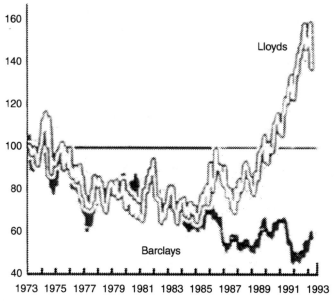

Figure 12.1 Share price of Lloyds and Barclays (relative to index).
Source: Datastream.

Table 12.2 Lloyds TSB ROE, 1993–2003

$ROE_{1993} = 21\%$	$ROE_{1996} = 33\%$	$ROE_{1999} = 29\%$	$ROE_{2002} = 23\%$
$ROE_{1994} = 24\%$	$ROE_{1997} = 37\%$	$ROE_{2000} = 28.4\%$	$ROE_{2003} = 33\%$
$ROE_{1995} = 25\%$	$ROE_{1998} = 31\%$	$ROE_{2001} = 29.1\%$	

Foreign asset disposal continued over the years: Corporate Banking Paris to
Crédit Agricole in 1997, Lloyds Brazil to HSBC and New Zealand operations to
ANZ in 2003, and, in 2004, the start of negotiations to sell the last piece of a
140-year presence in Latin America, the operations in Argentina. Domestic acquisitions went into pension fund management with the acquisition of Scottish
Widows, and consumer finance with the purchase of Chartered Trust. Over a
twenty-year period, Lloyds TSB had refocused on the United Kingdom, transforming itself into a dominant financial services firm. The massive exit from foreign operations in emerging markets (such as China and the countries of South
East Asia) could, of course, raise questions about the potential for future growth,
and whether or not short-term ROE targets and *shortermism* were not driving
factors. However, as indicated in Table 12.2, year after year, Lloyds TSB was
showing very high ROEs. Figure 12.2 shows the rapid increase in share price.

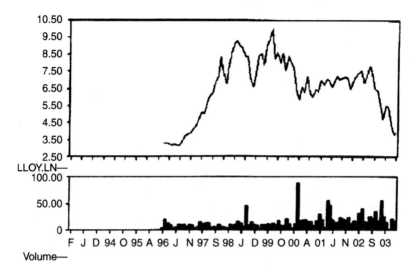

Figure 12.2 Lloyds TSB share price and volume, 1993–2003.

Source: Lloyds TSB Group LON (02/26/1993–02/28/2003) – Datastream.

In 1999, the share price of Lloyds TSB reached a peak of £10. The stated single objective of "doubling the share price every three years" appears to have been met. However, this seems to have been the end of the "golden" years. Since 1999, the price has fallen back to £4.50, despite a series of impressive ROEs. Although, the drop in share price could be due to the vagaries of stock markets, one can tentatively explain the source of the decline. It all started when the market became aware of the lack of an Internet strategy at the time of the "new economy" wave. Then came the end of the stock market bubble and losses in the pension business. Finally, and more significant, in light of the paper, was the decision of the British Competition Commission to rule out any significant merger for the four largest clearing banks, who had achieved a market share of 91% in liquidity management services to small and medium size enterprises, the SMEs (Competition Commission, 2002). With the inability to realize more cost-cutting driven domestic acquisitions, the market started to wonder about the new sources of growth. If past earnings growth was driven largely by capital gains on asset sales, cost cutting, and efficiency gains, these had reached a limit, and the market was getting anxious about the sources of future earnings growth.

The tale of Lloyds Bank, which started as a fairy tale of value-based management, is ending on a sour note as the market seems to be questioning the sources of future growth. It should serve as an example of the need to balance short-term earnings objectives with long-term sources of earnings growth: *in medio virtus*.

12.1.3   Interest rate level and growth[6]

A technical note on the sources of growth in banking concerns the current environment characterized by low inflation, low interest rates, and low profitability on the payment business. Indeed, the interest rate margins on deposits over the period 1980–2000 went down very significantly in most European countries. This is reported in Table 12.3. In Spain, for example, margins on savings deposits fell from 8.45% in 1980 to 2.37% in 2000. A similar pattern emerged in France, with margins on savings deposits falling from 5.3% to 0.92% over the same period. The evolution of margins on deposits did not arrive as a surprise. Indeed, it was widely anticipated that the arrival of a common European currency and an independent monetary policy, designed on the model of the German Bundesbank, would bring down inflation expectations, interest rates, and margins on deposits. The author, in an essay written two years before the arrival of the Euro, stated: "One can safely conclude that an objective of monetary stability and low inflation pursued by an independent European Central Bank will reduce the source of profitability on the deposit funding business" (Dermine, 1997). The effect is mechanical. Due to the drop in market rates, the inelasticity or "stickiness" of deposit rates implies an automatic reduction in interest margins.[7]

However, if, as documented in Table 12.3, the impact of low inflation on the margin on deposits is quite significant in a large number of countries, two additional effects of a low inflation environment might soften the impact of lower margins on deposits.

First, a low interest rate environment usually leads to much higher margin on personal loans because of the relative inelasticity of interest rates on personal loans. In Spain, for instance, loan rate stickiness raised the margin on consumer loans from 2.57% in 1980 to 4.67% in 2000. In Germany, margins on consumer loans appear to have increased from 4.32% in 1990 to 6.84% in 2000. A second positive impact of a low inflation environment is that the so-called "inflation tax" will be much smaller (Fisher-Modigliani, 1978; Dermine, 1985). A simple example will give the intuition beyond the inflation tax. Consider a case with no inflation in which equity is invested in a 3% coupon bond. After a 30% corporate tax rate is deducted, the revenue is 2.1% $((1 - 0.3) \times 3\%)$. The full profit can be paid as dividend as there is no need for retained earnings and higher capital since there is no growth of assets. If because of a 10% inflation rate, the same equity is invested in a 13% coupon bond, the profit after tax is only 9.1% $((1 - 0.3) \times 13\%)$, a figure too small to finance a necessary equity growth of 10%. No dividend can be paid in this case, and equity holders have suffered from an "inflation-tax."

Therefore, the impact of a low inflation environment on the profitability of banks will depend on the relative importance of reduced margins on deposits, higher profit on personal loans, and on the significance of the "inflation-tax."

In the next section, we review the strategy debate on focus versus diversification.

Table 12.3 Intermediation margin (%), 1980–2000

	1980	1985	1990	1995	2000
Belgium					
Treasury-bill	14.4	10.7	10.4	5.36	3.34
Margin on savings deposits	9.4	5.7	4.9	0.72	0.75
Margin on consumer loans				6.92	3.63
Retail intermediation margin				7.64	4.38
Margin on corporate loan	0.8	1.04	1.05	1.15	1.14
Netherlands					
Treasury-bill	9.2	6.85	8.13	5.18	3.34
Margin on savings deposits	4.2	3.5	5.63	3.13	1.84
Margin on consumer loans	5.3	1.65	3.62	2.32	2.91
Retail intermediation margin	9.5	5.15	9.25	5.45	4.75
Margin on corporate loan	3.05	−0.6	1.12	−0.18	0.41
Finland					
Treasury-bill	13.8	12.8	16.05	5.85	3.34
Margin on savings deposits	9.55	7.55	11.55	3.85	1.84
Margin on consumer loans	−3.64	−1.1	−0.45	4.09	2.75
Retail intermediation margin	5.91	6.45	11.1	7.94	4.59
Margin on corporate loan	−3.64	−1.1	−1.29	1.58	0.89
France					
Treasury-bill	12.2	9.5	10	5	3.34
Margin on savings deposits	5.3	3	5.6	0.66	0.92
Margin on consumer loans			5.4	3.03	4.85
Retail intermediation margin			11	3.69	5.77
Margin on corporate loan		3.83	1.19	2.28	1.75
Germany					
Treasury-bill	8.86	5.87	8.3	5.16	3.34
Margin on savings deposits			2.08	1.37	1.31
Margin on consumer loans			4.32	8.18	6.84
Retail intermediation margin			6.4	9.55	8.15
Margin on corporate loan	0.8	2.39	1.31	4.16	4.34
Spain					
Treasury-bill	12.2	12	14	8.33	3.34
Margin on savings deposits	8.45	8.25	11.58	5.58	2.37
Margin on consumer loans	2.57	5.03	3.18	5.62	4.67
Retail intermediation margin	11.02	13.28	14.76	11.2	7.04
Margin on corporate loan	−3.64	−1.1	−1.29	1.58	0.89

Source: Dermine (2003).

12.2   Focus versus diversification

The second main issue addressed in this strategy chapter is the issue of focus versus diversification. Traditional corporate finance theory states that no gains are to be expected from diversification in a world with perfect information and complete markets. Shareholders, holding a diversified portfolio of shares, can achieve the same results, in essence, by mimicking a diversified firm. Under this line of argument, cross-border mergers for reasons of diversification would have no merit, as shareholders could buy the shares of banks from two countries. Empirical evidence for the United States, consistent with this view, is that by DeLong (2001). She attempts to distinguish between focused mergers (same geography and activity) and non-focused mergers (different geography and/or activity). She reports that focused mergers create, on average, a gain of 3% in the combined value of the target and the bidder, while non-focused mergers destroy value.

To justify the gains from financial diversification, one has to turn to some types of market imperfections. Four motivations for corporate risk management and diversification have been advanced in the literature (e.g. Santomero, 1995; Froot and Stein, 1998; Dermine, 2004): managerial self-interest, non-linearity of taxes, cost of financial distress, and capital market imperfections. These are discussed briefly.

First, managerial self-interest refers to the fact that managers, having a significant fraction of their permanent income attached to the firm, cannot diversify risks adequately. Managers' risk aversion will lead to risk mitigation. Second, the non-linearity of taxes means that losses may not be fully tax-deductible, or that large profits could be taxed at a higher rate. In this case, a reduction of profit variance leads to a reduction of expected tax payments. Third, the cost of financial distress refers to the loss of value due to a state of distress. In banking, this could imply a loss of clientele or a loss of a profitable banking license (the "charter value"). Fourth, costs may arise from capital market imperfections. Because of asymmetric information, banks may find it costly to raise external funds. In such a context, losses could lead to a lower equity level, and missed profitable investment opportunities. Stabilization of profit can reduce the call for expensive external finance, and lead to the realization of profitable investments. An alternative explanation for the resources spent on risk control is linked to reputational risk. Because of opacity, investors cannot evaluate whether a reported loss is due to bad luck or to inferior management quality. In this context, stabilization of profit prevents a loss of value. So, even in the absence of bank regulation, there are several economic motivations for the control of risks and diversification in a bank.

The mathematics of financial diversification have been well understood since Markowitz (1959). An elegant expression of risk states that the standard deviation of total income is equal to the sum of individual risk, each of them weighted by the correlation between that risk and that of the entire firm.[8] Consider a bank present in three markets (say, three countries: Finland, Norway, and Sweden) with respective assets A in Finland, B in Norway, and C in Sweden, with

σ_A = standard deviation of return R_A on asset A (B, C), $\rho_{A,P}$ being the correlation between return on A (B, C) and the total bank, then the volatility, or riskiness, of total income, σ_P, is equal to:

$$\sigma_P = [A \times \sigma_A \times \rho_{A,P}] + [B \times \sigma_B \times \rho_{B,P}] + [C \times \sigma_C \times \rho_{C,P}]$$

The relationship indicates intuitively that, unless activities are highly correlated with the entire bank (correlation close to one), the sum of the risks is going to be less than the sum of individual risks. As a consequence, *ceteris paribus*, engaging in activities that are not highly correlated can bring about a reduction of volatility of income. Real economic benefits follow from stability of income since, as discussed earlier, market imperfections and opacity can raise the cost of external finance.

The expected gains from diversification across countries or activities will only materialize if correlations across sources of income are not too high. This becomes an empirical issue. Boyd and Runkle (1993) and Hughes *et al.* (1999) report that large banks, able to diversify credit risks across many states, exhibit a lower variance of profit in the United States. Other studies (Santomero and Chung, 1992; Boyd *et al.*, 1993), simulating a merger between banks and insurance companies, come to similar conclusions (a quite obvious result, since low correlation can only lead to more stable profits). Simulation results indicating the benefits of diversification must be viewed with caution for two reasons. First, there is an implicit assumption that the combined firm can be managed as efficiently as the separate firms. Second, as emphasized in an empirical study by Boyd and Runkle (1993), lower volatility of asset return is often combined with a lower equity base (higher leverage) so that the probability of default of large diversified institutions appears to be as high as that of smaller, less diversified but less leveraged, firms. At the international level, Berger *et al.* (2000) report very low correlations of the aggregate ROE of banking systems of the various European countries. Dahl and Logan (2002) analyze the overdue international claims of 28 UK-owned banks over the period 1987–2000. They report a significant gain from international diversification of credit risk exposure. Acharya *et al.* (2002), however, express caution in a detailed analysis of credit losses in Italy over the period 1993–1999 that the benefits of diversification might be lost with lack of expertise. Amihud *et al.* (2002) see no impact on the volatility of stock returns either before or after a cross-border merger.

A word of caution should be expressed here, concerning studies that focus on correlation and volatility of losses. As credit risk distribution is known to be highly skewed (many states of the world with fairly few loan losses, and few states of the world with periods of significant recession and substantial losses), it might be better to analyze the impact of diversification at times of deep recession. A standard approach in the management of trading risk is to simulate the impact of a large shock (*stress scenario*) on a portfolio. In Table 12.4, we report the provisions on loan losses (an imperfect estimate of loan losses) of the banking

Table 12.4 International diversification of credit risk, a simulation exercise: loan loss provisions as percentage (%) of total Loans

	1988	1989	1990	1991	1992
Austria	0.32	0.35	0.39	0.54	0.76
Belgium	1.38	1.35	0.64	0.88	1.09
Denmark	2.2	1.69	2.38	2.66	3.2
Finland	0.64	0.54	0.47	0.45	3.2
France	0.46	0.33	0.3	0.49	0.74
Germany	0.4	0.82	0.83	0.6	0.69
Greece	1.09	1.28	1.4	2.5	1.24
Italy	0.46	1.23	1.21	1.12	1.12
Luxembourg	1.48	1.55	2.17	1.72	1.62
Netherlands	0.39	0.34	0.39	0.46	0.43
Portugal	3.44	4.25	4.02	4.45	4.52
Spain	1.27	0.7	0.65	1.1	1.34
Sweden	1.72	1.51	0.75	3.2	6
United Kingdom	0.51	2.57	1.53	2.16	2.13
Diversified portfolio[a]	0.65	1.15	0.93	1.15	1.35

Source: Dermine (2003).

Note

a The diversified portfolio is a weighted-portfolio of loans of banks from each country, the weights being the 2000 GNP.

systems of several countries over the recession period 1988–1992. To study the potential benefits of diversification, we simulate the average loss on a GNP-weighted diversified loan portfolio. In the case of the United Kingdom, which experienced severe loan losses during that period (2.13% in 1992), one can observe that an internationally diversified bank would, *ceteris paribus*, reduce the loan losses by 37% (1.35% in 1992). Note that this is only a simulation. Part of the diversification benefit could disappear if credit management quality were to worsen in a large international organization.

12.2.1   Diversification at Lloyds TSB, the 1992 stress test case

In the first section of the chapter, we presented the strategy of Lloyds Bank over the period 1983–2000. Through a long series of sales of foreign assets, and purchase of domestic financial institutions, Lloyds TSB has created an efficient financial firm in the United Kingdom. In 1995, Sir Brian stated:

> By concentrating on fewer markets, we can simplify our business and reduce our overheads. Diversity carries with it complexity, and complexity creates cost, slippage and delay. Today's world is too competitive for us to handicap our people with extra costs, extra procedures and slippage in communication

and execution. Even more important, today's rate of change is too fast for us to tolerate the delays in decision making caused by having excessively complicated businesses. A sharper focus achieves better performance.

(Lloyds TSB Annual Report, 2005)

Given the prospects for demographics and economic growth in Western Europe, however, questions were raised about the growth potential, in particular when the Competition Commission will not allow additional mergers of significant size to take place. In the context of the earlier discussion, a second question must be raised about the strategy of Lloyds TSB, that of a lack of financial diversification, when risks are concentrated in one market. Again, the year 1992 provides a useful testing ground as it was the worst economic recession since the Second World War. Comparative data for British banks are presented in Table 12.5. An analysis of the profits of Lloyds TSB follows.

Table 12.5 indicates first that, due to asset disposals, the balance sheet of Lloyds TSB, for the financial year 1992, has been reduced substantially, in relation to those of its competitors. Also, while Barclays was severely affected by the recession, and both Barclays and NatWest equity were trading below net asset value, Lloyds Bank managed to have a market-to-book value ratio of 1.8, and an ROE of 16% during that recession period. If, at first glance, one could suspect a superior ability to control credit risk, this can be ruled out, as provisions for bad debt at Lloyds are more or less proportional to asset size. So, where was the profit coming from at a time of the worst recession since the Second World War? A careful reading of the 1992 Annual Report reveals that, indeed, UK retail banking at Lloyds was severely affected, making virtually no profit. Two main contributors to income were Lloyds Abbey Life (£298 million) and Problem Country debt (£193 million). The income on country debt came from a release of provisions, as the value of Brady bonds (LDC debt converted into bonds collaterized by zero-coupon US Treasury securities) were trading at a value substantially higher than previously provisioned Latin American loans. This is a perfect illustration of the benefits of diversification at work! The sources of diversification came from life insurance and exposure to country debt. We leave it to the reader to decide as to whether the exposure to LDC debt was a strategic choice, or a pure historical legacy dating from the early 1980s when Lloyds was an active lender to countries of South America.

Table 12.5 Profitability of Barclays, NatWest, and Lloyds in 1992

1992 Results (£m)	Barclays	NatWest	Lloyds
Total Assets	149,118	143,216	61,004
PreTax Profit	−242	405	801
MV/BV[a]	0.87	0.95	1.8
Provisions for Bad Debt	2,554	1,903	736

Note

a MV/BV = market value of shares divided by equity book value.

If focus may facilitate management attention and a better understanding of risks, it appears again that diversification can bring benefits at times of severe recession, and that a balanced firm must mix management focus with a healthy degree of diversification of income, *in medio virtus*.

12.2.2   The choice of corporate structure: societas Europeae?

Finally, to reap fully the benefits of cross-border banking, banks should be able to put in place an appropriate corporate structure. In theory, the European legislation with a single banking license would allow banks to operate with one corporate structure and branches in several countries. This would not only minimize the regulatory costs of having to comply with various regulators, but it would also avoid VAT payment on services provided by shared-services subsidiaries. However, the reality is that most of the large cross-border banks, such as the Scandinavian Nordea, the Dutch ING, and the German HypoVereinsbank (HVB) operate abroad with subsidiaries (Dermine, 2003).

Interviews conducted at ING Group and Nordea AB help to understand the choice of corporate structure.[9] Both banks express the view that, in effect, a single corporate entity would facilitate the exploitation of economies of scale. This is why, at Nordea AB, for instance, the asset management and securities business are put into cross-border structures with branches. The motivation to keep a subsidiary structure for banks is driven by eight arguments. The first four are of a temporary nature, likely to disappear overtime. The others are more permanent.

A first argument in favor of the subsidiary structure at the time of the merger is to keep "business as usual" and not to change the brand. This has a short-term timespan as both banking groups, Nordea and ING, are busy building their own brands. A second argument is that of reassurance of the local management that key functions will not be transferred. The reassurance of shareholders, in order to get their approval, is the third argument. MeritaNordbanken started with a dual listing in Stockholm and Helsinki. A dual structure reassures shareholders, as it gives both flexibility and continuity. The fourth argument is that of the need to reassure nations that they keep their bank. When acquiring the Norwegian Christiania Bank, Nordea stated that it would continue to operate as a legal entity. A fifth, and major argument concerns corporate tax. From an international corporate tax point of view, a subsidiary structure is often more flexible than a branch structure. That is, in case of future group restructuring, start-up losses are more easily preserved and taxable capital gains are more easily avoided in a subsidiary structure. Moreover, the conversion of a subsidiary into a branch could create a corporate tax liability. The sixth (surprising) argument is deposit insurance. One should be reminded that the deposit insurer of a subsidiary is the one in the host country, just as the insurer of a branch is the one in the home state. Moreover, in many countries, deposit insurance premiums are levied until the deposit insurance funds reach a certain level. After that, the premium is much reduced. If Nordea AB, based in Sweden, transformed its Norwegian subsidiary into a branch of its Swedish bank, it would have to contribute extra deposit insurance premiums to the home country Swedish deposit insurance fund in charge of protecting a larger pool of Swedish and Norwegian deposits. Apparently, the bank would not be able to collect the premiums paid to the Norwegian insurance fund. The seventh argument for a subsidiary structure is ring-fencing (protection from risk-shifting) and the ability to do a separate listing. Finally, the eighth, argument put forward in favor of a subsidiary structure is the ease with which to sell a business unit.

Of the eight arguments advanced to explain the choice of a subsidiary structure, four appear temporary (protection of the original brand, management trust, nationalistic feelings, and shareholder approval), two are due to the incomplete process of European integration (corporate tax and deposit insurance), but the last arguments are permanent features of business (asymmetric information and risk-shifting, listing, and flexibility). Two conclusions come out of this analysis of the factors governing the corporate structure. First, there are clear indications that much more work needs to be done on the corporate tax side to facilitate the creation of a European tax group by way of a branch structure. Second, the analysis indicates that the corporate structure of European banks is very unlikely to meet the single entity with branches textbook case, but will involve a web of branches and subsidiaries.

Nordea is an interesting test case. Nordea AB is the result of the merger of four leading banks in Finland (Merita), Sweden (Nordbanken), Denmark (Unidanmark), and Norway (Christiania Bank).[10] The group holds significant bank market shares in Nordic countries: 40% of banking assets in Finland, 25% in Denmark, 20% in Sweden, and 15% in Norway. Until March 2004, a listed holding company, Nordea AB, based in Stockholm, was the owner of banking subsidiaries operating in Scandinavia.

Very recently, Nordea AB announced its plan to move to a single corporate structure with the use of the Council Regulation on the Statute of a European Company[11] (*Societas Europeae*). The stated advantages are: regulation, book keeping, transparency, legal transactions, relations with rating agencies. In March 2004, the holding company in Sweden had received a banking licence. Progressively, the banking entities of the various countries will be housed into one single corporate bank entity, incorporated in Sweden. However, the corporate restructuring process is not easy. For instance, Finland has to change its law, as the financial contribution from branches are not the same as those of subsidiaries for the financing of bank supervision. Morever, as stated earlier, the deposit insurance is proving difficult. Mr Schütze, member of the Group executive Management, announced in June 2004:

> Nordea will apply to Internal Market Commissioner Frits Bolkenstein for a "grandfather clause" for the 1994 Directive to exempt *Ses* formed by the merger of existing banks in different countries from the home country requirement for deposit guarantees and thereby simply continue in local schemes.

> (Nordea, 2004)

It is not yet clear what the response of the EU Commissioner will be, but this would take us back to the situation before the 1994 *Deposit Guarantee Directive*. Its *home country* format was to ensure a matching of responsibility and account-ability between bank supervisors and deposit insurers. If Swedish supervisors have the home country control task of supervising the whole Scandinavian group Nordea, while deposit insurers of various countries are in charge of insuring local deposits, the matching of supervision and regulation would again be lost (Baltensperger and Dermine, 1987).

12.3 Conclusions

The purpose of the chapter has been to discuss two issues in bank strategy: the trade-off between short- and long-term value creation, and the issue of focus versus diversification. The case of Lloyds TSB helps us to understand that value-based management has been quite successful for a large number of years, but that focus on cost-cutting and banking into one country can lead to problem of future growth. A balance must be found between keeping growth opportunities and short term profit. Second, we have reviewed the various arguments for control of risk and diversification in banking. If focus can facilitate management attention and speed of response, diversification of income can be particularly welcome, partic-ularly at the time of a strong recession. A simulation of credit portfolios diversi-fication during the deep recession of 1992 shows that international diversification of credit risk across Europe would have helped banks from the United Kingdom or Sweden. The case of Lloyds TSB in 1992 reveals that the bank was greatly helped in 1992 by the holding of international Brady bonds, but also by domes-tic diversification into non-bank activities, namely life insurance. Finally, a call is made to European authorities to facilitate the creation of a single corporate entity, the *Societas Europeae*. Whether one looks at the trade off between short- and long-term corporate objectives, and focus versus diversification, the *in medio virtus* rule is to be highly recommended.

12A.1 Appendix: value, economic profit, and growth

In this appendix, it is shown that the market value of equity is equal to the value of equity plus the discounted value of future economic profits.

The market value of shares = present value of future dividends discounted at the cost of equity, that is the opportunity return on shares (R_s)

$$\text{Market value of shares} = \frac{\text{DIVID}_1}{1 + R_s} + \frac{\text{DIVID}_2}{(1 + R_s)} + \cdots$$

Simple assumptions allow to visualize the key-drivers of the market value of equity.

Constant dividend–payout ratio, $p = \text{DIVIDEND/EARNINGS}$
Perpetual growth of dividends, $g = (1-p) \times \text{ROE}$

It can be proved (see below) that the market value of equity is equal to equity plus the discounted value of future economic profits.

$$MV = E + \frac{(ROE - R_s)XE}{R_s - g}$$

Under these assumptions, the market-to-book value ratio is equal to,

$$\frac{MV}{E} = \frac{ROE - R_s}{R_s - g} + 1$$

Proof

$$\text{Market value of shares} = \frac{DIVIDEND_1}{R_s - g} = \frac{p \times EARNINGS_1}{R_s - g}$$

$$\text{Market value of shares} = \frac{p \times ROE \times Equity}{R_s - (1 - p) \times ROE}$$

$$\text{Market value of shares} - E = \frac{p \times ROE \times Equity}{R_s - (1 - p) \times ROE} - E$$

$$\text{Market value of shares} = E + \frac{(ROE - R_s) \times E}{R_s - g}.$$

12A.2   Appendix: diversification and marginal risk contribution

If we define x_i as the assets invested in business (country) i, R_i as the return on asset x_i, then the total net income is equal to,

$$\text{Total income} = \sum_i R_i \times x_i$$

And the variance of total income, σ_p^2, is equal to,

$$\sigma_p^2 = \sum_i \sum_j x_i x_j \text{Cov}(R_i, R_j)$$
$$= \sum_i x_i \text{Cov}(R_i, R_p)$$
$$= \sum_i x_i \rho_{i,p} \sigma_i \sigma_p$$

Total risk, or volatility of aggregate income, σ_p, follows.

$$\sigma_p = \sum_i x_i \sigma_i \rho_{i,p}$$

Acknowledgment

The author is grateful to Jean Cropper for editorial assistance.

Notes

1 Market imperfections, such as a lack of competition or externalities, may demand public interventions.
2 On value creation in banking, see Dermine and Bissada (2002). On pitfalls with value centers in banking, see Dermine (2004).
3 The measure is not perfect as it includes both a cost and an income variable. Economic-based measures of cost efficiency, such as Data Envelopment Analysis (DEA), are superior measures of operational efficiency (Canhoto and Dermine, 2003).
4 In a meeting with the author, Sir Brian explained that the attempt to take over Standard Chartered Bank was, in fact, aligned with the strategy of being one of the four leading firms in any market which Lloyds Bank would choose to enter.
5 Midland was taken over by Hong Kong and Shanghai Bank (HSBC) in 1992.
6 This specific discussion addresses one of the issues allocated to Commission 2 "*Competitive Strategies*" of the SUERF Conference.
7 Inelasticity can be explained by oligopolistic equilibrium models of the banking industry (Gual, 2004).
8 Proof available in Appendix 12A.2.
9 In both cases, we were able to meet the general counsel, the tax and compliance directors, and executive directors in charge of the corporate structure.
10 Nordbanken and Merita merged in 1997 to create MeritaNordbanken. In March 2000, this group merged with Unidanmark. In October 2000, the Norwegian Government Bank Investment Fund decided to sell its shares in Christiania Bank og Kreditkasse to MeritaNordbanken.
11 OJ 2001. The directive came into force late 2004.

References

Acharya, V., I. Hasan, and A. Saunders (2002). "The Effects of Focus and Diversification on Bank Risk and Return: Evidence from Individual Loan Portfolios," forthcoming, *Journal of Business*.

Amihud, Y., G. DeLong, and A. Saunders (2000). "The Effects of Cross-Border Bank Mergers on Bank Risk and Value," mimeo, *Journal of International Money and Finance*, forthcoming.

Baltensperger, E. and J. Dermine (1987). "Banking Deregulation," *Economic Policy*, 4 (April), 63–109.

Berger, A., R. DeYoung, H. Genay, and G. Udell (2000). "Globalization of Financial Institutions: Evidence from Cross-border Banking Performance," in *Brookings-WhartonPapers on Financial Services*, 23–120.

Bose, P. and A. Morgan (1998). "Banking on Shareholder Value, an Interview with Sir Brian Pitman," *The McKinsey Quarterly*, No. 2, 96–105.

Boyd, J. and D. Runkle (1993). "Size and Performance of Banking Firms," *Journal of Monetary Economics*, 31 (February), 47–67.

Boyd, J., S. Graham, and R. Hewitt (1993). "Bank Holding Company Mergers with Nonbank Financial Firms: Effects on the Risk of Failure," *Journal of Banking and Finance*, 17(1), 43–63.

Canhoto, A. and J. Dermine (2003). "A Note on Banking Efficiency in Portugal, New vs Old Banks," *Journal of Banking and Finance*, 27(11), 2087–2098.

Competition Commission (2002). "The Supply of Banking Services by Clearing Banks to Small and Medium-Sized Enterprises in the UK." A Report presented to Parliament by the Secretary of State of Trade and Industry and the Chancellor of the Exchequer, March 2002.

Dahl, D. and A. Logan (2002). "Granularity and International Diversification: An Empirical Analysis of Overdue Claims at Banks," mimeo, Bank of England, 1–28.

DeLong, G. (2001). "Stockholder Gains from Focusing versus Diversifying Bank Mergers," *Journal of Financial Economics*, 59, 221–252.

Dermine, J. (1985). "Taxes, Inflation and Banks' Market Value," *Journal of Business, Finance and Accounting*, 12(1), Spring 1985, 65–74.

Dermine, J. (1997). "Eurobanking, a New World," Laureate (Second Prize) of the *1997 EIB Prize*, published in EIB Papers, 2(2), 31–44.

Dermine, J. (2003). "European Banking, Past, Present, and Future," in *The Transformation of the European Financial System* (Second ECB Central Banking Conference), eds, V. Gaspar, P. Hartmann, and O. Sleijpen, ECB, Frankfurt, 2003 (available in e-book: www.ecb.int/pub/pdf/TransformationEuropeanfinancialsystem.pdf).

Dermine, J. (2004). "ALM in Banking," in *Asset & Liability Management, Handbooks in Finance Series*, eds, W. Ziemba and S. Zenios, Amsterdam: North Holland.

Dermine, J. and Y. Bissada (2002). *Asset & Liability Management, A Guide to Value Creation and Risk Control*, London: FT-Prentice Hall.

Fisher, S. and F. Modigliani (1978). "Towards an Understanding of the Real Effects and Costs of Inflation," *Weltwirtschaftliches Archiv*, 114, 810–833.

Froot, K. A. and J. C. Stein (1998). "Risk Management, Capital Budgeting, and Capital Structure Policy for Financial Institutions, an Integrated Approach," *Journal of Financial Economics*, 47 (January), 55–82.

Gual, J. (2004). "The Integration of EU Banking Markets," CEPR Discussion Paper Series No. 4212, 1–41.

Hughes, J., W. Lang, L. Mester and C. Moon (1999). "The Dollars and Sense of Bank Consolidation," *Journal of Banking and Finance*, 23(2–4), 291–324.

Jensen, M. (2001). "Value Maximization, Stakeholder Theory, and the Corporate Objective Function," *Journal of Applied Corporate Finance*, 14(3), 8–21.

McTaggart, J., P. Kontes, and M. Mankins (1994). *The Value Imperative*, New York: The Free Press.

Markowitz, H. M. (1959). *Portfolio Selection: Efficient Diversification of Investment* (Cowles Foundation Monograph 16), New Haven, CT: Yale University Press.

Nordea (2004). "Pioneering the Move Towards a European Company," press release, 23 June (www.nordea.com).

Pitman, B. (2003). "Leading for Value," *Harvard Business Review*, 81(4), 41–46.

Salomon Brothers (1995). "Lloyds Bank/TSB: A Brilliant Strategic Stroke," European Equity Research, 27 October.

Santomero, A. (1995). "Financial Risk Management, The Whys and the Hows," *Financial Markets, Institutions and Instruments*, 4, 1–14.

Santomero, A. and E. Chung (1992). "Evidence in Support of Broader Bank Powers," *Financial Markets, Institutions and Instruments*, 1, 1–69.

13 European primarily Internet banks

The profitability outlook

Javier Delgado, Ignacio Hernando and María J. Nieto

13.1 Introduction

For the purpose of this chapter, primarily Internet banks are those that rely heavily, although not exclusively (e.g. telephone, ATM) on Internet as a delivery channel. For this reason, it is usual to refer to Internet banks as being 'primarily' Internet banks rather than Internet banks 'only'. For the reminder of this chapter, the terms 'Internet bank' and 'primarily Internet bank' will be used interchangeably. To date, Internet banks have been substantially less profitable than traditional banks worldwide and this seems mainly explained by their higher overhead expenses.

The objective of this paper is to identify and estimate the magnitude of technology-based scale and technology-based learning effects of European Internet banks that heavily rely on this new technology to develop their business model. These effects are considered additive to the general scale and experience effects that occur at new banks that use the existing technology (i.e branches, ATMs). To this end, we perform regression tests based on pooled annual data sets of Internet and newly chartered traditional banks in Europe, using two financial ratios as endogenous variables (return on assets (ROA) and non-interest expenses over average assets). Our results indicate that Internet banks display significant technology-based scale economies arising from their ability to control operational expenses more efficiently than the new traditional banks. However, we do not find evidence that Internet banks access experience effects as a result of the heavy usage of the Internet technology.

The rest of the chapter is organized as follows. Section 13.2 describes the Internet banking landscape in Europe, paying special attention to the differences and similarities in performance of Internet banks in the United States and Europe. Section 13.3 defines the four performance processes whose magnitude is being estimated: general and technology-based scale and experience economies. Section 13.4 describes the data and the analytical framework adopted to test for the existence of general and technology-based scale and experience economies available for Internet banks. Finally, Section 13.5 summarizes the regression results and presents the main conclusions.

13.2 Stylized facts of Internet banks in Europe

Most of the European Internet banks started to operate in the late 1990s but some institutions launched informational Web sites before and/or were using the telephone as a delivery channel. Market shares of Internet banks vary significantly per country. The differences across countries in Internet banking penetration appear to be largely explained by the differences in the availability of access to the Internet. According to an OECD study (2001), France, Spain and Portugal followed by Italy, Germany and Belgium are among the group of countries with a low rate of Internet penetration.[1] The Scandinavian countries have the highest penetration rates at over 50 per cent, comparable to that in the United States, and also show the highest levels of Internet banking use.

The situation in Spain and Portugal compared to that of other countries appears to be somewhat atypical as it shows a level of utilization of this distribution channel above that which would be expected from the level of Internet penetration. Thus, in these two countries, despite the low Internet penetration rate, the take-up of Internet banking is at levels above those in countries such as France, Germany or Italy. Somewhat in contrast, the United States has a relatively low level of utilization of this distribution channel for banking despite a high Internet penetration rate. Technical and financial safety is seen as a crucial factor for the taking-up of Internet banking in both sides of the Atlantic. As a result, many Internet banks have found it necessary to have some form of physical presence and/or maintain other channels such as the telephone, hence the term 'primarily Internet' bank.

Unlike the United States where most of the Internet banks were established as independent start-ups, most European Internet banks are part of an existing financial group. This fact is relevant when analyzing the financial performance of Internet banks in both geographical areas. In Europe, the long-term viability of Internet banks has to be contemplated in the context of the financial group often assuming the specialization of the Internet bank in some market segments (e.g. mutual funds).

The differences in Internet bank adoption rates in the United States and the European Union are mainly explained by the continued reliance of United States' households on paper cheques, which are less compatible with Internet banking and require physical bank offices for the collection and clearing of cheques. Moreover, the take-up of online brokerage, which is one of the main drivers used for these banks for acquiring new customers, did not flow through to banks in the United States, because they were restricted in the degree to which they could engage in securities activities.[2]

The profitability measured as ROA of the European Internet banks was negative on average over the period 1994–2002, although about half of those institutions included in this study were showing profits as of end 2001. This finding is consistent with the fact that no matter what technology a new bank is relying on, it is likely to perform worse than a mature bank for a number of years. A similar trend is found when analysing the non-interest expenses of Internet banks on both sides of the Atlantic. Costs associated with Web site development (i.e. software research and development expenses, amortization of purchased software, data processing) and promotion (i.e. marketing) to gain name recognition are higher in the case of primarily Internet banks, due to the fact that they are new banks, and to the nature of the distribution channel itself.[3]

The Internet delivery channel potentially increases and modifies traditional banking risks and influences their risk profile (see BIS, 1998, 2000; Ciciretti *et al.*, 2004). A major source of risk for banks is credit risk. However, there is anecdotal evidence showing lower lending activity of Internet banks as compared with mature traditional banks (see Delgado and Nieto (2004) for evidence in Spain). In general, market risk and liquidity risk are greater when customers can transfer their deposits from one institution to another rapidly to take advantage of higher interest rates (see Delgado and Nieto, 2004 for evidence in Spain). At the same time, strategic, legal and security risks, as well as reputational risks are potentially greater and differ somewhat from those faced by traditional banks.

The regulatory approaches to deal with consumer protection in general and technical and financial safety of Internet banking in particular are most relevant since safety is seen as a crucial factor for the taking-up of Internet banking in Europe. Nieto (2001) encourages regulators to deal with these concerns according to the principle of neutrality with regard to the distribution channel. This principle implies that rules on transparency of operations, data privacy, as well as accountability and, in general, on consumer protection should be neutral to the distribution channel. By tackling consumers' security concerns in this 'technology neutral' fashion, European authorities may encourage a larger number of consumers to use this delivery channel on a long-term basis.

13.3 Definition of general and technology-based scale and experience effects

The objective of our study is to test for the existence of four distinct but simultaneous performance processes at primarily Internet banks in the European Union: general scale and experience effects, which are common to all new chartered banks, regardless of their business models, and technology-based scale and experience effects which are specific to new banks that use primarily Internet as delivery channel (see DeYoung, 2001, 2002, 2005).

General scale effects reflect the improvement in financial performance of banks as their output grows (asset size is a proxy for output), mainly through lower per unit costs. General experience effects refer to the improvement in financial performance through learning-based developments in cost control, risk management and investment diversification among others, as young banks accumulate experience (age is being used as a proxy). However, at an empirical level, because age and size are positively and significantly correlated at young banks, it is not a trivial task to disentangle experience and scale effects.

Technology-based scale effects imply even better financial performance of primarily Internet banks as size increases, because Internet technology is scalable and certain banking activities become more scalable as they incorporate it (e.g. credit scoring models to evaluate credit risk of SMEs) (see DeYoung, 2001, 2002, 2005; Sato and Hawkins, 2001). Technology-based experience effects explain better performance of Internet banks as they age and customers gain experience in transacting over the Internet, while managers better understand the new technology. Both technology-based scale and experience effects are additive to the general scale and experience effects. If significant technology based scale and experience effects do exist, then the financial performance of primarily Internet banks will improve more quickly than that of the new traditional banks, which can only rely on general experience and scale effects.

13.4 The empirical framework

Our empirical analysis on the learning and scale economies in European Internet banks is based on annual audited public financial data from BankScope between 1994 and 2002.[4] Our data corresponds to three samples of banks chartered in the European Union: primarily Internet (13 banks), established traditional of comparable size (335 banks) and newly chartered banks, a subset of the previous sample (45 banks).

The primarily Internet banks are separately chartered individual (non-consolidated) institutions (i.e neither a trade name – a non-separate entity that uses a commercial name – nor a dedicated branch) that reported to the European Central Bank (ECB, 2001)[5] to have business models heavily reliant on the Internet as the most important delivery channel. All of these banks were active at the end of 2002 and fulfil the following two conditions: (1) to offer mainly, although not exclusively, basic banking services including taking deposits and granting credits and (2) to be a new start-up or an existing bank that changed its business model in order to operate primarily by Internet.[6] According to the BankScope data base, they all belong to some financial group. The average age of the Internet banks sample is 5.0 years.

The established banks of comparable size are also separately chartered individual (non-consolidated) institutions which fulfil the following conditions: (1) their business models rely mainly, although not necessary exclusively, on traditional delivery channels (2) they are also commercial banks and (3) their asset size is in the same range as that of the primarily Internet banks (between €20.8 billion and 74 million). Within the sample of established banks, a subset of banks was created including those institutions that, in addition to these conditions, were launched in or after 1990. This sample of newly chartered traditional banks consists of forty-five entities and it is used as a performance benchmark. As is the case for the Internet banks, most of the newly chartered traditional banks belong to some financial group and their average age is 6.1 years.

The combined data set (primarily Internet banks plus newly chartered traditional banks) is an unbalanced panel of 378 observations of 58 banks, over a nine-year period starting in 1994. The banks' age is in years and the first year of operation has been considered entirely even if the bank has not been fully operating for the whole year. To the degree that the newly chartered traditional banks sample contains banks that use Internet to some extent as a delivery channel,

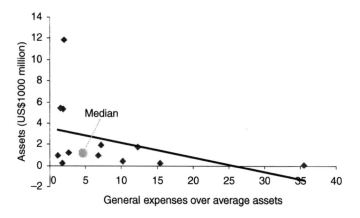

Figure 13.1 Internet banks: size and efficiency.

it will be harder to find evidence in favour of the existence of technology-based experience and scale effects at the primarily Internet banks.

Figure 13.1 shows the relation between asset size and the ratio of general expenses over average assets for the Internet banks in 2000. This figure, making use only of the cross-section dimension, suggests the existence of a negative relationship between asset size and the ratio of general expenses.[7] This relationship also holds when the two banks with extreme values of size and expenses are removed from the sample.

This result represents evidence in favour of the existence of technology-based effects. However, a regression analysis, controlling for the influence of other variables, is needed for rigorously testing the existence of such effects. More precisely, the regression framework attempts to identify and discriminate between the technology-based scale effects and the technology-based experience effects, showing whether the underperformance of Internet banks disappears as Internet banks grow larger and/or as they gain experience with the new business model.

Our empirical model consists of a reduced form equation allowing for the simultaneous existence of both technology-based scale effects (INTERNET × ln ASSETS) and technology-based experience effects (INTERNET × ln AGE).

$$
\begin{aligned}
\text{PERFORMANCE}_{it} \\
= \alpha + \beta \times \text{INTERNET}_i + \delta \times \ln \text{AGE}_{i,t} \\
+ \lambda \times \ln \text{ASSETS}_{i,t} + \gamma \times \text{INTERNET}_i \times \ln \text{AGE}_{i,t} \\
+ \eta \times \text{INTERNET}_i \times \ln \text{ASSETS}_{i,t} + \sigma X_{i,t} + \varepsilon_{i,t}
\end{aligned}
$$

where subscripts i and t represent index banks and time, respectively.

PERFORMANCE is alternatively ROA or non-interest expenses over average assets, two ratios that summarize the financial performance of the sample banks.

INTERNET is a dummy variable that equals 1 (primarily Internet banks) or 0 (newly chartered traditional banks).

The set of control variables (X) includes the real GDP growth and the inflation rate to control for the effects of macroeconomic conditions over the sample period (1994–2002) on the performance variables and country dummies to control for the effect of banks nationality on the performance variables (e.g. different absolute minimum capital requirements for licensing purposes across the European Union).

β indicates the different financial performance, at the means of the data, between primarily Internet banks and newly chartered banks when there are no significant technology-based effects. In the more general case, this performance gap would take the following form:

$$\beta + \lambda * \ln \overline{AGE}_{i,t} + \eta \times \ln \overline{ASSETS}_{i,t}$$

where $\ln \overline{AGE}$ and $\ln \overline{ASSETS}$ denote the mean values of the corresponding variables.

η and γ indicate the importance of any technology-based scale or experience effect, respectively.

λ and δ show the importance of general scale or experience effects, respectively.

As has been already mentioned, the colinearity between AGE and ASSETS (expressed in real terms) makes very difficult empirically separating experience and scale effects. For that reason, two alternative equations have been estimated, considering technology-based scale and technology-based experience effects in isolation, as a robustness test to investigate the potential effects of colinearity on the parameter estimates.

The regressions performed in this study use pooled data sets that combine the primarily Internet banks with the newly chartered traditional banks in Europe, and are estimated using both ordinary least squares (OLS) and generalized least squares random-effects (GLS-RE) estimation techniques. The random-effects approach includes, in addition to the usual random disturbance term, a bank-specific random disturbance term that accounts for the unexplained variation in the dependent variable that it is specific to bank i during the sample period.[8] The main results are in general robust to the estimation technique.

13.5   Main results and conclusions

Table 13.1 summarizes the most important results of the analysis that have tried to identify and estimate the magnitude of technology-based scale and learning economies of European Internet banks. The results indicate that, on the one hand, newly chartered traditional banks show significant evidence of cost related general scale economies. On the other hand, Internet banks show strong evidence of scale economies in terms of ROA. Our results show that an increase in asset size by 50 per cent results in a 1.85 percentage points increase in ROA. The primary source of the technology-based scale effects seems to be the ability of primarily Internet banks to control operational expenses even more efficiently than the new traditional banks. On average, a 50 per cent increase in asset size is associated with a 3.15 percentage points decrease in the ratio of non-interest expenses over average assets at primarily Internet banks, compared to only a 0.33 percentage

Table 13.1 Impact (p.p.) of an increase in asset size by 50 per cent

Impact on	Internet banks	Newly chartered traditional banks
ROA	1.59	—
Non-interest expenses over average assets	−2.61	−0.33

point decrease at newly chartered traditional banks. There is no conclusive evidence that either new traditional banks or Internet banks enjoy experience economies as they age.

The empirical analysis indicates that the success of the Internet bank model in Europe depends on the ability of these banks to save on overhead costs from technology-based scale economies and on whether these savings are sufficient to close the remaining profitability gap with traditional banks. Nonetheless, a note of caution must be introduced given the preliminary character of the findings of this study, which are based on only thirteen European Internet banks over a relatively short time horizon.

Finally, to the extent that Internet banks are struggling to prove themselves a viable business model, banking regulators and supervisors are encouraged to respond to the challenges posed by the incorporation of Internet in accordance with the principle of neutrality with regard to the distribution channel. It is in the realm of consumer protection in which, in order to protect consumers' interests, financial regulators are encouraged to specify for this distribution channel the general rules on transparency of operations and customer protection. By tackling consumers' security concerns, authorities may favour the use of this delivery channel by a higher share of the population, which would allow Internet banks to capture more of the potential scale efficiencies implied in our estimations.

Acknowledgements

The opinions stated herein are those of the authors and do not necessarily reflect those of Banco de España. The authors are grateful to the participants in the 25th SUERF Colloquium (Madrid, October 2004) for their valuable comments. Any errors, however, are entirely our own.

Notes

1 Internet penetration is usually measured as the percentage of the total population using the Internet in each country, while Internet banking penetration is the number of customers expressed as a percentage of the total population.
2 See Barth *et al.* (2003) for comparisons of the permissible range of banking activities across countries.
3 See Sullivan (2000), ECB (2001) and Delgado and Nieto (2004) for evidence in the United States, the European Union and Spain, respectively.

4 BankScope is a financial database covering 10,500 World Banks on CD-ROM with financial analysis software. It offers subscribers data up to eight years of detailed spreadsheet information, compiled by FITCHIBCA mostly from the balance sheet, income statement and applicable notes found in audited annual reports. It also includes data details on ownership, produced by Bureau Van Dijk, such as lists of shareholders and lists of banking subsidiaries.

5 The ECB launched a survey on e-banking activity in the European Union in 2002. The survey is not public. All thirteen primarily Internet banks (4 German, 3 Spanish, 2 Swedish, 2 Danish, 1 French and 1 British) reported to the ECB to operate mainly via Internet.

6 In the event of a change in business model (e.g. Patagon), two different banks have been considered: 'before' as a traditional bank and 'after' as an Internet bank.

7 A similar cross-sectional relationship between age and the ratio of general expenses to average assets is found.

8 As explained by DeYoung (2005), a fixed effect estimation approach is not feasible here, because the phenomena being tested for are themselves fixed effects. As a consequence, much of the variation necessary to estimate the coefficients β, γ and η in the equations would disappear in a fixed effects model.

References

Barth, J. R., D. E. Nolle, T. Phumiwasana, and G. Yago (2003). 'A Cross-Country Analysis of the Bank Supervisory Framework and Bank Performance', *Financial Markets, Institutions & Instruments*, 12(2), pp. 67–120.

BIS (1998). *Risk Management for Electronic Banking and Electronic Money Activities*, Basel Committee on Banking Supervision, March.

BIS (2000). *Electronic Banking Group Initiatives and White Papers*, Basel Committee on Banking Supervision, October.

Ciciretti, R., I. Hasan and C. Zazzara (2004). *Do Internet Activities Add Value? Evidence from the Banking Industry*, Rensselaer Polytechnic Institute Working Paper, mimeo.

Delgado, J. and M. Nieto (2004). 'Internet Banking in Spain Some Stylized Facts. Monetary Integration, Market and Regulation', *Research in Banking and Finance*, 4, pp. 187–209.

DeYoung, R. (2001). 'The Financial Progress of Pure Play Internet Banks', *Electronic Finance: A New Perspective and Challenges*, BIS Papers No. 7, November, pp. 80–86.

DeYoung, R. (2002). *Learning-by-doing, Scale Efficiencies, and Financial Performance at Internet Only Banks*, Federal Reserve Bank of Chicago Working Paper 2001–06, June.

DeYoung, R. (2005). 'The Performance of Internet-based Business Models: Evidence from the Banking Industry', *Journal of Business*, 78(3), pp. 893–948.

European Central Bank (2001). *E-Finance: Market Developments and Supervisory Issues*. March. Mimeo.

Nieto, M. J. (2001). 'Reflections on the Regulatory Approach to E-finance', *Electronic Finance: A New Perspective and Challenges*, BIS Papers No. 7, November, pp. 90–97.

OECD (2001). 'Electronic Finance: Economics and Institutional Factors', DAFFE/CMF (2001) 42.

Sato, S. and J. Hawkins (2001). 'Electronic Finance: An Overview of the Issues', *Electronic Finance: A New Perspective and Challenges*, BIS Papers No. 7, November, pp. 1–13.

Sullivan, R. J. (2000). 'How has the Adoption of Internet Banking Affected Performance and Risk in Banks? A Look at Internet Banking in the 10th Federal Reserve District', *Financial Industry Perspectives*, Federal Reserve Bank of Kansas City, December, pp. 1–16.

14 Bank risks and the business cycle

*Lieven Baele, Olivier De Jonghe,
and Rudi Vander Vennet*

14.1 Introduction

Bank risks are inherently cyclical. As financial intermediaries, banks are exposed to different types of risk such as credit and interest rate risk. Since the underlying sources of these risks are closely connected to the business cycle, bank health is related to the economic conditions in which they operate. Banking crises, or significant deteriorations in overall bank health, typically occur in economic downturns. For a large sample of developed and developing countries, Kaminsky and Reinhart (1999) show that banking crises occur as the economy enters into a recession, often following a prolonged boom in economic activity fueled by increased bank lending. However, while financial crises have often been preceded by sharp fluctuations in the macroeconomy and in asset prices, it would be a mistake to seek their origin exclusively in macroeconomic instability. While macroeconomic conditions may often be the proximate cause, banking problems usually emerge because of existing weaknesses in the banking system that have taken some time to build up (Llewellyn, 2002). In Europe, the typical example is the Scandinavian banking crisis in the early 1990s caused by a combination of imprudent lending and asset price collapses. An analysis of the time profile of bank risks in the Scandinavian banking crisis reveals that risks were gradually building up in the overlapping periods of financial liberalization, intensified competition, changing macroeconomic conditions, resulting in the ultimate banking crisis (Hyytinen, 2002). Moreover, while banking crises are often caused by an economic downturn, they may also amplify the recession. In most cases, banking crises are associated with a significant decline of real activity, sometimes caused by a credit crunch. As the profitability of financial institutions declines and confidence wanes, financial institutions tend to seek higher rewards for risk-taking or even withdraw from such activity altogether. Rising risk aversion or a crisis of confidence can have pronounced adverse effects on the real economy especially when the capital base of financial institutions has been eroded. The propagation mechanism results in falling bank loans and generates persistent declines in aggregate investment and output (Chen, 2001).

This seemingly inevitable sequence was not observed in the recent downturn over the period 2000–2003. Although economic growth in Europe, and especially in the large core countries of the European Monetary Union (EMU), declined substantially, some analysts question whether this period can be characterized as a recession (see the Business Cycle Dating Committee of the Centre for Economic Policy Research). Nevertheless, the economic slowdown was accompanied by a series of events that are usually very harmful for bank health (see BIS, 2004). The most important feature was the protracted stock market decline from mid-2000 onward, amplified by the September 2001 attack, slack consumer and business confidence, a relatively high number of corporate failures, and the accounting scandals that erupted from mid-2002 onward (also in Europe, for example, Ahold and Parmalat). Hence, there is every reason to assume that economic conditions were harmful for the risk profile of European banks. Yet, the banking system as a whole has proved to be very resilient. There were few, if any, bank failures or systematic problems among European banks that have prompted regulatory interventions or bailouts. Also, the number of actual rating downgrades of major European banks by rating agencies over the 2000–2003 period was very limited; from mid-2003 onwards some banks received a rating upgrade (FitchRatings, 2003).

This raises a number of questions that are important for the banks themselves, and also for regulators and bank supervisors, who care about the systemic stability of the financial system. Why was bank health less impaired in the recent downturn? A number of hypotheses have already been forwarded. Was it because the downturn was mild and commercial banks received ample assistance from the central banks in the form of historically low short-term interest rates? Was it because banks have become better at managing their risks and could rely on new markets for risk mitigation? Was it because banks entered the downturn with much healthier balance sheets than has been the case in previous recessions? Or have banks opted for corporate strategies that have enabled them to sustain profits even in otherwise unfavorable market conditions? These are the main explanations that have been forwarded by bank analysts and academic researchers (see, for example, Jordan and Rosengren, 2002).

Adequacy of absorption capacities of systemically important financial institutions has been a key element explaining the banking systems' initial resilience to the recent downturn and several shocks such as corporate and sovereign defaults. Buffers have been built up in recent years in terms of capital and profitability, the extent of those cushions differing from one banking system to the other. Most major financial institutions appeared to have had relatively favorable capital and liquidity positions prior to the slowdown. Increased use of new and innovative risk management techniques during the 1990s may have helped to avoid excessive risk exposures whereas the use of new financial instruments allowed credit risk to be more widely spread. Other factors, it has been argued, have also been important in explaining the resilience of financial institutions. They include that the slowdown was relatively shallow, a commercial property boom was absent and that much of the financing for the (technology) boom was obtained through capital markets rather than banks. However, as a result of recent developments, the profitability cushions and surplus capital in the financial sector have been eroded to some extent. As problems have continued to accumulate, some institutions may have come closer to critical thresholds, especially as the problems are not confined to a single area, but have been affecting several areas at the same time. Downward revisions of expectations for economic activity, trading losses due to stock market drops, a general decline in revenues from capital market activities, and deteriorating loan portfolios and record numbers of corporate defaults have all added to pressures on profitability and capital.

We try to assess some of these commonly advanced explanations for bank resilience on a broad sample of listed European banks in the 2000–2003 economic downturn. We identify banks with different strategies and different characteristics before the slowdown and investigate their risk profile before and during the economic downturn with market-based measures of return and risk. Banks are sorted in quintiles over the pre-downturn period 1996–2000 based on a number of observable characteristics related to their geographic location, their institutional type, or the initial balance sheet conditions with which they entered the downturn. Subsequently we investigate their return/risk profile during the economic slowdown of 2000–2003 using market-based measures such as the Q ratio, the Sharpe ratio, and the volatility of stock returns.

The rest of the chapter is organized as follows. In Section 14.2, we explore the link between bank return/risk and the business cycle. Section 14.3 subdivides the banks in relevant groups based on different criteria. Section 14.4 explains the empirical methodology and describes the sample of European banks. Section 14.5 discusses the main empirical results and the final section concludes.

14.2   Banks and the business cycle

In their role as financial intermediaries, banks are inherently exposed to changes in the overall economic conditions. From a theoretical point of view, banks are commonly characterized as delegated monitors, because they issue illiquid claims (loans) funded by short-term deposits with a relatively high degree of liquidity (Diamond, 1984). In their lending business, banks are exposed to default risk, caused by problems of asymmetric information, both *ex ante* (adverse selection) and *ex post* (moral hazard). In their role as maturity transformers, banks are exposed to interest rate risk because the average duration of their assets exceeds that of their liabilities. However, these risks are themselves influenced or even determined by business cycle conditions. In the literature, various channels have been developed through which economic conditions may have an impact on bank risk. First, there is an obvious association between the business cycle, the degree of asymmetric information, and bank default risk. Second, the economic environment may influence bank lending behavior and may alter the trade-offs between risk and franchise value. The third channel builds on the role of bank lending in the transmission of monetary policy. It should be kept in mind that these economic effects do not occur in isolation but in a changing regulatory framework. In the EU, the single market program, the harmonization of bank supervisory and capital adequacy rules, and the introduction of the euro can be regarded as milestones (Berger, 2003).

First, theories of imperfect capital markets (see, for example, Bernanke and Gertler, 1989 and Kiyotaki and Moore, 1997) argue that asymmetric information and agency costs are typically high during business cycle troughs and low during booms. The banking sector is especially vulnerable to adverse selection and moral hazard, both caused by asymmetric information. In an economic downturn, it becomes more difficult for banks to assess the creditworthiness of corporate borrowers. Since adverse economic conditions have a negative impact on the cash flows of borrowers, banks may suffer losses because some of their outstanding loans default. At the same time, the assessment of new loan applicants becomes more subject to type I errors because the net present value of new corporate investment becomes more uncertain. Moreover, the net worth of companies and the value of their collateralizable assets decrease. Since the value of collateral is likely to be procyclical, asymmetric information will be relatively high in business cycle downturns and relatively low in booms. This implies that bank intermediation becomes riskier during downturns through a reduction in the value of collateral attached to outstanding loans and an increase in the degree of asymmetric information.

Second, a shift in the risk profile of banks over the business cycle can also be caused by changing incentives on the part of banks. Economic downturns may produce the conditions in which banks have incentives to lower their lending standards and, hence, increase their riskiness. Rajan (1994) argues that bank managers with short horizons will set credit policies that are driven by demand side conditions, which could amplify business cycle movements. Hellman *et al.* (2000) show that banks have an incentive to gamble when their franchise value is harmed. Since this effect will be stronger in economic downturns, bank riskiness may behave asymmetrically. These risk incentives may cause lending cycles and associated swings in the riskiness of banks (see, for example, Kiyotaki and Moore, 1997 and Asea and Blomberg, 1998). Repullo (2004) and Schoors and Vander Vennet (2003) show that a gambling equilibrium may exist when the degree of asymmetric information increases, which is typically associated with recessions. However, they also show that this risky behavior is less likely to occur when capital adequacy rules are binding.

Third, there is evidence of a bank lending channel in most developed economies, although its importance *vis-à-vis* other monetary policy transmission channels remains disputed (see, for example, Angeloni *et al.*, 2002). Faced with adverse business cycle conditions, banks may elect to ration credit. This happened in a number of periods, both in the United States and in Europe. Peek and Rosengren (1995) argue that the recession of 1990–1991 in New England was reinforced by the reluctance of banks to lend. Also in the most recent business cycle downturn (2000–2003), banks have been accused of being excessively restrictive, both in the United States and in Europe (*The Economist*, 2002).[1] However, banks will react differently to monetary policy actions, depending on their financial strength and their access to internally or externally generated liquidity. Kashyap and Stein (1995) conclude that small banks seem more prone than large banks to reduce their lending, with the effect greatest for small banks with relatively low liquidity buffers. On the other hand, well-capitalized banks should find it relatively easy to access the interbank or the securities markets to raise funds in the face of a deposit shock. This implies that a restrictive monetary policy will have less impact on the loan supply of well-capitalized banks. Empirically, Kishan and Opiela (2000) show that the impact of monetary policy actions is different for banks with different sizes and capital ratios in the United States. Similar evidence is reported across the EMU banking systems in the 1990s (Altunbas *et al.*, 2002). Especially well-capitalized banks are expected to be less sensitive to the effects of monetary policy changes.

Based on these arguments we expect that the economic slowdown in the period 2000–2003 has a negative effect on the banks' risk profile, although differences may exist between different types of banks. Next to the negative risk effect, the economic slowdown is also expected to have an adverse impact on bank profits. The economic downturn is associated with increased realized loan losses and higher loan loss provisions (see BIS, 2004). Low inflation and low interest rates are typically associated with low interest margins (see Boyd *et al.*, 2001), a feature that is also caused by continuing deregulation and increased competition. Next to lower interest margins, banks also suffered from lower fee revenues due to the depressed stock market and the absence of merger and acquisition deals. The lower fees and commission from financial market trading and asset management were only partly compensated by revenues from bond market activity. As a result, bank profits were negatively affected, causing at least a temporary downward adjustment in bank market values. Consequently, the expectation is that the market-based performance indicators of bank returns and risk will be negatively affected by the economic slowdown. However, this does not imply that all banks will exhibit a similar return/risk behavior on the stock market. Banks can anticipate adverse shocks and can adapt their strategies accordingly. Therefore we need to consider banks with different institutional and strategic characteristics.

14.3   Types of banks

Since an aggregate deterioration of bank health may mask different performance across various types of European banks, we need to construct useful subsamples. In this section we subdivide banks into different groups based on observable characteristics that are assumed to capture a relevant part of their exposure to economic shocks. The subdivisions are based on economic theory and on frequently used categories by bank analysts. Some of the criteria are passive in the sense that the bank has little impact on that variable. An obvious example is geographic location. Other criteria are strategic in nature and can be managed by the bank. Examples are the degree of diversification, the level of capital adequacy, or the operational efficiency of the bank.

14.3.1 *Country affiliation*

Banks will be differently affected according to the magnitude of the economic downturn they are exposed to. Although the economic and monetary union has been accompanied by a certain degree of macroeconomic convergence in Europe, substantial differences in terms of business cycle conditions in different European countries remain. The typical example is the prolonged gap between Germany, the slowest growing country of the Eurozone (with even negative growth in a number of quarters), and a number of peripherical countries (such as Ireland or Spain) or non-EMU countries (such as the United Kingdom) that were much less affected by the recent slowdown. When poor economic performance in a country is caused by slack consumption and investment, local banks are assumed to suffer. Hence, as far as banks in different countries are primarily exposed to local business cycle conditions, country affiliation may be a useful criterion.

Of course, this is expected to be less the case for banks that have diversified internationally. Standard portfolio theory implies that internationally operating banks will be less vulnerable to abrupt changes in local business cycle or credit market conditions. The underlying rationale is that a geographic diversification of credit and market risk exposures leads to more stable revenues, assuming a non-perfect correlation of market movements and asymmetric business cycles across different countries or world regions. Banks from industrialized countries have indeed expanded their involvement in international lending, including loans to emerging markets, often in the form of syndicated lending. Part of this movement may be explained by increased competition in their home markets, leading to eroding interest margins and low domestic interest rates. Moreover, Western banks may also be induced to lend internationally because they enjoy deposit insurance, lender-of-last-resort services, and implicit guarantees, along with the expectation that international institutions such as the IMF will organize bailouts when the borrowing countries are hit by adverse macroeconomic events. However, since borrower information in developing countries is more opaque, the net exposure of internationally operating banks to moral hazard may actually increase, as was evidenced during some of the financial crises in the 1990s (East Asia, Russia, etc.). Finally, the risk benefits of geographical diversification rely on the assumption of low cross-border correlations. When, on the other hand, adverse credit market conditions prevail across most regions, as was the case in the recent downturn, banks may experience little risk benefits. Amihud *et al.* (2002) find that neither the total nor the systematic risk of banks engaged in cross-border bank mergers changes significantly relative to banks in their home markets. Moreover, even banks with significant activities abroad often remain dependent on economic conditions in their home market for the traditional intermediation activities of lending and deposit-taking.

14.3.2 *Diversification*

Banks have been allowed to broaden the scope of their activities beyond their traditional intermediation role of taking deposits and making loans. In Europe, the Second Banking Directive of 1989 allows banks to combine commercial banking, investment banking, asset management, financial advisory activities, and even insurance underwriting. All European countries allow universal banking or the formation of financial conglomerates in which commercial banking, insurance, and securities-related activities can be integrated, although different organizational models of universal banking coexist. Typically, banks have tried to lessen their dependence on interest income (from loans and securities) and have increased the proportion of non-interest income. The economic rationale again refers to standard portfolio theory. If the non-interest income sources are imperfectly correlated with the traditional revenues from intermediation, the bundled income stream will be more stable. ECB (2000) reports an inverse correlation between interest income and non-interest income in several EU bank markets, suggesting a high potential for diversification benefits. The general conclusion of merger studies among different financial services providers is that the combination of banking and other activities, especially insurance, may have a moderating impact on the overall riskiness of the conglomerate (Genetay and Molyneux, 1998; Kwan and Landerman, 1999; Cybo-Ottone and Murgia, 2000; Berger, 2003). DeLong (2001), however, finds higher abnormal returns for focusing rather than diversifying US bank mergers. For US banks, Stiroh (2002) finds that interest income and non-interest income have become more correlated in recent years.

Based on a different argumentation, a number of studies have provided evidence that universal banks could be less risky than their specialized peers. The closer ties with corporate borrowers and repeated lending may give universal banks access to private information which may improve the effectiveness of their monitoring efforts. The biggest advantage of universal banks may be in the *ex post* monitoring of firms facing financial distress because they can build up renegotiation reputation (Chemmanur and Fulghieri, 1994). If universal banks are better able to deal with financial distress, their cash flows will be less affected by adverse economic conditions. Specialized banks, on the other hand, are expected to be more vulnerable to economic fluctuations. Based on a large sample of European banks, Vander Vennet (2002) finds that the market betas of universal and specialized banks do not differ significantly in periods of economic expansion. In times of economic contraction, however, the market beta of universal banks is significantly lower than that of specialized banks. This finding is consistent with the conjecture that universal banks are better monitors and, hence, are less sensitive to shifts in the business cycle. The results are broadly in line with those reported by Dewenter and Hess (1998) for portfolios of relationship versus transactional banks in eight countries. Baele *et al.* (2004) use a regime-switching model and find that diversified banks have a lower sensitivity to shocks in credit market conditions in the recession state than specialized banks. Hence, our prediction is that diversified (universal) banks will exhibit less sensitivity to shifts in business cycle conditions than their specialized competitors.

The benefits of the formation of financial conglomerates depend on how diverse the different activities combined under one roof are, although the net effect of diversity may be ambiguous. On the one hand, the greater the extent to which activities differ within a financial group, the greater the revenue diversification benefits should be. In particular, life insurance companies are estimated to offer good prospects as matches for banks. The concept of 'bancassurance' has been applied by a number of European financial groups. On the other hand, the greater the heterogeneity of different activities within one group, the more substantial could be the costs of integrating different institutions (Berger, 2003). The recent difficult environment for financial institutions offers a good opportunity to investigate how these financial conglomerates performed. The period 2000–2003 was characterised by an economic downturn, a substantial stock market correction, financial asset deterioration more generally, record corporate default rates, the Argentina sovereign default, and several natural and man-made catastrophes, including most notably the September 11 attacks. One could argue that it is particularly during such a difficult environment that financial institutions are most in need of the benefits from diversified sources of earnings. On the other hand, difficulties in the insurance sector can also be the cause of financial stress in a financial conglomerate. Schick (2003) looks at developments, from the beginning of 2000 to end 2003, in equity market valuations of financial groups by comparing their share price developments with those of industry indices. The results from this type of exercise are mixed. There are some instances in which the financial-group index lies between the banking and insurance sector indices but most of the time the financial-group index lies above both indices. The fact that financial-group index always lies above at least one of the financial sector indices suggests that financial groups on average have realised some diversification benefits, as measured by equity market developments.

14.3.3 Capital adequacy

Another strategic option for a bank to signal financial strength is to maintain a relatively high level of capital as a protection against possible losses in its loan or securities portfolios. Banks in all European countries that are analyzed in this paper are required to maintain minimum capital levels as a proportion of their risky assets, calculated according to the current BIS standards. However, while the supervisory authorities impose a risk-based capital ratio of 8 percent, banks can signal their creditworthiness by holding levels of equity in excess of the required minimum. The excess capital serves as an additional buffer to cover unexpected future losses, thereby decreasing the risk of failure. In all standard models of banking, high capital levels are associated with a lower bankruptcy risk. Hence, the prediction is that banks with a relatively high degree of capital coverage should be better able to alleviate adverse changes in the business cycle and, consequently, will be judged by the financial markets to be less sensitive to shifts in business cycle conditions. Next to this positive risk effect, well-capitalized banks could also benefit from the potentially lower funding costs that this strategy may imply. This element of market discipline is expected to apply especially to the funds obtained in the professional and interbank markets, where competitive pricing based on perceived riskiness is standard practice. Berger (1995) documents a positive relationship between capital and earnings for US banks, a finding which he ascribes to the beneficial effect of capitalization on funding costs. Goldberg and Hudgins (2002) and Park and Peristiani (1998) show that uninsured deposits are exposed to market discipline. They find that riskier banks attract smaller amounts of uninsured deposits and pay higher interest rates on this type of funding than less risky competitors. For European banks, Sironi (2003) finds that investors in bank subordinated debt are sensitive to bank risk and that this effect has increased over the 1990s. This beneficial effect on bank profits may strengthen the positive risk effect of higher capital levels and, hence, affect the valuation of the bank by the stock market. Based on a regime-switching methodology applied to a sample of European listed banks, Baele *et al.* (2004) find that the stock returns and the conditional volatility of well-capitalized banks are significantly less sensitive to shocks in credit market conditions than those of relatively less-capitalized banks. The empirical question is whether or not the stock market judges banks with excess capital coverage to be less sensitive to the adverse economic conditions of the 2000–2003 period.

14.3.4 *Initial balance sheet and operating conditions*

Next to the degree of diversification and the level of capital coverage, banks may differ in other respects, related to the composition of their balance sheets or the efficiency of their operations. These features are the result of managerial actions and thus represent the dynamic initial conditions that banks have when entering an economic downturn. First, banks have different interest margins. This may partly be due to the legal and institutional environment, but primarily reflects the types of assets and liabilities of the bank. Banks with high interest margins are less vulnerable to profit shocks, hence we expect that their stock market performance will be less adversely affected than that of banks with small and vulnerable margins. However, it should be noted that interest margins in general have tended to decline in most European countries, due to increased competition and deregulation. Second, banks differ in terms of operational efficiency. Well-managed banks should have relatively low cost-to-income C–I ratios and, consequently, their profits should be better protected against unexpected bad times. Banking firms across the industrialized world have continued to enhance their efficiency through the rationalization of operations, consolidation and the adoption of new technologies, but the cross-sectional dispersion across banks remains high. Hence, the stock market may attach a different degree of confidence to banks with different observable levels of efficiency. Third, we also consider the composition of the balance sheet of the banks in the sample by ranking the banks according to their loan-to-asset (LTA) ratio and their asset quality, proxied by the loan loss provision ratio. The rationale is that banks with a solid presence in the lending market should be able to withstand economic shocks relatively unscathed. The LTA ratio may, however, also be a proxy for the degree of specialization of a bank in the lending business. Loan loss provisions, on the other hand, are an indication of the riskiness of the loan portfolio, but also of the bank's risk management and ability to anticipate and provision accurately for expected losses. The effect on bank stock returns of loan loss provisions has been shown to differ depending on the type of assets being provisioned (Blose, 2001). Nevertheless, there is also empirical evidence that many banks around the world delay provisioning for bad loans until too late, when cyclical downturns have already set in, thereby magnifying the impact of the economic cycle on banks' income and capital (Laeven and Majnoni, 2003).

14.3.5 Size, market power, and franchise value

Size or a dominant position in the loan and/or deposit market of the home country may confer specific advantages to a bank. In theory, banks with market power should have relatively high interest margins and this should operate as a protection against a profit shock caused by a recession. Large banks may also face structurally lower funding costs in professional markets because of their lower risk of default or implicit too-big-to-fail protection. Moreover, when banks are perceived to have market power in the pricing of their financial services, they will have a relatively high franchise value. A temporary economic slowdown should not be expected to affect their revenue-generating capacity in a fundamental way. Hence, their market valuation is expected to be relatively stable with less sensitive stock prices. However, regulatory changes can gradually erode bank market power and affect their franchise values negatively. Lower charter values, in turn, may induce banks to change their risk profile in terms of capital adequacy or lending risks, as Salas and Saurina (2003) show for the Spanish banking market. De Nicolo (2001) shows that charter values decrease in size and insolvency risk increases for most banks in twenty-one industrialized countries. Nevertheless, there is still widespread evidence that the largest European banks still enjoy some degree of market power, especially in the retail markets (Corvoisier and Gropp, 2002).

14.3.6 Hedging activity

Banks know that shifts in credit market conditions, that is, a deterioration of the creditworthiness of their borrowers, or shifts in asset market conditions may be caused by reversals of the business cycle. Consequently, they will try to mitigate some of the associated risk, for example, by hedging certain positions with credit or other types of derivatives. In recent years the deepening of securitization and risk transfer markets, especially the market for credit risk derivatives, has helped banks in Europe to spread strains across a larger and more diversified set of players, strengthening their resilience to adverse shocks (BIS, 2003). The rapid development of new risk transfer markets has enhanced the capacity of the financial system to absorb losses and supported its performance by helping to disperse risk across institutions and investors. The growth of securitization markets for bank-oriented credits was boosted by demand from institutional investors and advances in financial and communications technologies. The secondary market for syndicated loans has also grown substantially. Risk transfer techniques allow banks to diversify their risks better, which should also enhance financial stability. They contribute to a more sophisticated risk management by banks by allowing them to focus on their risk exposures on a portfolio-wide basis. The possibility of transferring risk, however, may also induce banks to take on additional risks and even to worsen asymmetric information problems by inducing banks to reduce their screening and monitoring efforts (Wagner and Marsh, 2004). Hence, while the off-balance sheet (OBS) activities of commercial banks have increased substantially over the last decade, it is not clear whether this trend has effectively produced less risk. Even a careful hedging strategy may not constitute an effective protection against unanticipated events (Peek and Rosengren, 1997; Froot and Stein, 1998). From time to time, regulators and supervisors express their concern about the ultimate distribution of risks attached to derivatives and similar instruments (BIS, 2003).

From this overview it is clear that banks with different institutional and financial characteristics may exhibit different sensitivities to changes in the business cycle, both in terms of profitability and riskiness. Since listed European banks have implemented different risk strategies, and we can use their stock returns to assess the sensitivities of their return/risk profile to pervasive shifts in credit and asset market conditions caused by the economic slowdown of 2000–2003.

14.4   Empirical methodology and sample

The sample consists of 280 listed European banks. We identify all European banks with a stock exchange listing in December 2003 and download their monthly stock market returns and market values from Datastream over the period 1996–2003. We require that the banks have at least 48 months of stock market data available in order to report meaningful return and risk statistics. The summary statistics of the number of banks per country and their average size and market value are presented in Table 14.1. Since listed banks are usually relatively large, the banks in the sample account for more than 80% of the total assets of the European banking industry. In some countries the coverage is more than 90% of domestic bank assets. To our knowledge, this sample is larger than the ones used in previous analyses of listed European banks. However, in interpreting the results, we have to account for the fact that the sample contains a considerable number of local savings banks, next to the sample of large commercial banks that is typically used in academic research and bank industry analyses. The bank accounting data is retrieved from the annual accounts available in the Bankscope database maintained by Fitch/IBCA/Bureau Van Dijk.

We distinguish between different types of banks based on observed characteristics. Two general categories are the country affiliation, that is, the country in which the bank is headquartered, and the institutional type of the bank (commercial bank, savings bank, investment bank, etc.). For the other subsamples, different ratios are used to construct a typology of banks. For the degree of diversification

Table 14.1 Summary statistics[a]

	Number of banks	Total assets[b]	Market value[c]
Austria	9	34,772	755
Belgium	7	157,121	7,153
Denmark	43	5,819	328
Finland	4	17,311	1,031
France	29	73,243	3,197
Germany	24	187,903	6,196
Greece	17	9,187	1,289
Ireland	5	28,440	4,059
Italy	41	35,674	2,509
Luxembourg	3	22,050	1,976
Netherlands	6	165,235	12,534
Norway	23	5,243	359
Portugal	11	10,874	1,402
Spain	18	38,073	4,660
Sweden	4	123,721	8,525
Switzerland	21	45,487	4,202
UK	15	185,043	20,985
Total	280		

Notes
a Values in million USD.
b Average over the period 1996–2003.
c Average over the period 1996–2003.

we use the ratio of non-interest income in total revenues. Non-interest income captures revenues from fee business, market trading, advisory activities, and commissions received from affiliated insurance companies. This should be a good proxy for the income derived from non-traditional banking activities such as investment banking, insurance, or asset management. Hence the ratio proxies for the degree of functional diversification of a bank. Capital adequacy is calculated as total equity divided by total assets. For a subset of banks we can also calculate the tier 1 ratio and use this as a robustness check. In terms of initial conditions, we focus on the net interest margin (defined as interest revenues minus interest expenses divided by earning assets), the C–I ratio (total interest and operating costs divided by total interest and non-interest revenues), the LTA ratio and the loan loss reserves – total loans ratio. These characteristics are intended to reveal specific strengths or weaknesses of banks when they are confronted with an economic slowdown. We also rank the banks by size (log of total assets) to investigate any market power or size-related effects. Finally, to proxy for hedging activities by banks we use the ratio of OBS exposure to total assets.

For each of the indicator variables, all the banks in the sample are ranked and subdivided in quintiles. For the identical subsample of banks allocated in each quintile, we report a number of statistics on the stock market returns and the market values for two distinct periods. The first period covers from January 1996 to February 2000 and is considered to be the period of strong economic growth and high bank profitability. The second period runs from March 2000 to March 2003 and is the period characterized by a significant slowdown of the economy, weak asset markets, and a series of shocks (terrorist attack, accounting scandals). The exact dating of the business cycle or asset market conditions is always somewhat arbitrary. We opt for this period because (1) the signs of an economic slowdown became apparent from mid-2000 onward, (2) equity and bond markets anticipated the slowdown with market corrections starting early 2000, (3) a series of (consumer and producer) confidence indicators started to decline from mid-2000 onward, and (4) bank performance started to deteriorate from mid-2000 onward (FitchRatings, 2003). We situate the end of the downturn period for banks in March 2003 because (1) the geo-political uncertainty and the associated uncertain economic outlook for the US and European economies were partly lifted by the outbreak of the Iraq war and (2) bank performance and its outlook exhibited a turnaround from the second quarter of 2003 onward (FitchRatings, 2003). The variables we report are the average stock market return of the banks in each quintile in the two periods, the volatility of the stock returns (standard deviation) as a measure of risk, the Sharpe ratio (calculated as the average returns divided by their standard deviation), and the Q ratio (calculated as the market value of each bank's equity divided by the book value of net assets). The Q ratio is often used as a proxy for the franchise value of a bank, that is, the discounted stream of its future net cash flows (Keeley, 1990). As such, a Q ratio above one would indicate that the bank is expected to generate profits over the longer term and is considered a good stock market investment opportunity.

To gain further insight in the sources of volatility, we decompose the equity returns of individual banks in three components: an equity market component, an interest rate component, and a purely bank-specific part. The sensitivity of bank stock returns to those on the broad equity market is a measure of systematic market risk, and follows directly from the well-known Capital Asset Pricing Model (CAPM). Flannery and James (1984), Dewenter and Hess (1998), and Vander Vennet (2002) showed, however, that banks are not only exposed to market risk, but also to interest rate risk. In the banking literature, the exposure of bank stock returns to interest rate movements is mostly seen as being the result of a maturity mismatch between assets and liabilities. More generally, however, interest rate exposure of bank stock returns may be understood as the result of intertemporal hedging demand (Merton, 1973). Investors require a premium for stocks that are expected to do worse in business cycle downturns. As argued before this is clearly the case for banks. Since the term structure of interest rates is known to contain useful information on the future state of the economy (see for example, Ang *et al.*, 2005), interest rate variables are frequently used as proxies for intertemporal risk.

Empirically, we estimate the following specification for each bank i:

$$r_{i,t} = \alpha_i + e_{i,t}$$
$$e_{i,t} = \beta_i \varepsilon_{m,t} + \gamma_i \varepsilon_{b,t} + \varepsilon_{i,t}$$

where $r_{i,t}$ represents the return on bank stock i at time t, α_i the bank-specific intercept, and $e_{i,t}$ the unexpected shock to the bank's stock price. $\varepsilon_{m,t}$ and $\varepsilon_{b,t}$ represent the time t return surprises for respectively the broad equity and bond market portfolio. The main parameters of interest are β_i and γ_i, which respectively measure the bank's exposure to market and interest rate risk. Finally, $\epsilon_{i,t}$ represents the part of the return surprise not related to movements in the overall equity and bond market. We use the broad European equity market index as a proxy for the market return and an index of government bond returns as a proxy for the interest rate factor.

14.5   Results and discussion

To investigate the impact of country affiliation on bank stock market performance, we first consider the (equally weighted) average stock market return and risk indicators for each country in two periods, one of favorable economic conditions (1996–2000) and the period of economic downturn (2000–2003). The findings are in Table 14.2. No distinction is made between different institutional bank types. The first observation is that banks recorded robust average returns in the expansion period, although there are considerable differences across countries. In the downturn period, however, the returns are much lower and even negative in some countries. This was notably the case in Belgium, the Netherlands and Greece, whose banking systems had experienced the strongest increase in the expansion period. Negative bank stock returns are also recorded in Germany, consistent with the dismal performance of the German economy over the period.[2] The pattern of relatively high returns in the first period and low or negative ones in the second is consistent with their characterization as expansion versus downturn periods. Since banks are exposed to the business cycle through various channels, their stock market performance closely tracks the changing economic environment. Another observation is that volatility is not systematically different across both periods. While one would expect the volatility of bank stock prices to increase in more uncertain times, this is not what happened on a cross-country basis. As a result, the Sharpe ratios for the bank/country subdivision are significantly higher in the expansion than in the downturn period. Finally, the average Q ratio for the banks ranked according to country of origin has declined somewhat in the downturn period indicating that investing in bank stocks, in general, was considered by stock market investors to be less valuable than in the boom period. It remains to be seen whether this constitutes a structural downward shift of European bank charter values.

Table 14.3 considers the stock market performance of banks subdivided by institutional type. A similar pattern is apparent, bank stock returns are higher in the expansion than in the downturn period. This is consistent with the theoretical link between bank performance and conditions in the economy and the asset markets. The return decline is especially noteworthy for commercial banks and non-bank credit institutions, although their average returns remain positive in the downturn period. Bank holding companies, real estate banks, and investment

Table 14.2 Value/return/risk of banks: countries

	Period 1/1996–2/2000			Period 3/2000–3/2003				
	Average return (%)	Volatility	Q ratio	Average return (%)	Volatility	Sharpe ratio	Q ratio	Q_E/Q_B
Austria	9.12	15.71	1.04	5.67	12.66	0.45	1.02	0.99
Belgium	14.74	29.27	1.03	-13.16	36.58	-0.36	1.00	0.98
Denmark	6.30	14.73	0.98	19.12	18.43	1.04	1.00	1.02
Finland	13.67	21.78	1.00	12.49	18.75	0.67	0.99	0.99
France	7.55	21.07	0.97	13.61	25.70	0.53	0.94	0.98
Germany	5.13	19.01	1.03	-20.70	37.04	-0.56	1.02	0.99
Greece	48.22	55.10	1.31	-47.65	45.72	-1.04	0.99	0.77
Ireland	17.57	26.16	1.03	28.39	35.68	0.80	1.07	1.04
Italy	19.48	29.77	1.13	-3.91	31.20	-0.13	1.03	0.95
Luxemburg	16.05	18.51	1.04	-0.94	20.60	-0.05	1.03	0.99
Netherlands	18.17	32.32	1.07	-17.68	43.80	-0.40	1.01	0.95
Norway	9.16	20.20	0.97	1.75	21.37	0.08	0.97	0.99
Portugal	17.03	31.49	1.04	-5.12	22.00	-0.23	1.02	0.98
Spain	18.01	26.81	1.12	3.12	23.24	0.13	1.07	0.96
Sweden	15.49	31.07	1.03	2.91	32.40	0.09	1.02	0.98
Switzerland	3.30	21.83	1.04	-0.28	21.03	-0.01	1.00	0.97
UK	17.82	35.71	1.15	-2.21	38.75	-0.06	1.04	0.93

Notes
Average return is the annualized average monthly stock market return over the period, volatility is the standard deviation of the monthly stock returns, Sharpe ratio is average return divided by volatility, Q ratio is the market value of equity divided by the book value of net assets, Q_E/Q_B is the Q ratio at the end of the period divided by the Q ratio at the start of the period.

Table 14.3 Value/return/risk of banks: types of bank according to their institutional type

	Period 1/1996–2/2000			Period 3/2000–3/2003				
	Average return (%)	Volatility	Q ratio	Average return (%)	Volatility	Sharpe ratio	Q ratio	Q_E/Q_B
Commercial banks	14.43	25.24	1.06	3.61	26.30	0.14	1.02	0.98
Savings banks	8.77	19.30	0.98	3.51	22.39	0.16	0.97	1.00
Cooperative banks	10.08	16.76	0.97	5.37	23.53	0.23	0.94	0.97
Non-bank credit institutions	17.84	47.31	1.34	2.40	43.41	0.06	1.04	0.82
Bank holding companies	18.08	32.55	1.06	−9.60	33.27	−0.29	1.01	0.96
Real estate banks	4.93	21.23	1.01	−11.74	36.59	−0.32	0.99	0.99
Special government banks	−1.73	18.28	0.97	−2.15	17.70	−0.12	0.97	1.01
Investment banks	32.71	37.06	1.66	−38.44	49.19	−0.78	1.08	0.76
Medium/long-term banks	−0.94	11.88	1.00	3.60	16.36	0.22	0.98	0.98

Notes

Average return is the annualized average monthly stock market return over the period, volatility is the standard deviation of the monthly stock returns, Sharpe ratio is average return divided by volatility, Q ratio is the market value of equity divided by the book value of net assets, Q_E/Q_B is the Q ratio at the end of the period divided by the Q ratio at the start of the period.

banks suffered the most significant decline in returns, with strongly negative returns in the downturn period. For investment banks, declining asset prices and very weak activity in the markets for underwriting and mergers and acquisitions have undoubtedly contributed to this phenomenon. Real estate banks were hit by the depressed conditions on the housing and commercial property markets, although real estate prices remained buoyant in some countries and interest rates were relatively low. For bank holding companies with stakes in insurance, the returns were negatively affected by the severe decline of insurance companies' net worth. The pattern of declining stock market returns is, however, not typical for cooperative banks, medium- and long-term banks and, to a lesser extent, savings banks. These banks succeed more or less in maintaining stock returns in the second period that are, on average, not below those in the boom period, albeit at a modest absolute level. This result is largely driven by a subsample of small, locally operating banks that remain primarily engaged in traditional intermediation activity. Local retail banks were helped by sustained household spending and mortgage refinancing, both spurred by relatively low interest rates. European retail banks were able to expand consumer credit and household mortgages, activities that proved to be particularly profitable in certain countries. The volatility indicator is again not systematically different across the two periods, although the institutional bank types that experience negative returns in the downturn period also saw the dispersion of their stock prices increase as a reflection of increased risk. The consequence is that Sharpe ratios were healthy in the boom period, with bank holdings, investment banks, and commercial banks leading the pack, while the Sharpe ratios become low or negative in the second period. It is noteworthy that the return volatility of savings banks, cooperative banks and medium-term banks is lower than that of all other bank types and that, as a consequence of their positive returns, these bank types exhibit positive, albeit rather low, Sharpe ratios. Consistent with the country findings, Q ratios were revised downward in the second period as a reflection of the worsened investment outlook in bank stocks in general.

In the different panels of Table 14.4, we explore several bank characteristics and their relationship with stock return performance over the expansion period (January 1996–February 2000) and the downturn period (March 2000–March 2003). First we focus on capital adequacy. It has been argued that banks with a relatively high degree of capital adequacy should be better shielded from adverse economic or asset market shocks. Hence, we expect that banks with higher capital ratios will be judged by stock market investors as less risky and better able to make use of any remaining profitable lending opportunities. In panel A the banks are ranked in quintiles based on the ratio equity – total assets. Capital adequacy ranges from an average of 3.49% in the lowest quintile to 14.62% in the highest quintile in the expansion period. Column 6 shows that the banks in the various quintiles were able to maintain their relative ranking; the average ratio in the second period ranges from 3.79% to 13.45% for the same sample of banks in each quintile. In the expansion period, the average bank stock returns are almost constant across the quintiles. This implies that banks with varying levels of capital adequacy perform similarly in good times. Nevertheless the standard deviation of the returns is lower for the well-capitalized banks, probably as a reflection of their lower risk. The resulting Sharpe ratios range from 0.40 to 0.66, indicating that investors do not view banks with different levels of capital as fundamentally different in economic benevolent times. In the downturn period, however, there is a clear link between the banks' return/risk profile and their capital adequacy. The equity-to-asset ratio and stock returns exhibit a positive and almost monotonic relationship. Obviously the stock returns in the second period are considerably lower, as a reflection of the adverse economic environment. But the average returns now range from −7.28% for the quintile with the lowest level of capital coverage to 7.83% for the well-capitalized quintile. Moreover, the worst-capitalized banks exhibit higher levels of return volatility, reflecting their higher riskiness. The net result is Sharpe ratios, as indicators of the return/risk trade-off, ranging from −21% to 34%. The Q ratio is highest for the quintile with the highest capital adequacy, and that remains the case in the downturn period. These findings are consistent with the hypothesis that well-capitalized banks are better able to withstand negative economic shocks and are viewed by stock market investors as less risky (see Dewenter and Hess, 1998; Vander Vennet, 2002; Sironi, 2003). The well-capitalized banks are rewarded for their risk-averse strategy with higher and less volatile returns. The findings based on the equity-to-total asset ratio as the indicator of capital adequacy are corroborated by those using the tier 1 capital ratio (see panel B). Together, these results also underscore the importance of Basle-type capital adequacy rules to induce discipline in bank risk-taking and to preserve stability in the banking system.

These results are largely confirmed in panel A of Table 14.5, which reports the estimation results for the sensitivity of bank stock market returns to the market and the interest rate risk factors. For each quintile, the table presents a market-capitalization-weighted average of sensitivities to respectively the equity and bond market portfolio. Both in the expansion and recession period, the exposure to the market factor, or market beta, is much larger for relatively poorly capital-ized banks. In both periods, the beta of the 20% best-capitalized banks is about half the market beta of the 20% worst-capitalized banks. Interestingly, market betas are not monotonically decreasing in relative capitalization: market betas are similarly high for the first 3 quintiles, and are only significantly smaller for the 2 quintiles containing the 40% best-capitalized banks.

The second dimension we explore is the degree of diversification. The indica-tor we use is the ratio of non-interest income to total revenues in order to capture the relative weight of non-traditional banking activities in the banks' portfolio. Those banks with a relatively high ratio depend more on revenues from asset management, financial market trading, investment banking, and insurance activ-ities. The argument is that, if the cash flows generated by those activities were suf-ficiently uncorrelated, the bundled revenues would be more stable and, hence, the riskiness of financial conglomerates would be lower. The data for the first period in panel C of Table 14.4 shows that a higher level of diversification is associated with slightly higher average returns, with comparable volatility across the

Table 14.4 Value/return/risk of European banks: types

	Period 1/1996 – 2/2000				Period 3/2000 – 3/2003					
	Ratio	Return	Volatility	Q	Ratio	Return	Volatility	Sharpe ratio	Q	Q_E/Q_B
Panel A: capital adequacy (capital/total assets)										
Q1	3.49	11.23	28.31	1.04	3.79	−7.28	34.57	−0.21	1.02	0.98
Q2	5.51	14.71	26.37	1.06	5.75	2.21	26.36	0.08	1.03	0.98
Q3	7.04	12.17	23.70	1.01	6.95	−0.23	25.71	−0.01	0.99	0.98
Q4	9.47	13.28	22.35	1.04	9.72	5.41	22.80	0.24	0.99	0.96
Q5	14.62	13.73	20.77	1.12	13.45	7.83	23.31	0.34	1.03	0.96
Panel B: capital adequacy (tier 1 capital ratio)										
Q1	5.96	11.92	30.83	1.04	6.48	−10.00	34.67	−0.29	1.01	0.98
Q2	8.09	15.32	25.80	1.06	7.61	6.36	25.83	0.25	1.03	0.98
Q3	9.38	13.44	23.55	1.02	8.25	4.02	24.15	0.17	1.01	0.99
Q4	11.71	8.50	19.73	1.00	10.56	10.43	22.07	0.47	1.00	1.00
Q5	20.86	14.33	19.92	1.12	16.03	11.29	22.28	0.51	1.03	0.97
Panel C: diversification (non-interest income/total revenues)										
Q1	8.10	11.37	28.46	1.04	9.05	−7.14	31.38	−0.23	0.99	0.96
Q2	13.77	7.75	19.55	1.01	14.28	4.92	23.30	0.21	1.00	1.00
Q3	17.42	13.21	21.58	1.05	18.99	7.22	21.62	0.33	1.02	0.98
Q4	21.47	12.92	21.33	1.02	23.15	6.95	25.51	0.27	1.01	0.99
Q5	34.67	18.16	29.64	1.15	37.66	−2.92	29.79	−0.10	1.02	0.92
Panel D: net interest margin										
Q1	1.22	7.25	24.95	1.01	1.19	−6.42	28.89	−0.22	1.00	0.98
Q2	2.13	14.03	24.50	1.04	2.11	0.60	29.37	0.02	1.00	0.96
Q3	2.96	19.03	27.48	1.11	2.74	−0.81	27.54	−0.03	1.03	0.95
Q4	3.84	14.37	26.82	1.07	3.52	−0.90	27.57	−0.03	1.01	0.96
Q5	6.08	9.10	17.66	1.03	5.69	14.71	19.53	0.75	1.01	1.00

Panel E: loans/total assets

Q1	36.90	26.73	35.75	1.18	43.42	-14.22	34.96	-0.41	1.02	0.90
Q2	52.11	12.76	26.00	1.03	57.04	0.96	28.86	0.03	1.01	0.99
Q3	60.00	11.24	22.44	1.05	64.74	5.31	26.13	0.20	1.02	0.99
Q4	70.28	8.54	19.42	1.01	70.55	9.99	21.70	0.46	1.01	0.99
Q5	84.80	5.33	17.71	0.99	84.56	5.78	20.95	0.28	0.98	0.99

Panel F: loan quality (loan loss reserves/net loans)

Q1	1.09	19.22	29.07	1.12	1.17	-1.36	29.09	-0.05	1.02	0.95
Q2	2.07	14.98	23.88	1.08	1.97	2.58	30.16	0.09	1.03	0.97
Q3	2.84	16.72	29.52	1.07	2.67	-11.98	32.70	-0.37	1.00	0.94
Q4	3.74	14.40	28.24	1.04	3.41	-3.92	28.03	-0.14	1.00	0.97
Q5	5.61	10.93	27.61	1.05	4.22	1.34	25.23	0.05	1.00	0.96

Panel G: operational efficiency (cost/income ratio)

Q1	47.63	15.05	25.41	1.12	48.97	1.43	26.61	0.05	1.03	0.95
Q2	59.37	15.49	24.20	1.05	61.33	0.76	26.60	0.03	1.01	0.96
Q3	64.55	10.06	21.63	1.02	66.79	5.88	23.60	0.25	1.00	0.99
Q4	68.36	11.17	21.86	1.01	64.99	4.28	24.80	0.17	1.00	0.99
Q5	75.72	11.86	27.69	1.05	74.38	-4.00	30.59	-0.13	1.00	0.96

Panel H: off balance sheet activity

Q1	3.65	8.69	22.65	1.03	4.62	0.09	27.27	0.00	1.01	0.98
Q2	10.78	12.56	24.27	1.05	13.10	-2.34	25.31	-0.09	1.02	0.97
Q3	18.87	11.84	23.02	1.02	25.31	4.95	25.79	0.19	1.00	0.98
Q4	28.22	11.03	20.74	1.03	30.59	8.36	23.88	0.35	1.01	0.98
Q5	83.36	19.47	30.08	1.13	65.60	-1.80	29.52	-0.06	1.02	0.94

Panel I: size (log of total assets)

Q1	5.17	8.05	15.82	1.04	5.39	14.77	19.08	0.77	1.00	1.00
Q2	7.31	13.65	25.55	1.10	7.59	0.14	25.87	0.01	1.01	0.94
Q3	8.55	10.23	18.86	1.02	8.72	7.85	21.08	0.37	0.99	0.98
Q4	9.82	18.35	28.11	1.06	10.00	-7.83	29.33	-0.27	1.01	0.96
Q5	12.17	14.89	33.96	1.05	12.42	-7.94	38.29	-0.21	1.02	0.97

Table 14.5 Bank sensitivity to market and interest rate risk

	Period 1/1996–2/2000			Period 3/2000–3/2003		
	Ratio	Market beta	Interest risk	Ratio	Market beta	Interest risk
Panel A: capital adequacy (capital/total assets)						
Q1	3.44	1.23	0.03	3.76	1.26	−0.43
Q2	5.52	1.24	0.13	5.77	1.02	−0.60
Q3	7.05	1.49	−0.08	6.89	1.13	−0.20
Q4	9.51	0.76	0.53	9.80	0.48	0.18
Q5	14.61	0.66	−0.20	13.41	0.65	0.18
Panel B: size (log of total assets)						
Q1	5.17	0.21	0.04	5.39	0.40	−0.37
Q2	7.34	0.61	−0.24	7.62	0.58	0.20
Q3	8.58	0.43	0.05	8.77	0.41	−0.10
Q4	9.95	0.81	0.11	10.12	0.49	0.08
Q5	12.25	1.34	0.04	12.52	1.25	−0.46
Panel C: LTA ratio						
Q1	36.28	1.30	−0.17	42.43	1.27	−0.70
Q2	51.49	1.32	0.25	56.13	1.08	−0.13
Q3	60.13	1.10	−0.02	64.40	1.20	−0.61
Q4	71.02	1.24	0.18	71.10	1.08	−0.13
Q5	85.31	0.18	−0.12	85.08	0.17	−0.04

quintiles. However, contrary to expectations, diversified banks do not perform better in the downturn period and the volatility of the returns in the respective quintiles is relatively high. The quintile Sharpe ratios seem to exhibit an inverse U-shape, which would suggest that there is an optimal level of diversification. The Q ratios are highest for the higher quintiles in the second period, but they also decline most in comparison with the first period. This leads to the conclusion that investors do not consider diversified financial institutions, or financial conglomerates, to be more safe or to be better equipped to withstand an economic downturn with more stable earnings. Somehow, this finding may be specific to the period under investigation because it has been characterized by a notably bad performance of insurance companies, primarily due to low investment returns and a series of catastrophic events entailing substantial claims. Nevertheless, the results indicate that the stock market does not view diversification as universally better than focused banking. Apparently, the negative correlation needed to absorb shocks in one activity did not materialize or was insufficient to make conglomerates safer investments. Although one period of economic downturn and financial market turbulence is insufficient to make conclusive statements about the relative merits of financial conglomeration, our evidence may be a useful part of a broader assessment.

A growing number of financial groups have been formed during the last decade. In Europe, many banks now own insurance companies, particularly life insurance companies, given their role in the long-term savings market. However, it may turn out that the synergy effects are not as high as previously thought. Difficulties in merging different institutions and corporate cultures may already be substantial during bull markets, but could be greater during bear markets. For those banks that have formed financial groups with insurers during the past few years, this is the first time that they own insurance companies in anything other than a bull market. Apparently, the level of correlation of the risk factors affecting operations in the different financial sectors are higher during such periods than many had predicted. Also, most European financial groups with investment banking arms have seen their ratings negatively affected, even though this was often also in response to the parent or subsidiary insurance company's financial difficulties. The insurance and reinsurance sector has been under particular pressure over recent years as a result of a large number of natural disasters, the terrorist attacks, falling equity prices, and the decline in investment income. Pressures seem to be particularly pronounced in the European insurance industry, reflected partly by the fact that European insurers have been much larger sellers of credit protection than insurers in the United States. These developments support the hypothesis that core banking activities provided more of a relief than non-core business for financial groups during the recent downturn.

In the following panels we examine various structural characteristics of bank balance sheets and the operational efficiency of banks. We first consider the net interest margin. Relatively high interest margins may be the results of the access to cheap sources of funding (e.g. savings accounts), better lending opportunities, superior borrower screening technology, market power, or a combination of these advantages. Presumably, banks with high margins should be better able to withstand a temporary worsening of economic conditions. Similarly, banks with a relatively high LTA ratio are supposed to have a high penetration in the local lending market and, hence, to be able to tap profitable lending opportunities. The ratio of loan loss provisions to total loans is an indicator of the quality of the loan portfolio. Low default provisioning should be reflecting good loan quality and be associated with less losses caused by defaulting borrowers. On the other hand, banks with a forward-looking provisioning strategy may benefit from accumulating sufficient reserves to absorb any realized losses. Finally, the C–I ratio is widely used as a proxy for the degree of operational efficiency of a bank. Banks with lean operations and low operating costs should be able to get through a slowdown without a fundamental deterioration of their profit-generating capacity and, hence, their franchise value.

Panels D to I show the results. Only the bank quintile characterized by the highest interest margins appears to have a profit advantage, since they exhibit high returns (14.7%) and a relatively low volatility in the downturn period, resulting in a Sharpe ratio (0.75) well above the other groups. A high LTA ratio appears to confer a distinct advantage on banks when times become more difficult; the second-period returns of quintiles 4 and 5 are high with lower than average dispersion, resulting in clearly superior Sharpe ratios (0.46 and 0.28). Presumably these banks benefit from established relationships with their borrowers, a feature which enables them to renegotiate loans at favorable conditions or even to expand their lending business profitably in periods of economic downturn. However, the LTA ratio may also proxy for the relative specialization of banks in the lending business. The interpretation would then be that banks with a focus on local lending were much less affected by the economic slowdown than more diversified banks. Panel C of Table 14.5 shows that the market beta is lowest for the banks with high LTA ratios. The reservation policy for anticipated loan losses seems to make little difference. While high loan loss reserves are associated with lower returns in the expansion period, there is no clear pattern in the downturn period. Hence, the stock market seems to attach little importance to the banks' loan loss provisioning strategy. The two quintiles with the lowest and the quintile with the highest loan loss reserves perform less badly, the first because of good loan quality, the latter probably because they have accumulated sufficient reserves to absorb losses due to defaulting borrowers. As far as operational efficiency is concerned, the evidence in panel G shows that low C–I ratios confer a slight advantage in terms of returns, as could be expected. However, no such effect is discernable in the downturn period, although the group of least efficient banks Q5 has a negative return. Although bank analysts keep stressing the continued focus on cost reductions as a tool to boost the bank's value, the effect of lean operations is not apparent in the second-period returns nor in their volatility. Nevertheless, the average Q ratio of the first quintile (banks with the lowest C–I ratio) is situated above those of the higher quintiles, indicating the implied long-term profit potential of efficient banks.

Finally, hedging activity and size appear to offer little protection against adverse economic shocks. As a proxy for hedging activity we look at the ratio of OBS exposures to total assets. It would be preferable to focus on derivatives trans-actions used by the banks to hedge certain exposures, but unfortunately this detailed information is unavailable. Panel H of Table 14.4 shows that the bank quintiles with relatively high OBS activity earn higher returns in the first period, but they also seem to be more volatile. Hence, OBS commitments offer profit opportunities in good times, but they are also considered to be more risky. In the downturn period, no clear advantage can be detected. The Sharpe ratios are essen-tially flat across the quintiles and the Q ratios are largely comparable. A similar conclusion imposes itself for size. Big seems to be beautiful in good times; the average returns for the two largest size deciles are relatively high, although the associated volatility is also rather elevated. However, big is certainly not beautiful in bad times. On the contrary, the smallest size quintile earns the highest returns with the lowest dispersion and the large banks seem to possess no "Q"-advantage over the longer term. Panel B of Table 14.5 shows that the market beta, or the sen-sitivity to broad market shocks, is highest for the larger banks in both subperiods. These findings should be interpreted carefully, however. Size turns out to be correlated with, for example, the degree of diversification and OBS exposure. Hence, the results may simply be a reflection of the relatively weak behavior of the diversified banks in the downturn period, largely due to losses suffered in their non-banking businesses.

14.6   Conclusions

Since the underlying sources of the risks that banks are exposed to are closely connected with the business cycle, bank health is related to the economic conditions in which they operate. The recent economic downturn (2000–2003) contained all the ingredients that usually provoke distress in the banking system: a protracted stock market decline, slack consumer and business confidence, a high number of corporate failures, accompanied by a series of man-made events such as terrorist attacks and accounting scandals. Yet, the European banking system as a whole has proved to be very resilient, with few, if any, bank failures or systematic problems among European banks that have prompted regulatory interventions or bailouts and a low number of actual rating downgrades. We investigate the potential causes for bank resilience on a broad sample of listed European banks in the 2000–2003 economic downturn. We identify banks with different strategies and different characteristics before the slowdown and investigate their risk profile before and during the economic downturn with market-based measures of return and risk. Banks are sorted in quintiles over the pre-downturn period 1996–2000 based on a number of observable characteristics related to their geographic location, their institutional type, or the initial balance sheet conditions with which they entered the downturn. Subsequently, we investigate their return/risk profile during the economic slowdown of 2000–2003 using market-based measures such as the Q ratio, the Sharpe ratio, volatility of stock returns and their sensitivity to broad equity market swings. Since an aggregate deterioration of bank health may mask different performance across various types of European banks, we need to construct useful subsamples. We subdivide banks into different groups based on observable characteristics that are assumed to capture a relevant part of their exposure to economic shocks.

We find that bank returns and risks differ across countries, consistent with the observed variation of cross-country macroeconomic performance in Europe. With respect to institutional type, we find that commercial banks and financial conglomerates fare less well in the downturn than traditional intermediaries active in retail banking. Also, banks with a focus on local lending and banks with relatively high interest margins seem to have benefited from that focus, relative to functionally and geographically diversified banks. The market-based return and risk measures support the conjecture that diversified banks were hit much harder in the 2000–2003 economic slowdown than their more specialized peers. Our results indicate that the stock market does not view diversification as universally better than focused banking. Apparently, the negative correlation needed to absorb shocks in one activity did not materialize or was insufficient to make conglomerates safer investments. Although one period of economic downturn and financial market turbulence is insufficient to make conclusive statements about the relative merits of financial conglomeration, our evidence may be a useful part of a broader assessment. Capital adequacy, on the other hand, clearly has a positive effect on the risk profile of banks. Banks with higher levels of capital are not only viewed as less risky, they also produce higher stock market returns during the economic downturn. This underscores the importance of Basle-type capital adequacy rules for the systemic stability of the banking system. Finally, we find that neither size nor hedging offers a structural protection against adverse economic conditions.

Acknowledgments

The authors thank Wim Boonstra, Jean Dermine, Michael Grote, Andy Mullineux, Theo Peeters, and Dirk Van Wensveen for useful comments at the SUERF 2004 Colloquium. The authors acknowledge financial support from the Programme on Interuniversity Poles of Attraction of the Belgian Federal Office for Scientific, Technical and Cultural Affairs, contract No. P5/2.

Notes

1 There is discussion whether a bank-led credit supply shortage has effectively materialized in the EU, the Eurozone or in specific countries. Based on the recently initiated Bank Lending Survey by the ECB, no hard evidence for a credit crunch is available, partly due to the offsetting effect of a more accommodative monetary policy stance.

2 The German banking landscape has traditionally been characterized by intense competitiveness, resulting in a comparatively low level of profitability. Interest rate margins have fallen and the average C–I ratios have remained excessively high. Accordingly, return on equity is low. Another part of the profitability problem is cyclical. Banks are suffering from the sluggish economy, which has caused the need for higher risk provisioning. Nevertheless, financial institutions were able to build up and still maintain considerable reserves, encouraged by tax regulations. Looking ahead, one of the most important tasks for German banks is to control costs. The adjustment process has started, manifesting itself in a least three ways. First, many banks have initiated aggressive cost-cutting programs. Second, banks have generally been raising the risk premiums in their loan business and, third, they have become more risk aware in their lending, consistent with the spirit of the upcoming Basel II.

References

Altunbas, Y., O. Fazylov, and P. Molyneux (2002). "Evidence on the Bank Lending Channel in Europe," *Journal of Banking and Finance*, 26(11), 2093–2110.

Amihud, Y., G. DeLong, and A. Saunders (2002). "The Effects of Cross-border Bank Mergers on Bank Risk and Value," *Journal of International Money and Finance*, 21, 857–877.

Ang, A., M. Piazzesi, and M. Wei (2005). "What Does the Yield Curve Tell Us About GDP Growth?," *Journal of Econometrics*, forthcoming.

Angeloni, I., B. Mojon, A. K. Kashyap, and D. Terlizzese (2002). "Monetary Transmission in the Euro Area: Where Do We Stand?," ECB Working Paper No. 114.

Asea, P. K. and B. Blomberg (1998). "Lending Cycles," *Journal of Econometrics*, 83 (1–2), 89–128.

Baele, L., R. Vander Vennet, and A. Van Landschoot (2004). "Bank Risk Strategies and Cyclical Variation in Bank Stock Returns," Ghent University working paper, No 04/264, Ghent University, Belgium.

Berger, A. N. (1995). "The Relationship between Capital and Earnings in Banking," *Journal of Money, Credit, and Banking*, 27(2), 432–456.

Berger, A. N. (2003). "The Efficiency Effects of a Single Market for Financial Services in Europe," *European Journal of Operational Research*, 150, 466–481.

Bernanke, B. S. and M. Gertler (1989). "Agency Costs, Net Worth, and Business Fluctuations," *American Economic Review*, 79(1), 14–31.

BIS (2003). "Credit Risk Transfer," Report by the Committee on the Global Financial system, January. Bank for International Settlements (available www.bis.org).

BIS (2004). Annual Report, Basel. Bank for International Settlements (available www.bis.org).

Blose, L. E. (2001). "Information Asymmetry, Capital Adequacy, and Market Reaction to Loan Loss Provision Announcement in the Banking Industry," *Quarterly Review of Economics and Finance*, 41, 239–258.

Boyd, J. H., R. Levine, and B. D. Smith (2001). "The Impact of Inflation on Financial Sector Performance," *Journal of Monetary Economics*, 47, 221–248.

Chemmanur, T. J. and P. Fulghieri (1994). "Reputation, Renegotiation, and the Choice between Bank Loans and Publicly Traded Debt," *Review of Financial Studies*, 7, 475–506.

Chen, N. K. (2001). "Bank Net Worth, Asset Prices and Economic Activity," *Journal of Monetary Economics*, 48, 415–436.

Corvoisier, S. and R. Gropp (2002). "Bank Concentration and Retail Interest Rates," *Journal of Banking and Finance*, 26(11), 2155–2189.

Cybo-Ottone, A. and M. Murgia (2000). "Mergers and Shareholder Wealth in European Banking," *Journal of Banking and Finance*, 24(6), 831–859.

DeLong, G. L. (2001). "Stockholder Gains from Focusing versus Diversifying Bank Mergers," *Journal of Financial Economics*, 59(2), 221–252.

De Nicolo, G. (2001). "Size, Charter Value and Risk in Banking: An International Perspective," IMF, Monetary and Exchange Affairs Department, Washington, DC.

Dewenter, K. L. and A. C. Hess (1998). "An International Comparison of Banks' Equity Returns," *Journal of Money, Credit, and Banking*, 30(3), 472–492.

Diamond, D. W. (1984). "Financial Intermediation and Delegated Monitoring," *Review of Economic Studies*, 51(3), 393–414.

Economist, The (2002). "Crisis? What crisis?" May 16.

European Central Bank (2000). "EU Bank's Income Structure," August (available http://www.ecb.int/pub/pdf/other/eubkincen.pdf).

FitchRatings (2003). "Outlook for Major European Banks in 2004: Calmer Waters Ahead," December (available www.fitchratings.com).

Flannery, M. J. and C. M. James (1984). "The Effect of Interest-rate Changes on the Common Stock Returns of Financial Institutions," *Journal of Finance*, 16(4), 435–445.

Froot, K. A. and J. Stein (1998). "Risk Management, Capital Budgeting and Capital Structure Policy for Financial Institutions," *Journal of Financial Economics*, 47, 55–82.

Genetay, N. and P. Molyneux (1998). *Bancassurance*, London: Macmillan.

Goldberg, L. G. and S. C. Hudgings (2002). "Depositor Discipline and Changing Strategies for Regulating Thrift Institutions," *Journal of Financial Economics*, 63(2), 263–274.

Hellmann, T. F., K. C. Murdock, and J. E. Stiglitz (2000). "Liberalization, Moral Hazard in Banking, and Prudential Regulation. Are Capital Requirements Enough?," *American Economic Review*, 90(1), 147–165.

Hyytinen, A. (2002). "The Time Profile of Risk in Banking Crises: Evidence from the Scandinavian Banking Sectors," *Applied Financial Economics*, 12, 613–623.

Jordan J. S. and E. S. Rosengren (2002). "Economic Cycles and Bank Health," Federal Reserve Bank of Boston (available http://www.bos.frb.org/bankinfo/conevent/slowdown/jordanrosen.pdf).

Kaminsky, G. L. and C. M. Reinhart (1999). "The Twin Crises: The Causes of Banking and Balance-of-payments Problems," *American Economic Review*, 89(3), 473–500.

Kashyap, A. K. and J. Stein (1995). "The Impact of Monetary Policy on Bank Balance Sheets," *Carnegie-Rochester Conference Series on Public Policy*, 42, 151–195.

Keeley, M. (1990). "Deposit Insurance, Risk, and Market Power in Banking," *American Economic Review*, 80, 1183–1200.

Kishan, R. P. and T. P. Opiela (2000). "Bank Size, Bank Capital, and the Bank Lending Channel," *Journal of Money, Credit, and Banking*, 32(1), 121–141.

Kiyotaki, N. and J. Moore (1997). "Credit Cycles," *Journal of Political Economy*, 105(2), 211–248.

Kwan, S. and E. Landerman (1999). "On the Portfolio Effects of Financial Convergence – A Review of the Literature," *FRBSF Economic Review*, 99(2), 18–31.

Laeven, L. and G. Majnoni (2003). "Loan Loss Provisioning and Economic Slowdowns: Too Much, Too Late?," *Journal of Financial Intermediation*, 12(2), 178–197.

Llewellyn, D. T. (2002). "An Analysis of the Causes of Recent Banking Crises," *European Journal of Finance*, 8, 152–175.

Merton, R. (1973). "An Intertemporal Capital Asset Pricing Model," *Econometrica*, 41(5), 867–887.

Park, S. and S. Peristiani (1998). "Market Discipline by Thrift Depositors," *Journal of Money, Credit, and Banking*, 30(3), 347–364.

Peek, J. and E. S. Rosengren (1995). "The Capital Crunch: Neither a Borrower nor a Lender Be," *Journal of Money, Credit, and Banking*, 27(3), 625–638.

Peek, J. and E. S. Rosengren (1997). "Derivatives Activity at Troubled Banks," *Journal of Financial Services Research*, 12(2–3), 287–302.

Rajan, R. G. (1994). "Why Bank Credit Policies Fluctuate: A Theory and Some Evidence," *Quarterly Journal of Economics*, 109(2), 399–441.

Repullo, R. (2004). "Capital Requirements, Market Power and Risk Taking in Banking," *Journal of Financial Intermediation*, 13(2), 156–182.

Salas, V. and J. Saurina (2003). "Deregulation, Market Power and Risk Behaviour in Spanish Banks," *European Economic Review*, 47, 1061–1075.

Schich, S. (2003). "The Health of Financial Institutions During the Recent Bear Market," *OECD Financial Market Trends*, 84, 57–71.

Schoors, K. and R. Vander Vennet (2003). "Rules versus Discipline: Capital Adequacy Rules, Monitoring Incentives, and Bank Behavior in Transition Economies," Ghent University Working Paper, mimeo.

Sironi, A. (2003). "Testing for Market Discipline in the European Banking Industry: Evidence from Subordinated Debt Issues," *Journal of Money, Credit, and Banking*, 35(3), 443–472.

Stiroh, K. J. (2002). "Diversification in Banking. Is Noninterest Income the Answer?," Federal Reserve Bank of New York, Staff Report No. 154.

Vander Vennet, R. (2002). "Cost and Profit Efficiency of Financial Conglomerates and Universal Banks in Europe," *Journal of Money, Credit and Banking*, 34(1), 254–282.

Wagner, W. and I. W. Marsh (2004). "Credit Risk Transfer and Financial Sector Performance," CEPR Discussion Paper No. 4265, February.

15 House prices and consumer lending

John P. Calverley

15.1 Introduction

This chapter explores the implications of housing bubbles and high household debt for monetary policy and for bank profitability. The paper presents data for a number of countries but focuses on the United Kingdom, where the rise in house prices has been particularly rapid, and on the United States, where nationwide house price growth has been more moderate but particular regions have shown rapid rises.

Rising house prices have been associated with a rapid rise in mortgage lending, both as borrowers gear up to afford higher house prices and as existing homeowners withdraw equity through mortgage equity withdrawal (MEW). For banks, this has brought a rapid growth in business, though competition is intense. The value of mortgages outstanding has doubled since the end of 1996, implying a 9.1% annual growth rate. In the 3 years to June 2004, the peak of the bubble period, the annual rise has averaged 13.5% pa. For monetary policy-makers, high MEW and relatively robust consumer confidence (both in general and about the outlook for house prices) have contributed to relatively strong consumer spending and low savings rates.

However, although heavy borrowing has taken household debt to a new high in relation to incomes, net wealth has held up well in recent years (despite the fall in stock markets since 2000), because of the rise in housing values. Moreover interest rates are much lower than in the past, so interest service costs are not necessarily onerous. Yet, if house prices were to fall significantly, household balance sheets could be under stress.

The key assessments then are: first, whether house prices are in a bubble or whether current elevated valuations are justified by changed fundamentals; and second, if a bubble now exists, can it be deflated gradually and without too much pain for borrowers, lenders, and the economy generally. The paper investigates 5 scenarios by looking at 5 possible paths for house prices and the house price–income ratio.

1 *You ain't seen nothing yet* There is more expansion to come and house prices and debt can continue to rise faster than incomes. Few economists will be

comfortable with this view because even those who have argued in the past that house prices are not yet overvalued now seem to view prices as fully valued.[1] If house valuations move still higher, there is a greater risk of trouble later. Nevertheless, this scenario cannot be ruled out for a period of time, raising the question of whether policy should address ways of trying to avoid it.

2 *A higher equilibrium*   The second view is that the last few years have seen a move up to a higher equilibrium level for house price–income ratios and associated higher debt/income due to lower interest rates and (in some cases) inadequate new housing supply relative to growing demand. But, going forward, the growth of house prices and household debt will revert to the rate of growth of incomes (e.g. 4% or so). This view suggests there is nothing to worry about, though for banks it does imply a slowdown in the growth of lending business.

3 *Stability in nominal terms*   House prices and debt will stabilise now, allowing the ratios to moderate over time as incomes grow. This is perhaps the best scenario (for those who think the ratios are too high currently) because it promises a gradual correction. The 'bubble mentality' will gradually dissipate and, over time, valuations will come back to more reasonable levels. As for Scenario 2 there is no crisis but lending business is weaker still.

4 *Autonomous house price collapse*   On this view, house prices are at risk of turning down sharply on their own, or with only an insignificant trigger, placing severe stress on household balance sheets, raising banks' bad loans and potentially bringing a sharp economic slowdown.

5 *House prices crash during the next economic downturn making it worse* On this view house prices are unlikely to turn down substantially on their own but, given another trigger for an economic downturn (e.g. a monetary policy mistake, a rebound of inflation requiring tight policy, or a shock to confidence) an accompanying crash in house prices could seriously exacerbate the downturn.

The chapter is organised as follows. Section 15.2 documents the rise in house prices in major countries and the accompanying rise in household debt. Section 15.3 looks at the case of the United Kingdom in detail, to address the question of whether the housing market is in a bubble or whether valuations are justified. Section 15.4 looks at the US case. Section 15.5 looks at the dilemma for monetary policy whereas Section 15.6 briefly outlines alternatives to monetary policy to resist bubbles. Section 15.7 returns to the five scenarios outlined earlier, analysing the implications for monetary policy and for banks. The concluding section makes an assessment of the most likely outcome for different countries.

15.2   Rising house prices and debt

Rapid rises in house prices are a widespread phenomenon among the industrial countries. In the eight years, 1995–2003, prices rose by a cumulative 193% in Ireland, 146% in the United Kingdom, 122% in Spain and 110% in the Netherlands and Australia (see Table 15.1). So far in 2004 prices have continued to rise faster than incomes in the United Kingdom and Australia. In the United

Table 15.1 Residential property price gains, 1995–2003

Property prices	1995–2003		2002 (%)	2003 (%)
	Cumulative (%)	Average p.a. (%)		
United States	61	6.1	6.9	8.0
Japan	−24	−3.3	−4.6	−5.8
Germany	−2	−0.2	1.0	−1.0
UK	146	11.9	23.9	10.0
France	60	6.1	6.7	16.4
Italy	42	4.5	10.0	10.7
Canada	42	4.5	10.3	11.3
Spain	122	10.5	17.4	17.3
Netherlands	110	10.2	4.5	3.6
Australia	110	10.2	18.5	18.9
Switzerland	3	0.4	4.9	2.8
Belgium	52	5.5	6.5	7.6
Sweden	82	7.8	9.2	6.1
Ireland	193	14.4	14.2	13.9

Source: Bank for International Settlements (2004, p. 138) and OECD (2004).

States the rise was 61%, rather more modest, though some areas, particularly on the coasts, saw greater activity. For example the eight-year increase was 107% in Massachusetts, 99% in California and 75% in New Jersey and New York. All these increases were well ahead of the cumulative rise in the consumer price level, ranging between 10% and 20%. The three major exceptions were Japan, still mired in falling prices, and Germany and Switzerland, where prices have been stagnant overall and down in real terms.

Rapid price inflation does not, in itself, point to a bubble. Prices were generally depressed in the early-to-mid-1990s, following a price bust in many countries after the 1990 recession, so that some of the rise may be legitimate catch-up. But measures of valuation, patchy as they are for housing in contrast to stocks, suggest that prices have now become unusually high compared with historical levels, in relation to both earnings and rents. One 2003 analysis, comparing house prices in relation to earnings with the average ratio from 1975 to 2002, found prices overvalued by 60% in Spain, around 50% in Britain, Ireland and the Netherlands, 28% in Australia and 14% in the United States (Capital Economics, 2003).

Another study based on rents found house prices–rents to be 20% above equilibrium in Britain and Spain and 7% in the United States (Ayuso and Restoy, 2003). This study was based on 2002 values so, with rents relatively static and prices up smartly since then, overvaluations relative to historical norms will have grown significantly. Owner-occupiers have been actively trading up in many countries and second homes have become more popular. Investors have also been avid buyers as property has taken over from stocks as the 'hot' investment. In Australia 1 household in 6 reportedly now owns an investment property.[2]

Table 15.2 Household debt trends, 1995–2003

	Household debt[a]	
	Cumulative change (%) *1995–2002*	*Nominal change (%)* *p.a. 2003*
United States	8.2	10.8
Japan	0.3	−0.1
Germany	4.2	1.0
United Kingdom	8.5	9.3
France	7.1	7.2
Italy	8.4	6.6
Canada	5.9	6.2
Spain	14.5	12.6
Netherlands	13.3	9.4
Australia	12.4	11.9
Switzerland	3.3	6.6
Belgium	3.5	2.2
Sweden	7.1	8.2
Norway	8.3	6.7
Denmark	8.2	8.2
Finland	7.0	12.3[b]
Ireland	—	—

Source: Bank for International Settlements (2004, p. 138).

Notes
a Broad financial accounts concept where available, otherwise credit from banks; partly estimated.
b 1990–2002.

Alongside the rise in house prices has been a rise in household debt over the same period (Debelle, 2004). The fastest rises have been in Spain (190%), the Netherlands (162%), Australia (153%), the United Kingdom (93%) and United States (92%), see Table 15.2. Such a rapid expansion of lending business has obviously brought great opportunities for banks, though competition has been fierce. But although margins for mortgages are under pressure, banks like mortgage business because it provides a good opportunity to cross-sell, particularly life insurance, home insurance, current accounts and personal loans or top-up mortgages.

House price growth and debt growth are broadly correlated as we might expect (Figure 15.1). As a result of the rapid rise in debt, the ratios of debt to income have risen in all these countries. For example the OECD calculates that debt to disposable income has risen to 139% in the United Kingdom and 118% in the United States from 107% and 94%, respectively in 1995 (OECD, 2004).

However, net household wealth has risen in both countries over the same period, reflecting increased holdings of both financial wealth overall and housing. Net wealth was of course higher during the stock bubble years, but rising house prices in recent years have to some extent offset the fall in stock prices. Overall then, household balance sheets appear to be in good shape. But this depends on house prices holding up. A significant fall in house prices, especially if combined

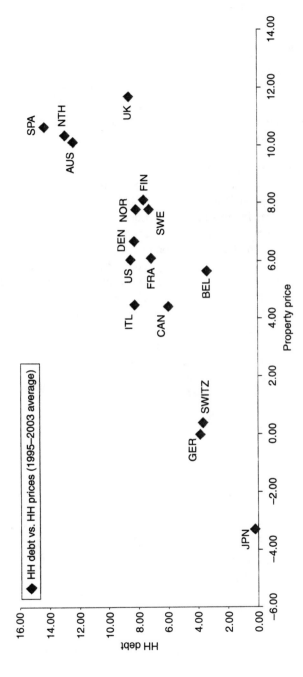

Figure 15.1 Household debt growth vs. house price growth, 1995–2003.

Source: Tables 15.1 and 15.2.

with a new decline in stocks prices, as might be expected in the event of a major economic downturn, could bring major problems.

15.3   The case of the United Kingdom

The United Kingdom has had one of the fastest rises in prices and now has unusually high valuations on any measure. The ratio of house prices to earnings in the United Kingdom has risen to an historical high (see Figure 15.2). Since the early 1970s, it has risen above 4 times incomes on 3 occasions, only to fall back sharply in subsequent downturns. In the early 1990s, after the pain of the 1990–1991 recession the ratio was unusually low so, the initial rise in prices in the mid-1990s was, arguably, legitimate catch-up.

Some analysts (not just industry insiders) argue that a step up in valuations is justified by a change in fundamentals (CEBR, 2004). The case rests mainly on a combination of changes in the structure of supply and demand and the effect of lower real and/or nominal interest rates. Common demand factors cited are increasing immigration, particularly to London, and greater household formation due to higher divorce rates or more young people moving away from home. On the supply side, the United Kingdom has seen very little response to higher prices due to the rigidity of planning controls which is particularly intense in Britain (Barker, 2004). There is also an argument that the quality of housing is not adequately captured in house price indices and so the ratios overstate the gain.

However not all the structural changes point to higher prices. For example, the tax treatment of housing in the United Kingdom is less favourable than in the

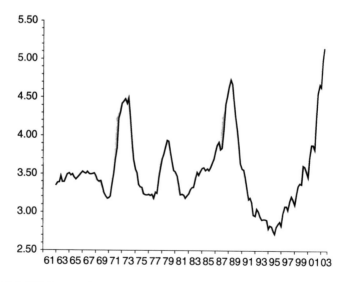

Figure 15.2 UK: house prices/average earnings.

Source: Datastream.

past, which would point to a lower equilibrium valuation. The Bank of England has calculated that the effects of the elimination of tax relief on mortgage interest should have reduced equilibrium house prices by 9% between 1990 and 2000 (Bank of England, 2000). Other tax changes since 1990, including increased stamp duty and the replacement of Poll Tax with Council Tax (property tax), would add to this reduction.

Further analysis of these specific factors is beyond the scope of this paper, but it is also worth remembering another point. Even if the demand curve for housing has shifted out as often claimed, is it correct to assume that the curve is highly inelastic? A rise in real house prices of more than 100% should surely encourage homeowners to reduce their demand for space. It should of course, but not necessarily, if a bubble mentality has taken hold. In a bubble rising prices means that demand is increased rather than reduced.

The argument that lower interest rates support a higher equilibrium house price deserves careful analysis. Theoretically, a lower nominal interest rate should have no effect if it is entirely due to lower inflation. There are, however, signs that homeowners do not connect house price inflation with ordinary inflation. For example, a 2002 survey from the United States of new homebuyers in four areas, Orange County, San Francisco, Boston and Milwaukee, found expectations for home price inflation over the next ten years to be 13.1% pa, 15.7% pa, 14.6% pa and 11.7% pa (Case *et al.*, 2003). Not only were these expectations well ahead of the historical record for these areas (5.6%, 7.1%, 8.3% and 5.6% respectively from 1982 Q1 to 2003 Q1) but of course average consumer price inflation and wage growth are likely to be considerably lower than in the past period.

However, the high nominal interest rates of the past meant that mortgage payments were effectively front-loaded and this may have constrained borrowers' appetite or lenders' willingness to fund large mortgages. Anecdotally, it would appear that many borrowers simply look at the initial monthly payment to see how large a mortgage they can afford. Similarly, lenders often link their willingness to lend to the ratio of the payment to after-tax income or equivalently, are willing to lend a greater multiple of salary as interest rates fall.

One simple way to forecast the impact of this tendency is to look at the extra mortgage that a fall in interest rates allows a given monthly payment to support. Since the mid-1990s average mortgage rates in the United Kingdom have dropped from about 7.5% pa to about 5.5% pa in 2002–2003 (and since back up to 6%). In the mid-1990s a loan of £100,000 (standard repayment loan of 25 years) would have required a monthly payment of £739. At 5.5% rates, the same monthly payment will secure a mortgage of approximately £120,000 or 20% more. The comparison is much more dramatic if we take a broader brush and compare with the 1980s. In the 1980s mortgage rates averaged closer to 12% at which this monthly payment would have supported a loan of only £70,000.

However, if real interest rates are not different, the burden of the mortgage will last for much longer, rather than rapidly dwindling relative to salary as was the case during past higher inflation periods. Similarly, for lenders it means that the period of potential strain for the borrower, where mortgage payments are a high proportion of income, will also last much longer.

More broadly, by paying much more for houses, whether knowingly or not, households are committing themselves to paying a much higher percentage of their income for housing services (over the life of the mortgage) than before. The effect is to create a one-off step up in housing valuations, though unless interest rates fall further, house prices should then slow down to move in line with earnings growth (Scenario 2).

Nevertheless, relying on the argument that it is the fall in *nominal* interest rates that has encouraged higher demand for housing services must imply either irrationality among households (not realising the extra cost), or that high interest rates imposed an artificial constraint in the past. While both are possible, most analyses of the impact of interest rates on house prices focus on *real* interest rates, where we are on sounder ground.

A study using an asset pricing model to explain the rise in British house prices found that the approximately 1.5% decline in *real* long-term interest rates from 1996 to 2003 could account for a rise in real house prices of a little under 40% (Bank of England, 2004). This is a substantial rise, though less than one-third of the actual rise in real house prices over the same period. The study attributes the remaining two-thirds mostly to a fall in the housing risk premium, that is, a more positive view of the outlook for housing.

However, looked at purely in terms of an investment, the decline in real long-term interest rates everywhere is at least partly due to a fall in the inflation risk premium. Yet, one of housing's greatest attributes as an investment is that it is a fairly reliable inflation hedge against unexpected inflation (more so than stocks for example). Hence, theoretically at least, it is not clear that all of the fall in real interest rates should automatically feed through into higher house prices.

Are there good reasons for a fall in the housing risk premium or is this another way of saying that there is a bubble? In the mid-1990s, the risk premium was naturally high in the United Kingdom, given the significant falls in house prices at the beginning of the 1990s. So the rise in house prices during the mid-1990s from particularly depressed valuations could fairly be linked to this. Further it could be argued that the good performance of the British economy over the last ten years, the avoidance of a major economic downturn, the significant fall in unemployment (from 10% in 1993 to 5% currently), the granting of full independence to the Bank of England as well as the maintenance of a floating exchange rate all further reduce the risk premium.

However there is a risk that the good performance of the economy cannot be indefinitely maintained (Scenario 5). It is now over 13 years since the last recession, the longest upturn for more than 100 years. Moreover the decline in the risk premium may also be due to the development of a bubble mentality. Accounts of bubbles through history have shown that, while they are of course characterised by rapid rises in prices and high valuations, they are also usually accompanied by various other factors, ranging from unusually low interest rates, through lending innovations to large-scale media interest (Calverley, 2004). All these elements

Table 15.3 Checklist: typical characteristics of a bubble

Rapidly rising prices
High expectations for continuing rapid rises
Overvaluation compared to historical averages
Overvaluation compared to reasonable levels
Several years into an economic upswing
Some underlying reason or reasons for higher prices
A 'new' element – e.g. technology for stocks or immigration for housing
Subjective 'paradigm shift'
New investors drawn in
New entrepreneurs in the area
Considerable popular and media interest
Major rise in lending
Increase in indebtedness
New lenders or lending policies
Consumer price inflation often subdued (so central banks relaxed)
Relaxed monetary policy
Falling household savings rate

Source: Calverley, 2004 (partly based on 'Bubble Trouble' HSBC Economics and Investment Strategy, July 1999).

seem to be present to a greater or lesser degree in the United Kingdom (see Table 15.3).

The existence of the first four items in the checklist has already been documented. The fifth item – that bubbles typically arise several years into an upswing – is clearly supported in the United Kingdom. Unemployment has trended down since 1991 with virtually no interruption. In 2001–2003, when most economies suffered a recession, the lowest year-on-year GDP growth rate in the United Kingdom was 1.5% and unemployment merely stabilised for a few months.

The underlying reasons for higher prices (item 6) may be the fall in interest rates, while higher immigration could be regarded as an underlying reason or perhaps a 'new element'. The subjective 'paradigm shift' could be that 'housing is the best pension', a view now widely held. And the drawing in of new investors is very clearly seen in the United Kingdom where 'buy-to-let' investment has become a major phenomenon. New entrepreneurs have emerged in the form of companies offering instant property portfolios or (expensive) courses on how to build a portfolio.

Popular and media interest is intense with numerous new TV programmes, with titles such as 'Location, location, location' and 'Property Millionaire'. The rise in mortgage lending has already been documented, and the household debt–income ratio has risen from 106% in 1995 to 139% in 2003 (OECD, 2004). New lending policies can clearly be seen in the easing of terms on investment properties. In the mid-1990s mortgages for investment property typically carried spreads well above owner-occupier mortgages alongside conservative lending criteria (whether linked to the borrower's income or the rental income). Now,

100% mortgages for 'buy-to-let' properties are advertised and rates are similar to owner-occupier mortgages.

A key factor in bubbles, to which we will return later, is that consumer price inflation is typically well-behaved so that monetary policy is relaxed. If consumer price inflation becomes a problem of course central banks raise interest rates to restrictive levels, which is usually enough to suppress a bubble and may cause it to collapse, particularly if the economy turns down too. This was the fate of the 1980s housing bubble when CPI inflation accelerated at the end of the decade.

The fall in the household savings rate, typically seen during a bubble, reflects both confidence that the rise in wealth is permanent and the high level of borrowing. It should be noted however that the fall in the UK household savings rate mostly occurred between 1997 and 1999, when London house prices rose rapidly but before nationwide house prices really took off so it is hard to argue that the house price bubble is the cause of a fall in the savings rate or robust consumer spending. It can however be argued that the improvement in household balance sheets combined with lower unemployment has allowed the savings rate to remain at low levels.

Bubbles are also often associated with strong exchange rates and this is supported in the United Kingdom. The real exchange rate has been strong since the mid-1990s and the current account balance has weakened since then. The high real exchange rate suppresses inflation, helping to keep interest rates lower.

The presence of all these factors in the United Kingdom now suggests that it would be unwise to rely on analyses suggesting that high house prices are fully justified by fundamentals. It is much more likely that at least part of the rise in prices constitutes a bubble.

15.4   Is there a US bubble?

The nationwide index for US home prices has marched upwards over the last 25 years, with prices never falling for more than a few months. Prices in certain areas, particularly on the coasts, have been much more volatile and have seen periodic bubbles and busts. Texas prices crashed after the fall in world oil prices in 1986 whereas California and New England prices fell sharply after the 1990 recession, with California impacted strongly by the defence cut-backs following the fall of the Berlin Wall.

However, just as in the United Kingdom prior to 1990, nationwide house prices did not fall because of the underpinning from ongoing consumer price inflation. Between Q1 1990 and Q1 1995 the nominal house price index climbed 7.6%. But with cumulative consumer price inflation of 17.9%, real house prices fell approximately 10%. In California, the nominal price decline of about 10% over the same period translates to a 24% decline in real terms.

After the price correction of the early 1990s the US market picked up gradually in the mid-1990s and then took off from the late 1990s. The 61% increase over the last eight years is a smaller increase than in many other countries but is well ahead of inflation of 20%. And many analyses now suggest that, on a nationwide basis, prices look high compared with past trends. One study based on rental yields found an overvaluation relative to past averages of 11%, as of Q3 2002 (Krainer, 2003). This estimate is similar to the estimate from the Bank of Spain mentioned earlier (Ayuso and Restoy, 2003). But, given house price and rent trends since then, I estimate this overvaluation rose to over 20% by mid-2004.

A comparison of prices to rents and prices to the median income also shows valuations to be historically high (Figure 15.3). Both ratios have been through cycles before, but are currently 10–15% *higher* than past cycle peaks and 20–25% above their averages. In prior housing market downturns in the 1980s and early 1990s these ratios fell about 10% over a 3–5-year period to cyclical lows. From current much higher levels, to return to past cyclical lows would require a fall of 25–30%. In past episodes, both incomes and rents were rising with general inflation and cushioned the blow. But in recent years, median incomes and rents have been rising only very slowly so this would imply a nominal house price fall of perhaps 15–20%.

However, some analysts question the idea of a bubble. One important point to note is that the OFHEO index of house prices looks at repeat sales of the same property but makes no allowances for any improvements or extensions in the property. Hence it probably systematically overstates the rise in house prices. Others argue that higher valuations are justified by improved fundamentals. For example, a report to Congress in 2003 argued that the case for a national bubble was unproven, though it did point to regional bubbles (Labonte, 2003). As for the United Kingdom, the focus is on the impact of low interest rates in justifying higher house prices, though as I have argued earlier, this is a questionable

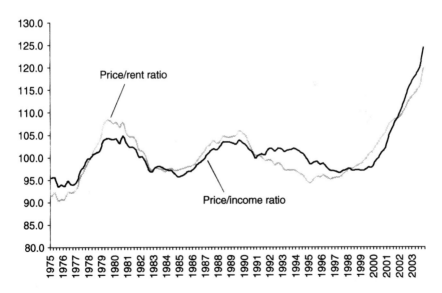

Figure 15.3 US: house price ratios.

Source: Goldman Sachs.

justification for high valuations except insofar as real interest rates are lower. In the United States, real interest rates on long-term bonds have been 1–1.5% lower since the beginning of 2000 than the average for the 1990s, which could account for part of the rise in prices (though part of this is presumably the reduction in the inflation risk premium as in the United Kingdom).

A run through the checklist of typical elements of a bubble, shows that many of them apply in the United States too, though the picture is somewhat more mixed than in the United Kingdom. For example, the United States is not several years into an economic upswing, as is common for a bubble. The current upswing only started in late 2001 and only became strong in 2003. Nevertheless, the survey of expectations described earlier suggests that confidence in house price inflation is well-entrenched after ten years of buoyant increases. And the 2001 recession was the mildest on record.

There has certainly been a major rise in lending, with mortgage debt up from $4523 billion at the end of 1999 to $6820 billion at end 2003. Of course, part of this increase reflects refinancing and mortgage equity withdrawal, but part will have fuelled house price increases. Higher borrowing is linked to lower mortgage rates but it is also true that, as in Britain, mortgages are more easily obtainable than ever before.

An important change in the last decade or so is the increased importance of the secondary market for mortgages. In the United States, it is now the norm for banks to originate mortgages and then sell them on to Fannie Mae or Freddie Mac. In 2003, the agencies' share of conventional mortgage debt stood at about 70%, more than double their share at the end of the 1980s.

Of course, to be eligible for purchase these mortgages have to meet strict 'conforming' criteria. Moreover the agencies themselves, which are privately owned, as well as investors in the mortgage-backed securities would suffer if there was a serious rise in defaults. Nevertheless it is hard to avoid the suspicion that loans are being made more easily now than in the past and this means more money chasing houses.

A 2003 survey of appraisers is revealing in this respect (Harney, 2003). Nearly 3 out of 4 randomly selected licensed appraisers told researchers that they had been pressured over the past year by a mortgage broker or loan officer to 'hit a certain value'. And if they ignored the pressure they faced the risk of a loss of business. One common tactic is 'pre-comping', where a loan officer asks in advance whether the appraiser thinks he or she can come up with comparable sales for a property to justify a specific target range for the mortgage. If the appraiser expresses doubts, the loan officer goes to another appraiser. Of the appraisers who reported pressure, 48% said the overvaluations demanded were 1–10% above the true value of the property while 43% said they were 11–30% above market value.

Returning to the checklist, in the United States, just as in the United Kingdom, there has been much talk of structural changes in demand for housing, related to immigration and faster household growth. There has also been a shift to investment in housing as an alternative to stocks. The household savings rate of course is low. It was already down to 2% at the end of the stock market boom and, contrary to expectations, has stayed low. Meanwhile consumer price inflation is subdued and monetary policy is strongly stimulative. Indeed it may be argued that the Federal Reserve has deliberately stimulated a housing boom to counter the depressive effects of the collapse of the stock bubble. US mortgage rates averaged 7–8% for much of the 1990s but fell below 6% in 2002–2004. Perhaps even more so than in Britain (because lower rates can be locked-in in the United States), there is a tendency to look at the monthly payment on a mortgage as the cost of buying a house, rather than making allowance for the fact that, with interest rates lower because of lower inflation, the potential upside for housing values is correspondingly lower.

US homebuyers of course enjoy tax relief on mortgage interest, though with lower interest rates and lower marginal tax rates this relief is worth less than in the past (which should imply lower valuations).

Overall the case for a US bubble is not as clear-cut as in Britain and is much more a regional phenomenon. However the principal states involved – California, Florida, Massachusetts, New Jersey and New York – account for 30% of the population and much of the higher-priced property in the United States. They also tend to be where the main 'opinion formers' in the United States live. So a slump in prices in these states, even if everywhere else showed stability, could have a considerable impact. But one very real possibility for the United States is that it is still in Scenario 1, where house prices and debt will continue to rise faster than incomes. The latest OFHEO price index data show a 9.36% gain for Q2 2004 over a year earlier.

15.5 Bubbles and monetary policy

Whether monetary policy-makers should react to bubbles has become a major subject of debate in recent years. Some policy-makers argue that it is impossible to be sure that a bubble is indeed a bubble and so asset pricing should simply be left to the markets. For others, it may be possible at times to identify a bubble, but usually only late in the day when deliberately pricking it would be dangerous and probably bring on the collapse that is feared.

Even if a bubble can be identified early, monetary policy, armed with only the interest rate instrument, cannot reliably hit two targets. The dilemma is illustrated in Table 15.4, showing a matrix of possible monetary policy responses. When the standard Taylor Rule (based on growth and inflation trends) suggests tightening while asset prices are perceived as bubbling as given in item 1 there is no dilemma and the bubble may well clarify the need for a rise in rates amidst the usual fog of uncertainty. However there is a question of whether interest rates need to be raised more than in the case of item 2 (where asset prices are calm). The Bank of England and the Reserve Bank of Australia (RBA) found themselves here in late 2003/early 2004. The Fed might have perceived itself here in 1999 in relation to the stock market but apparently did not. The view of the Fed then was that trying to restrain bubbles should not be a basis for policy.

Table 15.4 Monetary policy dilemmas with two targets

	House prices bubbling	House prices neutral	House prices falling
Taylor Rule suggests tightening	1 Tighten, and perhaps faster or more than strict Taylor Rule	2 Tighten	3 Dilemma. Tighten, but perhaps cautiously?
Taylor Rule suggests neutral	4 Not clear. Tighten a little? Or do nothing	5 Neutral	6 Not clear. Loosen a little? Or do nothing
Taylor Rule suggests loosening	7 Dilemma. Loosen, but less than otherwise?	8 Loosen	9 Loosen, and perhaps faster or more than strict Taylor Rule

Source: The author.

The opposite situation, where the Taylor Rule suggests loosening and asset prices are falling also presents no dilemma as given in item 9. Clearly there is a need to loosen and, again, the confluence of the two factors suggests rapid and aggressive easing. The Fed apparently did agree with the latter point in 2001–2003, leaving them open to the criticism that policy is asymmetrical and therefore tends to over-encourage bubbles.[4] If the British and/or Australian economies reach this position at some point we may imagine that they too will cut rates aggressively. Both countries would likely see a significant fall in the currency if they did so, helping to offset the economic slowdown.

The dilemmas really come to the fore in item 3 and item 7. A weak economy but with asset prices bubbling was the problem for the Bank of England in 2002–2003. The Taylor Rule (as well as geopolitical concerns) suggested loosening but house prices began to rise rapidly. The dilemma in item 3 has not been seen recently, but it could emerge in coming years if CPI inflation moves above target. However if economic growth is strong it is by no means clear that asset prices would fall (see below for more on this item). The situation in item 6 is perhaps more likely, where the Taylor Rule suggests policy at neutral but falling asset prices imply easing.

Overall, the rise in household debt burdens suggests that consumers may be more sensitive to higher interest rates than in the past, even though rates are low. Typical tightening cycles are likely to involve a smaller rise in rates than before. However one very important difference between Britain and the United States is that, in Britain more than two-thirds of mortgages are at floating rates whereas in the United States more than two-thirds are at long-term fixed rates. When interest rates are trending down, as for the last twenty years, the difference may not be so great because US consumers have been able to refinance at lower rates. But, on the way up, US mortgage holders are unaffected by rising rates, in contrast to the United Kingdom where higher short term rates quickly impact on mortgage payments.

Hence tightening cycles in the United Kingdom impact both on the cost of new loans and therefore potentially house prices, and the disposable income of existing homeowners (though there is some offset from higher deposit rates). In contrast, tightening cycles in the United States impact only on new borrowers. However, another difference between the two countries is that US home-building plays a larger role in the economy and is much more sensitive to interest rates. We will return to these issues later. First, we consider whether there are alternatives to monetary policy in restraining bubbles in the first place.

15.6 Alternatives to monetary policy

One possibility would be to use tax changes to lean against bubbles. However, not only would this be unpopular, but it might well not be effective. As noted previously, in the United Kingdom the tax burden has been raised on property in recent years (following the well-established fiscal formula of taxing whatever is buoyant), but this has not prevented prices rising rapidly.

Another approach sometimes proposed is to impose limits on loan-to-value ratios (LTVs). However, quite apart from the unattractiveness of restrictions of this sort, the evidence from Hong Kong is that it does not work. As early as 1991, the Hong Kong Monetary Authority (HKMA) reduced its guideline LTV limit from 90% to 70%. In fact banks were generally more cautious than this and as of September 1997, approximately the peak of the boom, actual LTVs were only at 52% (OECD, 2002). The HKMA also issued a guideline in 1994 that banks should limit their property exposure to 40% of loans. These measures probably did help to largely protect the banking system despite the subsequent 65% fall in house prices. Individuals lost much of their equity in housing but the default rate on loans was relatively low.

However this policy did not prevent a major bubble because there were enough new lenders entering the market to ensure that mortgages were easily available. Moreover buyers were often so keen to purchase that they took out personal loans at high interest rates to cover the down-payment. Perhaps, without the LTV limit the bubble would have inflated even further, but the Hong Kong experience strongly suggests that an LTV limit, on its own, is not enough.

A more attractive approach might be to try to restrain mortgage lending during booms. For example, countercyclical capital standards could be introduced, requiring banks to have higher capital ratios when asset prices are expensive and allowing lower ratios when they are inexpensive. In practice, banks tend to have pro-cyclical capital ratios, that is, lower capital ratios during booms and bubbles and higher ones during recessions and busts. And even if their official capital ratios are not pro-cyclical, risk assessment often becomes more relaxed while off-balance sheet (OBS) activity such as guarantees and derivatives may be stepped up, which comes to the same thing.

A similar result might be achieved by introducing stabilising provisioning rules requiring banks to make larger provisions when times are good and smaller ones when the economy is weak. Such a system was introduced in Spain in 2000 and has been avidly studied by regulators (Mann and Michael, 2002). However, this would require flexibility from accounting standards setters. Moreover, in most countries the tax authorities are reluctant to make such provisions tax deductible, because of fears that banks would use them as a tax avoidance measure. Spain has a complex system but it does allow banks to influence how much extra provisioning they make in the good times.

An approach which might satisfy the tax authorities, would be for the supervisors to determine the extra provisioning, based on the mix of lending and the behaviour of asset prices. For example, if house prices are seen as high, banks could be required to hold larger reserves against new mortgages. Such an approach needs to be mechanistic rather than discretionary, but then runs the risk of being inflexible.

The arguments here are separate from the issue of banking soundness. Of course bank supervisors might welcome either of these approaches because they would improve the incentives for bank soundness during the economic cycle. But it is easy to posit a situation where banks decide to relax their lending criteria in a way that adds fuel to a housing boom yet both banking management and supervisors regard the risk as acceptable from an individual bank's point of view. Losses on mortgage portfolios, at least for owner-occupiers, have historically been modest. This is true even during the recent experience in Hong Kong where home prices fell 65% from the peak in 1997 to the trough in 2003.

Moreover banks may find other ways to spread the risk. In the late 1980s, in the United Kingdom, insurance companies often insured the excess (at the mortgagee's expense) when LTVs pushed above a certain level (typically 80%). Many insurance companies took substantial losses on these portfolios in the early 1990s but it did not undermine their soundness. This underlines a typical feature of bubbles which is that new lenders come in to the market.

Many mortgages are now securitised so the risk is pushed back to investors including mutual funds, pension funds and insurance companies. Again, bank supervisors have no reason to discourage such business. Indeed quite the reverse. But investors in securitised mortgages may have a different level of risk aversion to that of banks, encouraging greater lending. Of course, higher risk loans do attract higher spreads, though there is a danger during bubble periods that investors are prepared to buy whatever the cost.

15.7   Five possible scenarios for housing, debt and the economy

1 *You ain't seen nothing yet*   The first scenario is where house prices and debt ratios continue to expand *faster* than incomes, providing support for consumer spending and the economy. MEW would also stay high, though it should be noted that if MEW and the savings rate are unchanged at a particular level, there is no new stimulus from this source. Consumer spending will expand at a percentage rate equal to income growth. In this scenario balance sheets expand but net wealth continues to grow. Banks can continue to make good profits from consumer business as the value of loans expands rapidly, and defaults should be limited since the economy too will be expanding while unemployment is stable or declining.

The bubble (if indeed it is one) gets bigger. Or in some cases, if a bubble has not yet developed, it starts now. Some other countries which have had smaller increases in prices and do not yet appear to be overvalued, for example Italy or Canada, might begin to enter a bubble. In part this might be due to the same conditions prevailing as in the existing bubble countries, particularly low interest rates and an increasingly competitive lending sector. But there may also be a degree of contagion as buyers from the United Kingdom and other bubble countries buy holiday homes or investment properties.

This is the scenario of the last several years but, while we would not expect it to continue indefinitely the limits for higher prices are not clear. Experience suggests that we should not expect a tightening of lending criteria to be the sole driving force for bringing it to an end, though it might perhaps play a role. However, with static lending criteria, potential borrowers would eventually reach their limit, especially first time buyers. Or, it could be that a rising trend for interest rates or a weakening in the economy leads to a scaling back of borrowing. Experience with bubbles in the past appears to show that, once a bubble mentality takes hold, with people speculating on a big scale, it comes to an end either because of a new external event or because the market reaches such an outrageously high level that greed gives way to fear.

2 *A higher equilibrium* The second scenario is that, after a step higher in valuations, house prices and debt then revert to a growth rate equal to incomes. As already noted, one of the consequences of this is that households will find their debt burden remaining relatively high for an extended period, only gradually eroding under the influence of inflation. But with the value of property rising (in line with incomes), housing as an investment still makes a positive return, though arguably not enough to justify the risk.[5] And the returns would seem very slow compared to the experience of recent years. For banks this scenario is less satisfactory than the first since the market is growing more slowly, only in line with earnings. Still, there would be no systemic problem with household credit.

One of the key questions is whether this is a stable scenario for the medium term. In practice markets never follow smooth equilibrium paths, so another way to test the stability of this scenario is to ask what would happen if house prices fell 5% or 10% in one year relative to earnings. Would they then pick up again, to stay in touch with the equilibrium track or is there a risk that the slide continues? The answer to this seems to depend on whether existing owners (occupiers or investors) would panic, whether potential buyers would expect a continued fall as 'bubble greed' gives way to fear, whether banks would sharply tighten lending criteria and whether a central bank response in the form of lower interest rates might be able to restore confidence if required. If the path is not stable then it slides into Scenario 4 or 5.

3 *Stability in nominal terms* The third scenario is perhaps the most benign from the point of view of central banks (at least those that worry about a bubble). It is that house prices and levels of debt stay broadly unchanged in nominal terms for a prolonged period allowing earnings to catch up and the overvaluation to be worked through. One argument in favour of this scenario is that even if the

willingness to buy houses turns down, homeowners and investors may simply stay put (though in the UK the latter would be making very poor returns – only the net rental yield of perhaps 2–3% pa). So the housing market may see a marked slow-down in turnover with little change in prices.

However, if house prices need a 30% fall to come back to reasonable valuations, this would imply a period of 7–8 years of stable prices. Moreover it must be questioned whether the housing market is likely to behave in this way. After major rises in prices, especially with signs of a bubble mentality, there must be a significant chance of a fall in prices. Still, this scenario is possible and perhaps most likely if some of the forces pointing to a fall in prices are offset by declining interest rates. For banks it would mean still weaker growth in consumer business, given lower housing turnover and a slowdown in MEW over time. Presumably delinquencies and defaults would tick up but not to a great degree.

The critical question for central banks is whether this stabilisation of prices would require an easing of policy to keep the overall economy on track. In the case of the United Kingdom, as noted above, the savings ratio has been quite sta-ble in recent years so the bubble does not appear to have added to consumer spending. But, if house prices stabilise, a savings rate of 6% is likely to mean net wealth falls in relation to incomes.[6] Moreover, MEW would presumably fall over time and we might also wonder whether there would be disappointment of consumer expectations of ever-higher house prices. In short, the savings rate would be expected to move up, though it is not clear how rapidly.

The Bank of England would probably welcome this, as would the RBA and probably the Fed. They would need to follow a looser monetary policy than otherwise and, overall, the economy would be likely to adjust in the direction of a lower real exchange rate, higher private savings and a smaller current account deficit. As long as the lower exchange rate did not trigger an inflation problem the outcome would be benign. However, in the case of the United States, we might wonder whether the rest of the world would be ready for the United States to start to grow its real net exports again.

4 *Autonomous house price collapse*   In this scenario house prices fall entirely of their own accord or with an insignificant trigger. The experience of past bubbles suggests this can often be the case. Accounts of bubbles sometimes refer to a period of eerie calm as the period of frenetic buying comes to an end, and then selling begins, gradually accelerating as panic sets in (Kindleberger, 1978). Critical state theory appears to provide a theoretical basis for this scenario, showing how bubbles can collapse without a major trigger (Sornette, 2003).

However, whether housing is likely to respond in this way can be questioned. Panic sales by owner-occupiers seem unlikely since people need somewhere to live. We might imagine that there could be a sudden rush to downsize if the bubble starts to burst. But, if prices fall by a moderate amount (10%?) people may give up trying to sell and stay put. The phenomenon of 'anchoring', identified in behavioural finance, is likely to be particularly prevalent in housing. Moreover past experiences of housing crashes usually have involved a major trigger, often the combination of higher interest rates and a recession.

However, the increased prevalence of investment in housing now could mean that there is a greater risk of panic selling, particularly in the United Kingdom and Australia where widespread investment in housing is a newer phenomenon than in the United States. There is also perhaps a greater risk, in the event of a major price correction, of repossessions as investors walk away or go bankrupt. In the United Kingdom the easing of bankruptcy rules in April 2004 might be a concern for banks. The risk of this scenario may also be greater in a low inflation environment, because the potential for nominal prices to fall is that much greater, leaving mortgage loans exposed.

Nevertheless, in the event of a significant fall in house prices, we would expect interest rates to be cut because of the risk of an economic slowdown. Lower interest rates would make it easier for investors to hold on by improving the running return from their investment (even if they face a capital loss). It should therefore mitigate the price fall as well as rebalance the economy in the way described in the previous scenario. But again, knowing how much to cut interest rates may be difficult.

Once house prices turn down (autonomously in this scenario) there begins a dynamic process as three forces interact: the downward psychology of a bursting bubble, the depressing effects on the economy of lower house prices and finally the stimulatory forces of easier monetary policy both for house prices and the economy. If the downward momentum of house prices from the bursting bubble is strong, cuts in interest rates may be unable to prevent house prices correcting substantially, but nevertheless may be able to keep economic growth near to trend. This benign outcome is most likely if the impact on the economy of falling house prices turns out to be modest and if other sources of demand in the economy (presumably exports and investment, since there is no room for increased fiscal deficits in the United Kingdom or United States) can take up the slack. As in the prior scenario, the authorities in the United Kingdom and Australia would probably welcome this outcome, with the bubble defused, the currency weaker and exports and investment stronger. However there is also the risk that the fall in house prices takes the economy down with it, most likely because the central bank responds too slowly. This scenario is more likely to bring a bumpy landing than the previous scenario.

For banks, the benign scenario of a correction in house prices without a slump in the economy would doubtless be less profitable than the previous scenarios. The consumer mortgage and lending business would contract and, at the margin, bad loans would go up. However, lower interest rates (which normally help banks' profits) would help as might improved returns on lending to business. Obviously the worst outcome is where both house prices and the economy slump together.

5 *House prices crash during the next economic downturn making it worse* In this final scenario the economy turns down, for one reason or another, and the

bubble in the housing market collapses leading to a potentially much more difficult economic downturn. This appears to be what happened in Japan and the United Kingdom in the early 1990s and threatened to be the case in the United States in 2001 with the stocks bubble. The Japanese authorities failed to respond to the problem fast enough and, of course, faced simultaneous bubbles in stocks, commercial property and residential property. The United Kingdom was unable to respond fast enough because of its 1990 entry into the Exchange Rate Mechanism. The United States, in contrast, responded very rapidly in 2001–2002 and, anyway, only had a stock bubble bursting.

An important issue is whether an economic downturn with housing collapsing would also see a major stock slump. It is reassuring that stocks have already fallen from their 2000 valuations and are now close to, or just above, mid-range historically (e.g. price–earnings ratios of 15–17 times). However, in the event of a simultaneous decline in the economy and in housing prices we could be sure that stock prices would also fall, perhaps down to the low end of the range (PE of 10–12). This would imply a new fall of 30% or more and would doubtless trigger wealth and confidence effects in itself. It would also seriously exacerbate the already existing problem of under-funded pensions, as well as, possibly, once again requiring many insurance companies to seek increased capital. Many pessimists on the US stock bubble are still waiting for this 'other shoe to drop'. Commercial property prices do not appear to be wildly exposed at present though they have been rising in some countries. Nevertheless they could fall too since a recession would quickly upset the supply–demand balance.

Overall, then the next economic downturn runs the risk of being particularly difficult if current high house price valuations have not been corrected before then (by Scenario 3 or 4). Central banks will need to stand ready to cut interest rates significantly and perhaps take other measures, such as quantitative monetary easing and direct purchase of government bonds and other assets, on the lines of the Bank of Japan's policy measures since 2001.

For banks this scenario is obviously the least attractive. The consumer lending business would contract sharply and delinquencies and default might be considerable. A large fall in bond yields and a substantial spread between short and long rates would help offset the problems, though, if deflation were to ensue and short rates go down to zero, the gap between short rates and bond yields would be unlikely to be as large as the 300–400 basis points seen in the United States in recent years. Consumer lending would, for sure, be a much less attractive business. One defining characteristic of this scenario would likely be a tightening of lending criteria, of course helping to make the situation worse.

15.8   Conclusion: what can we expect?

This paper has argued that a housing bubble exists in the United Kingdom and one is developing too in the United States. While we cannot completely rule out the argument that higher values can be justified by the low interest rate environment, other indications suggest that a bubble is present. How these bubbles will be resolved will play a major role in monetary policy and the course of the economy in coming years. The issue is already at the forefront in the United Kingdom and Australia. It is likely to become increasingly important in the United States. In the Eurozone, I would speculate that the *difference* between house price behaviour in Germany on the one hand, and in much of the rest of the region on the other hand, may become increasingly problematic.

For banks, it is rampant competition combined with the high profitability of mortgage (and related) business that has helped drive mortgage lending growth and house prices. But it seems certain that rapid consumer lending growth must come to an end at some point and some scenarios could also bring significant losses on consumer credit. The slowdown in growth is likely to be a reflection both of consumers being unable or unwilling to borrow further and banks tightening credit criteria for prudential reasons or under pressure from regulators.

The limits to further rises in house prices and debt (Scenario 1) are set by the interaction between the strength of the bubble mentality, up against the constraints of high valuations on buying together with the path of interest rates, and the economy. Further rises in house prices are perhaps most likely if interest rates stay low for a prolonged period while the economy continues to expand. At present, markets are expecting interest rates to rise in the remainder of 2004 and/or 2005 almost everywhere but if these expectations are scaled back, house prices could continue to rise faster than expected. A lower path for interest rates is most likely if inflation continues to come in below target or if there are periodic scares over the strength of the economic upturn.

In the United Kingdom and Australia interest rates have already moved up significantly, there are signs of a weakening of house prices and also housing valuations are particularly high. The potential for house prices and debt to continue rising rapidly therefore looks limited and so a continuation of Scenario 1 looks very unlikely. In the United States, interest rates have so far moved up rather less from their low point and valuations are not so extreme, except in certain locations, which suggests there is more risk of Scenario 1 continuing for a while (rises in prices faster than wages). Indeed this would be my expectation based on the view that US economic growth will remain close to, or just above, trend (3–3.5%) over the next 1–2 years, allowing the output gap to close only gradually and the Fed to normalise interest rates slowly while inflation remains quiescent. Later in 2005 and into 2006, if the output gap has closed, interest rates are likely to move higher, probably suppressing further rises in house prices.

In Spain, valuations do look particularly stretched. But interest rates are likely to move up the least over the next year, suggesting the risk of further house price rises. Overall then, the bubbles look more-or-less fully inflated in the United Kingdom and Australia but may have further to go in the United States and perhaps Spain. However this assessment has to be treated with caution: one of the characteristics of bubbles is that they often go on inflating far longer than analysts expect.

Taking the second and third scenarios together, stable ratios or stable levels, there is a good chance of one of these outcomes in the United Kingdom and

Australia. The Bank of England and RBA are focusing very carefully on housing and appear ready to respond to any significant fall in house prices with lower interest rates. In Australia in early 2004 and in the United Kingdom over the Summer of 2004, the central banks responded to very tentative signs of a housing slowdown by signalling a cautious approach to raising rates further.

However, there must also be a chance of the more negative scenarios developing at some point and in the case of the United Kingdom I would put the risk at 50% or perhaps more. Whether house prices will turn down completely autonomously on a large scale may be questioned though I believe this cannot be ruled out. More likely perhaps is the final scenario, where a downturn for other reasons becomes seriously exacerbated by a collapsing housing bubble. The usual reasons for an economic downturn are either higher interest rates in response to an inflation problem (Taylor rule tightening) or a slump in investment spending after a boom or in response to a shock. Neither appears imminent but the risks will increase over time, particularly for higher inflation. Output gaps are expected to disappear in the United States, United Kingdom and Spain in 2005 (OECD, 2004), though the Eurozone as a whole will still have a large output gap.

For central banks, the risks from house price bubbles will be increasing during 2005–2006, either from an autonomous decline or because an economic downturn emerges, which would be exacerbated by a large fall in house prices. High levels of debt as well as the key role of house prices mean that consumer demand may be especially sensitive to interest rates this time, particularly where much of the debt is at floating rates (e.g. the United Kingdom). Hence 'neutral' rates of interest may be lower than sometimes thought, for example nearer to 3% in the United States than 4% and nearer to 4.5% in the United Kingdom than 5–5.5%. And, if interest rates need to go above neutral to restrain the economy, the amount of tightening required might be quite modest.

For banks, the ideal consumer environment of strong borrowing, rising house prices, a growing economy and low interest rates looks set to come to an end soon. Hence the winning strategies of recent years are likely to be less successful in coming years. With luck there will just be a slowdown in business. But if a major recession occurs the environment could turn ugly. The outlook is for conditions to turn down first in the United Kingdom and Australia and only later in the United States and Spain.

The case of Spain is not comprehensively examined in this paper but a couple of comments follow from the scenario analysis. First, monetary policy in the Eurozone may well remain highly supportive for Spanish house prices, despite the already high valuations. Spain (like Ireland) resembles the Hong Kong case where the bubble was driven by negative real interest rates caused by the fixed currency peg, though the scale of new building is much more substantial than in Hong Kong. Second, Spain does not have control over its own interest rates, so in the event of Scenario 4 monetary policy would not be responsive (also Hong Kong's problem in 1998–2003). The Spanish authorities might therefore be wise to try to find non-monetary ways of limiting the bubble and also consider ways to limit the downside in house prices in case an autonomous bear market does begin at some stage.

Notes

1 In the United Kingdom, Douglas McWilliams of the Centre for Business and Economics Research has been one of the foremost (non-industry) proponents of the view that house prices can be at higher valuations than before and has consistently argued that the United Kingdom is not in a bubble and that prices would rise further. But CEBR's most recent analysis, published in August 2004, concluded that UK house prices are 3% overvalued, that is, about right. See www.cebr.co.uk

2 The *Economist*, 20 March 2004, p. 85.

3 For a discussion see Schwartz (2002).

4 The case for the defence rests partly on the fact that a substantial fall in a market is clearly likely to depress the economy to some degree whereas a rise in a market cannot be conclusively defined as a bubble and might be justified by changed fundamentals.

5 To take the UK example, if we posit 4% earnings growth (in line with the Bank of England's known comfort zone) and a 5% gross rental income giving about 2% after costs (maintenance, depreciation, agents fees, etc.), the investor earns 6% pa, only slightly above long-term bond yields.

6 In the United Kingdom, net wealth was 668% of incomes at end 2002 (OECD, 2004) with housing accounting for a little under half. A savings rate of 6% of incomes would not be enough to keep the ratio at 668% unless the stock market performed extremely well.

References

Ayuso, J. and Restoy, F. (2003). 'House prices and rents; an equilibrium asset pricing approach', Bank of Spain Working Paper No. 0304.

Bank for International Settlements (2004). 74th *Annual Report*, Basel, June 28, 2004.

Bank of England (2000). *Financial Stability Review*, June, London, pp. 105–125.

Bank of England (2004). 'Asset pricing and the housing market', *Quarterly Bulletin*, 44(1), pp. 32–42.

Barker, Kate (2004). *Delivering Stability: Securing our Future Housing Needs*, March 17. Available at www.barkerreview.org. Report commissioned by HM Treasury.

Calverley, John P. (2004). *Bubbles and How to Survive Them*, Nicholas Brealey: London, p. 13.

Capital Economics (2003). Reported in *The Economist*, November 29, p. 111.

Case, Karl E., Quigley, John M. and Shiller, Robert J. (2003). 'Home buyers, housing and the macro-economy', in Anthony Richards and Tim Robinson (eds), *Asset Prices and Monetary Policy*, Reserve Bank of Australia, Sydney.

CEBR (2004). *Housing Futures 2024*, Centre for Economics and Business Research, London, July 2004.

Debelle, G. (2004). 'Household debt and the macroeconomy', *BIS Quarterly Review*, March, 1–64.

Harney, Kenneth (2003). 'The nation's housing: appraisers pressed to overvalue', *Detroit Free Press*, September 14.

Kindleberger, Charles P. (1978). *Manias, Panics and Crashes*, New York: Basic Books.

Krainer, John (2003). 'House Price Bubbles', *Economic Letter*, No. 2003–06, March 7, Federal Reserve Bank of San Francisco.

Labonte Marc (2003). 'US housing prices: is there a bubble', Report for Congress, May 16, Washington, DC.

Mann, Fiona and Michael, Ian (2002). 'Dynamic provisioning: issues and applications', *Bank of England Financial Stability Review*, December 2002, pp. 128–136.

OECD (2002). *Turbulence in Asset Markets: The Role of Micro Policies*. OECD Contact Group Report, Paris, September.

OECD (2004). OECD Economic Outlook 2004/1 No. 75, June, table 10, p. 176.

Schwartz Anna J. (2002). 'Asset price inflation and monetary policy', NBER Working Paper No. 9321, November.

Sornette, D. (2003). *Why Stock Markets Crash: Critical Events in Complex Financial Systems*, Princeton, NJ: Princeton University Press.

16 Capital markets and financial integration in Europe*

Philipp Hartmann, Simone Manganelli and Cyril Monnet

16.1 Introduction

Capital market development and financial integration are of paramount importance for the European economy. For example, at the 2000 Lisbon Council they were included in the agenda intended to make the European Union (EU) the most competitive economy by 2010 (EC, 2000). The links between the size of the financial system and the level of economic development are well-documented (King and Levine, 1993). Moreover, increased financial integration, by reducing the cost of capital, will allow for a better allocation of resources. This may ultimately lead to increased economic performance. A study for the European Commission (EC), for example, estimates the potential impact of financial integration to be a 1% increase in EU GDP growth (Giannetti *et al.*, 2002). Finally, the transformation of the financial system can have an impact on the stability of the system itself, with possible consequences on the whole economy (Padoa-Schioppa, 2003).

It should therefore come as no surprise that European political and monetary authorities have a strong interest in capital markets and financial integration. European institutions have taken several initiatives to foster integration and development of the euro area capital markets. The most well-known of such initiatives is certainly the Financial Services Action Plan (FSAP). The EC launched the FSAP in 1999 with the explicit objective of actively promoting (and eventually achieving) the full integration of European financial markets, by providing homogeneous infrastructures and ensuring a level playing field for financial operators.

The European Central Bank (ECB) has also taken a proactive stance in this matter. The ECB is interested in the transformation of the European financial system for several reasons. First, capital markets represent one of the main channels through which monetary policy is transmitted. Second, payment and settlement systems play an important role in evolving financial systems. Third, structural changes in financial markets may in the transition be associated with risks to financial stability.

It is against this background that in 2002 the ECB and the Center for Financial Studies (CFS) established the ECB-CFS research network on 'Capital Markets and Financial Integration in Europe'. The network aims at stimulating top-level and policy-relevant research on the structure and integration of the European financial system and its linkages with the United States and Japan. It was launched in an effort to better understand the main processes under way in the transition from many different financial systems into a single one, to assess the quality with which the financial sector fulfils its functions, to analyse the relationships between these developments and those taking place in other major financial systems and to examine the implications of all these factors for the economy as a whole. While both empirical and theoretical research was envisaged, relevance for policy debates constituted another parameter for the work this initiative wanted to promote. The network was first established for a period of two years, which expired in April 2004. It has now been renewed for another three years, until end of 2007.

Within a relatively short period of time the network formed a coherent and growing group of researchers interested in the integration and development of European financial markets. Active contributors to this group have regularly presented the results of their research in the events organised and sponsored by the network.[1] Academic researchers, researchers from the main policy institutions and policy-makers participated actively in the workshops, either by presenting research results or through speeches and in policy panels. The network also stimulated a new research field on securities settlement systems, an area of high policy relevance that had not attracted much interest in the research community beforehand.

This paper brings together the main findings of the work done under the network and illustrates the issues to be tackled in the forthcoming years. It is structured as follows. The next section will describe in greater detail the organisation and the structure of the ECB-CFS research network. Section 16.2 will highlight the most interesting results and policy-relevant conclusions from the research papers presented under the auspices of the network. Section 16.3 presents the research agenda for the next phase of the network by discussing three new priority areas. Section 16.4 concludes.

16.2   Purpose of the network and main priority areas

In 1999, the EC presented a framework for action in the financial services industry to help achieve the benefits of the Single Market in financial services. The formulated objectives of this FSAP are to ensure a single EU market for wholesale financial services, guarantee open and secure retail markets and modern prudential rules and supervision. The Commission proposed forty-two measures and a timetable for their adoption with deadline 2005. In 2002, the date of creation of the ECB-CFS research network, the Commission reported that,

> Recent progress in the Council and the European Parliament on a number of proposals demonstrate that the political commitment to implement the FSAP on time is beginning to be translated into firm political agreements...Even if not all barriers have been removed, significant and irreversible progress towards a strong integrated European financial sector by 2005 is achievable – it is a prize that is now within our grasp.

Against the background of the FSAP, the ECB-CFS research network was intended to stimulate research in all areas relevant for the functioning of the European financial system. The work can be decomposed in three distinct, but related, broad areas of research: (1) European financial integration, (2) financial system structures in Europe and (3) financial linkages between the euro area/EU, the United States and Japan. A detailed description of key research areas was developed and made publicly available in the network 'roadmap'.[2]

To concentrate research resources and ensure policy focus, a limited number of areas within the three main broad research fields were initially given top priority for the first two years: (1) bank competition and the geographical scope of banking; (2) European bond markets; (3) European securities settlement systems; (4) the emergence and evolution of new markets in Europe (in particular start-up financing markets) and (5) international portfolio choices and asset market linkages between Europe, the United States and Japan.

Work on *bank competition and the geographical scope of banking* has been given priority because – despite the adoption of the 'single passport' principle – the euro area is still experiencing relatively few cross-border mergers compared with domestic consolidation and relatively limited cross-border corporate lending. Also supervisory structures and regulatory approaches pertaining to the banking sector underwent profound reforms whose effects should be analysed.

European bond markets have undergone rapid changes in the past few years, including the development of euro area-wide secondary market trading platforms, as well as the development of a more significant corporate bond market. These changes are so recent that their main sources and their wider implications are not widely understood. They may have important practical consequences, not least because bond markets constitute one key market for the conduct of monetary policy by central banks.

Despite the importance of *securities settlement systems* for financial markets, research was only at an embryonic stage when the network was set up. Moreover, the fragmentation of the European securities settlement industry, resulting in high cross-border securities trading costs, may well constitute the single most important obstacle to further securities market integration (see Giovannini Group, 2001, 2003). The rapid structural change in the European securities settlement industry and the very limited research available on these topics when the network was created made work in this area particularly important and relevant to policy-makers.

The area of *new markets* also received a very high priority. In 1998, the Commission (EC, 1998) reckoned that 'fewer technology-based enterprises are created in Europe and their prospects for growth are inhibited. Also, venture capital is underdeveloped in many European countries compared with the USA, in particular in the field of seed and early stage finance'. This highlighted the importance of the availability of a wide range of funding and investment possibilities for innovations and risk sharing – and hence ultimately for growth and welfare.

Priority was also given to *international portfolio choices and asset market linkages between Europe, the United States and Japan,* as the past few decades have brought an enormous expansion of international capital flows. As a consequence, global financial linkages have strengthened. While their impact on economies is far larger than traditional trade linkages, for example, knowledge about the driving factors behind international financial flows is still relatively limited.

16.3   Results of the network

This section reviews a selection of the main policy-relevant results of the work done in the context of the network, going through its five priority areas, as formulated in the network 'roadmap'. We start each of the following sub-sections with a paragraph summarising the key findings. We then elaborate on these findings in more detail.

16.3.1   Bank competition and the geographical scope of banking

Results reveal that, first, integration is not very advanced in many retail-banking markets. Second, some of the inherent characteristics of traditional loan and deposit business constrain the cross-border expansion of commercial banking, even in a common currency area. Hence, the implementation of some policies to foster cross-border integration of retail banking may be ineffective. Third, bank competition does not need to cause instability, but is likely to spur growth in developed countries, as more competition in the banking sector induces financially dependent firms to grow more. Fourth, theoretical research suggests that supervisory structures may not be neutral towards further European banking integration. Finally, a stronger role of area-wide competition policies could be beneficial for further banking integration.

As shown by Baele *et al.* (2004), the degree of integration varies in the different segments of the retail-banking markets. In the corporate lending market, following significant convergence in the run-up to European Monetary Union (EMU), short-term and medium- and long-term lending markets are still segmented, even more so for short-term lending (see Figure 16.1). Households mortgage loan rates seem to have become more uniform across countries, while the consumer credit segment remains highly fragmented (see Figure 16.2).

This price-based evidence is confirmed by quantity measures of cross-border activities within the euro area. Cross-border lending is still very limited in the retail-banking segment, as shown in Figure 16.3 and Hartmann *et al.* (2003).

The persistence in home biases in lending and borrowing to non-financial corporations and households is confirmed by evidence from Berger *et al.* (2002) that large multinational corporations still prefer small local institutions to global financial institutions for their local cash management – that is, short-term banking needs, including short-term lending, liquidity management, etc. To the contrary, one would expect multinational corporations to be the first beneficiaries of the services offered by global banks.[3] The disappearance of domestic banking business as a consequence of advancing financial integration therefore does not

Figure 16.1 Cross-sectional standard deviation of interest rates on short-term and medium- and long-term loans to enterprises.

Source: ECB.

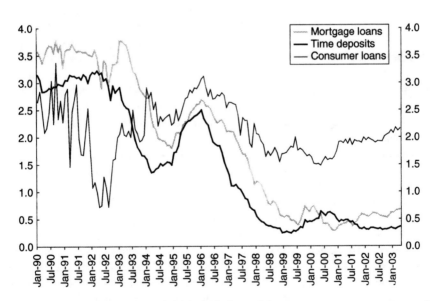

Figure 16.2 Cross-sectional standard deviation of interest rates on consumer and mortgage loans and time deposits.

Source: ECB.

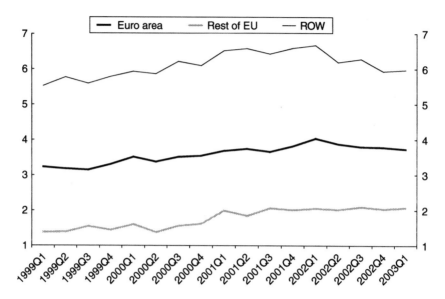

Figure 16.3 Cross-border loans (as a percent of domestic loans).
Source: ECB.

seem to be a likely development, at least not in the short run. In complementary work, Guiso *et al.* (2004) find evidence that even if financial markets become increasingly integrated, domestic financial institutions do not become redundant. Results suggest that local financial development – and therefore local banking – is an important determinant of the economic success of an area, even in an environment where there are no frictions impeding capital movements. All in all, we can conclude that traditional loan and deposit business appears to solve economic frictions in a way that is difficult to reconcile with very extensive cross-border expansions.

The other side of the coin is that domestic banks, potentially equipped with substantial local market power, constitute a break on greater financial integration. Some see cross-border mergers and acquisitions as a possibility to solve this problem. An active use of European competition policy, for example, taking an accommodative stance towards competition enhancing cross-border mergers could be a straightforward way to create room for such consolidation.

Degryse and Ongena (2004) suggest that bank relationships and industry specialisation are affected by competition. Bank branches facing stiff local competition engage relatively more in relationship-based lending. The effect of competition on industry specialisation is much less pronounced. A diversification effect seems to follow competition, as bank branches engage somewhat fewer borrowers in the same industry if local market concentration decreases.

As diversification tends to be associated with less risk, this result suggests a positive relationship between bank competition and financial stability. Carletti and Hartmann (2003) survey more systematically the literature on competition and stability and, indeed, conclude that the idea that competition is something dangerous in banking, since it generally causes instability, can be dismissed. Competition in banking should therefore be re-examined. The paper by Kaas (2003), for example, suggests that policies favouring competition from foreign banks would improve welfare, if local incumbent banks were less efficient. In related empirical work, Claessens and Laeven (2003) examine whether competition in the banking sector is beneficial for economic growth. The result depends on the degree of financial development. In less developed countries, sectors that are financially dependent grow slower when the banking system is more competitive, while in developed countries more competition is associated with higher growth. More precisely, financially dependent firms will grow by 1.5% more per annum if the country's banking sector is more competitive. These findings support the view that sufficient competition in European banking systems is an important ingredient for the financial system to play a stimulating role for overall economic performance.

In line with this conclusion, Carletti and Hartmann (2003) also argue that there should be well-defined arrangements about the relative roles of competition and supervisory authorities. Supervisory authorities often have some role in bank merger reviews, and those countries that have given only a weak role to competition authorities may be advised to ensure that competition concerns are not neglected.

More generally, the regulatory and supervisory framework seems to have implications for retail credit markets. First of all, Buch and DeLong (2003) find that regulation is a driving factor behind international mergers: banks operating in a more regulated environment are less likely to be the target of international bank mergers. Hence, some regulatory barriers can be impediments to further mergers and acquisitions. Second, Huizinga and Nicodeme (2003) find that international non-bank depositors appear to favour banking systems covered by explicit deposit insurance. Systems with co-insurance, a private administration and a low deposit insurance premium attract them. The sensitivity of non-bank deposits to deposit insurance policies opens up the possibility of international regulatory arbitrage. Third, Dell'Ariccia and Marquez' (2003) theoretical paper shows that a centralised regulator could increase efficiency at the cost of flexibility in applying different regulations to countries with heterogeneous financial systems. The benefits of a single regulatory framework therefore heavily depend on the symmetry in the financial systems of the relevant countries.

The dependence of the European financial system on banks only increases the importance of these issues. Contrary to the United States, whose system still relies more heavily on market finance, we can conclude that enough banking competition is important in European banking in order to support economic growth.

16.3.2   European bond markets

While the government bond market has integrated rapidly with the EMU convergence process, its full integration has not yet been achieved. The introduction of a common electronic trading platform reduced transaction costs substantially, but yield spreads of long-term sovereign bonds of the euro area are still heterogeneous. This is largely explained by different sensitivities to an international risk factor, whereas liquidity differentials only play a role in conjunction with this latter factor. Somewhat surprisingly in this context, the dynamically developing corporate bond market exhibits a relatively high level of integration. There is also increasing evidence that the introduction of the euro has contributed to a reduction in the cost of capital in the euro area, in particular through the reduction of corporate bond underwriting fees. As a result, firms may wish to increase bond financing relative to equity financing. The development of a larger corporate bond market is also important for monetary policy. For example, US evidence suggests that the rating of corporate bonds may contribute to the persistence of recessions, as rating agencies' policies affect firms asymmetrically in their access to the bond market over the business cycle. US evidence also suggests that liquidity conditions in stock and bond markets tend to be positively correlated.

As documented by Blanco (2002), the government bond market integrated significantly with the EMU convergence process and with some efforts to harmonise issuing procedures and conventions. However, full integration of the government bond market has not yet been achieved. For example, while the level of convergence in yields is impressive, yields of government bonds with similar, or in some cases identical, credit risk and maturity have not entirely converged. Typically, as shown in Table 16.1, yields on 10-year euro area government bonds may differ by around 15–20 basis points between different countries. Differences in liquidity as well as in the availability of developed derivatives markets tied to the various individual bond markets have been mentioned as possible explanations for these spreads.

To explain observed yield differentials between long-term sovereign bonds in the euro area, Favero *et al.* (2004) resort to an international risk factor (measured as the differential between high-risk US corporate bonds and US government bonds). There is a strong co-movement among European countries' yield differentials with Germany. As shown in Figure 16.4, this common trend appears to be highly correlated with this international risk factor. Somewhat surprisingly, they argue that liquidity differentials do not explain much of the yield differentials. Rather, the differentials are largely explained by varying sensitivities of local yields to the international risk factor. Liquidity only plays a role when interacting with the international risk factor.

Most European government bonds are now traded on MTS, the single international platform. Cheung *et al.* (2004) conduct a microstructure study of trading in MTS, showing that national order imbalances appear to be diversifiable across all market participants. More precisely none of the national order imbalances in the government bond markets of Germany, France, Italy or Belgium affect benchmark (German) yield innovations.

Governments have also a lot to gain from integration and well-designed markets. The institutional design of markets is very important for their integration and the prevailing prices. Specifically, differences in the microstructures and

Table 16.1 Average yield spread for 10-year government bonds relative to Germany

	Austria	Belgium	Finland	France	Greece	Ireland	Italy	Netherlands	Portugal	Spain
1993	18.4	70.6	30.1	25.5	1,685.7	119.9	467.2	−16.2	468.1	369.9
1994	16.6	88.8	217.5	35.3	1,402.7	122.9	365.8	0.2	361.2	313.3
1995	28.4	63.1	194.0	68.6	1,042.6	160.2	535.7	4.9	462.1	442.7
1996	11.3	27.8	88.3	11.6	842.0	115.0	313.1	−5.9	235.5	252.2
1997	3.3	10.1	76.5	−7.1	454.4	65.1	118.0	−7.3	71.8	73.9
1998	16.3	19.1	24.6	8.5	393.3	24.5	33.7	7.0	28.6	27.8
1999	20.3	26.2	22.6	11.8	190.8	21.6	25.1	14.1	31.2	24.2
2000	29.9	33.3	20.3	13.9	82.2	25.2	33.3	15.2	35.1	27.0
2001	27.4	32.0	22.8	13.3	48.9	19.3	37.5	14.9	35.8	28.8
2002	16.8	19.8	18.2	8.4	32.3	21.6	24.2	11.1	22.6	15.2

Source: ECB.

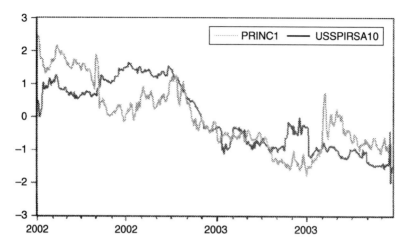

Figure 16.4 First principal component of euro-area government yield differentials and the spread between the 10-year fixed interest rate on swaps and US government bond yield.

Source: Favero *et al.* (2004).

issuing procedures of European Treasury bill markets across countries and changes of those features over time affect yields in treasury auctions, and thus the cost of funding for governments. As shown in Biais *et al.* (2004), regularly issuing bills significantly reduce yields. Also, when bills are traded on a centralised, transparent electronic limit order book, such as MTS, their liquidity rises and the yields decline significantly. Governments could therefore enhance liquidity and reduce yields and the costs of their funding, by efficiently designing treasury securities and issuing procedures as well as by promoting and accommodating modern cross-country trading systems. According to the estimates provided by Biais *et al.*, governments could save up to €350.19 million by improving the microstructure of the Treasury markets.

The corporate bond market in the euro area is surprisingly well-integrated, as first documented by Baele *et al.* (2004). They show that in this rapidly expanding market, the country where a bond is issued has only marginal explanatory power for the cross-section of yield spreads, once a number of systematic risk factors is accounted for. Quantity-based indicators also tend to support this conclusion. Between 1998 and 2002, the share of bond market funds (both government and corporate) with European-wide investment strategies increased dramatically from below 20% to above 60%, indicating a drastic reduction in the home bias of bond portfolios in the euro area. In contrast, home bias still seems to characterise cross-Atlantic portfolios of corporate loans. Evidence from Carey and Nini (2004) suggests that interest rates of syndicated corporate loans in Europe are on average 30 basis points lower than in the United States. The difference is both economically and statistically significant. Since systematic differences across the two markets in loan and borrower characteristics do not explain it, they describe this pricing difference as a puzzle, encouraging further research that focuses on why borrowers do not cross borders.

Another set of results presented at network events relates to the effects of the euro on European corporate bond markets. In particular, there are more and more evidences showing that the euro has contributed to reductions in the cost of corporate bond financing, and therefore in the cost of capital more generally. For example, Tsatsaronis and Santos (2003) show that the introduction of the euro led to a reduction in the underwriting fees of international corporate bonds issued in the new currency (see Table 16.2). This reduction was largely due to greater contestability of the investment banking business in the post-EMU European market. There is a global downward trend in fees over the 1994–2001 period, with value-weighted average fees for 2001 standing 86 basis points below their 1994 levels. This 37% reduction is largely attributable to a sharp drop in the euro-denominated segment. As a result, underwriting fees for euro-denominated corporate bonds are now at the same level as in the dollar segment of this market.

Bris *et al.* (2003) show that the introduction of the euro has lowered firms' cost of capital, by further increasing capital markets integration in Europe and by eliminating currency risks among the countries that joined EMU. More precisely, they show that firm valuations for large firms in the euro area (as measured by Tobin's Q between 1998 and 2000) have increased by 7.9% per year relative to firms in non-EMU countries, after controlling for firm, country and time specific effects. These developments point to further growth of European corporate bond markets.

Table 16.2 Average fees by nationality of borrower and currency of denomination, 1994–2001

Nationality of the borrower	Currency of denomination					
	Legacy currency		*Euro*	*US dollar*	*Other*	*All currencies*
	Foreign currency	*'Home' currency*				
Before the euro						
US	1.715		1.750	1.168	1.350	1.351
Euro-area	1.945	1.504	1.103	1.304	1.295	1.492
Other	1.786		2.000	1.160	1.168	1.227
Total	1.780	1.504	1.602	1.139	1.199	1.291
After the euro						
US			0.886	0.669	0.644	0.706
Euro-area			0.779	0.804	0.808	0.791
Other			0.597	0.757	0.653	0.652
Total			0.772	0.686	0.694	0.716

Source: Tsatsaronis and Santos (2002).

Corporate bond markets are also tied to the business cycle. According to Santos (2003), rating agencies' policies affect firms asymmetrically in their access to the bond market over the business cycle. The idea is that the 'quality' of the signal produced by the rating agencies varies with the firms' creditworthiness. Since rating agencies are more likely to produce split ratings on bonds of mid-credit quality issuers, the impact of recessions is not uniform across firms: it increases the cost of capital, most for mid-credit quality firms. As ratings become increasingly uncertain in recessions, the information becomes more asymmetric. Uncertainty related to the quality of firms then raises the cost of access to capital.

16.3.3   European securities settlement systems

European securities settlement infrastructures are highly fragmented and further integration and/or consolidation would exploit economies of scale that could greatly benefit investors. It is not clear, however, whether direct public intervention in favour of consolidation would lead to the highest level of efficiency, for example, because of the existence of strong vertical integration between trading and securities platforms ('silos'). In contrast, promoting open access to clearing and settlement systems could lead to consolidation and the highest level of efficiency. Finally, regarding concerns about unfair practices by Central Securities Depositories (CSDs) towards custodian banks, regulatory interventions favouring custodian banks should be discouraged, as long as CSDs are not allowed to price discriminate between custodian banks and investor banks.

The two Giovannini reports (2001, 2003) stressed the need to progress with securities settlement infrastructures, especially regarding cross-border settlement. Legal and technical barriers to further integration were highlighted. Given the already very comprehensive practical work of the Giovannini group in analysing barriers to consolidation, the network focused on somewhat different issues. Two points were particularly addressed. First, there is a lot to gain in Europe from further consolidation of securities settlement systems. Second, in addition to the barriers highlighted in the Giovannini reports, there may be intrinsic features of the securities trading and settlement industry that prevent consolidation.

Settlement in Europe is 33% more costly than in the United States, as the average cost per settled transaction is $3.86 in Europe and only $2.90 in the United States. This difference is partly explained by the segmentation in the European market, as the average cost for operating an international CSD in Europe is $40.54 relative to $3.11 for a domestic one, while it is only $2.90 in the United States (see Schmiedel *et al.*, 2002). Hence, looking at the exploitation of economies of scale in Europe and the United States, the latter is operating at a much more efficient level.

European settlement infrastructures show a strong potential for cost saving, as illustrated by Table 16.3. Costs will rise by a factor of only 0.68 when the number of instructions increases by 1, while the same measure for the United States is 0.94. Hence, Europe has much more to gain from further consolidation. However, given the level of complexity in EU international securities settlement systems,

Table 16.3 Cost scale elasticities for a single instruction in securities settlement

Median	0.696
Europe, Canada	
All	0.682
Excluding ICSD	0.639
ICSD	0.696
US	0.944
Asia, Pacific	0.741
Loglinear model median	0.744

Source: Schmiedel *et al.* (2002).

the effectiveness of settlement industry infrastructures may benefit from the simplification of the procedures for cross-border settlement, as for instance advocated in the second Giovannini report (2002).

Koeppl and Monnet (2004) argue, however, that lifting all legal and technical barriers to consolidate may not suffice to insure that the best forms of consolidation will take place. They analyse theoretically the role of vertical 'silos' in securities market organisation for efficient horizontal consolidation between components of the silo, that is, exchanges and back-office operations such as clearing and settlement. An efficient merger is characterised by the lowest cost of clearing and settlement. They show that it is impossible to achieve such a merger when silos are in place. The reason is that lack of information on the cost structure of the competitor raises the cost to achieve an efficient merger. These additional costs can never be covered with the revenues of the merger, as they increase with the revenues. However, competition can be used to achieve efficient consolidation. The authors show that exchanges can achieve an efficient merger by each outsourcing its own settlement operations, as long as each settlement system competes for settling all trades of the merged exchange. Hence, they argue that fostering competition and open access to securities settlement systems may be an adequate policy.

Regarding the efficient design of the structure of securities settlement systems, Holthausen and Tapking (2004) tackle pricing strategies of CSDs relative to custodian banks. Both CSDs and custodian banks provide the same service, but custodian banks often need to resort to CSDs. In an environment where CSDs do not price discriminate custodian banks from usual investor banks, Holthausen and Tapking show that CSDs can increase the cost of custodian banks by increasing the variable part of their price schedule. However, although still sub-optimal, they also show that the equilibrium market share of CSDs is closer to the optimal level than in the case where there are no custodians. They conclude that regarding concerns about unfair practices by CSDs towards custodian banks, regulatory interventions favouring custodian banks should be discouraged, as long as CSDs are not allowed to price discriminate between custodian banks and investor banks.

Iori (2004) looks at the efficiency and stability of alternative designs for securities clearing and settlement infrastructures. Using the plausible assumption that settlement takes place in batches throughout the day and that settlement can be delayed, she finds that increasing the frequency of settlement (and therefore approximating real-time settlement) increases the likelihood of failure but reduces the systemic effects of a failure. As a consequence, the shorter the interval between settlement batches, the more stable gross settlement systems are compared with net settlement systems, and vice versa.

With these papers on securities settlement systems being presented in its events, the network stimulated a new research field that is particularly important for current policy concerns in relation to European financial integration. The network will continue its efforts to promote further research in this area.

16.3.4   The emergence and evolution of new markets in Europe (in particular start-up financing markets)

Relative to the United States, European 'new markets' and start-up financing are relatively little developed and integrated. However, new markets and venture capitalists are the most important intermediaries for the financing of projects with high risk and with potentially very high return. The analysis carried out within the network reveals that European start-up financiers are mostly institutional investors, while US venture capitalists are mostly rich individuals. Also, new equity markets are essential for the development of start-up financing in Europe, as they provide an exit strategy for start-up financiers, who can then sell new successful firms using initial public offerings. The legal framework affects the development of venture capital (VC) firms. For example, very strict personal bankruptcy laws constrain early stage entrepreneurs, reducing demand for VC finance. More generally, firms tend to be more valuable in the context of good corporate governance practices. Therefore, the development of the single European market for financial services should be promoted by good corporate governance.

Da Rin (2003) illustrated the key characteristics of the European VC industry. Over the 1990s, the level of investment in the European VC industry was about half of the one in the United States, showing the relative underdevelopment of this industry in Europe. Also the characteristics of this industry differ across the two continents. The European landscape of VC firms is highly captive (that is owned by an industrial company or financial intermediary), as shown in Table 16.4.

Typically, these types of VC firms invest less in early stage and high-tech projects, providing less soft support to private companies relative to individual ones. There is also evidence that European VCs aim at selling their firms. As shown by Da Rin *et al.* (2004), the creation of New Markets could therefore foster the creation of VC firms, as additional exit opportunities create further incentives for VCs to invest. However, Da Rin also reported findings that European VC might actually not make a difference for sales growth of the companies they are financing. Table 16.5 shows that when controlling for the ownership structure at the time of an initial public offering (IPO) – by including a dummy variable that takes on the value of one when different categories of shareholders are

Table 16.4 Fund level survey data: European VC industry is highly captive

Investor type	Average holding	Proportion of VC funds in which this investor type is present
Banks	0.40	0.44
Corporate investment	0.25	0.23
Financial investment	0.30	0.31
Government	0.53	0.28
Individuals	0.45	0.24

Source: Da Rin (2003).

Table 16.5 Robust regression-dependent variable sales growth rate

Independent variable	Coefficient		Std. error
Germany	0.5408	***	(0.1341)
Foreign sales	−0.0629		(0.1218)
Age	−0.0012	***	(0.0004)
Leverage	−0.1001	***	(0.0273)
Capital raised	0.0019	***	(0.0004)
Founders	0.2280	*	(0.1308)
Managers	0.4152	**	(0.2031)
Venture capital	0.1099		(0.1479)
Corporate venture capital	0.6610	**	(0.3762)
Constant	0.3641	***	(0.3101)
Number of observations	355		
F (14; 340)	5.32		
p-value	0.000		

Source: Bottazzi and Da Rin (2002).

Notes
*, **, *** denote 10%, 5% and 1% significance levels for the significance tests of the parameters in the table.

present – VC does not significantly affect sales growth rate. While VC-backed companies raise more capital at IPOs, they do not tend to grow faster than others.

Tykvová and Walz (2003) bring additional evidence that firms backed by bank-dependent and public VCs have significantly lower market value relative to firms backed by independent VCs. In general, firms backed by independent VCs perform better and display a lower return volatility than firms of other VCs or non-venture-backed ones.

VC firms are investing very locally and with a very few exceptions have less than 10% of foreign partners. Also, the cross-border investment of VC firms is less than 2%. Finally, less than a third of funds originate from foreign investors. Most foreign investors are from the United States and are concentrated in only a small number of firms (Da Rin, 2003). This shows a low degree of integration in this sector in Europe. As for the characteristics limiting integration in retail credit markets, the nature of the VC industry, which is quite different from that of other financial intermediaries, may provide an explanation. VC makes localised and undiversified investments; VC is based on human rather than financial capital and VC has a small number of investors. However, financial integration could indirectly restructure the VC industry through its effect on the allocation of funds and the changes in the EU economic structure, notably on the listing ability of new firms. In this regard, financial integration may improve exit channels for VC and reallocate talent and human capital.

Corporate governance of new firms and the legal framework surrounding early finance can also greatly affect the VC industry and the development of New Markets. Cumming and Armour (2003) find that severe personal bankruptcy laws discourage early stage entrepreneurs and therefore significantly reduce the demand for VC finance. Also, according to Giannetti and Simonov (2003) investors are more likely to buy stocks of a firm when the ratio of control to cash flow rights of the principal shareholder – expected to be positively correlated with the extraction of private benefits in a firm, and therefore used as a proxy for bad governance – is lower. Improved corporate governance has a stronger effect on sophisticated investors, like financial institutions and foreign investors, while large domestic investors and individuals that are board members, do not base their investment decisions on corporate governance grounds. Finally, Desai *et al.* (2003) stress the importance of the institutional framework for entrepreneurial activity in Western, Central and Eastern Europe. The authors identify a particular sensitivity of entrepreneurial activity to institutional factors (corruption/fairness, protection of property rights, well-functioning legal system) for countries of Central and Eastern Europe. In particular, less corruption and better protection of property rights increase entry and reduce exit of firms. This supports the view that well-designed institutions foster entrepreneurial activity partly through the positive impact on relaxing capital constraints. Corporate governance is therefore an important factor for understanding portfolio choice across countries.

There is one feature of European governance structure that seems to be better than its counterpart in the United States. The dual board system often adopted in Europe separates the monitoring and the advising roles of the board of directors. Adams and Ferreira (2004) argue that revealing information and getting advice enables the manager to make better decisions, but this might increase his chances of getting fired when this information changes the board's opinion about his ability. This trade-off provides a rationale for the board to reduce its monitoring activity up-front whenever it is not too costly to induce the manager to reveal his information. The authors show further that the first-best level of monitoring can nevertheless be attained when a dual board system is used.

16.3.5   *International portfolio choices and asset market linkages between Europe, the United States and Japan*

At a global scale, asset market linkages have increased recently. For example, major economies such as the United States and the euro area have become more financially interdependent. This phenomenon can be observed in stock and bond markets as well as in money markets, where the main direction of spillovers has recently been from the United States to the euro area. Country-specific shocks play now a smaller role in explaining stock return variations of firms whose sales are internationally diversified. Increases in firm-by-firm market linkages are a global phenomenon, but they are stronger within the euro area than in the rest of the world. Various other phenomena also increase market linkages and therefore the likelihood that financial shocks spread across countries. One example is the use of global bonds. Finally, nowadays more direct access of unsophisticated investors to financial markets may increase volatility.

Brooks and Del Negro (2003) reported in the Launching workshop that the degree of co-movement across national stock markets has increased dramatically in recent years. They find that the ability of country-specific effects to explain international variation in asset and sales growth and return fell significantly during the late 1990s, while the explanatory power of global industry effects increased and in some cases surpassed that of country effects, as shown in Figure 16.5. Yet, this question is not settled. Although there is some ground to believe that international linkages are becoming stronger, country effects are still large. Where firms are located seems to still matter more than what they actually produce, although there is evidence that at the European level, industry effects are gaining further importance.

Stronger international linkages may be explained by growing cross-listings. Halling *et al.* (2004) reported that more companies are listing their shares, not only in their domestic stock exchange, but also on foreign exchanges. They find that cross-listing initially raises trading volume in foreign markets, but a declining trend then follows (Figure 16.6).

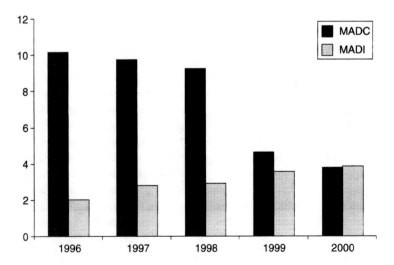

Figure 16.5 The relative importance of country and industry effects in global asset growth. (Mean average deviations are measured in per cent per year and based on annual US Dollar total asset growth.) Mean average deviations for country (MADC) and industry (MADI) effects.

Source: Brooks and Del Negro (2002).

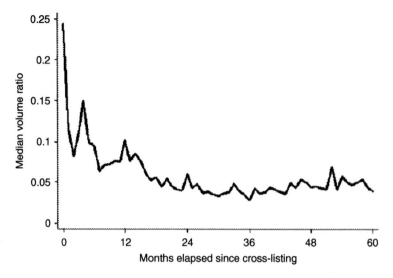

Figure 16.6 Monthly ratio of foreign to domestic volume in the five years after cross-
listing, median values.

Source: Halling *et al.* (2004).

Although this would suggest a return to the dominance of the domestic market,
the decline in foreign trading is quite slow for certain companies. Foreign trading
volume turns out to be higher for export-oriented companies and for companies
which cross-list into foreign exchanges with lower trading costs and better insider
trading protection. Also small, high-growth and high-tech firms tend to have
relatively higher foreign trading activity.

Investors, as firms, are seeking ways to exploit financing capacities of all
markets by creating new instruments, such as global bonds, that can be simultaneously traded in multiple markets. Miller and Puthenpurackal (2003) reported
that global bonds are likely to be an expanding form of finance, as this instrument
reduces the cost of debt capital. According to their study, borrowing costs for
globally tradable bonds are 15 basis points lower than on comparable US domestic bonds. Moreover, issuing costs of global bonds are 13 basis points lower than
those of US domestic bonds. Making these types of instruments more attractive
will undoubtedly bring additional linkages between Europe, the United States and
Japan, thus increasing the risk of volatility spillovers among the different markets.

Examining the effects of monetary policy announcements and macroeconomic
news on interest rates in the money markets, Ehrmann and Fratzscher (2004)
already found evidence that the spill-over effects are stronger from the
United States to the euro area than vice versa. They also find that since the introduction of the euro the cross-Atlantic interdependence of money markets has
steadily increased over time, as shown in Figure 16.7. In a similar vein, Fleming
and Lopez (1999) examine whether information from other trading centres affect

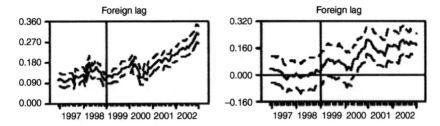

Figure 16.7 Rolling window parameter estimates of the effects of a change in the United States (German, left panel) money market rate on the German (US, left panel) money market rate. Germany and US, January 1993–February 2003.

Source: Ehrmann and Fratzscher (2004).

intra-market variances for US treasury bonds in London, New York and Tokyo. They find strong evidence that volatility spills over from New York to London and Tokyo but not the reverse.

Increased volatility spillovers may become worrisome with the 'democratisation' of access to financial markets. Guiso *et al.* (2003) find evidence that lower access costs bring less sophisticated investors in stock markets, with the potential consequence of inducing greater volatility. For example, unsophisticated investors can react excessively to market signals because of the limited ability of small investors to withstand financial pressure. This suggests considering policies that can reduce volatility, such as improving the flow of accurate financial information.

Cross-border asset holdings are also encouraged by the harmonisation of securities regulation, as shown by Vlachos (2004). Institutional or cultural differences have negative effects on bilateral asset holdings, but results for regulatory differences are robust even after taking these effects into account. Hence, with increased cross-border asset holdings, local markets will be populated with investors that have more diverse information and portfolios. The presence of heterogeneous investors in stock markets has been analysed by Albuquerque *et al.* (2004), who show that this investor heterogeneity is crucial for explaining international portfolio choices. They propose a model of international portfolio choice where investors are heterogeneous, both within a country and across countries. Bringing the model to the data, their main finding is that domestic heterogeneity of investors is much more important than cross-country heterogeneity.

16.4   Future steps: continuation of the network

Despite the wealth of results reported in the previous section, there remain open questions to be examined, some of which have only arisen recently. This section briefly mentions some open questions and new developments to be addressed in the continuation of the ECB-CFS network.

So far an assessment of the impact of the FSAP could not be undertaken. While most FSAP measures have passed at the European level on time (before the end 2004 deadline), their implementation at the national level is still pending (deadline end 2005). The effects of the FSAP will only unfold in the coming years, including its effects on central bank policies. Further work on capital markets and financial integration in Europe should analyse those effects.

An area that is relatively little developed concerns the effects of financial integration and the modernisation of financial systems on the real economy, notably on economic growth. This dimension is particularly relevant in the context of the Lisbon Agenda and the FSAP. It is the ambition of the network organisers to also stimulate more research in this area. The same applies to the implications of financial integration for financial stability in Europe.

Finally, an important recent development is the enlargement of the EU. New issues arise with the integration of new member states and with their envisaged future adoption of the euro. Their financial development is not identical to the ones of many of the earlier member states and the process of financial integration is likely to advance in a different fashion in those countries.

The ECB and the CFS concluded that further research is needed in those areas, and that the network on 'Capital Markets and Financial Integration in Europe' provides a good structure within which to pursue this work. The two institutions therefore agreed to continue the network for three further years. To cover, inter alia, the issue mentioned earlier three additional areas will be added to the main priorities of the network: (1) the relationship between financial integration and financial stability; (2) EU accession, financial development and financial integration and (3) financial system modernisation and economic growth in Europe. The remainder of this section presents these three research areas in more detail.

16.4.1   The relationship between financial integration and financial stability

While an integrated area offers more opportunities to share risk and to allocate capital, it may be less resilient to unexpected and uninsurable shocks, as they may propagate wider and faster. Moreover, it is of interest to know whether greater integration could increase the risk of cross-border contagion in a financial crisis. With the integration of European financial markets going forward, it is important to understand what type of integrated financial structure is the most resilient. The ECB has an obvious interest in this. As in accordance with Article 105(5) of the Treaty, the European System of Central Banks (ESCB) shall 'contribute to the smooth conduct of policies pursued by the competent authorities relating to the prudential supervision of credit institutions and the stability of the financial system'.

Furthermore, a comprehensive review of the EU arrangements for financial regulation, supervision and stability is currently underway (ECB, 2003). The review, which should contribute to the further integration of the EU's institutional financial architecture, was initially triggered by the report (2001) of the Lamfalussy Committee on the regulation of European securities markets.

The work of the research network on the relationships between financial integration and financial stability will seek to bring additional elements in shaping a view regarding what this new financial architecture should be. In particular, important questions are the following: Are market-based or bank-based financial structures more resilient to shocks? How can financial regulations be designed so as to be conducive of integration while still ensuring financial stability? What is the link between financial integration and contagion risk? What are the mechanisms that can trigger contagion and financial fragility? How and to what extent do financial crises impact on economic activity? Finally, how does competition in the financial services industry affect the ability of the financial system to withstand shocks?

16.4.2 EU accession, financial development and financial integration

As expressed by the President of the ECB,

> Assessing the impact of EU enlargement on the European economy is a complex question. Despite the considerable complexity surrounding this issue, one thing that is clear is that EU enlargement will provide new opportunities to trade and investment flows. Many of these effects are visible because of the high degree of economic integration already reached between the present Member States and the acceding countries.
>
> (ECB, 2004)

Further financial integration is likely to follow swiftly the political and economic integration of these countries in the EU. There are many ways in which this financial integration can take place. One way, which currently seems to be a dominant one, is that foreign financial institutions acquire financial institutions of new member states.[4] Another way would be the cross-border provision of financial services. Clearly the first is likely to be faster than the second, and may develop accession country financial systems faster as well. The example of the 'old' EU member states suggests that there are many obstacles to the direct provision of financial services abroad, in particular in retail markets. The heavy presence of foreign financial institutions may, however, pose other challenges for the new member countries, for example, in the area of financial stability and supervision. All these developments will determine financial structures, development and competition in financial services across the enlarged EU.

Important questions for further work within the network are therefore the following: What factors explain differences in financial structures across new and old EU member states? What role is financial integration taking in this development? What is the relation between financial integration and financial development? Who benefits from financial development in the process of integration? Are there any risks to financial stability during fast changes in financial structures and institutional arrangements? How will financial integration among accession countries advance relative to integration between accession countries and the previous EU countries?

16.4.3   Financial system modernisation and economic growth in Europe

The capacity of financial systems to promote economic growth depends not only on their level of integration, but also on their quality and the efficiency with which they channel savings into investment. In other words, when tackling the issue of economic growth, it would be too narrow to place the focus entirely on the level of integration. Although several financial systems can be very financially integrated, they may not be developed in such a way as to achieve a greater volume or efficiency of financial intermediation, and therefore may not improve the growth performance of the economy. Financial modernisation and financial development, however, improve efficiency of financial intermediation, and are processes influenced by many other factors than financial integration. As the network has contributed to these issues on the link between finance and growth only to a relatively limited degree so far, they have now been added as a separate priority area.

Work could focus, in particular, on the following issues: How can one further improve the structure of highly developed financial systems? How can one measure the performance with which the financial system performs its functions? What are the costs and the benefits of modernising the financial system? What is the best form of corporate governance? What are the implications of uniform accounting standards? How to incorporate improvements in the structures of the financial system? How to effectively enforce rules?

16.5   Conclusion

In response to the growing need of understanding the dynamics and implications of the integration and development of the European financial system, the ECB and the CFS launched a research network on 'Capital Markets and Financial Integration in Europe'. This paper described the scope, the findings and the future initiatives of this network.

The ECB-CFS research network aims at stimulating top-level and policy-relevant research on the structure and integration of the European financial system and its linkages with the United States and Japan. By acting as a hub for researchers working in these fields and by actively promoting research in specific areas of interest, the network managed to bring together in a continuous fashion a large number of researchers who shared their most recent results and to stimulate new research on these issues. After two years of activity, the work done under the ECB-CFS research network helped to shed more light on the process of European financial integration, on effects the euro had on the European financial system and on the role of financial linkages between the major economies. One of the most tangible achievements of the network was the stimulation of new research on securities settlement systems, an area of high policy relevance, playing a key role in the process of financial integration. It had not attracted much attention in the academic community beforehand.

Enlargement of the EU, the impact that financial integration may have on financial stability and the relationship between financial system development and economic growth are some key areas in which the network will concentrate its efforts over the next three years. Many important questions remain on the agenda, key policy issues need to be tackled and many challenges lie ahead. We hope that this article also conveyed a sense of the research excitement that is growing around European financial markets and that this may help the network to continue stimulating new insights in this important area of research.

Notes

* Any views expressed in this paper are the authors' only, and do not necessarily reflect those of the European Central Bank or the Eurosystem.
1 Further information on the network and papers of past workshops can be downloaded from the network web site, www.eu-financial-system.org
2 The roadmap is publicly available at www.eu-financial-system.org/roadmap.pdf
3 Degryse and Ongena (2004) also point to informational and political barriers that limit mergers and acquisition in banking.
4 See 'Financial Sectors in EU Accession Countries' (ed. Christian Thimann), ECB, 2002.

References

Adams R. and D. Ferreira (2004). 'A Theory of Friendly Boards'. Mimeo. Stockholm School of Economics. Paper presented at the Final Symposium of the ECB-CFS Network hosted by the ECB.

Albuquerque R., G. Bauer and M. Schneider (2004). 'International Equity Flows and Returns: A Quantitative Equilibrium Approach'. ECB Working Paper No. 310. Paper presented at the Final Symposium of the ECB-CFS Network hosted by the ECB.

Baele L., A. Ferrando, E. Krylova, P. Hoerdhal and C. Monnet (2004). 'Measuring Financial Integration in the Euro Area'. ECB Occasional Paper No. 14. Paper presented at the Final Symposium of the ECB-CFS Network hosted by the ECB.

Berger A., D. Qinglei, S. Ongena and D. Smith (2002). 'To What Extent Will the Banking Industry be Globalized? A Study of Bank Nationality and Reach in 20 European Nations'. Paper presented at the Launching Workshop of the ECB-CFS Network hosted by the ECB.

Biais B., A. Renucci and G. Saint-Paul (2004). 'Liquidity and the Cost of Funds in the European Treasury Bills Market'. Mimeo. University of Toulouse. Paper presented at the Final Symposium of the ECB-CFS Network hosted by the ECB.

Blanco R. (2002). 'The Euro-area Government Securities Markets. Recent Developments and Implications for Market Functioning'. Bank of Spain Working Paper No. 120. Paper presented at the Launching Workshop of the ECB-CFS Network hosted by the ECB.

Bottazzi L. and M. Da Rin (2002). 'Europe's "New" Stock Market'. IGIER Working Paper No. 218, Bocconi University.

Bris A., Y. Koskinen and M. Nilsson (2003). 'Capital Structure and the Euro'. Mimeo. Yale University. Paper presented at the Launching Workshop of the ECB-CFS Network hosted by the ECB.

Brooks R. and M. Del Negro (2003). 'Firm-level Evidence on Global Integration'. Federal Reserve Bank of Atlanta Working Paper No. 2003–8. Paper presented at the Launching Workshop of the ECB-CFS Network hosted by the ECB.

Buch C. and G. DeLong (2002). 'Cross-border Bank Mergers: What Lures the Rare Animal?', *Journal of Banking and Finance*, 28(9), 553–568. Paper presented at the Final Symposium of the ECB-CFS Network hosted by the ECB.

Carey M. and G. Nini (2004). 'Is the Corporate Loan Market Globally Integrated? A Pricing Puzzle'. Federal Reserve Board, International Finance Discussion Papers No. 2004–813. Paper presented at the Final Symposium of the ECB-CFS Network hosted by the ECB.

Carletti E. and P. Hartmann (2003). 'Competition and Stability: What's Special About Banking?', in P. Mizen (ed.), *Monetary History, Exchange Rates and Financial Markets: Essays in Honour of Charles Goodhart*, Vol. 2, Cheltenham: Edward Elgar, 202–229.

Cheung Y., F. de Jong and A. Menkveld (2004). 'Euro-area Sovereign Yield Dynamics: The Role of Order Imbalance'. ECB Working Paper No. 385. Paper presented at the Final Symposium of the ECB-CFS Network hosted by the ECB.

Claessens J. and L. Laeven (2003). 'Competition in the Financial Sector and Growth: A Cross-country Perspective'. Mimeo. University of Amsterdam. Paper presented at the Final Symposium of the ECB-CFS Network hosted by the ECB.

Cumming D. and J. Armour (2003). 'The Legal Road to Replicating Silicon Valley'. Mimeo. University of Cambridge. Paper presented at the Third Workshop of the ECB-CFS Network hosted by the Bank of Greece.

Da Rin M. (2003). Key lecture on 'European Venture Capital' delivered at the Third Workshop of the ECB-CFS Network hosted by the Bank of Greece.

Da Rin M., G. Nicodano and A. Sembenelli (2004). 'What Drives the Structure of Private Equity Investment'. Mimeo. University of Turin. Paper presented at the Third Workshop of the ECB-CFS Network hosted by the Bank of Greece.

Degryse H. and S. Ongena (2004). 'The Impact of Technology and Regulation on the Geographical Scope of Banking', *Oxford Review of Economic Policy*, 20(4), 571–590.

Dell'Ariccia G. and R. Marquez (2003). 'Competition Among Regulators and Credit Market Integration'. Mimeo. University of Maryland. Paper presented at the Launching Workshop of the ECB-CFS Network hosted by the ECB.

Desai M., P. Gompers and J. Lerner (2003). 'Institutions, Capital Constraints and Entrepreneurial Firm Dynamics: Evidence from Europe'. NBER Working Paper No. 10165. Paper presented at the Final Symposium of the ECB-CFS Network hosted by the ECB.

EC (1998). 'Fostering Entrepreneurship in Europe: Priorities for the Future'. COM (98) 222 final.

EC (2000). 'The Lisbon European Council – An Agenda of Economic and Social Renewal for Europe', Contribution of the European Commission to the Special European Council in Lisbon, 23–24 March 2000, Brussels, 28 February.

ECB (2002). 'Financial Sectors in the EU Accession Countries', in Christian Thimann (ed.), Frankfurt am Main.

ECB (2003). 'The Integration of Europe's Financial Markets'. October 2003, Monthly Bulletin, 53–65.

ECB (2004). 'The Challenges for the European Economy in 2004'. Speech by Jean-Claude Trichet, President of the European Central Bank, Conference organised by Foro de la Nueva Economia and The *Wall Street Journal*, Madrid, 29 January 2004.

ECB and CFS (2004). 'Research Network on Capital Markets and Financial Integration in Europe – Results and Experience after Two Years' Frankfurt: ECB, December.

Ehrmann M. and M. Fratzscher (2004). 'Equal Size, Equal Role? Interest Rate Interdependence between the Euro Area and the United States'. ECB Working Paper No. 342. Paper presented at the Second Workshop of the ECB-CFS Network hosted by the Bank of Finland.

Favero C., M. Pagano and E. Von Thadden (2004). 'Valuation, Liquidity and Risk in Government Bond Markets'. Mimeo. Paper presented at the Final Symposium of the ECB-CFS Network hosted by the ECB.

Fleming M. and J. Lopez (1999). 'Heat Waves, Meteor Showers, and Trading Volume: An Analysis of Volatility Spillovers in the U.S. Treasury Market'. Federal Reserve Bank of New York Staff Reports No. 82, July 1999. Paper presented at the Third Workshop of the ECB-CFS Network hosted by the Bank of Greece.

Freixas X., P. Hartmann and C. Mayer (eds) (2004). 'European Financial Integration', Special Issue of the *Oxford Review of Economic Policy*, 20(4), 475–489.

Galati, Gabriele and Kostas Tsatsaronis (2003). 'The Impact of the Euro on Europe's Financial Markets', *Financial Markets, Institutions and Instruments*, 12 (August), 165–221.

Giannetti M. and A. Simonov (2003). 'Which Investors Fear Expropriation? Evidence from Firm Investor Base'. CEPR Working Paper No. 3843. Paper presented at the Second Workshop of the ECB-CFS Network hosted by the Bank of Finland.

Giannetti M., L. Guiso, T. Jappelli, M. Padula and M. Pagano (2002). 'Financial Market Integration, Corporate Financing and Economic Growth'. Report prepared for the EU Commission. Paper presented at the Second Workshop of the ECB-CFS Network hosted by the Bank of Finland, European Economy, Economic Papers, No. 179.

Giovannini Group (2001). 'Cross-border Clearing and Settlement Arrangements in the European Union'.

Giovannini Group (2003). 'Second Report on EU Clearing and Settlement Arrangements'.

Guiso L., M. Haliassos and T. Jappelli (2003). 'Household Stockholding in Europe: Where Do We Stand and Where Do We Go?' *Economic Policy*, 18(36), 123–170.

Guiso L., P. Sapienza and L. Zingales (2004). 'Does Local Financial Development Matter?', *Quarterly Journal of Economics*, 119(3), August 2004, Paper presented at the Launching Workshop of the ECB-CFS Network hosted by the ECB, 929–969.

Halling M., M. Pagano, O. Randl and J. Zechner (2004). 'Where is the Market? Evidence from Cross-listings'. Mimeo. University of Vienna. Paper presented at the Final Symposium of the ECB-CFS Network hosted by the ECB.

Hartmann P., A. Maddaloni and S. Manganelli (2003). 'The Euro-area Financial System: Structure, Integration and Policy Initiatives', *Oxford Review of Economic Policy*, 19(1), 180–213.

Holthausen C. and J. Tapking (2004). 'Raising Rival's Costs in the Securities Settlement Industry'. ECB Working Paper No. 376. Paper presented at the Third Workshop of the ECB-CFS Network hosted by the Bank of Greece.

Huizinga H. and G. Nicodeme (2003). 'Deposit Insurance and International Bank Deposits'. CEPR Discussion Paper, No. 3244. Paper presented at the Launching Workshop of the ECB-CFS Network hosted by the ECB.

Iori G. (2004). 'An Analysis of Systemic Risk in Alternative Securities Settlement Architectures'. Mimeo. King's College, London. Paper presented at the Final Symposium of the ECB-CFS Network hosted by the ECB.

Kaas L. (2003). 'Financial Market Integration and Loan Competition: When is Entry Deregulation Socially Beneficial?', Mimeo. University of Vienna. Paper presented at the Third Workshop of the ECB-CFS Network hosted by the Bank of Greece.

King R. G. and R. Levine (1993). 'Finance and Growth: Schumpeter Might be Right', *Quarterly Journal of Economics*, 108(3), 717–737.

Koeppl T. and C. Monnet (2004). 'Guess What? It's the Settlements!'. ECB Working Paper No. 375. Paper presented at the Third Workshop of the ECB-CFS Network hosted by the Bank of Greece.

Miller D. and J. Puthenpurackal (2003). 'Security Fungibility and the Cost of Capital: Evidence from Global Bonds'. Mimeo. Ohio University. Paper presented at the Third Workshop of the ECB-CFS Network hosted by the Bank of Greece.

Padoa-Schioppa T. (2003). 'Central Banks and Financial Stability: Exploring a Land in Between', in V. Gaspar, P. Hartmann and O. Sleijpen (eds), *The Transformation of the European Financial System*, European Central Bank, Frankfurt.

Santos J. (2003). 'Why Firm Access to the Bond Market Differs Over the Business Cycle: A Theory and Some Evidence'. Federal Reserve Bank of New York Working Paper (September). Paper presented at the Third Workshop of the ECB-CFS Network hosted by the Bank of Greece.

Schmiedel H., M. Malkamaki M. and J. Tarkka (2002). 'Economies of Scale and Technological Developments in Securities Depository and Settlement Systems'. Bank of Finland Working Paper No. 26. Paper presented at the Third Workshop of the ECB-CFS Network hosted by the Bank of Greece.

Tsatsaronis K. and J. Santos (2003). 'The Cost of Barriers to Entry: Evidence from the Market for Corporate Euro Bond Underwriting'. BIS Working Paper No. 134. Paper presented at the Launching Workshop of the ECB-CFS Network hosted by the ECB.

Tykvová T. and U. Walz (2004). 'Are IPOs of Different VCs Different?'. CFS Working Paper No. 2004/02. Paper presented at the Third Workshop of the ECB-CFS Network hosted by the Bank of Greece.

Vlachos J. (2004). 'Does Regulatory Harmonization Increase Bilateral Asset Holdings?'. Mimeo. University of Chicago. Paper presented at the Final Symposium of the ECB-CFS Network hosted by the ECB.

Index

Note: Page numbers in italics indicates illustrations.

eBooks – at www.eBookstore.tandf.co.uk

A library at your fingertips!

eBooks are electronic versions of printed books. You can store them on your PC/laptop or browse them online.

They have advantages for anyone needing rapid access to a wide variety of published, copyright information.

eBooks can help your research by enabling you to bookmark chapters, annotate text and use instant searches to find specific words or phrases. Several eBook files would fit on even a small laptop or PDA.

NEW: Save money by eSubscribing: cheap, online access to any eBook for as long as you need it.

Annual subscription packages

We now offer special low-cost bulk subscriptions to packages of eBooks in certain subject areas. These are available to libraries or to individuals.

For more information please contact webmaster.ebooks@tandf.co.uk

We're continually developing the eBook concept, so keep up to date by visiting the website.

www.eBookstore.tandf.co.uk